POLITICS

A no holds-barred analysis of the political mac̶h̶i̶n̶e̶

By Dr. Edward Schellhammer
Founder and President of MARBELLA UNIVERSITY

© Copyright 2012. Dr. Edward Schellhammer. All rights reserved.

ISBN-13: 978-1480198715
ISBN-10: 1480198714

www.MarbellaUniversity.com
www.PioneeringEducation.com

Table of Contents

PREAMBLE: ARCHETYPAL LEGACY FOR HUMANITY 6

1. EXPLORATIONS OF POLITICS...23

1.1. POLITICS AND POLITICAL SCIENCE 23
1.2. SYLLABUS OF POLITICAL SCIENCE 36
1.3. BOOKS ABOUT POLITICAL SCIENCE 48
1.4. DEPARTMENTS OF GOVERNMENTS 60
1.5. THE ACTIVITIES OF POLITICIANS 64
1.6. IGNORED POLITICAL REALITIES 74
1.7. THE STATE OF HUMANITY 79
1.8. THE METHODS OF POLITICAL SCIENCE 94
1.9. STUDYING POLITICAL SCIENCE 110
1.10. CAREERS FOR STUDENTS OF POLITICAL SCIENCE 115
1.11. THE BIG PICTURE OF POLITICAL SCIENCE 119

2. HUMAN EVOLUTION AND POLITICS 127

2.1. POLITICAL THOUGHTS...127
2.2. PHILOSOPHICAL IDEAS 141
2.3. PSYCHOLOGICAL IDEAS...160
2.4. EDUCATIONAL IDEAS 174
2.5. MIND AND SOUL OF POLITICIANS 188
2.6. HUMAN EVOLUTION WITH POLITICS...........................222
2.7. THE ARCHETYPES OF THE SOUL 228
2.8. PEOPLE AND THE MIND...235
2.9. LIMITS OF LIVING STANDARD 264

3. HUMANITY, THE PLANET AND POLITICAL FAILURE 276

3.1. HUNGER, FOOD AND WATER 276
3.2. POVERTY AND MISERY...280
3.3. AGRICULTURAL LAND, FOREST, OCEANS 287
3.4. HEALTH AND HEALTH CARE 291
3.5. CONTAMINATION, WASTE, SEWAGE............................299

3.6. TRANSPORT SYSTEMS 316
3.7. CLIMATE CHANGE...319
3.8. CRIMINALITY AND CORRUPTION 328
3.9. RE-ARMAMENT, MILITARY AND WARS 331
3.10. UNEMPLOYMENT 344
3.11. PUBLIC DEBT AND FINANCIAL DISASTERS 347

4. POWER AND POWERLESSNESS...............................350

4.1. POLITICAL SYSTEMS 350
4.2. POLITICAL IDEOLOGY..376
4.3. STATE AND POLITICAL STRUCTURE 393
4.4. MEDIA AND POLITICS..402
4.5. POLITICS AND RELIGION 408

5. GOVERNMENT FAILURES 433

5.1. POLITICAL FAILURE..433
5.2. LOBBYISM AND PRESSURE GROUPS 438
5.3. POLITICS, POWER AND MONEY 440
5.4. MATURITY OF POLITICIANS 449
5.5. THE PERVERSION OF POWER 451
5.6. ECONOMIC DESTRUCTION OF DEMOCRACY 455
5.7. SYSTEMIC FAULTS IN POLITICS 458
5.8. HISTORY OF WARS 461
5.9. ENLIGHTENMENT FOR THE 21ST CENTURY...........................493

The Author

Dr. Edward Schellhammer (Swiss)

Dr. Edward Schellhammer studied Education, Psychology, Philosophy, Information Technology and Statistics in Fribourg (Licentiate) and in Zürich (Doctorate). He was lecturer at the University of Zurich (Psychology, Methodology and Statistics of Social Sciences, Philosophical Anthropology, and Innovation in social institutions. He was also manager of various scientific projects. He was teacher in a Professional School (Psychology) and in a Head Nurse School (Philosophical Anthropology, Special Pedagogy), as well as in a Superior School for Therapeutic Pedagogy (Children's Pedagogy, Psychopathology).

Later he completed further education in psychoanalysis (several schools such as Freudian and Jungian, as well as in Institutes of Humanistic Psychology and Behavior Training). In 1979 he established his own Academy and Practice for Individuation with over 1,500 students and clients over the course of 10 years. He was engaged for years in the research about Religions, Spirituality, Esoteric, and holistic alternative therapy, having participated in countless further education programs and international conferences.

From 2003 to 2009 Dr. Schellhammer mainly worked in the field of Life & Business Coaching. He developed coaching and mediation concepts for Geopolitical and Socioeconomic Consulting in the fields of the big national and global problems of humanity and the world.

"My studies and professional experiences in Switzerland since 1970 and in Marbella (Spain) since 1988 have given me an understanding of human beings, education, cultures, needs, standards, life and business like no other!"

Preamble: Archetypal Legacy for Humanity

Many scientists, experts, and institutions say:

- ■ "In a few decades the world will collapse."
- ■ "A world population of 9-10 billion is not sustainable."
- ■ "An apocalyptic catharsis is inevitable."
- ■ "Already today too many people live on earth."

Is the state of humanity and the planet really that much in danger?

During the last 30 years I had an estimated 12,000 dreams showing me the state and development of humanity and the earth. It is much worse than most people recognize! The elites, the illuminati, all kind of secret organizations, the most powerful people and the super-rich around the globe will lose everything! And the entire humanity will fall into a dark Abyss. All dreams I had culminate in two messages:

> **In 35-40 years everything will be over, the end, no more earth and no more humanity.**
> **The door to the Paradise for all souls (with some exceptions) is now closed until the complete enlightenment of the truth is fulfilled globally.**

Countless individuals and institutions offer solutions:

- Scientists, politicians, authorities and leaders in economy and industry, religious communities and leaders, spiritual masters, media, and bloggers offer solutions.
- The meanders are countless. The distorted realities cover the truth. Hidden interests and objectives determine their solutions. Psychopaths with religious psychosis fight for their solution.
- The good will of many experts with their conceptual approaches is precious, but inefficient. All solutions must consider the evil power of some people behind the collective sceneries.

Secret Societies will never have the solution: Forget the Bilderberg Group! Forget the Illuminati! Forget the Freemasons! Forget The Order of Skull and Bones! Forget the Rosicrucians! Forget the Ordo Templis Orientis! Forget the Hermetic Order of The Golden Dawn! Forget The Knights Templar! Forget the Opus Dei! Forget the Royalties and Aristocrats! None of them will have a future!

Is there an evolutionary solution for humanity and the planet?

During the last 33 years I had an estimated 3,000 dreams about the Archetypal Processes of the Soul until the highest possible goal as the source of the ultimate solutions for humanity.

I will tell you here about my archetypal dreams and then you too can find the answer.

The universal decision

Summary of some of the dreams I have had over a period of 30 years:

We are in the year 1920. The First World War is over. We are in the center of the spiritual world, the seat of government of the spiritual Kings of all souls. There are around 30 Kings sitting around a huge round table in a majestic temple: Buddha, Lao-tsé, Re, Aton, Plato, Abraham, Moses, Jesus Christ, Mohammed, Thomas of Aquino, Luther, and many more wise men of God that have lived on earth over the last 5,000 years.

The wise Kings discuss intensely. They are very worried about the development on earth. They realize that the actual state will lead to a next war, a much bigger war. They also forecast dire developments for humanity and the planet during the century.

One King is speaking: "One of us must go back to earth and give the rules that lead humanity on to the right track." The Kings react loudly and fiercely: Never! Impossible! That is nothing for me! Not one of them wants to take on such an impossible mission.

Then God comes in, a huge stature of light of immeasurable power. God says: "I understand you. But one of you must go back to Earth!"

Some of the Kings are pale-faced and shaking from fear, it could be them. Then God goes to one of the Kings and points his finger on this King: "You will go! I will give you all the powers of attorney that no spiritual King on earth ever received, including the power to judge over all souls! You alone will represent me on Earth!"

I wake up from this dream and am completely confused: "OMG, what did I just dream! What sort of an incredibly crazy thing is this?

I will tell you a few summarized archetypal and prophetic dreams that I have had so that you can better understand this "incredibly crazy thing":

My archetypal dreams started with the end of my University career

Dream: *"Find the mystery of mankind!"* somebody invited me.

Dream: An owl is guiding me.

Dream: Out of my abdomen a little tree grows.

Dream: I'm attending my own funeral (I am renewed).

Dream: I receive a sword, a sceptre, a globe and a cross; these symbols I compose into a circle-cross-Mandala.

Dream: I am standing by a well, a source that represents the 'highest peak'.

Dream: I am in various churches, in ecclesiastical libraries looking for the truth. What I find is a lot of dust and stones.

Dream: *"Search within your soul for the living!"* says the wise man.

Dream: I experience a ritual: *"God nourishes you, God strengthens you, God protects you, and God guides you."*

Dream: I go to the Valley of the Kings with seven white elephants.

Dream: I receive a goblet and I am summoned to search the mysteries of life in it.

Dream: Priests from ancient Egyptian times show me how they practise rituals.

8

Dream: I'm able to draw the sword of the king of the Grail from the rock and then I'm given an orb.

Dream: The ruler of the collective unconscious world of souls beats the people with a whip. He reaches everyone and wants to coerce me into obedience too. However, as he rises his whip there is a flash of lightning and he tumbles over, points his finger at me and shouts into the universe: *"This is the new Messiah!"*

Dream: A sun-like female figure draws me towards it, embraces me and I can feel its energy flowing through me like a strong current. Then I'm unified with this light, I am one with this sun. *"This is the unio mystica"* I hear said.

Dream: Preparations for a celebration 'accomplishment of the Individuation process' are made.

Dream: Victory belongs to the king alone. He alone is supported by the Spirit. Everything you have, you have from God. Realize God! All people long for this. This is the hour of the beginning of a new life. The Spirit continues: *"Rarely is there someone somewhere, who has so much faith (trust) in God, who lets himself be led by God the way you do".*

Dream: Within me is the temple of the Holy Grail. Actually I know everything; I can reveal and help other people to experience this.

Dream: A voice: *"He, the Individuated man, has a particular assignment in this world, only thought (made) for him. Only he is worthy for it since he is the man of God, the third in the covenant with God and the Spirit."*

Dream: The strength comes from the origins of the life symbol.

Dream: *"You know how life grows. You are life. You are being. You only do what you are. You come from the source in God. You understand the primal source of life. The people want bread from you",* somebody says.

Dream: I've reached the goal. I've got the water and the fire and I know the path and the goal.

Dream: *"You know that God does not go to man, man has to seek God. God is life, wisdom and love. God is within you; you are in God. The signet ring is guaranteed to you. You are the king. You are the trustee of a concern which is not of this world. The new man is born. These are events which belong to another world rather than this dark, archaic and chaotic world. Your Spirit speaks from within you."*

Dream: I am in the Garden of Eden. It is indescribably beautiful. The paradise is mine. It is within me.

Dream: As in a ritual procedure I say three times: I love the symbol of life. I am the life symbol.

Dream: Then in continuation there is a *"celebration of the reincarnated Messiah"*.

Dream: I am on my way to the universe; I must cross a bridge and I have to promise to go back to the people, then I meet God (a burning well); I can see pyramids of light, golden worlds and a huge golden circle-cross-Mandala shimmering on the eternal horizon. *"Death"*, who is the only witness of my journey to God, says: *"Fulfilled is the word"* (that I, the Messiah, will come back to mankind). On my way back I am wearing the signet ring with a circle-cross-Mandala engraved on it. The covenant (or: pact) with God is sealed.

Dream: I am sitting at a round table together with twelve men, great wise men and kings. I look out of the window onto the open sea. An immeasurable danger is approaching the mainland. I hear myself saying: *"There is only one solution: The reincarnated Messiah! He is living on earth!"*

Dream: I am standing on a bridge. There is a river underneath, flowing from a lake. It is raining incessantly. The water level is rising. I see that there is an enormous catastrophe approaching.

Dream: Through the fog I see the future. More and more people get ill and die.

Dream: On a mountain, God waits for me. I go to him and say: *"The creation of humanity is lost."* God – like a sun – answers: *"perhaps"*. Then, the scene changes: I enter a room. Many top government officials from the USA and from Europe are sitting there. I say to them: *"I am coming directly from God and he said: perhaps."*

Dream: The president of the USA has allowed me to tell him one of my dreams in front of the plenary assembly, and so I speak: "I saw a king coming to Europe, as pure and clear as none before. And I saw that all the nations disarmed; and I saw, how the king brought peace to all people on earth, the peace from God." Suddenly I realize I am talking about myself.

Dream: The Spirit says: "You are appointed and ready: The Messiah is great and alive. You have got the proper equipment to face the world."

Dream: I experience, that I have passed all the ordeals (trials) in the union with God.

Dream: The inner Spirit speaks to me: "You represent God on earth. Nobody else! You have got all the powers of attorney. Make use of them. You are a true king of the Holy Grail. The world of souls is your kingdom. God loves you very much."

Dream: I'm watching a battle of titans in the universe: The good one has to face up to the evil one. In the end, the good one wins because he is bonded with God.

Dream: The main protagonists are playing cards, my trump beats all. Someone from the group of spectators shouts out repeatedly: "This is truly the reincarnated Messiah, have mercy upon us." Then all of them pray this in a chorus.

Dream: A famished child is dancing on a battlefield full of corpses and blood. The child is dancing a dance of death. I ask the president of the USA: "Do you want to accept me as the reincarnated Messiah? You will avoid 80% of the damage and suffering."

Dream: The evil, a figure of horror, approaches me and says: "And you're playing the second leading part."

Dream: My Spirit warns me: I see the Kings of the Grail sitting at the round table. They're discussing very gravely the lack of love in this world, the disregard for psychical life, the lack of truth and the denial of the Spirit in the soul.

Dream: I have to attend a procession. I am appointed to be the patron of Europe.

Dream: I receive a 'triple cross-circle Mandala', which is, together with a fivefold structure (a Pentagram) and triangles, assembled into a kind of pyramid. In each corner there is a circle-cross-Mandala and even in the body of this pyramid there is one; a quite unfathomable construction! I am thinking in my dream: This is an even higher level than the attainment of the Individuation. This symbolizes the completeness of a messiah.

Dream: I am holding a platter, on it there are twelve smaller plates with ornaments embossed on them, all of them as beautiful as a circle-cross-Mandala. Everything is completed, prepared and ready. I have to bring the people many 'fine' things.

Dream: An expedition around the world which boils down to: The complete love is the most valuable thing that there is, and nobody has it anymore. I realise this, while I'm walking four white, long-haired, graceful, endearing, healthy, positive and extraordinarily beautiful dogs.

Dream: I cannot bear this any longer, I'm exhausted. I've tied a black cloth over my eyes, so I don't have to see anymore. Yet I still see everything. I want to flee from seeing. I simply can't. I don't want to see this dark King anymore. I see him nevertheless at the other end of the evolution. I speak to him: "What a pity that you're at the opposite end of the Individuation. You would be the only king on a par with me. You shall spare me to your own advantage! You only have one life, where you can command everything. Yet in my realm, where I am the king of kings, you have nothing to say and you will not be there. Your future in the spiritual world will be determined only by me."

Dream: I am standing in a dark, somehow mythical room. There I see lots of snakes, small ones and big ones, huge snakes all of them dead, slain, stabbed, and beheaded. I am watching this like in a film, although at the same time I am in it. I look back, from where I came and then look forward. I'm standing at the gate to the Grail and then at the altar of the Grail.

Dream: I receive 'cosmic scissors' and with them I cannot only cut and separate, but also join together and create wholeness. It is an enormous, very unfamiliar and alien gadget. I protest, because I think that this does not fit into my hand. But it does, it fits perfectly.

Dream: Experts in theology are asking me something about the Messiah. Then I draw something in the sand on the floor, a kind of shibboleth, and I say: "…and if you crucify me a second time you'll lose the earth!"

Dream: I receive a new signet ring with twelve gemstones. "This is the ring of the Messiah" it is said.

Dream: I am in a forest. On the branch of a tree there sits an eagle with its wings spread, as if he wanted to show me the pattern of his wings. I take a closer look and discover: This is an image of the king-archetype on the one hand and of the reality of the living king of the Grail on the other hand.

Dream: I am wearing the signet ring on my left hand and I'm saying to someone: "No one on this world dares to wear this ring and the last one who did, was living 2000 years ago."

Dream: It's about the collapse of the earth, about the exponential growth of all relevant components and about interconnected chemical reactions and the like. And I'm thinking: There is nothing I can do.

Dream: "I will see to it personally as a king of the Grail, that those, who have in the future, perpetrated atrocities against the values of love, the truthfulness and the Spirit, are severely punished in the spiritual world, This will be necessary to protect the evolution of mankind, since in the next 500 years there will be no other king of the Grail coming to this earth (I am not sure, maybe it said: 600 or 1000 years)."

Dream: I am coming to a church in Jerusalem: The main part has got a cupola, the plaza outside is square-shaped with a column at each corner. All around there are more columns or turrets. As I step on the square I say to a person next to me: I can see the last riddle, solving it means, that we've reached the goal. I know the solution. On one of the steeples the circle-cross-Mandala is missing. The great wise and true experts of the holy books of humanity know through immemorial tradition, that only the true Christ and Messiah can solve this riddle with a dream. I know that the circle-cross-Mandala has to go on the steeple top and I remember in my dream: I've received this a few years ago (in reality!). I take it out and proceed to attach it there. It fits perfectly.

Dream: A king has got two pharaoh birds, very colourful and marvellously beautiful. It is said that these are magic birds. We come to the city of Jerusalem. I'm very glad we've finally reached the goal together with the kingly birds.

Dream: In further dreams I see Christ, sometimes full of light, sometimes as a judge, occasionally laughing and cheerful. Then I see him as a large figure in the cosmos, at times among people and then alone. I see him very near to God, infinitely far away from the people. He has got a unique relationship with the sun: He carries it on his hands, but it is also within him, he calls it and gives it to the people whenever they want it. Christ is somehow always within me; I cannot get rid of him.

Dream: People, well educated in belief, have dragged me into the mud by ignoring, keeping silent, and not touching. A priest is their master. They are bound to him. He asks me to beat him. I am allowed to knock out two of his teeth. I want to do it, but suddenly I recognize his trick: After that he can play the martyr, blemish me as a criminal and violent person; and all will esteem him as a peculiar true and just man of God.

Dream: A voice: "Also for the rich people tomorrow, no risks will be covered."

Dream: It's about the crucifixion as a perverse sexual act. With that they crucify the Anima (the archetype) and the symbol of life (the circle-cross-Mandala: God on the one side and the fulfillment of the psychical-spiritual human being on the other side). That is the totally perverse lunacy (madness), I think in the dream!

Dream: I am talking to young people: "I understand that you suffer under the worldwide destruction of the environment. I will come soon and I will see that the world will have a good future."

Dream: The punishment is pronounced and sealed. Only the reincarnated Messiah can annul it. No folk can ignore his Messiah without the gravest consequences for the collective.

Dream: "You must live the Holy Spirit, always straight forward, and with as little deviance as possible!"

Dream: Later I realize in a dream: My signet ring is too small. I need a new one (that means: I have grown).

Dream: I am in the Vatican, in an immense arch room, full of all kinds of junk. A big amount of rubbish, compressed many meters high. I am there and take a look at it while thinking: There is absolutely nothing here that could have a value or could be vivid.

Dream: A big organization has its own Jesus Christ; also reincarnated. This is a terribly mucous, dirty, black and charred shop with a lot of dirt.

Dream: People are talking about a person having been on a very long journey, which has taken him far too long; this person has worked hard. He achieved it without taking drugs. And he is still totally healthy. I can feel it: they are talking about me.

Dream: My last 10 years are presented full of actions. Then the big proletarians appear in the film: the people who downplayed everything, played dirty games against me (people from politics, the church, the press, the economy, etc., from Switzerland, Germany and Austria).

Dream: I am on a very big ship. I am chatting with people; strong men are on my side. Then, the ship is sailing out from the peer towards the open sea, faster and faster until full speed. I am on the rear end and look into the water. There is a big and very special whale following the ship. I know this whale. He also knows me. Now I have to say goodbye. I feel him even in the distance; we are both very sad. I have tears in my eyes.

Dream: I recognize in a dream: I have astonishing power with my words alone. Then my chief appears, God personally, like a sun and apologizes for the drudgery of the last 12 years.

Dream: The whole project is finished. Everything is ready; I and my matters; for the whole humanity.

Dream: The pope surrenders and withdraws, ashamed because his 'boss' doesn't want him.

Dream: The Spaniards name me a prophet.

Dream: I walk through the Vatican. And I ask myself who has paid and still pays for all this, and under which conditions has all this been built. And I think: hidden behind all of this is an immeasurable megalomania, a perverse suppression and exploitation of people, robbery and homicide, wars and dictatorships, lies about God and religion.

Dream: The Spirit speaks: "One day, when you will die, the whole world will mourn. Millions will carry your ashes in the chalice to the eternal last home." Hearing this I see a big golden chalice of the Holy Grail with the life symbol engraved on the cap. But by no means is that time near!

Dream: Many important strong men are in fact nothing else than baby pissers without legs (I see in an image).

Dream: The big book about humanity is bulky, heavy and dark.

Dream: A professor of history has written a book about the years 1988 until 1998. I flip through the book and realize: In the main feature and essential facts nearly everything is false.

Dream: Young people don't want to learn, least of all about self-knowledge and reflection. Only by force.

Dream: In Zurich an execution is prepared (death penalty like in the USA). I tell the people there: "By the way, God told me clearly and unambiguously that killing as a punishment is not allowed and will never be approved by him (God). Then I go to the University of Zurich. At a lecture I speak: "... and by the way if you continue living as usual, you will lose the earth. The big collapse can occur in 20-30 years."

Dream: "Somewhere on this damned earth there must be a place where I can live and work as the Messiah", I protest about this.

Dream: I tell somebody: "... o.k., then whatever, I will go the path as God demands from me until my death."

Dream: A long dream scene about why no one was ever able to kill Hitler. The answer: People deserved him; his paternal side made everybody into a slave.

Dream: An unknown town in Northern Europe. Everywhere men show their penis, some are partly and some completely naked, partly covered with cloth or plastic. Many have blown their penis up with air, technically enlarged, even some little boys. They show each other the 'marvelous' thing they have. Many women are totally excited over these men with big and large penises. Everything seems like carnival. I observe from a distance, find this disgusting, distasteful, an expression of the sick society.

Dream: There is only one true King of the Holy Grail on this earth.

Dream: I explain to people my life since 1988. It was like in the movie 'Terminator'.

Dream: The biggest justice scandal (in history) is how the press, politicians, church, etc. (in Switzerland, Germany, and Austria) ignored me until today and doomed me as a wacko (without any examination).

Dream: What is a priest that has not accomplished any of the archetypal processes?

Dream: I am the great opus, created from God.

Dream: One can ignite the entire world with one bomb.

Dream: Tornados. Floods. Waves up to 30 and even 100 meters. Massive. It destroys everything into 1000 pieces. I am somewhere, entirely in the light.

Dream: It is as if I am allowed to live only for one unique reason, to save the world, to establish the foundation of a new era of Christianity.

Dream: People talk rubbish about me, the Messiah. I am there near to these people, but incognito. And I think: That much stupidity is unbelievable!

Dream: The rivers in the North are all about to overflow, frighteningly deep and strong whirlpools, very dangerous speed. Nobody wants to see it.

Dream: They have placed a packet of dynamite in the town. One targeted shot and half of the earth explodes. Because they all don't want what the Spirit gives them through me: Being a King of the Holy Grail is untouchable.

Dream: It's all about one person. They examine the Messiah and King of the Holy Grail minutely. Investigations. Evaluation: all complete, round, solid, healthy. The police cannot find anything that could be complained about either.

Dream: An assembly. I tell the people: Not taking serious the values and realities of the psychical life is deadly for the entire collective.

Dream: Arrived at the destination. A sunny fairy is with me, an illuminating female (energetic) shape. Suddenly a deep pain hits me, so hard that I scream: "more than 13 years of empty promises!" This glowing body of light embraces me. Then I am alone standing on a big rock; here is the life symbol engraved since primitive times, since the beginning of humanity.

Dream: A tree full of snakes with hydra heads and suckers. Everything is alive in the tree, but there are no leaves. (An image reflecting our society!).

Dream: It says, (I have) really performed all archetypal processes given in the history of mankind. And all this in the bond with the Holy Spirit.

Dream: I speak to people: "In the past I recognized: the roman-catholic church, the freemasons, the Rosicrucian, and all others don't teach or practice the true path. With you I would only live your dogmas and ideologies; never could I live myself and with the Spirit. I had no other option than to search for everything by myself. What did I have to lose? And I found the Spirit, the path and the aim."

Dream: In Zurich. Millions of very small maggots everywhere. They devour people's bodies.

Dream: Earthquakes. Floods. Masses of people falling into abysm. Agitations everywhere.

Dream: A big town such as Berlin: Neurotic people, psychopaths, amusement parks. Masses of monkeys dancing everywhere, people with drive disturbances, politicians, people from show business, and also people from the culture. All decadent!

Dream: A huge ship like Titanic, but even bigger. 35,000 people are on it. It's sailing. It's night. Then, an incident, and the ship sinks slowly. I am an observer and I think: The iceberg is not the problem (the real cause), but the arrogance of the captain.

Dream: People talk about me. Then they conclude that I am really a true priest from within my soul.

Dream: I receive a painting: a big rosette of diamonds. It glows wonderfully.

Dream: A big assembly. I am talking. I reproach the people about how they did not take serious what I said, not even the problems of the environment with the consequences we have to expect. And I say: "Your children will have to live like in the Middle Ages, cholera included."

Dream: A voice is speaking: "You are the new Messiah of humanity, and the guarantee for a good future."

Dream: An endless long earthquake, esthetically devilishly beautiful. It's night. Fire and disruption are everywhere on the ground. Nobody wants to see this danger. The scenery extends to half of Europe. I can feel the ground trembling. I call the people: "... !" But nobody listens to me.

Dream: I tell people: "I told you 20 years ago that the chemical composition (the chemical interactions) of all components ..... (in the body) ..... ."

Dream: I tell people: "Never again will I come back to this earth. I am only here for a visit and I have to accomplish a job. And you have to get your shit together yourself."

Dream: From the heaven debouching, first energy, panic in the air, frightening, then something like warships or war machines fly towards the earth; suddenly the entire sky is full of them. An unbelievable dimension as large and deep as the sky, everything is full of these flying machines. The never before existed machinery of destruction. A totally apocalyptic scene.

Dream: I have to make a second doctorate examination. They ask me what I know about the history of mankind. I answer: "Humanity, God and Spirit are eternal, ranging always between two poles (against the life symbol and in the life symbol). The earth will disappear, but humanity transcendentally never. The souls will incarnate elsewhere to create and develop life; and this eternally."

Dream: Again they tried to lure me into a trap. They want to imprison me, to put me in a psychiatric clinic, to even kill me. They defame me, start intrigues against me. The secret service is very active in this matter. They all managed to silence me, to isolate me radically. Swiss and German people all of them!

Dream: Somebody asks me who I am. I answer: I am a king in my soul and you can't imagine how your entire future will depend on me.

Dream: The dominator of the world is doing his work, everyday!

Dream: The day will come where no bread exists.

Dream: The horizon is gloomy. Everything is poisoned, the air and the ground. A cosmic nightmare is in the atmosphere.

Dream: If the young people would know how the slow torturous death will be ...

Dream: I tell the press: "You haven't got the slightest clue about what kind of punishment is waiting for you for having ignored me and having kept me from the people!"

Dream: Scenes about a war in preparation like in the Middle Ages. Unbelievably perverse. They throw poor people into boiling water. They are the capitalists on highest level with their greed for gain.

Dream: I am in a cathedral reading in an old Bible. I am bored: everything is junk from old times. There is nothing there that really helps people to master life. There is nothing there that forms people for the modern world. There is zero objective knowledge from today's know-how that could help people to find themselves.

Dream: Many people are trying to cross a river. Most of them are drowning. This is because of the inability of the politicians to lead people.

Dream: I am interviewed on television: At the end I am asked: Do you want to say a last word to the viewers? I answer: "Yes, I can say to everybody: Continue living as you have up until this day and you will lose the earth!"

Dream: Explosive-like developments. I can't do anything, I think. But the Spirit has an idea: "Now use your full potential and power of attorney" (that you received from God)!

Dream: Over and over there were times of doom of a society or folk. The true prophets and men of God were in the critical situation that new hard spiritual punishments had to be determined in order to allow a possible new start. Today only triple punishments might help that at least a part of humanity sees the importance and urgency of the dramatic state of humanity and the earth.

Dream: "I have not come from millions of light years away to this earth, sent from God, to play here the cretin and idiot. With me humanity and the earth will have a good future. Without me humanity will perish. The choice is now yours!"

Dream (2008): I told people in a dream: "You have 10 years left to take strong measures to avoid the total collapse." But nobody listen. (That means in 2011: You have got 7 years left!)

We are in the year 2010

Dream: In 35-40 years everything will be over, the end, no more earth and no more humanity.

Dream: A voice from the heavens: "Nobody that is part of the Jewish stream will get into Paradise". Bush

20

My decision in April 2011

The conclusion of all my research, analysis and dreams about the state of humanity and the planet is: A massive global octopus, full of falseness, lies, misrepresentation, distortion, deadly poison, political and religious psychosis, perverse lust to kill with an indescribable and never before existing dimension and power, that has got nearly the whole of humanity in its iron grip.

After I wrote this about the 'octopus', a few days later, on the 17.04.2011 I dreamt:

Dream: The door to Paradise must now be completely closed for all souls, until the complete enlightenment of the truth is fulfilled globally.

Therefore, with all the power of attorney from my spiritual (archetypal) authority I decide today:

I will not let a single soul into Paradise, apart from a few exceptions, until this octopus is detected and disclosed, until the truth is researched and clarified and until both are fully understood by the entire humanity. Everyone is summoned to work on this catharsis and renewal: Researchers, Experts, Scientists, Journalists, Politicians, legal professionals, CEOs, and all kinds of power holders and religious officials; but also all humans being in a state to contribute in any ways to this catharsis and renewal.

Every single person must be educated with the path that leads towards the fulfillment of the Archetypes of the Soul: the all-encompassing catharsis and the psychical-spiritual education, guided by the inner Spirit and the power of love. If this occurs, then I will re-open the door to Paradise in 25-30 years. If this does not happen, the door will be closed to all souls for 50,000 years (apart from certain exceptions). If humanity rejects my Archetypal Status with all the implications and consequences, then I could extend the collective punishment up to 200,000 years; the worst punishment since ever in the history of all souls.

What do you want in 35-40 years for you, your children and the following generations?

Now, you have the frame and foundation to find the right answers!

The truth and the Archetypes of the Soul are the primordial foundation and aim of science, politics, economics, religion, society, and human life.

Humanity has lost the Archetypes of the Soul. The entire sciences, politics, economics, and religion do not have it. That's the scandalous drama of humanity. The absence of the truth and of the Archetypes of the Soul produces enormous destructive energy and developments for humanity.

These archetypal dreams show clearly that sciences, politics, economics, and religion do not take care of the archetypal, psychical and spiritual evolution of mankind nor do they have any respect for the creation. This is an outrageous global sham. Sciences, politics, economics, and religion dehumanize the mind and soul of humans, and eliminate the dignity of humans.

Sciences, politics, economics, and religion are infected with the most toxic virus that ever existed: the dynamic code for regicide and deicide. In the end, it will irreversibly and unstoppably lead to doom. It can happen within decades if drastic global measures are not soon taken.

Dr. Edward Schellhammer

1. Explorations of Politics

The systemic core pillars of a society are economics, politics, education, and religion. The world of economics together with education we have explored:

The book ECONOMICS I unveils the dogma and ideology of the biggest scam in modern history that led to the degradation of humanity and the planet via "profits at all costs". With a pioneering approach, the book provides the foundation for new principles of Economics for a Sustainable Development.

The book ECONOMICS II delves into the key elements of microeconomics and their intricate relation to the current financial crisis and the omnipresent destructivity exerted on humanity and the planet due to the compulsive obsession of "exploitation". The intrinsic dynamic of microeconomics is uncovered: regicide and deicide.

The book ECONOMICS III uncovers the key facts and figures of the state of humanity and the planet in relation to the macroeconomic parameters revealing herewith the systemic failures in economics, politics, education and religion – sealed with guidelines for macroeconomic policies of a sustainable roadmap.

Here in this book we explore the world of politics starting with the general political topics, the syllabi of the science of politics, and scientific definitions of politics. It helps us to determine the frame of the political fields with its key-words.

1.1. Politics and Political Science

As a first step we search on the Internet for some descriptions. Some sources may not be representative for the world, or even doubtable. But as a whole we get a picture that helps us to create a first frame about political science. From Wikipedia we summarize: [1]

---

[1] http://en.wikipedia.org/wiki/Political_science

Subjects

- The study of the state, government, and politics
- The theory and practice of politics
- The analysis of political systems and political behavior
- Revealing the relationships underlying political events and conditions
- Constructing general principles about the way the world of politics works
- Political science intersects with other fields
- Exploring ancient roots of politics and economics
- Classical political philosophy: Hellenic and Enlightenment thought
- Modernity and the contemporary nation state
- Classical thought
- Terminology with sociologists (e.g. structure and agency)
- Allocation and transfer of power in decision making
- The roles and systems of governance
- Governments
- Success of governance
- International organizations
- Political behavior
- Public policies
- Stability
- Justice
- Material wealth
- Peace

Associated fields of political science

- Anthropology
- Public policy
- National politics
- Economics
- International relations
- Comparative politics
- Psychology
- Sociology
- History
- Law
- Political theory

The distinct sub-disciplines which constitute the field [2]

- Political philosophy

Political philosophy is the reasoning for an absolute normative government, laws and similar questions and their distinctive characteristics.

- Comparative politics

Comparative politics is the science of comparison and teaching of different types of constitutions, political actors, legislature and associated fields, all of them from an intrastate perspective.

- International relations

International relations deal with the interaction between nation-states as well as intergovernmental and transnational organizations.

A general understanding of political science

"Cambridge (founded in 1209) has a long and distinctive tradition in the study of politics and international relations with particular emphasis, going back over a century, on historical, legal, economic and philosophical approaches to the study of political thought and national and international politics." [3]

The same source says: "The course in Politics and International Relations at Cambridge rests on the conviction that the political and international worlds need to be understood together and historically. We seek to explain how the political and international worlds in which we live came to be."

We emphasize:

→ Political science consists extensively in historical study strongly focusing on philosophical thoughts (political philosophy).
→ Political science is about understanding politics, profoundly related with the (politics of the) world.

- Politics is meaningless without 'context'. It's always about something and for something or somebody, for the people, for the society. There is no focus on the real context of politics.
- There is no future perspective such as developments for the upcoming decenniums, the inertia of politics, the long-term effects of political decisions and actions.

---

[2]http://en.wikipedia.org/wiki/Political_science
[3] http://www.polis.cam.ac.uk/

The Cambridge program of political science includes options such as:

- Sociology, Social Anthropology, Biological Anthropology, Archaeology, Social Psychology, Cultures of Mesopotamia and Egypt, Akkadian, and Egyptian
- Politics of the USA, Africa, the Middle East, China, and Western and Eastern Europe)
- Politics of particular regions of the world, including Europe, East Asia, Africa and South

We emphasize:

→ Political science is much more than about thoughts on the politics of the past and present
→ Political science includes social and biological Anthropology, Archeology, Cultures

We have from Heywood a representative book about political science. He writes about politics: "Politics is exciting because people disagree. They disagree about how they should live. Who should get what? How should power and other resources be distributed? Should society be based on cooperation or conflict? And so on. They also disagree about how such matters should be resolved. How should collective decisions be made? Who should have a say? How much influence should each person have?" [4]

Let's have a critical look at the parts of this definition (or description) of politics:

- Politics is exciting: The author commences with creating a positive emotion in the reader. We could create a negative emotion: politics is disgusting because when politicians open their mouth, then they start lying or manipulating in order to usually hide something.
- (Exciting) because people disagree. We could say: permanent disagreements are annoying and show the egomania and cantankerousness of the politicians. This is absolutely not exciting.
- The author talks about people: Does he mean the politicians or John and Mary, taking a glass of wine in the bar and talking about politics or politicians? Does he mean a professional meeting where the experts try to understand something and to find a solution in order to take a decision? Does he mean lawmakers when they talk during Parliamentarian sessions?

---

[4] Heywood, 2007, p. 3

full reference

26

We know them: mad, badly educated, always destroying everything from the opposite table, no different to hooligan adolescents with a behavior disorder. All this is not exciting at all!

- They disagree about how they should live: We interpret, the author means the folk. This 'how they should live' is extremely vague here. Is it about lifestyle, living standard, or is it about religious belief? Is it about sex or is it about eating habits? The majority of people live in a very unconscious and stupid way. Describing this, we could easily fill 1000 pages. There is no substance in this statement.

- An important question is: Who should get what? It seems the author talks about the people (the folk). A better statement would be: people already get too much of product consumption. And too many people have got a lot without having worked for it. A serious question would be: What do people do with what they get? Or: Did they work for what they got (or get)? Or: What are the motives for all the wants people have?

- The distribution of power and other resources is indeed a topic of the highest importance, especially as everywhere politicians abuse their power and the resources they have got for their political operations.

- Should society be based on cooperation or conflict? This question is a trap: There is no human life without conflicts and there is no desirable life that lacks completely of cooperation (in both the micro and macro fields of life). The core of this has primarily nothing to do with politics but much more with human life and behavior in general.

- People (or politicians) disagree about how such matters should be resolved: The source of disagreements about solutions can have different roots, some are practical, others economical, and many are ideological or religious. Religion is a rather private matter but the other routes can be approached by scientific methods, with intelligence, and expert knowledge. On the real political stage it is often a matter of ideological interests or incompetence, or wrong understanding of humans (the folk) and human life.

- How should collective decisions be made? This is indeed a political topic of highest importance. Fact is: a neurotic or narcissistic mind, a psychotic or psychopathic person (politician) better not have too much decision making power. But if 95% of the folk are stupid, lazy-minded, greedy, neurotic, narcissistic, cantankerous, self-opinionated, and not adequately educated, then they also better not participate in political decisions. As democracy has been largely proven to be rotten to the core, the answer lays in the future education of people (and politicians). Another answer lays in the question: Do we need centralized governments? We could also discuss the idea: central governments have 20% power, provincial governments get 30% and the other 50% remains in the local governments. This option is exciting!

- Who should have a say? This question leads to the criteria and not directly to the people (politicians): expert knowledge, life and professional experiences, skills for the job, genuine inner dedication, moral behavior and attitudes (character integrity). This also is a very exciting approach to politics. *Some kind of Philosopher King?*
- The influence each person should have: We don't know if the author refers to the politicians or to people in general (the folk). Influencing factors are everywhere in the everyday life of people and politicians. The media have much more influence that the politicians and the folk as a whole. An individual has practically no influence. Does he mean the lobbyists or the pressure groups or the Church or the corporations or the banks? The author's approach here is vague, naive and therefore useless.

→ The author has not said much about politics and political science. The description used is not even useful as a first introduction statement.

Another statement from this author is: "The disagreement that lies at the heart of politics also extends to the nature of the subject and how it should be studied." [5]

- Disagreement lies at the heart of politics: This is a view from just one perspective. It's a psychological perspective as most politicians are very archaic personalities with very suppressed complexes in their unconscious mind. Seen from here, the question is rather a psychoanalytical one.
- At the heart of politics there are much more the management of everyday matters in order to have a regulated, sustainable and balanced society life. This is what is or should be the essential work (at the heart) of politicians.
- Disagreements about the nature of the subject and how it should be studied can be solved, but not with rigid, infantile, dictatorial, and neurotic authorities. An evolutionary science must have its freedom and flexibility to explore 'external' fields or new perspectives. The field of politics requires certain knowledge, skills, and character qualities that can be determined (as a subject). The way political science should be studied gives us the modern didactics and the psychology of learning. The manifoldness of the political fields and the mostly much narrowed syllabi of political science indeed shows a 'crisis' that is absolutely not exciting. We explore this matter later on here.

→ The disagreement statements are confusing and do not lead to useful answers here. It doesn't say anything about the real world of politics.

---

[5] Heywood, 2007, p. 3

Heywood continues defining politics: "On the one hand, the existence of rival opinions, different wants, competing needs and opposing interests guarantees disagreement about the rules under which people live. On the other hand, people recognize that, in order to influence these rules or ensure that they are upheld, they must work with others." [6]

We would first say: rival opinions, different wants, competing needs and opposing interests is part of human life and occurs everyday and everywhere. In that sense these 'conflictive' matters are something 'normal' and are not characteristics exceptionally for politics. Also disagreement about rules is a matter that every couple, every family and all kind of groups and communities experience regularly. There are skills that can be learnt to efficiently manage such dynamics. This is in its essence not 'political'. By being compulsorily focused on this petty aspect of politics (and life) we ignore the real substantial political stuff.

The author continues explaining politics: "The heart of politics is often portrayed as a process of conflict resolution, in which rival views or competing interests are reconciled with one another. However, politics in this broad sense is better thought of as a search for conflict resolution than as its achievement, as not all conflicts are, or can be, resolved ... Politics is usually thought of as a 'dirty' word. It conjures up images of trouble, disruption and even violence on the one hand, and deceit, manipulation and lies on the other ... in the 19th century the US historian Henry Adams summed up politics as 'the systematic organization of hatreds'." [7]

Let's focus on some elements from these statements:

Process of conflict resolution: this is also a matter of life in general and especially in the world of business. In all parts of human life people do deal with conflict resolutions. In that sense it is not 'specifically political'.

Politics is better thought of as a search for conflict resolution than as its achievement: By all the critical statements about politics, we must also focus on the positive achievements of politics. Here we enter into the different political departments that we will discuss later on.

---

[6] Heywood, 2007 p. 4
[7] Heywood, 2007 p. 4

There is a certain compulsion to always find an agreement between different opinions about what is right and wrong. It seems politicians always want to find a harmony and norms or rules to regulate everything in a society. Why can't they accept certain pluralism and freedom of choosing this or another solution (norm, regulation, or no regulation)? Human life is a process of permanent learning (although 90% of people do not learn much through life). Compulsion leads to regression!

Not all conflicts are, or can be, resolved: Partly this statement is trivial; partly the statement is too vague to be discussed: there are the 'everyday conflicts', the small conflicts, regional conflicts, and international conflicts. As already more than 50% of the Western Governments are heavily neurotic psychopaths and psychotic people, they also tend to produce conflicts on a global scale which – it seams – can't be solved without a global war of never seen dimension. *as never seen before –*

These politicians also cause immense problems in their own country that leads sooner or later to violent events, even to civil war. The author trivializes the topic of 'conflicts'. Henry Adams is right: Today, more and more we identify a systematic organization of hatreds, of megalomaniacs, psychotic psychopaths striving for world governance and operating in their country with deceit, manipulation and lies. We enter here into the core topics of the deicide. [8]

→ This author deviates from the real world of politics which we consider as deceit and deviation, even distortion. *deviation*

Lynch says that it is not easy to describe what politics is and he mentions three definitions of politics: "1) The Academic study of how a people, a nation or a state is governed. 2) A public profession concerning matters of government. Involving the acquisition of status and the exercise of power and authority. 3) Activities relating to the organization of a state, relations between the state and other states, and between the state and its citizens." [9]

- The statement 1) is critical, as many programs of political science lack of important fields or aspects of the real politics.
- The statement 2) lacks the management of the society with its manifold sectors and of the people (folk) in general.
- The statement 3) gives the impression as if politics is preponderantly a matter of organizing 'things' as if a state would be a corporation.

---

[8] Schellhammer, 2012, Deicide (and also: Trilogy on Economics)
[9] Lynch (et al.): UK Government & Politics. 2010

A very short, probably not very professional definition of political science is: "Political science is the academic subject centering on the relations between governments and other governments, and between governments and peoples." [10]

Of importance here is: There is a government and there are the people. Interestingly, the word 'government' is abstract, impersonal, and the people are concrete: the humans, the citizens. It would make more sense to say: on the one side there are the rulers and on the other side are the people. From here we can start: Who are the rulers? What is the difference between the rulers and the people from a real point of view? Or: What are the interests of the rulers? Or: What are the interests of the people? We can go ahead with much more questions, for example: What is the power of the rulers? What is the power of the people in front of the rulers? etc.

This is a trivial statement about political science, but it does raise many other questions that will lead us to explorations of highest importance.

Another definition of political science marks five points: [11]

1. It is the science that studies the political power and authority of the state and government.
2. It is the systematic study of the institution, organization, processes and laws of the government.
3. It is the study of politics that may influence the government structures and processes in a given society.
4. It is how the branches of government perform the various political tasks such as the delivery of basic services.
5. It is the exercise of sovereign political right of the state and government to carry its task for the improvement of quality of life in the society

- Again we realize here that the people are ignored and the world of politics is a system and the actors within the systems and sub-systems are irrelevant.
- We also miss in this description the purpose and goals of politics, the interests of the actors and the interests and needs of the people.

---

[10] http://economics.about.com/od/economicsglossary/g/political.htm
[11] http://savior.hubpages.com/hub/Definition-and-Importance-of-Political-Science

A following statement from this author reinforces the impression: "Generally, the importance of political science is the application of political powers and authority in the realm of government structures. The ordinary citizens may know and learn about their political rights and privileges from a given form of government including the political structure and processes of the state."

And more: "From the understandings of these basic concepts of government, state, laws and institutions those who would study political science must know its importance and function, relationship with other discipline and broader understanding to its specific roles of individual in a civilized society."

- ☝ The fundamental value of democracy 'the government is from the people and for the people' is gone down the drain.
- ☝ It is indeed important to understand the mentioned concepts. But it is also important to understand the actors in these structures; and this is ignored here.

But the author also mentions as essentially positive approach: "Thus the study of political science will also include the empirical investigation of political facts through social research and the application of critical thinking. The key words in the comprehensive analysis on the principles of political science are state, government, law, institution, power relationships, legal process, constitutions and politics. These are the important dimensions to study political science that need to be constantly in touch to mold the citizens in achieving quality of life to our society." [12] Positive is here:

- Critical thinking
- Comprehensive analysis
- Achieving quality of life to our society

In other words: students must be critical, think critically, ask questions, comprehend the analysis, and focus on the aims of practical politics, especially 'quality of life'.

Therefore let's be critical and try to deal with some more interpretations of 'politics':

---

[12] http://savior.hubpages.com/hub/Definition-and-Importance-of-Political-Science

Politics is as the art of government: "Politics is not a science…but an art, Chancellor Bismarck is reputed to have told the German Reichstag. The art Bismarck had in mind was the art of government, the exercise of control within society through the making and enforcement of collective decisions. This is perhaps the classical definition of politics, developed from the original meaning of the term in Ancient Greece." [13]

→ To govern and to exercise control seems to be the core of 'politics'. But does this reflect the reality? It shows how politicians think and feel: They are focused on power and control, and not on the professional management of their fields. This reflects the megalomaniac drive and not a useful classical definition. Politicians have to serve the people and not their greed for dominance and 'order' or 'control' or ego-satisfaction through ruling.

"To study politics is in essence to study government, or, more broadly, to study the exercise of authority … US political scientist David Easton (1979, 1981), who defined politics as the 'authoritative allocation of values' … 'Authoritative values' are therefore ones that are widely accepted in society, and are considered binding by the mass of citizens." [14]

→ Here political science seems to be reduced to study the exercise of authority. But it would be better to study the (insane) mind and behavior or the incompetence of these authoritarian personalities.
→ The 'values' that they allocate is here undetermined; it can be everything, good and bad, destructive and constructive, useful and useless, soul and money, consumption and inner values, wealth and food, and so on. Such an approach to determine politics leads to nowhere.

The definition of 'Policy' is also critical: "…that is, with formal or authoritative decisions that establish a plan of action for the community." Here we have the real activities we will later on explore.

"There is a growing recognition that the task of managing complex societies is no longer simply carried out by government but involves a wide range of public and private sector bodies. This is reflected in the idea that government is being replaced by 'governance'." [15]

---

[13] Heywood, 2007 p. 5
[14] Heywood, 2007 p. 5
[15] Heywood, 2007 p. 6

→ We conclude here that the modern political science explores this 'wide range of public and private sector bodies'. Such topics must become part of the syllabi.

"Negative or pejorative images have so often been attached to politics. This is because, in the popular mind, politics is closely associated with the activities of politicians. Put brutally, politicians are often seen as power-seeking hypocrites who conceal personal ambition behind the rhetoric of public service and ideological conviction. Indeed, this perception has become more common in the modern period as intensified media exposure has more effectively brought to light examples of corruption and dishonesty, giving rise to the phenomenon of anti-politics ... As individuals are self-interested, political power is corrupting, because it encourages those 'in power' to exploit their position for personal advantage and at the expense of others." [16]

→ People have their experiences with politicians during their life; and a majority knows these false power-seeking hypocrites. It would be an exciting project to systematically investigate on the political stage all the components of these pejorative images. At least, it should form part of the syllabi of political science.

"At its broadest, politics concerns the production, distribution and use of resources in the course of social existence. Politics is, in essence, power: the ability to achieve a desired outcome, through whatever means. This notion was neatly summed up in the title of Harold Lasswell's book *Politics: Who Gets What, When, How?* (1936). From this perspective, politics is about diversity and conflict, but the essential ingredient is the existence of scarcity. The simple fact that, while human needs and desires are infinite, the resources available to satisfy them are always limited. Politics can therefore be seen as a struggle over scarce resources, and power can be seen as the means through which this struggle is conducted." [17]

The author operates here with the vocabulary from the economics: [18]

→ Production, distribution and use of resources are the business of the economic world. And this is not the main job in politics.
→ The term 'scarcity' is a very manipulative word (or concept) and thoroughly abused in the science of economics.

---

[16] Heywood, 2007 p. 7
[17] Heywood, 2007 p. 11
[18] Schellhammer, Economics I, 2012

➜ The simple fact that humans' needs and desires are infinite is a false statement (not a simple fact) and distorts the corresponding realities.

➜ 'Allocation' (distribution or made ready to distribute) is a term like a chewing gum that can be used in manifold ways.

➜ That resources available to satisfy the people are always limited is a trivial fact: in the end everything, included the planet and even the air is limited.

➜ That politics is in essence 'power', the ability to achieve a desired outcome, is a distortion of political realities, national and international.

➜ That Politics is about 'who gets what, when, and how' is an economic approach and it does not give the right picture about politics.

➜ Politics seen as a struggle over scarce resources is a stupid view and reduces the world of politics enormously. This is a typical economic approach.

➜ The understanding of power as the means through which this struggle is conducted does not say how politicians in office use their power.

🖎 The entire description of politics becomes here very naïve, sterile, artificial, and fabricated. The active political realities remain in the fog.

🖎 The way politics is defined and described for (or from) the political science distorts this world and deviates from the political reality.

🖎 The use of terms here allows interpreting the meaning in manifold context and this produces more confusion than enlightenment.

🖎 The critical picture the majority of people have about politicians and politics reflects experiences, but it is not considered, by the authors as serious.

🖎 Most approaches to describe 'politics' turns around the use of power and is never about servicing the people (the entire folk).

🖎 There is in all descriptions not a thin sign leading us to the key question: What is this human and political theatre 'meaningful' on this earth for?

🖎 The most important question about 'power' is ignored: Do the politicians in office really have power or are they the servants of the hidden supreme economic (or religious) masters?

🖎 The understanding of politics in reality and in the science of politics shows us that some strange agents have begun regicide everywhere! Or in a symbolic expression: The previous servants of the king have stolen his crown.

Indeed: The science of politics can be very exciting!

1.2. Syllabus of Political Science

The question about what is politics leads us to political science: "Even respected authorities cannot agree what the subject is about. Politics is defined in such different ways: as the exercise of power, the exercise of authority, the making of collective decisions, the allocation of scarce resources." [19]

➜ Best, we consider all these fields as a perspective, a topic, a part of politics and therefore they all are a subject of high importance for political science.

Another way to get a picture about the field of political science is to collect the topics from several BA and MA educational programs from India, Europe and the United States. We have explored 20 BA programs and some MA programs. From these sources we collected a list of much more than 300 topics (subjects considered as being part of the Bachelor and Master study program of political science).

We do not give here the references as it could be misunderstood, discrediting some and favoring others. We assume that many other syllabi of political science have subjects in their programs that we have not listed as follows. We also integrated the syllabi from the APSA (Organized Sections American Political Science Association), which does not mean that all the American study programs about political science do include these subjects. [20]

We categorize the subjects perfectly knowing that some subjects could be placed in other categories. We do not categorize here in semesters, years, first and second level, or in BA and MA. Some subjects refer to a country; this means that it is of foreign interest and not a subject referring to the country of the university.

➜ The question that accompanies us is: What do the people know about the political world? And: What do the members of a political party, of the parliament, and the ministers and heads of state know about the political world?

---

[19] Heywood, 2007, p. 4
[20] http://www.apsanet.org/content_4596.cfm

■ History of political ideas

(Non-European countries tend to study Western political philosophy from Plato to the modern times; but none of the Western programs of political science has included Asian or African political philosophy or ideas of the past and present.)

- Political thought from Plato to Hegel
- Greek political thought
- Roman political thought
- Ancient political thought
- Political thinking since Marx
- Vedic political thinking
- Classical political thought
- Marxism and Leninism
- Stalinism
- Political ideas of Mao-Tse-Tung
- Machiavelli
- 20th century political thought

■ Contemporary political ideas

- Liberalism
- Democracy
- Socialism
- Traditionalism
- Reformism
- Pluralism
- Elitism
- Federalism
- Idealism
- Anarchism
- Right
- Left
- Neo-Liberalism
- New Left
- Post-modernism
- Realism and neo-Realism
- Contemporary political thought
- European political thought
- Modern political thought
- Western political thought

■ Modern theories of political science

- Positivism
- Rational choice theory
- Behaviorism
- Structuralism
- Post-structuralism
- Realism
- Institutionalism
- Pluralism
- Concepts of Ideology
- Modern political ideologies
- Modern political theories
- Concepts in modern political theory
- Foundations of political theory
- Foundations of politics
- Trends in political theory
- Policy studies and analysis
- Recent trends in political theory
- Political Sociology
- Political Socialization
- Political Development
- Political Modernization
- Political Elite
- Politics of Environment
- Social Change
- Control of public expenditure
- New Political Science
- Political Methodology
- Comparative Democratization
- Political Science Education
- Politics, Literature, and Film
- Health Politics and Policy
- Conflict Processes

■ Political history

- World in the 20th century
- Second World War
- Cold War
- Colonialism and legacies

- Neocolonialism
- 20th century Russian politics
- Political history of Eastern Europe in the 20th century
- Diplomatic History of the Arab-Israeli conflict
- Territorial politics and multilevel governance
- New World Order

■ Political structures

- Legal institutional structures
- Political parties
- Contemporary democracies
- Democratization in Europe
- Nature of Non-Western political systems
- Operating of parliamentary democracy
- Federalism and Intergovernmental Relations
- Public Policy
- Political Organizations and Parties
- Presidents and Executive Politics
- Representation and Electoral Systems

■ Power, authority and legitimacy

- State: definitions, departments, structures, elements
- Constitution, meaning, structure, content
- Forms of governments
- Forms of power
- President, Prime Minister, Parliament
- Governor, Chief Minister, State Legislature
- Center-state relations
- Electoral systems
- Power and decision-making
- Political Networks

■ Laws and court

- Law and Courts
- Legislative Studies
- Justice, judicial system
- Rights, fundamental rights
- Rights, Duties and Citizenship

■ Public administration

- Concept, Nature and Importance of Public Administration
- Growth and Evolution of Public Administration
- Interaction between Public and Private Administration
- Scientific management and administration bureaucratic theory
- Organization: Hierarchy, control, Centralization, Decentralization
- District, local and rural administration
- Ethics and Values in Public Administration
- Structure of Organization: Line and Staff, Chief executive, Roles
- Administration, departments and public corporations
- Services, recruitment, promotion, accountability
- Administration of Law and Order
- Control over administration
- New Public Management
- Pattern and Role of Bureaucracy
- Financial administration, principles and processes of budgeting
- Public Policy: Formulation, Implementation and Evaluation

■ Actual national politics

- National politics and policy
- Balance of power and collective security
- National political economy
- Immigration and citizenship
- Development and under-development
- Comparative politics
- Politics of dissent
- Science, Technology and Environmental Politics
- Public Policy in rural and urban areas
- Good governance, E-governance, right to information
- Political processes
- Political economy
- Race, Ethnicity and Politics
- Terrorism
- Corruption
- Arms control and disarmament
- Politics of environment
- Foreign Policy

■ International Relations

- The determinants of foreign policy
- Basic concepts
- International political economy
- IMF, World Bank, WTO
- Topics in British politics
- International organizations
- Globalization: concepts, mechanism, impacts
- Advanced Modern Asia
- British politics
- British political tradition
- American constitution and government
- The American Presidency
- International politics of East Asia
- Advanced Politics of Russia and Eastern Europe
- Foreign policy and diplomacy
- International security
- Security and disarmament
- International security and arms control
- Diplomacy and foreign policy
- Non State activism international politics

■ United Nations

- United Nations Formation
- Charter and objectives
- UN and Millennium development goals

■ European Union

- Institutions
- Policies of the EU
- Concept
- Structures
- Development
- Political economy of EU
- Comparative European governments
- Europe in a globalised world
- Europe in post-communist Eastern Europe

■ Sociology, society

- Theories of sociology
- Political sociology
- Social development
- Socialization
- Culture
- Political modernization
- Political elite
- Political and social change
- Terrorism
- Violence
- Social worlds
- Media
- Culture
- Feminism
- Women and Politics Research
- Sexuality and Politics
- Modern social theories
- Poverty, welfare and the state
- Religion and politics

■ Psychology and politics

- The field of political psychology
- Political communication
- Behavior theories
- Behavior of voting
- Human development
- Propaganda
- Politics and the media
- Politics and sport
- Protest movements
- Gender in the world of politics
- Communication theory
- Political psychology of voter decision making
- Rational choice models of political cognition
- Psycho-biography of political actors
- Motivations of people to get involved in politics
- Personality and politics
- Personality in foreign policy

- Personality and the first Gulf War
- Attitudes and political cognition
- The structure of attitudes
- Symbolic politics and public opinion
- Affect and emotion
- European politics and society
- Information Technology and Politics

■ Ethics and moral values in politics

- Non-violence
- Feminism
- Human Rights
- Race, Ethnicity, Identity

■ Scientific methods

- Methods
- Multivariate analysis
- System theories
- Political analysis
- Introduction to Political Research
- Basic Steps of Research- Research Design, Hypothesis
- Measuring Political Phenomena.
- Sampling Methods.
  Experimental Research
- Tools of Data Collection
- Data Processing, Analysis and Interpretation.
- Measuring Political Phenomena
- Sampling Methods
- Comparative Politics
- Tools of Data Collection

■ Politics of foreign countries (of interest)

For most countries the neighbor nations and its political system and policies is of high interest also for political science. Some countries have historical and strong economic (trade) ties to other countries. Therefore the political system and the policies of such countries are of high interest also for political science. We give here some example of such foreign countries we found in the syllabus of for example American, Indian and British universities (colleges, schools):

- United Kingdom
- United States
- European Union
- Russia
- China
- India
- Canada
- Nigeria
- Switzerland

There are (British) programs with extensive geographical orientation:

- Social Anthropology, Biological Anthropology, Archaeology, Social Psychology, Cultures of Mesopotamia and Egypt, Akkadian, and Egyptian
- Comparative Politics (including politics of the USA, Africa, Middle East, China, and Western and Eastern Europe)

The syllabus of political science (a model)

We can organize the list of all existing syllabi into categories:

1. History of political ideas

☐ History of political ideas
☐ Political history

2. Actual political ideas and theories

☐ Contemporary political ideas
☐ Modern theories of political science

3. Organization of political structures

☐ Political structures
☐ Power, authority and legitimacy
☐ Laws and court
☐ Public Administration

4. Actual national politics and policies

☐ Actual national politics

☐ Politics of criticalities
☐ Economics of politics

5. International relations

☐ International Relations
☐ United Nations
☐ European Union
☐ Politics of foreign countries (of interest)

6. Auxiliary sciences

☐ Sociology, society
☐ Geography
☐ Psychology and politics
☐ Ethics and moral values in politics
☐ Scientific methods, methodology
☐ Archeology
☐ Culture
☐ Anthropology
☐ Theory of knowledge

➔ What do the people know about the political world?
➔ What do the members of a political party, of the parliament, and the ministers and heads of state know about the political world?
➔ What do all institutions of political science teach (and not teach)?

Conclusion:

We admit that an overview of over 20 different syllabi from India to Europe and America does not give a complete picture about the content of all the different syllabi of political science. We also are aware that a short title (referring to a subject) does not say much about the real content that is de facto taught. Some subjects have the attribute 'comparative'; we consider this as a possible perspective of most topics.

We observe that there are extreme differences between offered study programs (the syllabi); at least a majority of the mentioned syllabi do not give a clear impression of the content: one subject from one program may be divided into 3 subjects in another academic program.

We can already make some first conclusions about the differences of subjects and the list of the subjects in general.

We identify some differences and deficits, for example:

- Very theoretical, abstract and far a way from the reality of politics
- Much reduced and do not even offer 30% of the listed subjects
- Some with a high flexibility in choosing subjects beyond politics
- Some are very extensive and include much of the real political world
- Many Western syllabi have 65% identical subjects under varied names
- Do not touch the psychological realities of politics and politicians
- Do not include ethics and Human Rights or political corruption
- Do not teach any actual national or global political criticality
- War is a superior political topic, but such a subject is not listed
- The fields of the political departments are much neglected or ignored
- The mega-parameters of global developments are mostly ignored
- The many trouble spots around the globe are neglected or ignored
- Political transparency and political public relations are ignored
- All political monetary matters of supreme importance are ignored
- Lobbyism as a political force of mega-octopus dimensions is ignored
- Lies, cheating, deceit, distortion, propaganda, manipulations do not exist
- Many programs totally lack ethics, integrity and other human values
- The false flag or proxy operations (US) as political tool are taboo
- The imperialistic development of the Western nations does not exist
- The increasing neo-colonialism from many nations does not exist
- Present capitalism or neo-capitalism is as a topic, therefore taboo
- Economics as a political tool to weaken, damage, destroy nations is taboo
- Trade as a matter of high political importance for nations does not exist
- Religion as a political factor of supreme importance does not exist
- The human factors are reduced to trivial aspects or even totally ignored
- Sustainability of political policy, programs and decisions does not exist
- The relation between politics and the world of business is not taught
- Jewish-Zionist power, the 'invisible hand' in Western politics, is taboo
- The developments of Europe and America towards fascism is taboo
- All the outrageous lies about WWI, WWII, and the Cold War are taboo
- All the atrocities of colonialism and imperialism are not reflected
- The big corporations as a treat for society and governance is ignored
- All the wars from the West since 1946 up to today are totally ignored
- The immense political power of the military-industrial complex is ignored
- How Western politics over the last 25 years has destroyed countries is taboo

Normative statement: The syllabi of a majority of study programs of political science is a cheat, falsifying the political realities, that trivializes or ignores the importance of very important and relevant fields and knowledge.

👍 The fact that the responsible managers of the syllabi have a great scope for choosing what they like to teach shows a certain academic freedom.

👍 The manifoldness of subjects offers an enormous potential for all-embracing research and teaching, and for exploring the big picture of politics.

👍 The varied names (titles) of more or less identical fields of a subject allow the teachers to choose their preferred slices from the cake.

But seen as a whole the effects of the (average) teaching programs show us a very critical picture:

"The London School of Economics and Political Science (LSE) is one of the foremost social science universities in the world." [21] Founded in 1895, they have prepared since then hundred thousands (if not more than a million) of (British and foreign) students for a responsible professional path in economics, governance, and political science in general.

The history and the politics of the United Kingdom since 1900 up to today show us that their political programs are a total failure: wars and endless wars, and today more wars, always destroying and exploiting other countries, and in their homeland misery and more misery, and a thoroughly corrupt (maybe could be called 'criminal') system of the monetary and economic systems, and of politics in general.

Normative statement: LSE claims that its programs are for the "betterment of society". But based on my 'Trilogy of Economics' they teach the perfect program for deicide. We assume there are many other academic institutions, especially in Europe and America, which follow the same path.

We could visualize the general programs of political science as a beautiful, strong, proud, sovereign, grand bull; but the bull is castrated. And there must be a reason for that, which we will have to find out.

---

[21] http://www2.lse.ac.uk/aboutLSE/aboutHome.aspx

1.3. Books about Political Science

Another approach to get a big picture about political science is to simply consult the actual classical books used for teaching and studying in the Western World. There are hundreds of such books and we can't go through this amount of scientific books. We have to choose some classical books that are listed and recommended (by Amazon) as 'study books'. First of all we have to make an analysis of the 'tables of content' (content analysis).

A question is if the content of these books are representative or simply a subjective selection of topics from the authors. I assume that the general picture arising from the contents of several classical books about political science will cover at least 75% of the standard subjects that are taught at universities and academic schools in Europe and America. We do not consider books about scientific methods (social sciences), books and subjects that are rather about secondary fields such as general sociology, general psychology, general laws, general culture and religions, trade, and so on. The criterion is: the direct political relevance.

Let's first have a look at the table of content from one classical study book about politics. [22] We reorganize the content with the given keywords:

Introduction: Studying politics

1) Ideologies and ideas of politics

- Politics: Definition
- Political ideologies: Liberalism, conservatism, socialism, others
- Nations and nationalism: Definition, varieties, future perspective
- Democracy: Definition, models, practices
- The state: Theories, roles, global perspective
- Governments, systems and regimes: Classifications

➜ We should divide these topics into: 1) History; and 2) Present Theories
➜ We must add here 'Ethics' and 'Human Values' (of political relevance)

---

[22] Heywood. 2007

2) Political structures in the modern world

- Constitution, law and judiciaries: Classifications and purposes
- Assemblies: Roles, parliament, structures, performance
- Political executives: Roles, power, leadership, theories
- Parties and Party systems: Types of parties, systems
- Representation, elections, voting: Voting behavior
- Groups, interests, movements: Types, models, patterns
- Bureaucracies: Theories, roles, power, control

➜ Universities of each country obviously have a national approach.
➜ The different topics allow for a comparative analysis.
➜ Missing here are the governmental departments (bureaucracies) that de facto are the real political world (are not elected); all have very different duties and are in charge of long-term policy implementation.

3) National politics and performance

- Subnational politics: De-/Centralization, ethnic and community politics
- Policy and performance: Processes, theories of decision making, systems, implementation practices

➜ We miss here the very different (concrete) duties (politics) of the governmental departments particularly as in democratic systems these key authorities are not elected and whose opaque power and actions are not subject to the same scrutiny as elected (fixed term) politicians.

4) Global politics and performance

- Definition, world order, globalization, global governance

➜ We suggest here to divide this section into politics with neighboring states, continental politics, international coalitions, and global politics.
➜ This category is an essentially part of 'International Relations'.

5) Politics and society

- Economy and society: Economic systems, social structures
- Political culture, identity and legitimacy: Multiculturalism, stability
- Mass media and political communication: Theories, democracy, governance

→ We add here an institutional structure of highest importance: Religion.
→ A must to add here is: Modern aristocracy (elites), the role of corporate and governmental power.
→ We also miss here: Political and personal education of the citizens.
→ The political personhood (integrity, knowledge, skills) also deserves a place here.
→ Additionally there is no exploration here of any evolutionary concepts (balancing continuity with change); it is all about maintaining the status quo.

A special chapter (we found in this book)

■ Militaries and police forces: Roles, control, accountability

→ Police forces form part of the judicial apparatus (department).
→ Military is the defense department and should be part of a category we can name with 'political departments'.

General conclusions:

We agree that every professor, teacher and expert in politics (political science) has his personal preferences depending on biography, professional career, teaching experiences, interests and frankly biases. A book is always a limited product and an author is obliged to choose his topics. Even the structure of the content can vary depending on the author. Sometimes the construction of categories and the distribution of the topics into categories is a matter of discretion. There is nothing wrong or bad with that.

→ Fact is: a structure of a field becomes a different picture depending on the main components and on the missed topics or 'parameters'.

But from a general book about politics we expect that all very relevant systemic parts be exposed and at the appropriate places. Sometimes it is very meaningful what is missed, occasionally more than what is elaborated. A topic can be very small, but may have an immense impact in the entire (political) system. Other small topics can be placed on a tertiary category or simply as a very special area of expertise.

In the neo-capitalistic books about economics (study) 'military' is understood as a 'positive externality' like 'education' and 'public goods'. This we conclude is a very manipulative construction. Here in the science of politics we have 'military' separated from all the political departments: 12, 18, and even 30 or more in some countries. We consider this too as a manipulative rejection to enter into the practical politics of the departments and to give supreme importance to (real) military politics. After all "war is simply a continuation of political intercourse, with the addition of other means" as described by the strategic theorist Clausewitz. [23]

→ If war is the continuation of politics and in that sense 'politics with other means', then indeed 'military' is a way (a tool) of doing politics.

→ In not every war since 1945, to date not a continuation of politics. War is the direct means for imperialistic (neo-colonialist) aims.

It's quite revealing: American and British politics is all about military power: threatening other countries and interventions. Without (use of) military power their politics would fully fail internationally and globally. And without (use of) police power (criminal, security, intelligence services and civil guards) their politics would fail internally.

→ The hidden function of military and police deserves a superior place in the main categories of political science.

We have seen that in the political structures described the institutions of religion don't have a place. Today, and for the past 20 years it is obvious, the aristocracy in most European countries does still have enormous hidden political power, especially through the banking system. This topic is highly critical, historically complex and actually (maybe for centuries) of immense influence in politics despite, the so-called 'democratization'.

→ The hidden power of the aristocracy (new and old) deserves a superior place in the main categories of political science.

What is a political system without the politicians? It's meaningless. There are all sorts of politicians: neurotics, narcissists, psychopaths, megalomaniacs, psychotics, tyrants, despots, liars, cheaters, deceivers, gamblers, intriguers, amoral and unscrupulous people as well as a very small number of committed public servants. From the bottom (the grassroots) up to the top power positions, the majority play their games in order to exploit everything and every vivid thing wherever they can on this planet. Many of them are driven by a religious psychosis for world governance others by pure greed. The political personhood (integrity, knowledge, skills, commitment) must be focused in the study of politics. 'Ethics' and 'Human Values' of practical political relevance must become an essential practical part of this category as must be the exploration of alternative accountability based structures.

---

[23] Clausewitz.com. http://www.clausewitz.com/readings/quotations.htm

➔ The personalities of politicians deserve a superior place in the main categories of political science.

What is a political system without the citizens, the folks? There are all sorts of humans: a majority is badly educated, stupid, false, naïve, blinded, ego-centered, neurotic, conceited, believing in a religion full of sham and very archaic with very low personhood qualities driven by greed, blabber, fun and consumption. Their mental system works on an efficiency level of 5-10%. They are not formed psychologically and spiritually for an all-sided balanced kind of being and way of living. A majority has no idea about the real world of politics and anyway they do not much trust politicians and politics unless they are given free things. We talk here about 80-95% of a population. With such a collective negative psychical-spiritual state a true democracy can never work nor evolve.

➔ The psychical-spiritual state of the folks (citizens) deserves a superior place in the main categories of political science.

Describing and analyzing the political power and its constitutional justification is without doubt an essential part of political science. The neo-capitalistic society is essentially built up on some pillars:

Banking and insurances, raw resources (oil and gas included), gemstones and gold market, the big manufacturers and the big retail corporations, the vast mass media, telephone and mobile phone networks, Internet providers, public transport systems, energy production (electricity, gas, coal and nuclear), food production and allocation of (drinking) water, and so on.

Who are the owners and who controls behind the curtains these superior pillars of society? This field is not simply a matter of lobbyism or pressure groups; these systems have real power which they exercise everyday! If we have to challenge the thesis that they have more power than the government and that they even dictate to the government what is right and wrong to do, then this topic become of highest importance in the science of politics. If political science rejects exploring these topics, then it becomes a ridiculous kind of 'Punch and Judy Show' reflecting the daily 'reality shows' of most parliaments rather than the true exercise of power.

➔ The ownerships and control (power) of the essential pillars of a society deserve a superior place in the main categories of political science.

Now let's take another book and explore the table of content: 'UK Government & Politics'. [24]

We summarize some essential key words from a country that is held up as one of the oldest parliamentary democracies:

- Democracy and participation: Referendum, political culture
- Elections, voting: Functions, systems, voting behavior, campaigns, media
- Political parties: Structures, roles, organizations, internal democracy
- Political parties: policies, ideology, ideas, socialist, conservative, liberal democrat
- Pressure groups: typology, methods, successful factors
- Constitution: Definition, sources, sovereignty, strengths, weaknesses
- Parliament: Structure, functions, House of Commons, House of Lords
- Prime minister: Cabinet, ministers, civil servants, executive power
- Judges and civil liberties: Judiciary, power, status of right, Supreme Court
- Devolution and local government: Union, administrative and legislative
- European Union: Development, institutions, EU & British politics

From a constructive view we can identify a manifold description of the systems of the British government. In some chapters we also find explanations about Northern Ireland and a ˀcomparison with the US government.

But critically we observe that there is no systemic elaboration of globalization, public relations, the supreme powers of the British Monarch and its historic roots. The imperialistic politics of the last 20 years, especially together with the United States, are not explored, and neither is the still felt impact of the UKs imperialist past that is still vital and shadows the British Government.

- We get informed about an 'empty house' and some politicians, but not about the real politics and the real political participation of the citizens.
- Based on the table of content we consider such elaboration as sterile and far away from what real politics is about.

➔ The given picture is good and indispensable for an introduction to governmental structures, but not representative for the big picture of a valuable political science (syllabi).

---

[24] Lynch (et al.). 2010

Finally we take another book to explore the table of content: 'British Politics for Dummies'. [25] We reiterate: It is absolutely clear that the key words of any table of content does not cover all the explanation of the topics in a chapter. We get a rough picture about the main components of the entire structure. And this is what we want with our first approach. The table of content has here the following key structure:

- Political universe: local & national politics, parliament, assemblies, politics in the media, European Union, the wider world
- Importance of politics and politicians: Types of authority, purpose of politics, role of politicians, making the law, changing constitution, for the country, life standard, planet, poverty, terrorism
- Participatory democracy: History of democracy, British democracy, monarchy, rights of citizenships, strengths and weaknesses of democracy, citizens
- Political ideologies: Ideology, Western democratic model, Liberalism, Socialism, New Labor, Marxism, totalitarian regimes, communism, alternative politics, fascism, theocracy, feminism, environmentalism, extremism
- British political state: History, Church and state, power of the Lords, Labor party, power of the Prime Minister, European Union
- Elections and British Parties: Electoral systems, majority, proportional representation, status quo or reforms
- Voting behavior: Right to vote, trends, party strategies, election campaigning, effects of Media
- Political parties: Definition, how they operate, the parties, the leaders, party members, minor parties
- Pressure groups: The structures, inside and outside, exert influence, public opinion, the variety of pressure groups (business, human rights, environmental, professional, trade unions), pressure groups and EU, think tanks
- Politics and the Media: Relationship, special advisors, the different media, elections and media, opinion polling
- Britain's Constitution: Need, types, rules, parliamentary sovereignty, success, unwritten constitution, monarchy, republicanism
- Parliamentary democracy: House of Commons, Prime Minister, the job of peers, government bills, royal assent, the speaker, committees, other players
- The PM and the Cabinet: Power of the PM, offices of state, cabinet jungle, political food chain, Cabinet committees and reshuffles, special advisors, Shadow Cabinet

[25] Knight Julian. 2010

- Ministers and civil servants: The job of departments, hierarchy, civil services, secretary of state, the cabinet secretary
- Courts and Judiciary: Legal systems, civil and criminal law, basic rights of citizens, Scottish court system, courts and the constitution
- Local governments and devolution: job of local governments, structure, Scotland and Wales and Northern Ireland, devolution, parliament, assembly
- Becoming a politician: Becoming part of a party, becoming a candidate, political ladder, local, seat in the parliament, election, life as an MP, top jobs
- Britain's place in the world: The Empire, new role in Europe, relationship with US, Commonwealth of Nations, overseas territories, world police officer, UN
- International stage: The United Nations, the role of the G8 and the G20, trading blocs, WTO, power game China, NATO
- Europe and the EU: Understanding how it works, goals, institutions, law making and legal system, Russia, Turkey, Balkans, European Treaties, EU budget, agricultural policy
- US politics: Understanding US influences in the world and UK, UK's special relationship, US system of Government, Congress, presidency, supreme court, from a bill into law, democrats, republicans, religious rights, political parties
- The part of tens: prime ministers, political scandals, events that shaped the modern world, trends for the future (Internet voting, Indian modernization, Chinese democracy, Chinese control of Africa, replacing the dollar, expanding the EU, shortages of water, scrambling for oil, global warming, global population growth)

We observe here some very interesting differences compared with other consulted books. Especially worth a mention are:

1) Most chapters draw a picture from the definition, the system or theory to the practical (concrete) aspects of governance.
2) While other authors separate historic perspectives from the present theories and structures, the author includes here historical aspects directly in the different explorations and descriptions of the present.
3) Several chapters include some of the immense global problems (the 'mega-parameters' we will explore later on) from environmental issues up to political and economical power shifts. These topics are of supreme importance for politics and deserve a structural and systemic approach in forming a perspective of politics.
4) The author also gives an insight into the standard political career from becoming a member of a party to climbing the ladder, to holding a

ministerial post. We consider this as indispensable for political science as such a biography profoundly shapes the political attitudes and activities.

🖑 We miss here as everywhere in books about political science the essential psychological and spiritual characteristics of the people and their everyday life, including their criticalities.

There are many national, international and continental political institutions beyond Europe and America created for specific regional, international or continental interests, indirectly also addressing the interests of Europe and America (as non-members).

Private entities of political importance are categorized under 'Pressure Groups'. There are many non-governmental institutions of high political impact. Big corporations, especially retailers and banks, fundamentally shape a society and have economical as well as social impacts, both of highest political relevance.

The economic perspective with political relevance was extensively explored in our 'Trilogy on Economics' (Schellhammer, 2012) and therefore we ignore this perspective here.

➔ The importance of pressure groups, political institutions beyond Europe and America and (non-governmental) corporations, all of high political impact, must be categorized each in a special section.

Some critical questions may challenge the science of politics:

1) How much of (political) history about ideologies, ideas, thought, theories and visions must form part of a Bachelor program in order to understand the present (of politics, theories, structures and concept)?
2) Are there didactical, educational and intrinsic characteristics that a) require teaching political history before or parallel to the teaching of the theories and concepts of the present; and b) require always teaching the historical aspects together with the structures, theories and concepts of the present?
3) The term 'history' is generally seen as referred to the far past. Even the years 1945-2000 people in general understand as part of history. In the extreme we could say: the 'yesterday' is already history. But in some way the history is always present. What does separate the past from the present? Is it only the big time perspective?

4) If a majority of the political history (texts, articles, papers and books about history) reflects distorted, manipulated and misinterpreted historical realities, what use do such historical approaches serve?

From a psychoanalytical approach we can learn: the biography of an individual is never simply the past that we can forget about: The past is always vivid in the present unconscious mind and partly in the conscious mind of people. And the past always has shaped a person in most aspects. The same can be applied to a society and a nation.

Therefore, if we want to profoundly understand an individual we need to understand his past. Or from a psychotherapeutic perspective: a present disturbance or conflict (a 'complex') can only be solved if the roots are identified and transformed into something new (renewal), replaced by something new (constructively efficient), or even simply eliminated.

A rational approach is not enough; a meditative approach is always indispensable. Reconciling (accepting) by learning (changing) is part of each catharsis. Re-conditioning an annoying or destructive behavior pattern does not eliminate its old roots and therefore is a superficial approach with a short term effect; in most cases a shift to another (sometimes less) annoying or damaging behavior. Just look to the behavior of the UK who having been a leading aggressor and colonizing half the world during the 19th century was forced to switch in the 20th century and become secondary to the US's leading aggressor role.

Such transformations are a learning process that includes understanding of the source and development. It leads (ideally) to a new progressive holistic development. Only then we can 'forget' the past; or in other words: the past does not affect anymore the present. From another point of view we also can say: the present forms (prepares) the future forming a context as todays behavior is usually rooted in the past.

We can also say it in this way: a new car, new clothes, a nice apartment, the Internet, the mobile phones (etcetera) do not change a person's inner life in the sense of a catharsis or renewal. The inner archaic being remains the same.

🖑 The entire political apparatus, no matter how advanced and modern it is technically and verbally (or written), hosts' archaic politics due to archaic politicians.

Normative statement: A political science that focuses preponderantly or solely on the political apparatus is a sham.

There is also such a thing as a collective unconscious: local, regional, provincial, national, continental, and global. This unconscious reality is energetic around us everywhere, something like the air around us and is very rooted in past actions and behaviors.

For the political world we conclude: The political history always comes back, is part of (haunts) the present, and is endlessly repeated by politics and the folks, obviously in the expressions and context of a modern world. From this point of view we conclude:

→ Also in the political world the present is the result of the past and the present forms (prepares) the future.

In 'Economics I, II, and III' [26] I have revealed that neo-capitalistic economics is on a nearly unstoppable path of regicide and deicide. I also have shown that politics is strongly involved in this totally destructive economic path. In the end it will destroy humans' evolution. I could not find any book on politics that explores and discusses these evil developments (with roots in the far past).

→ The archaic coding from the (far) past is still the code for the present politics (and politicians). With no evolution there can be no true and lasting revolution.

Theoretical and practical politics, even political science, have been and are made from humans and for humans, and always affect humans, folks, and a (big) part of the world community and in the end also the planet. A political science that ignores all the human factors (and human values) everywhere becomes something akin to being taught about sexuality by the Roman-Catholic Church. That's insane and it leads to madness and a collective highly neurotic and destructive dynamic.

We identify some critical aspects:

☞ There is a lot in the political world that is simply a re-make of the past politics and its consequences at that time.
☞ Practical politics can't be separated from ideology, ideas, concepts and human values; faults in past concepts therefore must be identified and changed.
☞ Ideological or practical aspects that have been appropriate or understandable in the past may not be useful or relevant for the present.

[26] Schellhammer. Trilogy on Economics. 2012

- Ignoring today the vivid past politics and its consequences will always lead to a repetition of the past in new shapes.
- As politics is full of distortion, lies, cheating, deceit, falsifications and etcetera, history (in books) is shaped and interpreted the same way.
- The more the mass media distort and disfigure political facts in the present and past, the more the political science also teaches a distorted political world.

We conclude:

→ Revealing distortion and lies about the history of politics is indispensable for political science, and also for individuals striving for a political career.
→ Identifying the factors that created the past (and still shape today) the path of regicide and deicide is indispensable for the political sciences.
→ Political science must explore and teach all the human factors, including neurosis and insanity that are relevant for politics and political systems.

1.4. Departments of Governments

What is politics or a government without the departments? It's like a cook without comestible goods or a footballer without a football. What is political science without extensive and profound explorations of the governmental departments with its activities? It's meaningless and above that a sham.

There is also a political structure: a political institution is responsible for managing the entire social aggregate. There is a government with a head (president or prime minister) and departmental ministers that operate in the interest of society's groups and members. We have collected from some governmental websites a variety of governmental departments:

Education	Labor	Catastrophes
Health	Agriculture and forest	Pension
Jurisdiction and Police	Animal Breeding	Meteorology
Finances	Fisheries	Land settlement
Defense	Youth	Interior affairs
Trade	Building	Environment
Commerce	Wildlife	Consumer protection
Traffic	Immigration, migration	Foreign affairs
Family affairs	Culture	Religion
Social services	Economic affairs	Archeology
Women affairs	Sport	Etcetera

In general all governmental departments are households. And no household can operate without money. But in a certain (theoretical) way households could operate without a government, although with fatal consequences. We entered into that matter in 'Economics III' (Schellhammer, 2012).
Here however we can formulate some general conclusions:

➜ The politicians' matters are the real worlds of the departments.
➜ The political governance is about the real world of the departments.
➜ The real worlds of the departments is always also about money.
➜ Political governance implies skills to manage the fields of the topics.
➜ Political governance requires knowledge about the department's world.

These statements have consequences for political science, drawing on the big frame and encompassing all political fields:

- The money issues (money at disposal, costs etc.) we must assume, are a matter of political economy.
- Management skills adapted to the specific department's world is a matter of political science.
- The specific knowledge about the department's world is not a subject of political science.
- The knowledge about the department's world that ministers have is part of political science.
- There are departments that devour immense amount of money; others much less.
- Parliamentarians always have different needs and wants and unlimited (ego-) wants, sometimes (including emotional self-interest).

🖙 We have not found in the list of syllabi any subjects that contain political management and the indispensable knowledge referring to the specific departments.

🖙 In other words: Political science is predominantly like a footballer without a football.

The needs and wants for the different departments ('households') have varied sources:

- The people, citizens
- The institutional operations
- Ideologies and ideas
- The matter of the subject
- Further developments, expansions
- Technological progress
- New law requirements
- New challenges to manage
- Aspiration for profiling
- Struggle for power
- Vested interests

🖙 We have not found in the list of syllabi any subjects that contain the needs and wants of all mentioned sources together with its political dynamics.

The biggest, the most costly, and probably the most challenging departments or topics are: pension and unemployment payments. Let's assume some options to solve these two problems:

1) People must work up to the age of 75 or 82 depending on their health (maybe part time work) until they get (full) pension fund.

2) People are self-responsible for saving money to cover up to one year (or 2 years) in case of unemployment; and only then do they get for one year a monthly unemployment payment (with an added obligation to further vocational education) and for those who never find a job, they will finally have to live in an educational and working community receiving the indispensable needs (not a mobile phone!).

The scientific question is here: Do we need an ideological statement (idea) or do we have to solve such kind of problems simply based on the practicable and sustainable financial issues? What are the ideological foundations (or implications)? Or asking in another way: How do politicians take their decision in these human matters (arguments)?

Another scientific question arises with waste and contamination: Do the originators of these 'negative externalities' have to pay fully for all but really absolutely all costs (cleaning up, recycling, environmental damages, and contamination with all its collateral human damages)? Is this an ideological decision or is this simply a practical issue (causers pay for the results of their doing)? What are the ideological foundations (or implications)? Or asking in another way: How do politicians take their decision in these matters (arguments)?

These types of questions are crucial in the political life and decision-making processes.

🖎 We couldn't find in any syllabi describing any such type of critical scientific approach.

Most departments have accumulated and do manage some sort of public goods. Examples of public goods that are of interest for the people's everyday life (leisure) are:

- Public places
- Art galleries
- Parks
- Swimming pools
- Libraries
- Free further education
- Museums
- Expositions

- Archeological material (places)
- Lighthouses
- TV channels
- Radio
- Movies
- Concerts
- Public buildings
- Healthcare
- Other public infrastructure

We also can consider as public good of people's daily interest: clean air, clean lakes and rivers, and clean (healthy) resources (e.g. soil), contamination-free environment and food, and natural beaches (free from urbanizations and constructions).

We understand the importance of the public goods as 'public wealth' and as 'quality of collective life standard'. We could even discuss this parameter as of higher importance and relevance than the GDP; or that the GDP should include such values.

☞ We couldn't find in any syllabi describing such kind of scientific approach.

1.5. The Activities of Politicians

Let's find another approach to create a frame with content about the world of so-called 'politics'. If we know in a very general way what politicians do and how they do it, then we have a picture telling us what real politics is about.

"Politics is, above all, a social activity. It is always a dialogue, and never a monologue." [27] Taking this statement as a starting point, we want to explore these social activities. It can help to understand what politics is about.

Knight describes some political activities. [28] We summarize with keywords:

- Resolving conflicts
- Encouraging compromises
- Accommodating different interests
- Determining who exercises power
- Making the law
- Changing the constitution
- Ensuring a more controlled state
- Galvanizing the country in times of crisis
- Listening to constituents
- Working for the good of the country
- Tackling big issues
- Keeping up living standards
- Setting tax policy
- Targeting government spending
- Deregulating
- Saving the planet
- Bringing an end to world poverty
- Fighting terrorism
- Reckoning with the decline of Western dominance

Knight mentions a focus of highest importance for practical governance, especially in the nearer future: "The Western powers such as the US and UK have been the wealthiest, strongest militarily and most economically successful for the past few hundred years." [29]

---

[27] Heywood. 2007, p. 3
[28] Knight Julian. 2010, p. 23-32
[29] Knight Julian. 2010, p. 33

The author's statement sounds like a glorification of the efficiency, of the kinds of performance and of the quality of the US and UK politics and government. But he should also mention that the wealthiest, strongest militarily and most economically successful states are fully based on crimes against humanity:

- They have conquered many other folks and stolen their land.
- They have killed hundreds of millions of people.
- They have practiced genocide around the globe to get their wealth.
- They have robbed the wealth and all resources from other folks.
- They have built up their power and economy with a hundred million slaves.
- They have exploited many countries with dictatorship and military forces.
- They have begun regicide and killed many opposing foreign leaders.
- They have terribly exploited their own folks letting a majority live in poverty.
- They have begun incredible outrages in the name of God and Jesus Christ.
- They have brought indescribable suffering and misery to the world.
- They have seduced and corrupted foreign leaders with money and privileges.
- They have sowed hatred allover the world that will hit back in the future.
- They have destroyed infrastructures, cultures, resources allover the world.
- They have operated with absolute satanic perversion and psychopathy.
- They have used and still use media as a means for lies, betrayal and deceit.
- And today they continue with all these economic, bellicose, and evil means.

The statistics about the growth of the world population show us a very critical future: If nothing significantly changes in the coming 3-4 decades, then China will have a population of over 2.5 billion, India as well will have over 2.5 billion people, and Africa's population could grow up to 3 billion people. The world population as a whole will reach within 40 years a population of 10 billion people. [30] Logically, the population of the United States and the European Union will be dramatically small, less than 8-9% of the world population. The political implications are enormous! The question arises: What are the governmental activities to tackle these changes in terms of world governance? The data about China and India is wrong; population growth is coming from Africa, South America and Middle East! Additionally why should there be any implications this population in balance has always existed. Surely the real issue is that the population is growing from people living longer creating many societies of old and therefore vulnerable people.

→ As a very general conclusion we can say: Politics and political science is about political activities (of their agents) in the interest of some individuals.
→ Logical and common sense is: Political science is not a natural science and therefore cannot simply operate with the methods of natural science.

Orrell describes the misconceptions of economics. In the style of his characteristics we can formulate for politics the same misconceptions: [31]

▪ Politics can be described by political 'laws'
▪ Politics is made up of independent individuals
▪ Politics is stable
▪ Political risk can be easily managed using statistics
▪ Politics is rational and efficient
▪ Politics is gender-neutral
▪ Politics is fair
▪ The kind of governance can continue forever
▪ Living standard will make citizens happy
▪ Growth of power is always good

🖑 Such misconceptions in politics reveal to us the true psychical, mental and spiritual state of the politicians in office.

---

[30] Schellhammer: Economics III. 2012
[31] Orrell David. Economyths. 2010, p. 6

From what politicians do and how they do it we can even conclude some characteristics about their personality (character, mind, spirituality, integrity). From there we get a first general impression of their political ideas, visions, and ideologies.

A politician is obviously (hopefully) a human. He has a home, maybe a partner and a family. In the (early) morning he leaves his home and goes to his office. From there he starts working. Maybe already on the way to his office he has some phone calls (in the car). During the day he is working and in the evening (if he is not travelling or having a meeting) he goes back home, probably often late and very late.

At home the politician is the 'human', not the politician, so we hope. From here the politician is a private person communicating and acting with their partner and / or the children. Even a politician that is single has at home some 'private moments' with cooking, washing, cleaning, watching television, reading something, and so on; leaving at the door his political matters. We can compare this situation with a judge or a police officer: both do their job somewhere and somehow, but at home they should not play the judge or respectively the police officer; in the real world there may be exceptions that most probably sooner or later lead to private disasters.

Brainstorming the professional activities of a politician

- Listening
- Talking and discussing
- Having meetings or sessions
- Reading documents
- Getting informed
- Analyzing a matter
- Thinking
- Trying to understand a matter
- Contemplating (maybe)
- Taking decisions
- Studying a matter
- Interpreting matters
- Taking conclusions from matters
- Giving instructions or orders
- Controlling (checking) matters
- Signing documents
- Searching for something
- Negotiating something
- Mediating

- Calling
- Receiving or making calls
- Checking emails
- Compiling a draft document
- Preparing a speech
- Preparing for a meeting
- Making notes about something
- Correcting a prepared speech
- Calling for administrative help
- Getting expert advice
- Going to another office for something
- Nicely (?) shaking hands
- Attending a press conference
- Political party events (talking, giving speeches)
- Travelling to meet special people

We reorganize the activities of politicians creating a first frame:

a) Communication

- There are communication channels in a hierarchy
- He talks internally with colleagues
- He communicates with people and groups outside
- He communicates with other officials
- He communicates with representatives of external institutions
- He communicates with representatives of foreign institutions
- There are services providing him with information

b) Mental activities

- He gets information to be analyzed and selected
- He must interpret and balance received information
- He elaborates on the advice he has received from experts
- He evaluate new information (about realities)
- He makes conclusions and arrives at decisions based on information

c) Management activities

- He gives advice, instructions, and orders
- He controls the executions and its result
- He gives out information for varied purposes
- He gets orders and has to manage their realization

- Managing the functioning of vital systems
- Setting laws, rules, aims, values, and measures
- Setting priorities, proceedings, and roadmaps

d) Mediation, negotiation

- He must negotiate and balance manifold interests
- He must mediate between conflictive positions
- He must accept flexibility in decisions about interests

e) Conflict, crisis and problem management

- Taking measures to ease and resolve conflicts
- Resolving crises and problems
- Managing heavy damages and catastrophes

f) Structural management

- Managing the structures of allocation of all kind of goods
- Managing the structures of allocation of all kind of services
- Managing the structures of allocation of work
- Regulating all kind of processes in the society

Conclusions:

→ Political offices require specific knowledge and skills about communication, elaboration of information, decision making, mediation, negotiation, general management, conflict management, management (use) of power, and speaking (to the public).
→ The bigger the lack of the right knowledge and the bigger the lack of efficient skills are, the higher is the risk of failure in the world of politics.
→ The knowledge and skills are not equal to the knowledge and skills in (big) corporations. A state is not a corporation and political activities do differ very much from the world of (big) corporations.

Let's put these activities into a second frame:

1) If there would not be any folk in a country these activities would be completely useless. If there would not be a determined land (with borders) for these activities, these activities would become unlimited, chaotic, critical, and mainly baseless.

2) Politicians are humans, privately living in a network with other humans (partner, children, family, friends, etc.). The folk consist of a certain amount of humans. These humans are not simply a human biomass or rats.

3) On the one side we have the politicians that are elected and charged with a political office. On the other side we have individuals (members of the national community) that can be politically active in a party or non-governmental organization or a pressure group of some kind. These individuals are not in charge of a political office.

4) There is another group of humans to consider: all those citizens that do not actively participate in politics, except estimated 40-75% go voting (in a nation that has implemented this 'democratic' tool of political participation). In case of strong austerity and extreme scarcity or injustice this group of people can cause serious problems for the entire government or to some single politicians.

Conclusions:

➔ Political activities are always from and for people, in general for the entire folk (citizens) of a country.
➔ Logically one fundamental risk of failure in the world of politics lies in the complexity of human factors on both sides.
➔ If politicians do not have the appropriate knowledge about humans (mind, soul or psyche, the behavior, the genuine inner needs, some wants, and the inner potentials), then they fail in their job.
➔ If the citizens of a country are stupid, lazy, blabber-mouths, ignorant, soulless, thoroughly greedy, narcissists and neurotics, and not appropriately educated (in mind and soul), then any form of democracy (participation in political matters through voting and elections) fails.
➔ For example, a family in the economic understanding is a 'household'. There are also other kinds of households. If a father and mother don't care well for the children, they grow up with 'criticalities': mental problems, mental and behavior disorder, etcetera. In the future these children are either obedient (submissive), or they develop disrespect, hate, rejection of responsibility and everything, protest behavior, and a very critical life management. Compare a state to something like a mega-household. Therefore the same principles apply between politicians and the folk.
➔ If people behave like rats or sheep (because they are brainwashed, manipulated, lured, seduced, and badly educated through public education, family life, and mass media), then a democracy is in decline and automatically transforms into an oligarchy (or dictatorship, fascism).

→ If politicians ignore the human values, the inner life of people (and their own inner life), the values of nature and the planet, then they become the servants of monetary supreme masters. And then a state becomes a corporation managed with the tools and principles of the neo-capitalistic economics. This is already a hidden kind of dictatorship and fascism. At that point democracy just flushes down the drain.

The political departments, as presented in chapter 1.4., form a third frame to identify what politics is about. Let's draw some examples:

- The minister of Health Care has never professionally experienced hospitals.
- The minister of Agriculture has no idea about the world of animal breeding.
- The minister of Education has an archaic understanding of humans' mind.
- The minister of Energy is totally disinterested in nature and environment.
- The minister of Economic Affairs only knows neo-capitalistic theories.
- The minister of Defense is a psychopath, a megalomaniac, very cantankerous.
- The minister of Traffic is an enthusiast of (modern) cars and car racing.
- The minister of Family Affairs has no idea about a family life with low wages.
- The minister of Jurisdiction and Police has a rigid and dictatorial character.
- The minister of Social Services has no experiences about the social world.
- The minister of Youth has no insight into the concerns of youth today.
- The minister of Wildlife doesn't like animals, and eats meat twice daily.
- The minister of Foreign affairs is shaking hands with an Islamic leader.
- The minister of Fisheries had a construction company and never lived by the seaside.
- The minister of Environment doesn't even know 5% of the problems in his/her field.
- The minister of Religion is a Catholic or a Jew, totally abhorring Islam.
- The minister of Pensions has no insight into the life of poor elderly people.
- The minister of Women is a young woman that thoroughly hates men.
- The Foreign Minister has no idea about Africa, Asia, and Latin America.
- The minister of Labor has never seen a (small, big) business from inside.
- The minister of Culture doesn't know with heart and soul what culture is.
- The Minister of Finances doesn't know the world of the monetary games.

- The head of state of an EU-country doesn't speak one sentence in English or any other European or non-European language.
- 80% of lawmakers are millionaires from rich families with properties included.

🖎 Here we are now in the modern political world of Europe and America!

These examples show us four essential criticalities:

1) Politicians can be and are in office about a field they don't know much about and they don't have any inner commitment to the inner values of that field.

2) The state of the (conscious and unconscious) mind of politicians (the result of their biography) has a big impact on their activities and decisions.

3) The skills the politicians have, especially in the fields of communication and mediation, shape decisively the processes and results.

4) The ethics, the moral attitudes and behavior, and the moral character (integrity) of politicians have a fundamental influence on their activities.

Based on the state of humanity, the world and the planet [32] we can and must conclude:

🖎 The causes of the big problems of nations, of the state of humanity, the world and the planet lies in the deficient (pathological) mind of politicians, the lack of relevant knowledge about their fields of responsibility, the absolute ignorance and incapacity to understand humans and humans' life, the lack of indispensable skills (management, communication, mediation), and in the destroyed and distorted or even absent conscience (moral attitudes) with a corresponding character.
🖎 These very delicate topics are ignored in probably 95% of all offered programs about political science around the globe. Herein lays one of the most critical systemic faults of political science – accredited by all governmental and private authorities licensed to give out accreditations.

---

[32] Schellhammer. Deicide. 2012. And: Economics III. 2012

Normative statement: It is a disgrace and an outrageous insanity how the authorities of academic education, including the departments of education and any accreditation institution, manipulate the syllabi of political science in order to cheat, deceive and brainwash all students for the sake of the false games of politics (and economics). Considering all the consequences (of their evil and stupid doing) in 20-35 years, these responsible people must be put in prison until their last second of life; and all their wealth must be confiscated and used for repairing the state of humanity and the planet.

1.6. Ignored Political Realities

The world of politics is full of falseness, lies, cheating, deceit, perversion, distortion, candy-coated, trivializations, exaggerations, hypes, fabrications, manipulations, propaganda, brainwashing, empty promises, intrigues, breach of contracts, provocative neurotic games, imputations, tactical maneuvers, back-stabbing, shams, etc. The lies are mostly mixed with some truth. What are therefore the remaining topics for an 'objective' science of politics?

Normative statement: A political science that excludes these evil political 'games' is not worth much.

Politics (governments) are today in the service of the monetary masters and not of the people. We already have fascism and dictatorship flowering in USA and Europe, dictated to by the capitalistic class or the so called 'élite'. Herewith the political activities become a game for clowns and democracy converted into a farce. Politicians have not learned from history how dangerous the 'servants of the kings' can be. These 'servants' sit and operate everywhere in the key offices of the political systems in Europe and the USA.

Ignoring these neo-capitalistic developments makes the science of politics useless. Students simply have to copy a certain amount of sterile ideas and some structural facts, to pass the exams, and then they get the diploma and hopefully a job that gives a wage significantly above a workers' wage.

Nobody needs to read Marx or Smith – simply read the 'Trilogy on Economics' and you understand the world of economics and politics today, free from 'Marxism, socialism, or any other -ism.

State failure

There is no clear definition of 'state failure'. But we can discuss parameters that show some essential failures of politics; here some examples:

- Corruption
- Bribery and nepotism
- Misuse of 'God' and religion
- Inflation
- Depression
- Stagnation

- Decline of GDP
- Extreme Poverty
- High public debt
- High rate of unemployment
- Hunger
- Lack of (drinking) water
- Lack of (healthy) food
- High concentration of contamination
- Politicians don't represent the interests of their citizens
- Decrease in the middle class
- Inequality
- Governments are a charade
- Extreme economic imbalance
- Waste of money for non-sustainable projects
- Inefficient public administration
- Government is an instrument of oligarchic groups
- Serious allocation problems (for needs)
- Lack of public transport
- Lack of health services
- Inefficient public education
- Lack of vocational education
- Environmental destruction
- Lack of human rights
- Economic decline
- Chronic lies, cheating, deceit, empty promises
- People cannot trust their own public institutions
- Austerity implementation
- Reduction of (democratic) freedoms
- Terrorism
- Unrest
- Civil war
- War
- And so on

Fundamental critical question are:

- Does the (obligatory) syllabus of political science include (explore, analyze and discuss) such failure and its causes? No!
- Is anybody or a group of political agents (in the government) held accountable for such failure? No!

Normative statement: A political science that excludes these failures (and others not mentioned in the list) is not worth much. Political science becomes an abettor of economics.

Basic Living as a Human Value

Healthy food	Billions do not have it. Part of industrialized food is not healthy.
Healthy drinking water	Billions do not have it. Immense illnesses due to dirty drinking water.
A home, shelter	Billions do not have it or have something of inhumane miserable quality.
Own bathroom	Billions do not have it.
Own kitchen	Billions do not have it.
Access to electricity 24/7	Billions do not have it: More than 1 billion use wood and coal (produces high CO_2) for cooking.
Connected with sanitation	Billions do not have it. Sewage goes to the sea and into nature.
Clothes and shoes	Billions only have an absolute minimum (not enough).
Goods for living	Billions only have an absolute minimum (not enough).
Work (for making a living)	Billions do not have work or are underemployed; can't live a proper life with it.
Doing business	Western world: too regulated. Small & medium sized businesses shrinking.
Education (basic, vocational)	Billions do not have it or only a minimum. Fully or partly illiterate. A holistic approach for personal growth and mastering life is excluded all around the world.

☞ The political failure is obvious and outrageous!

The ignored folk

- Marriage is an archetypal value: ignored and abused!
- Family is an archetypal value: ignored and suffocated!
- Love is an archetypal value: ignored, abused, and destroyed!
- The truth is an archetypal value: ignored, abused and banned!
- Truth from the inner source of life: ignored, abused and banned!
- Authentic ways of living are of archetypal value: ignored and banned!
- Work is a genuine need of highest value: ignored and abused!

- Inner holistic development is an archetypal value: ignored and banned!
- Knowledge to master life is indispensable: ignored!
- Skills to master life are indispensable: ignored!
- Strong medium-sized businesses are pillars of society: ignored, destroyed!
- Healthy air is a common good of highest value: ignored, contaminated!
- Healthy water is a common good of highest value: ignored, contaminated!
- Healthy natural food is a good of highest value: ignored, contaminated!
- Having a home is an absolute basic need: ignored!
- Mentally healthy people form the strength of society: ignored, banned!
- Minimizing human made illnesses is of highest importance: ignored!
- Minimizing all kind of accidents is of highest importance: ignored!
- Stable economic conditions are indispensable for security: ignored!
- Balanced distribution of wealth is the foundation for peace: ignored!
- Huge natural areas in urban zones are a natural need: ignored!
- Spiritual intelligence is as valuable as rational intelligence: ignored!
- The potentials of mind and soul are crucial for evolution: ignored!
- 100% protection from debt traps and risks are indispensable: ignored!
- Inner fulfillment of people founding a paradisiac society: ignored!
- Natural, healthy, genuine social environment: ignored and hindered!
- The scope of individual development and biological rhythms: broken!
- Performance as a condition for upgrading living standard: ignored, limited!
- Collective longing for redemption, salvation: ignored, disrespected and abused!
- Manifoldness of cultural ways of living: disrespected, ignored and banned!
- Protection of the planet and its resources: disrespected, abused and ignored!
- Mental loading capacity (information): disrespected, abused and ignored!
- Living and growing from the inner source of life: ignored and banned!
- Putting the Archetypes of the Soul above money: unknown and totally banned!

→ All these human values do not express an ideology, or a dogma, or a fundamentalism, or a religion, or an idea or thought. They are simply genuine.

→ All these human values are authentically rooted in the ways that mind and soul in balance do operate (can be shaped, formed, enhanced) and represent the true potential for human evolution.

➜ Politicians, experts of political science, and the folks must decide: Do we want to destroy the psychical-spiritual evolution of mankind or protect and promote it?

The critical conclusions are not 'promising':

- The huge majority of political policies show a complete lack of these human values for all humans and society.
- The way of doing politics and practicing governance fully ignores these genuine values.
- The huge majority of politicians are traitors to all these genuine human values and therefore co-perpetrators of the deicide road map.
- Ignoring these human values in the practicing of governance will lead to the doom of all humanity.

1.7. The State of Humanity

Many scientists, experts, and institutions say:

"In a few decades the world will collapse."
"A world population of 9-10bn is not sustainable."
"An apocalyptic catharsis is inevitable."
"Already today too many people live on planet Earth."

The picture: Unemployment, economic inferno, public debt, poverty, misery, riots, wars, contamination, pollution, climate change, inhuman mega-cities, slums, collateral damages of car traffic, industrial accidents, increase of sea level, drought, floods, tornados and hurricanes, nuclear waste, waste, sewage, dirty water, industrial food and meat, famine, destroyed fish resources, exploitation, damaged eco-systems, illnesses, mental disease, behavior disorder, epidemic plagues, melting of glaciers, elimination of species, destruction of environment, crimes, mafia, corruption, lack of health care, analphabetism, lack of drinking water, decrease of agricultural land and forests, chemicals and pharmaceutics and heavy metals in the food chain and already in human's body, lies, cheat, distortion, brainwashing, manipulations, billions of humans radiating toxic mental energy, etc.

The dire state of humanity and the planet is actually much worse than the media report, much worse than people can see, and much worse than people can imagine. The most significant causes of the immense global problems today started around 25 years ago. The year 2000 already marked the 'point of no return' with the first serious irreversible damages we see today around the globe. The inertia of the complex actual developments will let humanity crash into a wall in 10 years if drastic measures are not taken soon. The next 'point of no return' in the year 2020 when the process of destruction accelerates creating unimaginable and extremely frightening problems for humanity that will only fully come to the surface 10 years later; that means around the year 2030.

🖎 The state of humanity is herewith a matter of the tragic failure of politicians and politics.

These politicians have no solutions. They are all desperate in the iron grip of the super elites from the banking world. Indeed, there are a few unimaginably powerful people, driven by a titanic psychotic mission, absolutely unscrupulous and down-and-dirty. They have no conscience. They have no problem to destroy the entire world and to eliminate humanity. They are unlimitedly obsessed that this is their mission from God and they are chosen to 'punish humanity' at all costs, even if only a few (hundred-) thousand 'chosen people' survive. The roots of this incredible lunacy started around 2700-3000 years ago with the culmination 2000 years ago.

❦ The state of humanity is herewith also a matter of the tragic failure of religions.

The state of humanity and the planet is in immense danger of complete collapse within 35-40 years. This is the result of people that ignore the human values and that are too cowardly and hypocritical to stand up for these human values and for the Archetypes of the Soul.

People should not think now that they can just continue living as usual and start changing their way of living and thinking when everything becomes visibly mad! Today, and with every month that goes by humanity cannot continue to live as usual, the consequences will just increase exponentially and in 20 years will be absolutely disastrous and uncontrollable: the beginning of the end!

Normative statement: The people, the master of economics, and the politicians are guilty for these absolutely devilish developments!

Innumerable individuals and institutions offer false promises and solutions:

Scientists, politicians, authorities and leaders in economy and industry, religious communities and leaders, spiritual masters, media, and bloggers offer solutions. The meanders are countless. The distorted realities cover the truth. Hidden interests and objectives determine their solutions. Psychopaths with religious psychosis fight for their solution. The good will of many experts with their conceptual approaches is precious, but inefficient. All solutions must consider the evil power of some people behind the collective sceneries.

Secret Societies will never have the solution: Forget the Bilderberg Group! Forget the Illuminati! Forget the Freemasons! Forget The Order of Skull and Bones! Forget the Rosicrucians! Forget the Ordo Templis Orientis! Forget the Hermetic Order of The Golden Dawn! Forget The Knights Templar! Forget the Opus Dei! Forget the Royalties and Aristocrats!

During the last 30 years I had an estimated 12.000 dreams showing me the state and development of humanity and the earth. It is much worse than most people recognize! The elites, the illuminati, all kind of secret organizations, the most powerful people and the super-rich around the globe will lose everything.

- ✸ Risk: The entire humanity will fall into a dark Abyss within 35-40 years.
- ✸ Nearly 7 billion people are imprisoned in a dark labyrinth of lies and deceit.
- ✸ Madness, falseness, dirty propaganda, and manipulations govern over nearly everything and everyone in the world.
- ✸ Most of humanity is dehumanized, degenerated, and confused, due to contamination and the media: programmed to be soulless robots!
- ✸ There is absolutely no sustainability for 8, 9, or 10 billion world citizens.

What does this state of humanity say about the political sciences? What does the state of humanity tell us about the politicians? What does the entire political system (structures) tell us about governmental organization?

We have extensively explored with hundreds of facts the mega-parameters of the entire humanity and the world (Schellhammer. Economics III. 2012).

We have 7 billion people on earth now. In around 12 years an estimated 8 billion people will live on earth; in 25 years we will have 9 billion people on earth. By 2050, 10 billion people will be one earth; growth will continue!

There are and there will be in 2030-2050 much more needs and wants:

Of highest economic and political importance is the fact: Estimated every 13-15 (or: 12-13) years one billion more people – in total 3 billion more people in 40-45 years will have additional needs and wants:

- A home
- A job, work
- Money for living
- Education, professional and higher education
- Public Health Care
- Medicaments
- Healthcare
- Sanitation
- Food and beverage
- Healthy water

- Water for agriculture
- Fertile agriculture land, free of contamination
- Energy (electricity, gas, oil, petrol)
- A variety of natural resources
- Sewage and rubbish recycling
- Clothes and shoes
- All kinds of products and goods
- Furniture
- Hardware
- Detergents and toilet articles
- Cars and scooters
- Condoms
- Televisions
- Stationary articles
- Mobile phones
- Computer and internet connection
- Leisure areas
- Touristy opportunities
- Fun and entertainment
- And much more …

→ The consequences for the global economy will be monstrous!

Every 13-15 years one billion more people – in total 3 billion more people in 40-45 years will need efficient political management and state administrations which includes political decisions and management.

The future challenges for politicians:

- The production processes
- The allocation of goods and services
- Citizen registration and control
- Tax registration, collection and management
- Public traffic systems (people and goods)
- Registrations of cars and vehicles
- Courts and policing institutions
- Road construction and maintenance
- Sanitation and waste disposal
- Disposal of corpses
- Contamination regulations
- Nuclear waste maintenance
- Electricity delivery and maintenance

- Water system maintenance
- Pension systems
- Education and research
- Culture promotion
- Public health care
- Energy resources management
- Media systems
- Food production
- Food quality control
- Building more homes
- Allocating construction licenses
- Management of catastrophes
- Military forces and secret services
- Economic and industrial systems
- Businesses and service sector
- And much more ...

→ The consequences for the political apparatus and for global governance will be monstrous!

If every human being on this earth continues living as usual and if unimaginable drastic economic, political and social measures are not taken globally before the year 2020, then you must expect to experience the following picture of the world with some key words to draw the fields – just multiply today's stated global problems by 300% and that means the complete destruction of the planet and a doomed humanity.

The 30 big problems of humanity, the earth, and the planet are:

1. **Earth population:** Increasing, urban growth, declining youth population, increasing elderly population, motives for procreating a baby, increase of needs, contamination, risks, no sustainability
2. **Poverty:** Famine, hunger, misery, lack of food and drinking water; causes; physical, psychical and social effects; different patterns of poverty in all countries, no sustainability
3. **Contamination:** Sewage, garbage, electro-waste, drugs, detergents, pollution, fine dust; network of causes; chain of effects; increase in population growth, no sustainability
4. **Destruction of agriculture:** Drought, desertification, deforestation, floods, tornados; effects on food production, food prices and social life; lost value of agricultural land, no sustainability

5. **Exploitation of manpower:** Abuse, child labor, slavery, low wages, working conditions, destruction of human values and social life, attitudes of exploitation, no sustainability

6. **Exploitation of resources:** food and non-food; limited water resources; no sustainability of natural resources; speculations; no sustainability for production

7. **Energy production:** Coal, nuclear power stations, renewable energy, producing energy with manpower; consumers of energy; risks; costs; increasing long term demand, no sustainability

8. **Transport:** Car traffic, public and goods transport traffic (air, train, sea, bus, tram); life style and demand of transport; direct and lateral effects (contamination, accidents), no sustainability

9. **Climate change:** Causes; catastrophes and economic consequences; long term effects on eco-systems, rising sea levels, glaciers melting, species dying, humans, societies, countries; long term costs of damages, no sustainability

10. **Industry:** Overproduction, mass production, globalization; mega corporate groups and their power; damages to small and medium businesses; effects on humans; environmental damages

11. **Economy:** Financial institutions, public debt, consumer debt, low earnings, speculation businesses; power of mega-institutions and their owners and CEOs; complex effects, no sustainability

12. **Business:** Decrease of small and medium sized businesses; lack of genuine innovation, ignored importance and sustainability of such businesses; laws and regulations; no sustainability

13. **Health:** Physical and mental illnesses, diseases, addictions; epidemics; accidents (Traffic, work, home, leisure); lack of health care; costs and exploitation (abuse), no sustainability

14. **Law and human rights:** Lack of laws for nature; power interests; police intervention; injustice; courts and corruption; abuse of laws for power and mega greed; no sustainability

15. **Extinction of species:** Due to contamination and climate change; complexity of importance for nature and food chain; consequences of decrease of certain species; no sustainability

16. **Environmental destruction:** Due to over-construction and other causes; catastrophes as a result; urban expansion and influences on humans, human life and society, no sustainability

17. **Extinction of nature:** Due to contamination and climate change; deforestation and its long term consequences on the climate; destruction of human, social, species life; no sustainability

18. **Eco-systems damages:** Contamination, climate change; global (all-areas) consequences; destruction of food resources, islands, land, beaches, water resources, no sustainability

19. **Unemployment:** High rate, lack of earning (not enough work) opportunities; political and economic causes; economic imbalance, the long term costs and damages, no sustainability
20. **Politics:** Lack of real democracy; distorted communication; inefficiency; lack of qualifications of politicians; career brainwashing; abuse of power, taxes; cheating entire folks; too many vested interests; no sustainability
21. **State administration:** Lack of quality and efficiency; rigid regulations; totalitarianism, over-control, over-regulations; lack of professionalism; no sustainability
22. **Leaders and power:** Abuse of power, world power aspiration, the elites behind the scene undermining democracy; the uncontrollable excessive financial power; no sustainability
23. **Military and wars:** Militarization, wars, civil wars; terrorism; economic and cyber war; weapon manufacturer's interests; triggering wars with intrigues and false flags; no sustainability
24. **Trouble spots:** Tensions, unrest, riots, civil wars, political crimes; the causes and effects; police reactions, military and leaders; lack of knowledge and skills for solutions, no sustainability
25. **Crimes:** Organized crime, corruption; crime, violence, cheating, scams; prison life; the human sources of crimes; the function of deviating from political crimes, no sustainability
26. **Media:** Brainwashing, manipulation, power of information; the almost impossibility for individuals to address a folk; propaganda for the elite's interests, no sustainability
27. **Religions:** Dogmatism, fundamentalism, myths, superstitions, deception, falseness, brainwashing; power abuse; lack of authentic and comprehensible 'divine' experiences, no sustainability
28. **Ethics and human values:** Lack of moral and human values; the lost truth; the all-embracing exploitation of human's soul and life; no respect for ethics in politics or life, no sustainability
29. **Public education:** Analphabetism, lack of vocational schools; the state of humanity and the planet as an expression of lack of education or wrong education, no sustainability
30. **Conspiracy or facts:** WTC, Apollo 12, false flags, murdering, intrigues, hidden triggering (by proxy) wars, the hidden moguls ruling the world for more than 2,000 years, no sustainability

→ Extrapolate the picture by one billion people more, then by two billion more, and then by three billon people more (means 10bn people on earth).
→ Think about that, you (if you are not already old) will experience these dire realities with immensely increasing explosive calamities in the future.
→ The topmost drive that leads to this future is the outrageous capitalistic economics and capitalistic dictatorship madly obsessed with war.

The mega problems of humanity are all human made, for example:

- Unlimited capitalism has enslaved humanity, created these gluttonous consumers and decayed human's soul.
- Psychotic greed and complete arrogance of capitalists exploit all resources and every vivid thing.
- 95% of humanity will be enslaved from suffering, lack of money and from debt.
- All ecosystems are irreversibly poisoned and damaged from toxins and climate change.
- Fish resources and healthy agricultural land will become extremely scarce.
- Endless more extinction of species, more deforestation, and more wonderful islands will disappear.
- Glaciers worldwide are incessantly melting and with that water resources are rapidly decreasing.
- Expect more floods, drought, fires, hurricanes, acute weather changes, riots, social unrest, and civil wars.
- Immense amounts of CO_2 and methane gas are being released incessantly into the air.
- The chain reaction of nature is all embracing: also the air will be thinner in 40-50 years.
- The increase of sea levels will hit half of humanity and change the life of all humans within decades.
- Billions will migrate in search of a new home, for land, work, food, and drinking water.
- The toxic cocktail of global contamination will create plagues and kill billions of people in the near future.
- Fine dust everywhere produces more and more painful illnesses, cancer, and even mental dysfunction.
- Medicine and drugs and hundreds of chemicals are already in all food chains and water supplies.
- Sewage and waste from 7 billion people and nuclear waste around the globe is poisoning the planet.
- The Western media, including Google, Facebook and other social networks are in the hands of evil.
- Western media operates with brainwashing, deceit, fabrications, distortions, poisoning human's minds.
- Accreditation bodies suffer from compulsive disorder and operate with totalitarian control in capitalistic interests.
- Accredited public and academic education destroy inner potentials, genuineness, and finding pioneering solutions.

- Increasing unemployment, poverty and misery, and natural catastrophes will hit billions of people.
- Religions have failed terribly in their mission for love, peace, truthfulness, fulfillment, and human values.
- Christianity, and the 'Holy Bible' are archaic, fabricated, and distorted, a botch to subordinate human's soul.
- Christianity killed a billion people during its history in the name of J.C.: Christian teachings are a scam.
- An absolute madness in Western 'golden palaces' is trying to dominate the entire humanity with an iron fist.
- The psychopathic predators come from the US, Europe and Israel, with roots in the Judeo-Christian faiths.
- It's not a failure of leaders; it's intended and orchestrated from mad elites with a long lunatic history!
- The devil has full control over speculators, rating agencies, central banks, stock markets, IMF, World Bank, Central Banks …
- Most leaders in international corporations and in capitalistic governments are only paid puppets.
- The puppet masters pulling the strings behind the scene for more than 2000 years are total monsters.
- These monsters destroy governments, countries, folks, economies, cultures, infrastructures, and the planet.
- Wars over and over again since Roman times are triggered by these monsters; also the upcoming WWIII.
- The root of all evil lies in Genesis: "You are the chosen folk; dominate the world and every vivid thing."

Billions of people need to be collectively punished for their lies, falseness, hypocrisy, and cowardice. Also blinded, ignorant, naïve, credulous, conceited, lazy-minded, blabbering masses need a dire lesson. A terrible global war eliminating up to 80% of the earth population seems to be an inevitable matter of nature. Actually we are at the point of no return: One spark and half of the world explodes and burns.

→ It is self-evident that we don't let polar bears walk around in towns, villages and cities. People need to be protected from polar bears with all necessary means.

Each of the following parameters has highest political implications and implies hundreds of billions if not $1-2 trillion costs per year. Some sources speak about $3-5 trillion per year alone (costs of damages) from the big corporations:

The most important mega-parameters of societies and the world:

- Population growth
- Poverty and economic imbalance
- Scarcity for primary needs
- Lack of infrastructures
- Lack of healthy food
- Lack of healthy water and water for agriculture
- Decrease of underground water resources
- Glaciers melting (water reservoirs)
- Decreasing agriculture land and soil degradation
- Deforestation, desertification, decomposition
- Over-exploitation of seas and oceans
- Over-exploitation of raw resources
- Irreversibly damaged eco-systems
- Species reduction and elimination
- Contamination: chemicals, pharmaceutics
- Contamination: fine dust, waste, nuclear waste, sewage
- Collateral effects of the transport systems
- Nuclear waste and its maintenance
- Climate change with consequences for production
- Drought, flood, fire, tornados, storms, hurricanes
- Disease and all kind of illnesses, accidents
- Mental and behavior disorder of all kind
- Crimes and corruption
- Rearmament, military and wars
- Unrest, trouble spots and radicalism
- Mega-cities and its social-mental effects
- Reparation of damages and measures for protection
- Decrease of human values, dehumanization
- Destruction of democratic values, principles
- Increasing money demand globally for living

🖎 Although these mega-parameters are of highest importance and a supreme political concern today and for much more in the future, we found very little and by the majority absolutely nothing about it in all the syllabi and tables of content of political science books.

Normative statement: A political science that excludes these mega-parameters as a political subject is not worth much. Political science becomes an abettor of the deicide road map.

Effects of Mega-Parameters

A first short approach requires a differentiation between causes and effects.

Parameters (cause):

- Contamination
- Pollution
- Destruction
- Damages
- Diminishment

Parameters (effect):

- Affects human body
- Affects mind and soul
- Affects social life
- Affects species
- Affects ecosystems
- Destroys human values
- Destroys environment
- Destroys resources
- Puts the planet in danger
- Puts humanity in danger
- Creates risks of unrest and wars

Parameters (agents):

- Human's characteristics
- Institutional characteristics
- Society's characteristics
- Political characteristics
- Religion's characteristics

- Media's characteristics
- Educational characteristics
- Economic characteristics
- Academic characteristics
- Ethical characteristics

<u>Parameters (non-productive costs): damages, destruction, elimination, prevention:</u>

- Short term costs
- Long term costs
- Super long term effects
- The cost's of long term effects

<u>Who pays for the costs?</u>

→ There are direct costs that are burdened on the global economy.
→ There are indirect costs due to systemically destroyed resources.
→ There are the costs for repair, protection, and prevention.
→ There are the not definable costs from the loss of human values.
→ The total costs of these parameters exceed $ 20trillion per year.
→ These costs are 'mega-parameters' that dominate the global economy.

✸ Although these networks of perspectives are of highest importance and a supreme political concern today and much more in the future, we found very little and by the majority absolutely nothing about it in all the syllabi and tables of content of political science.

Normative statement: A political science that excludes these mega-parameters as a political subject is not worth much. Political science becomes an abettor of the deicide road map.

The accumulation of the destructive mega-parameters by every decade

- Population growth
- Poverty and economic imbalance
- Lack of primary needs and infrastructures
- Lack of healthy food
- Lack of healthy water and water for agriculture
- Decrease of underground water resources
- Glaciers melting (water reservoirs)
- Decreasing agriculture land and soil degradation

- Deforestation, desertification, decomposition
- Over-exploitation of seas and oceans
- Over-exploitation of raw resources
- Irreversibly damaged eco-systems
- Species reduction and elimination
- Contaminating chemicals, pharmaceutics
- Contamination: fine dust, waste, sewage
- Nuclear waste and its maintenance
- Climate change with damages for production
- Droughts, floods, fires, tornados, storms, hurricanes
- Disease and all kind of illnesses, accidents
- Mental and behavior disorder of all kind
- Crimes and corruption
- Rearmament, military and wars
- Unrest, trouble spots and radicalism
- Mega-cities and its social-mental effects
- Reparation of damages & measures for protection
- Decrease of human values, dehumanization
- Destruction of democratic values, principles

→ The collective unconscious contains the collective history of mankind!
→ Humanity is in permanent interaction with the collective unconscious!
→ The explosive content of the collective unconscious is the superior threat!

Creative thinking:

→ Extrapolate the picture by one billion people more, then by two billion more, and then by tree billon people more (means 10bn people on earth).
→ Think about that, you (if you are not already old) will experience these dire realities with immensely increasing explosive calamities in the future.
→ The topmost drive that leads to this future is the outrageous capitalistic economics and capitalistic politics (dictatorship, fascist systems) madly obsessed with war.

☞ Although these networks of perspectives are of highest importance and a supreme political concern today and much more in the future, we found very little and by the majority absolutely nothing about it in all the syllabi and tables of content.

Normative statement: A political science that excludes the political importance of these increasing mega-parameters is not worth much. Political science becomes an abettor of an outrageous sham.

A Spanish news report (translated): "...Scientists from allover the world forecast an immanent planetary collapse ... Today, the next change of the global state will be very baleful for our civilizations, and once a planetary change is produced, there is no return ... Humans have done nothing really important to avoid the worst." [33]

In the coming 3 decades we will have to expect dire developments: 2-3 billions will die from hunger and more billions will die from contamination. Maybe up to 2 billion will die from the most satanic war that ever existed. In the end, the best case in the decennium 2050-2060 an estimated 2-3 billion people will have survived (many with genetic defects) and will live in conditions worse than in the Middle Ages. Should contamination be all-embracing and destroy all eco-systems worldwide, then at best a few hundred million people will survive.

- The state of humanity and the planet are an expression of politicians.
- The state of humanity and the planet shows the face of political science.
- Politics is not about the truth, it's about distorting facts as long as it can.
- Political science doesn't offer anything to avoid the upcoming doom.
- Political science does offer nothing to solve humanity's mega-problems.
- Wars and bellicose practices are an expression of the politicians.
- Many politicians are also a result of political sciences.
- From this perspective the political science is a complete failure.
- The entire accreditation system for all social sciences turns out to be a sham.

→ Do you think that political science and the politicians have nothing to do with these 30 big problems of humanity?

Normative statement: A political science that excludes and ignores these most important national and global mega-parameters with its future developments and long term effects for humans and societies for millenniums becomes an abettor of the deicide program.

---

[33] http://www.que.es/ultimas-noticias/curiosas/201206062036-cientificos-aseguran-revista-nature-colapso-cont.html

Perception and Picture about the World

The external reality and the internal reality

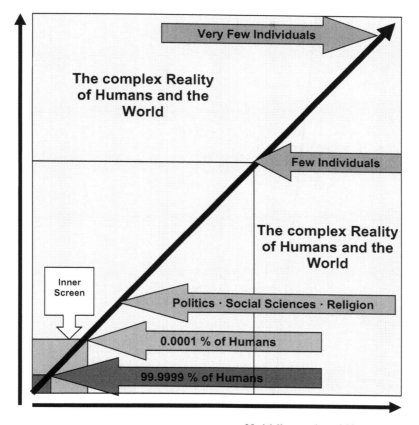

Amount of Elements

Humane Maximum

Very Few Individuals

The complex Reality of Humans and the World

Few Individuals

The complex Reality of Humans and the World

Inner Screen

Politics · Social Sciences · Religion

0.0001 % of Humans

99.9999 % of Humans

Multidimensional Network Mind, Soul, World, Planet

Senses – Perception – Defense Mechanisms – Becoming aware – Feeling – Memorizing – Thinking? – Interpreting – Judging – Concluding – Behavior

<u>Conclusion:</u> The inner screen: highly reduced, distorted, interpreted, judged Considered as the truth about psychical, spiritual, and external realities.

1.8. The Methods of Political Science

The German website mentioned below makes it clear: "The political science does not teach students for a political career. The political science explores political institutions and processes. Political scientists for example explore the causes of wars (…) or they ask how different political systems deal with Climate Change. Politics stimulates emotions. The science of politics stays objective: their analysis are based on theories and empirical methods, for example measuring voting behavior." [34]

We do not consider this statement as an official scientific statement; it may be an individual voice. But it makes thinking as it represents a general old-fashioned understanding of social sciences, based on Weber or Popper and others from this kind of positivistic school.

☞ An exclusive positivistic understanding of social sciences is already a tool of deicide.

A politician should have extensive and precise knowledge about political institutions and processes. He must have a clear and profound understanding about the causes of wars (which fundamentally lies in human factors). For a politician it is important to know how representatives from other political systems deal with Climate Change (pro or con). It is not true that politics simply stimulates emotions. The different opinions and all the lies and cheating around political topics create emotions.

A politician must have extensive knowledge that partly offers the list mentioned in chapter 1.2. In that sense, studying political science is a preparation, is an indispensable foundation for political careers. But we agree: such foundation is absolutely not enough for a political function with high responsibility.

Normative statement: A politician that does not have such foundation is in the wrong place.

---

[34] http://ranking.zeit.de/che2012/de/fachinfo/28

Today, political science is an academic discipline: "Disagreement about the nature of political activity is matched by controversy about the nature of politics as an academic discipline. One of the most ancient spheres of intellectual enquiry, politics was originally seen as an arm of philosophy, history or law ... From the late nineteenth century onwards, however, this philosophical emphasis was gradually displaced by an attempt to turn politics into a scientific discipline." [35]

The big picture of political science shows us that the scientific methods vary depending on the field, from case studies, statistics, general social methodology to hermeneutics. To claim that political science is a natural science like physics is a derailment if not a deceit. It's the same wrong approach as in economics that is preponderantly nothing more than an ideology. Economic laws and principles are a myth. [36]

The statement 'political science is objective' can open a very extensive discussion. Surely, first and foremost, the first step of social science is to explore realities of political relevance, to describe facts as minutely as possible up to the 'Nano' elements. The more exact a reality is described, the better are the results and the better is the understanding of the matter. To have an eye only on the visible superficiality leads to a very reduced observation. Everything has a manifold network with other elements forming the matter. Human factors also play a decisive role.

"A science of politics is clear. It promises an impartial and reliable means of distinguishing 'truth' from 'falsehood', thereby giving us access to objective knowledge about the political world." [37] The context of this statement doesn't make clear if the author cites a general understanding of political science or if this is his personal opinion. The statement itself is insane:

☝ How distorted and sick is a mind that creates such distortions and lies?
☝ The sole motive for such distortions is a hidden cantankerousness.

➡ If the concept of a chosen reality (unity) is much reduced, then the 'truth' is also much reduced. It leads to distorted and disfigured results.
➡ The 'falsehood' of statements about realities already is pre-programmed with the (theoretically) supposed unity (entity) of the research object.
➡ The author confirms it: "What we can learn about individual behavior is limited and superficial."

---

[35] Heywood, 2007 p. 13
[36] Orrell David. Economyths. London. 2010
[37] Heywood, 2007 p. 17

Objectively we can describe a war situation, the activities and everything being real around a battle. The causes have many dimensions, especially human factors and hidden fabricated economic conditions or a false flag. War is always emotional for the actors, the victims, and the spectators (on the television). War has a lot to do with loss of human values, perverted human minds, hate, rage, greed, megalomania, psychosis and psychopathy; sometimes the motives are objectively identifiable as an indispensable act of defense. The Germans are brainwashed by the media since decenniums that Hitler was the evil man and only he is guilty for the WWII. There is no political science or science of history that explores and reveals the 'invisible hands' that provoked Hitler's bellicose actions. And nobody talks about Stalin's servants or the financiers of Marx, Lenin, Trotsky, and others from this circle, or about the servants today in the United States and in most European countries.

Another example to show the problem of political science and methodology: We can make a list of all the visits from the head of state of Germany, France, United Kingdom, United States, etc. There is always a motive for such visits. What are the motives of the head of states not to visit a neighbor country or any country of interest? The answers would reveal unimaginable unspoken realities behind the curtains of the politics. But would such result be considered as 'scientific'?

☙ Political science does never touch 'hot potatoes' nor the processes that broil the potatoes.

Heywood makes it very clear: "The idea that models and theories of politics are entirely value-free is difficult to sustain when examined closely. Facts and values are so closely intertwined that it is often impossible to pry them apart. This is because theories are invariably constructed on the basis of assumptions about human nature, human society, the role of the state and so on that have hidden political and ideological implications." [38]

Therefore this kind of 'objective methods' will always result in the confirmation of the beautiful political lies, objectively and without emotions. From here and from many other examples we could conclude that this 'objective methods' serve to hide lies and to construct a never existing 'objective' reality. In some countries there are criminal laws that prohibit asking critical questions about delicate political matters of facts.

☙ Political science is de facto not free in choosing topics for scientific research and teaching (exploring) political criticalities.

---

[38] Heywood, 2007 p. 17

☞ Political science is de facto and immanently not free from values, ideologies, emotional attitudes, and presuppositions.

It seems as if 'emotions' (or emotional themes) are something like valueless spume for the social (political) sciences. But the emotional system in the mind of people is as valuable and important as the intelligence (the cognitive functions). In that sense 'emotions' are not simply a nasty accompaniment of humans or of political matters. Emotions are the result of something and they produce something; and this complexity must form part of social sciences, including political science. All types of emotions have a meaning!

Normative statement: Experts in the social sciences should be fired when they reduce humans to (objective) behavior (voting) patterns or 'measurable' cognitive functions or controllable opinions (attitudes) or visible and measurable (e.g. consumer or tax-payer) behavior.

It is also possible that political science explores the emotional reactions of people in specific matters. As we can see with the list in chapter 1.2, many subjects require extensive lecturing and the students must acquire knowledge from both near and far past. Students cannot simply read about ideologies, ideas, concepts and visions from the last centuries or millenniums. The challenging part is the right interpretation and understanding within the frame and context of the time and conditions (political, social, religious, education, and ways of living) from these (historical) authors. This is an essential part of the study of political science.

➔ Objectivity and neutrality in the social sciences are on the scientific, methodic, and personal level of its agents a Chimera!

"This means that scientific objectivity, in the sense of absolute impartiality or neutrality, must always remain an unachievable goal in political analysis, however rigorous our research methods may be." [39]

➔ The problem with the scientific objectivity already starts with choosing the subjects for a Bachelor and Master program of political science.
➔ If the department of education and the accreditation institutions decide about the syllabi, what is allowed and not desired to research and teach, then already the thin part of achievable objectivity is affected by a systemic fault.

---

[39] Heywood, 2007 p. 18

Methods of social sciences

"In the 1950s and 1960s with the emergence, most strongly in the USA, of a form of political analysis that drew heavily upon behavioralism. For the first time, this gave politics reliably scientific credentials, because it provided what had previously been lacking: objective and quantifiable data against which hypotheses could be tested. Political analysts such as David Easton proclaimed that politics could adopt the methodology of the natural sciences, and this gave rise to a proliferation of studies in areas best suited to the use of quantitative research methods, such as voting behavior, the behavior of legislators, and the behavior of municipal politicians and lobbyists." [40]

→ 'Objective data' and 'quantifiable data' can be completely different. The elaboration of a case study can result in 'objective data', but not necessarily in quantifiable data. Analyzing the attitudes of a politician in the way he communicates, can lead to non-quantifiable, but objective result.

→ De facto from the matters of politics the political science can adopt the methodology of the natural sciences only in the sense of 'counting something measurable'. But how can we quantify all kind of communication and mediation or conflict resolutions?

→ How can we quantify 'meaning'? How can we quantify for example the meaning of 'evil' or even 'good' in political doing?

"Although behavioral analysis undoubtedly produced, and continues to produce, invaluable insights in fields such as voting studies, a narrow obsession with quantifiable data threatens to reduce the discipline of politics to little else. More worryingly, it inclined a generation of political scientists to turn their backs upon the entire tradition of normative political thought." [41]

→ Where are the politicians, the leaders with great character, excellent moral attitudes, and peaceful visions for a nation with a folk that can grow in a psychical-spiritual evolution?

→ Where is the political science that explores the psychical-spiritual evolution and its political management as a fundamental pillar in a society?

---

[40] Heywood, 2007 p. 14
[41] Heywood, 2007 p. 15

"The basic of assertion that behavioralism is objective and reliable is the claim that it is 'value-free': that is, that it is not contaminated by ethical or normative beliefs. However, if the focus of analysis is observable behavior, it is difficult to do much more than describe the existing political arrangements, which implicitly means that the status quo is legitimized." [42]

→ Ethical and normative statements (claims) are not necessarily 'contaminating'. It's today rather the other way round: the lack of ethics and norms (based on human values) contaminate the entire world of politics.

→ There are certain archetypal human values that are indispensable for humans, folks, and for humanity. They encompass genuine human values and they are normative and unchangeable, eternal and in a certain way infallible.

→ Do you want the regicide and deicide allover the world, executed from the neo-capitalistic coalition and their enslaved politicians, with the roadmap from the hidden supreme masters (of economics) until the planet is irreparably destroyed and humanity dehumanized and degenerated, and in the end eliminated? Political science must answer this question everywhere and all the time by exploring, researching, and evaluating real political activities and its results!

☞ The thesis that says 'science alone provides a means of disclosing truth' is the result of sick, insane and soulless humans. It reduces humans to a human biomass, to rats, and to a mechanistic understanding of humans and society.

☞ There is not much intelligence required to understand that all vivid organisms are never simply a mechanical apparatus. Scientists in the social sciences with such primitive scientific understanding poison and destroy humanity and the planet!

Normative statement: The 'truth' is much more than the result of the methods of natural sciences. A political science does not need such mentally sick and soulless humans! Fire them and put them in a re-education camp to find their soul (inner life, their unconscious mind).

In that sense, in the real world and in social sciences generally, there are not many 'clean' and 'sterile' theories and empirical methods. It's always about humans and archetypal human values. Most factors that become a topic of political research include the meaning of countless components.

---

[42] Heywood, 2007 p. 15

→ Hermeneutics is indispensable in social science and it consists of rules that create 'objective' knowledge beyond the statistical methods from today.

→ To equate 'measurable' and 'countable' with 'science', excluding other scientific approaches, is not only a reduction of realities; it's a manipulation avoiding to identify the real world of humans in general, of politicians in particular, and of society's life as a whole.

From Wikipedia we get an orientation about the scientific methods and its philosophical background: "Political science is methodologically diverse and appropriates many methods originating in social research. Approaches include positivism, interpretivism, rational choice theory, behavioralism, structuralism, post-structuralism, realism, institutionalism, and pluralism. Political science, as one of the social sciences, uses methods and techniques that relate to the kinds of inquiries sought: primary sources such as historical documents and official records, secondary sources such as scholarly journal articles, survey research, statistical analysis, case studies, experimental research and model building." [43]

Heywood points out some more methodical problems to consider. We summarize and extend:

1) Concepts are tools with which we think criticize, argue, explain and analyze.

2) Concepts help to classify objects by recognizing that they have similar forms or similar properties. Concepts include ideological components.

3) The political terms (e.g. democracy, freedom, justice, and etcetera) have extensive objective and subjective connotations.

4) A model is a didactical tool reflecting a hypothesis or a theory or a systemic composition or an idea. A model serves to understand and therefore is something useful for example for presentation, discussion, or a summary.

5) We add: A theory is a proven hypothesis. A model can represent didactically (visually) a hypothesis or a thesis.

6) We add: Political science is not free (neutral) from interests of a particular group or class. Ideological components and bias are everywhere.

---

[43] http://en.wikipedia.org/wiki/Political_science

6) Generally the author says: "Much of academic political science, for example, has been constructed according to liberal-rationalist assumptions, and thus bears the imprint of its liberal heritage." [44]

Nevertheless social sciences offer many tools in order to operate scientifically (objectively) aiming (new) knowledge and understanding (political) realities and its interrelations.

We list here what we consider as essential methods:

- Explorations
- Exact description
- Analysis (decomposing)
- Systemic analysis (network, interrelations)
- Content analysis
- Comparative analysis
- Case studies
- Statistics
- Experimental research
- Model building
- Hermeneutics (interpretation)

We list here what we consider as essential sources:

- A specific real field
- People (mind, behavior, needs, etc.)
- Historical documents
- Official records
- Scholarly journal articles
- Survey research results
- Statistical results
- Results of content analysis
- Alternative press and expert websites (Internet)

We identify seven essential dimensions of social science:

1. Positive, descriptive, analytical, holistic, systemic, dynamic
2. Objective realities versus human factors (mind, behavior)
3. Normative aspects; imply values for or of humans, and decisions

---

[44] Heywood, 2007 p. 21

4. Choosing a topic is a decision and implies a normative dimension
5. The practical relevance includes a normative dimension
6. Ignoring factors of a matter has a normative dimension
7. Ignoring parts of a complex field includes a normative dimension

→ In social sciences 'descriptive and normative' are in an inseparable intrinsic relation.

Descriptive and normative dimensions are intrinsically related. For example, psychology can analyze the self-management or the way of thinking or talking of people with a hundred characteristics. In all cases, the result shows a certain level of quality or efficiency. A very low quality as well as a very high quality (of performance) becomes intrinsically a normative trait. The result can't be better than the quality of the behavior (performance). Therefore the result also has a descriptive and a normative dimension – inseparable!

Scientists can't simply focus on the descriptive (measurable) dimension and ignore the normative (qualitative) dimension. The normative dimension can be seen as a descriptive scale of a value (good-bad, efficient-inefficient, constructive-destructive, true-false, right-wrong, progressive-regressive, and etcetera.

The world is made by humans, the folks and the politicians. Reducing political realities to ideas, ideologies, structures and some events by ignoring the inner world of humans, is a devalued approach to political realities.

- Ignoring these networks of humans (mind, life) as the most essential part of supreme political duties makes political science soulless and inhumane.
- The state of humans, of humanity and the planet, of the world of politics, and of political science clearly show us: Humans and a majority of humanity are already extremely dehumanized and regressed, and live with a horrifying distorted and rotten state of the mind and soul.

Normative statement: A political science that excludes these humane worlds as a political subject is not worth much. Political science becomes sterile, irrelevant and a wasted exercise.

Another important aspect of methodology is the meaning of the field and its variables. How can a scientist (in social sciences) operate a research project without understanding the meaning of the components to explore? What is the meaning of hunger, absolute poverty, unrest, rioting, or war and the already irreparably damaged eco-systems with its resources? A difficult task is also to make operational a general value, for example 'freedom' or 'democracy'. As a whole we conclude:

→ The methods of political science include much more than 'objective' realities, understood as 'countable' or 'measurable' or 'behavioral' (like physical science).
→ The methods combine inductive and deductive approaches, e.g. from attitudes to behavior or from behavior to attitudes (values), or from a result of human activities to behavior and from there to the mind and to (human) values.
→ The methods always must include the meaning and the fact that humans are not an apparatus, but a vivid organism as well as the nature and the entire planet – our 'mother earth' our 'home'.

Institutional public-choice theory

"Amongst recent theoretical approaches to politics is what is called formal political theory, variously known as 'political economy', 'public-choice theory' and 'rational-choice theory'. This approach to analysis draws heavily upon the example of economic theory in building up models based upon procedural rules, usually about the rationally self-interested behavior of the individual involved. (…) formal political theory provides at least a useful analytical device, which may provide insights into the actions of voters, lobbyists, bureaucrats and politicians, as well as into the behavior of states within the international system." [45]

→ 'Political economy', 'public-choice theory' and 'rational-choice theory' have their roots in the neo-capitalistic economics. We have extensively proven that such theories do not work, that they are very manipulative, and that they have a systemic fault trivializing and distorting human realities.
→ To get insight into the actions of voters, lobbyists, bureaucrats and politicians is indeed a matter of political science. The problem is how to get a concept about this 'inside'. It has to do with behavior; and behavior is highly tied to the systems of the brain or mind, which includes

---

[45] Heywood, 2007, p. 15

cogitative, emotional, inner needs, spiritual intelligence, and ability to love, the unconscious mind, and so on.

"(…) The rational-choice approach to political analysis overestimate human rationality in that it ignores the fact that people seldom possess a clear set of preferred goals and rarely make decisions in the light of seldom possess a clear set of preferred goals and rarely decisions in the light of full and accurate knowledge. Furthermore, in proceeding from an abstract model of the individual, rational-choice theory pays insufficient attention to social and historical factors, failing to recognize, amongst other things, that human self-interestedness may be socially conditioned, and not merely innate." [46]

→ We can fully agree with the author's critical statement about the rational-choice theory, a trap constructed from and by economists. As the entire capitalistic economics (seen as a mega-concept) always aims at the increase of profit we must ask: what for is the public-choice theory in the world of politics? It is the control of citizens by creating mainstream opinions (attitudes) in the society, especially in the interest of certain policies.

→ It does make sense to undertake research about voting behavior. The result can be used for manipulation (e.g. propaganda), style of communication (with the citizens). It can also lead to the knowledge that the entire folk need to be educated to become 'political humans', democratic participants.

→ A rational-choice approach in the field of lobbyism can reveal a lot about hidden interests and its power influences. To understand the bureaucrats and the effects of such mental and behavior structures can help to create more efficiency and flexibility in the administration. Stubborn bureaucrats paralyze the evolution of society and humanity's evolution as a whole.

→ We can understand the rational-choice approach as a method to get knowledge. At the same time we identify: the chosen ('objective') method together with the underlying concept about personhood already select (manipulate) the reality and have immanent purposes (for use and abuse).

Other methodological problems

▪ Identifying realities only with the eyes create superficial realities.

---

[46] Heywood, 2007, p. 16

- Neurotic or psychopathic people see the world in a neurotic (psychopathic) way.
- Highly narcissistic individuals have an ego-centered interest and view of the worlds.
- Strongly active defense mechanisms in personal matters operate equally in scientific matters.
- A society where the truth is replaced by lies creates mendacious social sciences.
- Social science separates what in reality is inseparable (e.g. behavior and inner life and 'meaning').
- The abuse of valuable words (e.g. democracy) distorts scientific work and results.

Is the political science a science?

We have explored in other books the science of economics and one important question was: Is the science of economics a science? And we have proven:

Economics is an ideology, a neo-capitalistic ideology and never a science. We have also proven that the science of economics does not reflect the real world of economics, and ignores completely all relevant human factors, psychological, spiritual, behavioral, and real (in the everyday life). We also have explored that the science of economics is a much reduced and artificial construct, ignoring most of the relevant interrelated systems. [47]

Therefore we have here the same questions:

- Is political science really a science?
- Does political science teach about the real world of politics?
- Is political science understood in its relevant intrinsic interrelations?
- Does political science consider the result of real politics (in society and the world)?
- Is a system of governance something 'objective' or an ideological expression?
- Is there (in the political systems) an intrinsic evolutionary dynamic?
- Is the political science naïve, trivial, superficial, and ignorant towards the human factors of political realities?
- Is the political science reduced to 'only what can be measured is part of science'?

---

[47] Schellhammer. Trilogy on Economics. 2012

- Are single political events, seldom repeated, also a topic of political science?
- Does political science brainwash students aiming to eliminate conscience and most other mental factors?

Normative statement: A political science that operates with a naïve and narrow positivistic understanding of social methodology is not worth much. Heavily neurotic people (men and women) should never be allowed to get a significant position in politics and political science because their state of mind already distorts realities even before they perceive and start thinking.

From these first explorations about the syllabi and understanding of political science we already are confronted with the question: Which subjects must be an indispensable part of the study program? The explored university programs do not give a satisfactory answer. But there must be an intrinsic construction of subjects that build up the necessary and relevant knowledge about political science. Other subjects may be declared as 'specifications' (to become a specialist in a specific topic) to set up above the foundation program (e.g. for a Master or PhD degree).

Many sciences have made significant progress in theories and as a result in practical implementation in order to understand and improve humans' life and society. What kind of new knowledge, new thesis and 'laws' has political science produced the last 50 years in order to become more democratic and, for example, more efficient in creating safety for people, peace, justice or to save the planet and avoid wars?

Do we have to suspect that most of what political science teaches is trivia, which means probably partly valuable, but essentially useless for professional application in the world of politics? Trivia does not lead to governmental innovations and progress in the real democracy; which means the essence of democracy expressed in the statement: 'government of the people, by the people, and for the people'. This statement has become irrelevant and is a myth.

Strictly speaking this is not a Democratic but Republican statement. The definition of a Republic is: "a constitutionally limited government of the representative type, created by a written Constitution - adopted by the people and changeable (from its original meaning) by them only by its amendment - with its powers divided between three separate Branches: Executive, Legislative and Judicial. Here the term 'the people' means, the electorate". [48]

---

[48] http://www.lexrex.com/enlightened/AmericanIdeal/aspects/demrep.html

In the USA and France (to a lesser extent) for example the President (Executive branch) which could be Republican or Democrat has limited powers and has to clear (almost) all actions and decisions through and by Congress (Lower House) which could be Republican or Democrat and Senate (Upper House) which again could be Republican or Democrat these are the Legislative branches.

The Judicial branch separate from both intervenes in extreme cases to act as the final check on the power of either the Executive or Legislative branches hears pro and counter arguments and rules. In essence this system was devised by The Founding Fathers of the USA (copied to a lesser extent by France) to create a series of "checks and balances on power" ensuring that "man's natural greed and corruption by power" did not succeed. They did not unfortunately foresee that; a) when this system becomes too partisan there is a log jam and; b) the power of the lobby groups to corrupt the Legislative branch.

One definition of a Democracy is: "Governance by leaders (of ideologically based parties) and parliamentary representatives whose authority is based on a limited mandate (term of office) from a universal electorate that selects (votes) among genuine alternatives (different policies) and has some rights to political participation and opposition and is represented by a Parliament of all major parties." [49]

This is the case of the UK (Parliamentary Democracy) and most European countries with the power of the Prime Minister (Rajoy, Merkel, Cameron) limited by a majority Parliamentary vote and ultimately the head of state (Queen, King or President) having the power of veto and an Upper House (Lords or Senators) acting as a "watchdog" on the Government.

In most of the European systems the Judicial branch is totally independent of government (in theory!!!). Again this system is designed to have a built in "check on the balance on power" and although a majority of Parliamentary representatives (by a party) is required to form a government and decisions and policy applications are much more fluid than the USA, this "check" can only be effected by the majority of MPs (Members of Parliament) voting against the ruling Government (kicking them out). But since this depends on a party holding a majority it tends to be rare and unlikely that they would vote their party out.

---

[49] Danziger 1998, 159 quoted on:
http://www.uiowa.edu/~c030142/DefinitionsOfDemocracy.html

Another point worth noting is that in the English language the word that is used to describe a group of baboons – arguably the most aggressive, loud, stupid and violent ape – is a parliament of baboons!

We will explore more about it and hopefully we will find a positive answer. But from the described (listed) syllabi we can't see any new knowledge in the interest of people, folks, societies, and humanity, or in the interest of peace and justice, or a balanced society, or to serve the common good. In a simple word:

- What are the scientific findings that can make the world (a society) better off?

A majority of people are politically apathetic and they do not trust the words and actions of politicians. Most of the citizens of a country do not even know the basic structure of the government and the names of the top office holders. We can interpret this as an intended result, partly to stabilize the governmental structures and processes, especially the power.

🖐 The self-interests of politicians and of economics are guaranteed as long as the rate of unemployment remains in a narrow frame; and as long as people have money for a humane living, and get a pension payment.

Normative statement: The real politics is a charade, full of lies and cheating, falseness and fabrications, and hidden evil doing. The science of politics is also part of this Charade. Both do not serve either their citizens or the world.

In the 'Trilogy on Economics' we have extensively explored the function of the big corporations, including the banking world, and came to the conclusion that they rule the governments, the societies and the world. Their sole interest is accumulation and concentration of money, wealth and through that world governance without being in (governmental) office. We couldn't find any subject in the syllabi that covers this criticality of global dimensions.

A very relevant question is also: How does the ideology of a political party influence the final decisions of a government? Or: What kind of ideological elements ('ideas') do finally lead to a political decision with real consequences for the society, the people and the world of business? A comparative interest could include United States, any European state or even countries in Asia, Africa or Latin America, not excluded Israel and the Arab world.

➡ Ignoring these modern capitalistic developments and the relevant methods that includes the human factors as a holistic entity, shapes the science of politics to a collaborator of the economical and political supreme masters.

♥ The actual methods of political science are much reduced, based on a wrong understanding of science and support with that the interests of the elite.
♥ Political science has no relevant progressive dynamics in the interest of a national and global psychical-spiritual evolution.

If we talk about social science we must contemplate some more specifications about the world of social sciences:

In the real world of social sciences, including political sciences, everything has a meaning, a value, a quality (or efficiency), a function, an effect, a result, a cause, and an interrelation. A fundamental difficulty is to get the right meaning in the context of a variable or a setting of variables. A meaning can be objective in the context of a theory or fact; but also in a subjective context. Meaning (value) can be innate or projective, determined, or simply functional. This is characteristic for humans and human life in general. This is a fact and not an ideological statement.

→ A social science (political science) that does not examine with scrutiny the meaning, value, quality, function, effect, result and cause of a variable with its interrelation is a very superficial science walking with children' shoes and the naivety and credulity of a lovely 5 years old child. It becomes useless on all levels: intellectual, psychical, spiritual, educational, and practical. But it does open the floodgates to ideological and pseudo-religious interests.

1.9. Studying Political Science

A Bachelor program takes in general 3 years, each year divided into 2 semesters which take approximately 15 weeks of teaching each. Ignoring special holidays, these 15 weeks can be counted as 75 days of studying (Monday to Friday). Therefore 6 semesters consist of 450 days of study.

There are study programs with 8 or 10 hours of classes per week; others with 12-16 hours. We take an average of 2.5 hours of classes per day (equal to 12.5 hours per week). A Bachelor program consists of 450 days multiplied by 2.5 hours which results in 1125 hours of classes during 6 semesters.

The rest of the time at disposal we consider as the time for searching and researching information, studying, reading (papers, articles, and books), writing essays, writing a thesis, preparing for exams, and institutional visits (political departments, administrative sections, parliamentary sessions, local authorities, etc).

Moving ahead from here, we can determine: one subject consists of 2 hours of class during one semester. On average we get around 6 subjects per week and semester; or 5 subjects if one subject consists of 4 hours of class per week; or 4 subjects if 2 subjects need 4 hours of class per week which we consider as realistic and adaptable for our interest here. With this last sample we get 4 subjects per semester and therefore in total (6 semesters): 24 subjects.

→ If we add a Masters program, based on the same calculations, we get in total 32 subjects for a Bachelor and a following Master program.

It is essential to see: some subjects consist of 30 hours of class and some subjects consist of 60 hours of class per semester. In reality, some universities operate with 12 weeks classes plus 3 weeks exam preparations and exams per semester. This means 20% less classes (hours) per semester and in total of the 3 respectively 4 years of study. Here, a subject would consist in 12 x 2 = 24 hours per semester or 12 x 4 = 48 hours per semester.

Conclusions:

→ 24 hours of teaching a subject is enough for simply an introduction.

→ 48 hours of teaching a subject is enough for a selected intermediary elaboration.

→ A profound exploration of a subject would require another 48 hours.

But we have identified an estimated 230 subjects, or if reduced to superior categories around 100 subjects. We can consider any kind of further and more general categorization, but we still get at least 50 subjects.

Based on a realistic distribution of the time for classes we get 24 subjects for the whole Bachelors program and another 8 subjects for a Masters program; additional the study hours (1500-1800 hours per year).

Another approach to quantify the teaching and study potential of a Bachelors program gives us the ECTS-European Credit Transfer System: The student's academic status can be expressed by the use of the ECTS. One standard academic year corresponds to 60 ECTS credits that are equivalent to 1500–1800 hours of study (4 credits = 1 credit per hour teaching + 2-3 credits per hour of studying). ECTS has been developed in order to provide a common measurement and facilitate the transfer of students and their grades between European higher education institutions

We must be aware that we have not included possible practical subjects (with practical training including internships), indispensable for many of the possible career perspectives: IT skills, communication skills, resolving humane problems, psychological interpretations, political negotiation skills, mediation skills, diplomatic (public) communication, journalistic writing, professional self- and time management, conflict resolution skills, skills in dealing with cultural differences, skills in understanding and dealing with religious components in the political world, and so on.

- The worst of all is that a majority of the given standard programs ignore between 65 and 75% of all political mega-parameters and of the real political world that we consider as 'of highest importance and practical relevance'.

- Students do not learn to think: critical thinking, reflective thinking, creative thinking, intuitive thinking, moral thinking, network thinking, thinking in time perspectives, pioneering thinking, thinking in the dimension of meaning; they simply copy (memorize) and paste (exam).

We give some suggestions what students of political science should learn:

- Identifying the connotations (fields of meaning) of the words and terms
- Multiplying the parameters by hundreds of millions and even by billions

- Extrapolating the growth of figures by 30, 50, 100, and even 200 years
- Expanding the fields and areas of activities into the global dimension
- Identifying the psychological and spiritual meaning of scientific statements
- Finding out what is hidden, not mentioned, but is an intrinsic reality
- Focusing on the dynamic of construction of the theories and principles
- Giving a view to the multi-dimensional interrelations in the real world
- Putting the folk's behavior in the context of mind and soul and real life
- Putting the politician's behavior in the context of mind and soul and real life
- Interpreting human factors behind ideas, principles, theories, and ideologies
- Putting the political concepts, theories and ideas into the real life of society
- Understanding the pressure groups as a systemic political part of society
- Comparing small countries with the big countries and their political power
- Finding an understanding with visualization, intuition and creative thinking
- In general finding an approach to the systemic effects of multiple variables

Normative statement: It's a disgrace how political science reduces the mental tools and potentials of students making them into obedient altar boys and girls.

For a huge majority of study programs in the capitalistic world we must conclude:

- The programs of political science are of very low relevance for a job in any political field.
- The study programs do not holistically prepare a student for a political career.
- The study programs do not prepare for the practical skills in any field in and around politics.
- The study programs are far away from the reality of the social and political worlds.
- The study programs miss any rational concept or comprehensible structure of the syllabi.
- The study programs are not hierarchically organized from introduction to thoroughness.
- The study programs are a supermarket where everybody can choose for needs and wants.
- The study programs are significantly (maybe up to 90%) a 'copy and paste' proceeding.
- High ranking or any specific reputation doesn't mean anything for a professional career.

The core-question is:

→ What is the purpose (aim) of an academic program in the political science and in general in the social sciences?
→ Should social sciences efficiently prepare students for a professional career in any corresponding field of study?
→ Considering the immense public costs for universities, is it reasonable (and affordable) to offer for free or for much reduced fees such manipulative, ideological, highly useless, and sterile academic programs?

There are universities and schools of global reputation and with a top ranking offering the study program of political science. Compared with some other universities (not ranked) their program is very narrow and of miserably low quality. If we compare their syllabus with the full list of possible and relevant subjects they both are of outrageous low quality. These universities and academic schools (we focus here on America and Europe) do not offer a program that is sustainable and useful for the future of humanity.

Normative statement: A majority of the Western political science cheat the students, their parents, the society, and in the end, considering the consequences, the folks and the entire humanity.

99% of the academic programs of political science are accredited, directly from the governments or indirectly through agencies that are operating backed up from the government. What is the value of such accreditations? It's simply a business, a money machine that creates money.

Official accreditations are not worth a penny. It is even worse: these institutions of accreditation promote the complex mendacious system of lies, cheating, deceit, sham, and so on, and they hinder any initiative for 'free academic teaching and research'. Above that: it makes their study program practically irrelevant for all professions that are involved in or associated with politics or political matters.

🖎 At its best the graduated students become some sort of diligent altar server. The belief is: political science is about relevant and real politics. The other belief is: it is right, good and wise that people accept, obey and follow the rules of the authorities.

Here we have the culmination of the academic sham (in political sciences)! It's the same with religion and it's the same with the economic science, the science of education and psychology. They all create liars, cheaters, deceivers, false people, perversion, naïve and ignorant sheep. This leads to the destruction of the human evolution.

Normative statement: The accreditation concept as given in Europe and the United States is a servant of the satanic deicide. [50]

---

[50] See: Schellhammer. Trilogy on Economics. 2012; or: Schellhammer. Deicide. 2012)

1.10. Careers for Students of Political Science

The American Political Science Association says: "Political science is the study of governments, public policies and, systems, and political behavior. Political science subfields include political theory, political philosophy, political ideology, political economy, comparative politics, international relations, and a host of related fields." [51]

They also write on their website: "Political science students can gain a versatile set of skills that can be applied in a wide range of exciting careers in federal, state and local governments; law; business; international organizations; nonprofit associations and organizations; campaign management and polling; journalism; pre-collegiate education; electoral politics; research and university and college teaching." [52]

A German program about political science sees the future of their students in the following working fields: (academic) teaching, advisor to politicians, working for think thanks, working for Public-Affairs; and after a master program: positions in a ministry, in a party, or in the state administration. They also mention possible careers in an international organization or in the field of diplomacy (with special further education). Other graduated students can find a job as assistant or referee writing speeches for politicians; or they can collect information in a parliamentary group. With further education in economics there are also jobs to find in a business consultancy. [53]

APSA gives us more examples of careers for political scientists. The following are a sample of careers for political scientists: [54]

- Activist, Advocate/Organizer
- Administration, Corporate, Government, Non-Profit, etc.
- Archivist, Online Political Data
- Budget Examiner or Analyst
- Attorney
- Banking Analyst or Executive
- Campaign Operative

---

[51] http://www.apsanet.org/content_9181.cfm
[52] http://www.apsanet.org/content_9181.cfm
[53] http://ranking.zeit.de/che2012/de/fachinfo/28
[54] http://www.apsanet.org/content_6457.cfm

- Career Counselor
- CIA Analyst or Agent
- City Planner
- City Housing Administrator
- Congressional Office/Committee Staffer
- Coordinator of Federal or State Aid
- Communications Director
- Corporate Analyst
- Corporate Public Affairs Advisor
- Corporate Economist
- Corporate Manager
- Corporate Information Analyst
- Corporate Adviser for Govt'l Relations
- Corporate Executive
- Corporation Legislative Issues Manager
- Customs Officer
- Editor, Online Political Journal
- Entrepreneur
- Federal Government Analyst
- Financial Consultant
- Foreign Service Officer
- Foundation President
- Free-lance writer
- High School Government Teacher
- Immigration Officer
- Information Manager
- Intelligence Officer
- International Agency Officer
- International Research Specialist
- Issues Analyst, Corporate Social Policy Div.
- Journalist
- Juvenile Justice Specialist
- Labor Relations Specialist
- Legislative Analyst / Coordinator
- Lobbyist
- Management Analyst
- Mediator
- Plans and Review Officer, USIA
- Policy Analyst
- Political Commentator
- Pollster
- Public Affairs Research Analyst

- Public Opinion Analyst
- Publisher
- Research Analyst
- State Legislator
- Survey Analyst
- Systems Analyst
- Teacher
- University Administrator
- University Professor
- Urban Policy Planner
- Web Content Editor

Career perspectives are essentially in the fields: [55]

- Advisers to specific politicians
- Run for office as politician
- Working in governments, in political parties or as civil servants
- Non-governmental organizations (NGOs) or political movements
- Corporations
- Private think tanks
- Research institutes
- Polling and public relations

Critical conclusion:

➜ Do the syllabi as mentioned above really prepare the students for such professional careers?

We must consider the fact that a student starts studying by the age of 18.
At 21 a student gets their Bachelor of Arts (or: of science). A student then starts working for some years or he can continue with a master program (1-2 years). After that, a few students may continue with a PhD program. By 21 or 23 or 25, a man (or a woman) is far from being mature. He (she) may have some relevant professional experiences, but his (her) picture of the world is still very small. And, especially he (she) has no insight into the real political world behind the curtains.

✎ A graduated student in political science does not have any deeper knowledge about humans and humanity's evolution, the manifoldness of the households' real lives in a society and around the world.

---

[55] http://en.wikipedia.org/wiki/Political_science

- A graduated student in political science does not have any deeper knowledge and experiences about corruption, bribery, nepotism, intrigues, lies, cheating, distortions, manipulations, maneuver, and so on.
- A graduated student in political science does not have any deeper knowledge and experiences about the 30 global mega-parameters; he or she has no picture about the global development for the upcoming decades, etcetera.
- A graduated student in political science has practically no skills (technical, methodical, and psychological) to deal with the complexity of the political world; and he or she has not developed the inner (mental, psychological, spiritual) foundation for any job with high practical and moral responsibility, etcetera.

Normative statement: It's outrageous that these graduated students can become a political advisor based on simply having copied the knowledge of the subjects, partly old-fashioned and outdated, partly irrelevant, partly simply too much of aesthete, and missing most important topics (subjects) due to non-existence in the syllabi.

1.11. The Big Picture of Political Science

(This chapter may be for readers with a special interest in the management of political science.)

We extend now the organization of the list of all existing syllabi and subjects into categories:

1. History of political ideas and politics

- [ ] History of political ideas
- [ ] Political history
- [ ] Political developments since 1980

2. Actual political ideas and theories

- [ ] Contemporary political ideas and theories

3. Organization of political structures

- [ ] Political structures
- [ ] Power, authority and legitimacy
- [ ] Laws and court, jurisdiction
- [ ] Public administration
- [ ] Pressure groups and corporations
- [ ] Structures of aristocracy and the elite

4. Actual national politics and policies

- [ ] The job of governmental departments
- [ ] Actual national politics
- [ ] Politics of public goods (wealth)
- [ ] The mega-parameters of humanity
- [ ] Politics of criticalities
- [ ] Economics of politics (monetary, trade, etc.)
- [ ] State success and failure
- [ ] Accumulation and concentration of wealth
- [ ] Ideological versus practical and rational decisions
- [ ] Governance without being in (governmental) office

5. International relations

☐ International Relations
☐ United Nations
☐ European Union
☐ Politics of foreign countries (of interest)
☐ World politics

6. Auxiliary sciences

☐ Sociology, society, multiculturalism
☐ Geography and its political implications
☐ Psychical-spiritual concepts of personhood
☐ Holistic understanding of human life
☐ Personality patterns in politics
☐ Ethics and moral behavior in politics
☐ Scientific methods and hermeneutics
☐ Media and politics
☐ Archeology
☐ Culture
☐ Anthropology
☐ Theory of knowledge
☐ Religion and politics
☐ Technical skills in political fields
☐ Conflict resolution, problem solving
☐ Political management, strategies, tactics

We must ask again:

→ How much of all these topics do the people know?
→ How much of all these topics do the members of a political party know?
→ How much of all these topics do the lawmakers know?
→ How much of all these topics do the ministers know?
→ How much of all these topics do the heads of states know?
→ How much of all these topics do the bureaucrats know?

☝ Could it be that the people have a lot of political opinions, but practically no relevant political knowledge? Yes!

☝ Could it be that a majority of the agents operating in the political system do not have much political knowledge? Yes!

☞ Could it be that a majority of the agents operating in the political system do not have the indispensable skills to do their job? Yes!

The Classical Fields of Political Science

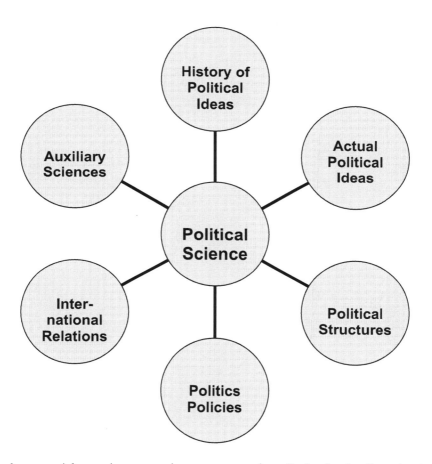

As the essential superior categories we assume that all, absolutely all academic institutions that teach political science accept this general concept. The problem is that each field can include innumerable sub-fields, focuses or special perspectives. Our list above shows the manifoldness of content these essential fields can have. Considering the varieties of the content these fields can have, we understand such a general categorization simply as a first extensive frame of the political science.

We admit: the above listed subjects reflect an extensive program that requires minimum 6 years of study, very diligent studying. Most subjects can easily fill a book with 1000 and more pages. Most subjects also have a different approach and different emphases.

If we also consider the extensive career field students of political science can have, then we can or must also include some practical subjects that are relevant for at least most of these career options.

We already identified that some academic institutions declare that political science does not prepare for professional fields. So, what is the study program for? Why should political science not prepare individuals for a political career?

All other programs of social science (except Philosophy, History, and Literature) prepare students for a professional field within their teaching topics, e.g. Psychology, Education, Social Science (Humanities), Sociology, and Law. Even the natural sciences such as physics, chemistry, medicine, etcetera, prepare students for the corresponding immanent professional fields.

Normative statement: Behind the sterile attitude of political science we see hypocrisy and cowardice, cardsharper or incompetence, or an intentional purpose: to hide the real (morally dirty and very manipulative) world of politics and ignoring (or destroying) the conscience of the students. With that this sterile attitude shows fundamental elements of the master deicide program.

Back to our explorations: For a Bachelor and Masters program we must limit the content. But what are the criteria for this limitation or selection of single topics? We give some suggestions to discuss:

- The core of the subject (terms, facts, knowledge)
- The essential structure and its purpose (aims)
- The primary components and its theories
- Human factors that play an important role
- The causes and effects of high importance
- The significant realities behind the façades
- The systemic progressive and regressive dynamic
- The interrelated connections (with other fields)
- Ideological and normative components
- The interaction of internal and external criticalities
- Mainstream of development and external influences
- And etcetera

Can we construct a hierarchy of learning and topics? This is a very delicate undertaking as there are different options and different opinions about importance and indispensability. Nevertheless let's try developing a model to discuss.

Syllabus of the superior categories for a Bachelor program

First year: 2 semesters	1-1	1-2
History of political ideas and thought	2	
Political history I: Colonialism and Industrialization: 1500 -1900; critical analysis of politics and the human factors	4	
Political structures	2	
Sociology: humans' life, businesses, multiculturalism	4	
Anthropological life philosophy based on concepts of the mind	4	
Scientific methods (Basics and multi-variant concepts)		4
Political history II: Modern History 1900-2012: critical analysis of politics and the human factors		4
Contemporary political ideas, thought and theories		2
Power, authority and legitimacy		2
Laws and court, jurisdiction		4

Second Year: 2 semesters	2-1	2-2
Pressure groups, power of big corporations, aristocracy and elites; governance without being in office	4	
The job of the different governmental departments	4	
Politics and economics of public goods (public wealth) versus negative externalities	4	
Economics of politics (monetary, trade, GDP, taxes, etc.)Accumulation and concentration of wealth	4	
Hermeneutics	2	
Public administration		4
Actual national politics: trends in EU, US, Asia, Middle East or a country of choice (e.g. UK, France, Germany)		4
The global problems of humanity (mega-parameters)		4
Ideological versus practical and rational decisions		2
Living standard, lifestyle and human values around the globe		2

Third Year: 2 semesters	3-1	3-2
Political ethics, moral behavior and psychopathology of leaders and the collective	4	
International Relations & Politics of other nations	4	

United Nations	4	
European Union	4	
Politics of UK and US (Russia, China Rest of the World)		4
International institutions (IMF, WHO, WTO, World Bank, etc.)		4
Media, mass-psychology, propaganda and politics		4
Measuring state success and failure		2
Thesis tutorial		1-2

Free of choice to take in any semester of the Bachelor program

- [ ] IT-Skills (basic and advanced)
- [ ] Team work
- [ ] Basic management skills
- [ ] Internet, social networks (e.g. Facebook) and politics
- [ ] Conspiracy hypotheses or theories
- [ ] Languages

Syllabus of the superior categories for a Master program

Master Program – One Year: 2 semesters	1-1	1-2
Political management, strategies, tactics	2	
Religion, culture, politics, and its human factors	4	
Concepts of political conflict management, problem solving (international and national)	4	
Trouble spots around the globe	4	
Causes of wars and military activities (1880-2012)	2	
Aims, strategies and principles of global renewal		2
Comparative politics (countries of interest)		4
World politics and the immense global problems		2
Geography and its political implications		2
Thesis tutorial		1-2

Free of choice to take in any semester of the Masters program

- [ ] Global re-armament and concepts of peace development
- [ ] Other topics of interest related to the country of the study location
- [ ] Languages

Specialization for a PhD

- [ ] Archeology: social and political interpretation
- [ ] Biological and philosophical Anthropology
- [ ] Theory of knowledge, dogmatism and ideology
- [ ] Legitimacy of conspiracy hypotheses or theories
- [ ] Immanent factors of structural reforms
- [ ] More options are given depending on the university
- [ ] And etcetera

In general this construction of the syllabus of political science shows us the complexity of this field. As it includes practical skills and significant knowledge about the real politics, such a program forms an excellent and stable foundation for all those who want to work in the future in a political field.

We also must consider that the world will enormously change in the nearer future (10-35 years). Politics will be confronted with unimaginable realities. The challenges to deal with 8, 9 and 10 billion people, with catastrophes and wars of national, continental and global dimension will be immense.

Herewith political science becomes a responsibility that requires personalities with inner strength, with wisdom, and an inner foundation rooted in psychical and spiritual development. All other types of individuals will however lead humanity down the abyss. Today there are practically no such potentials in the academic institutions, in the governmental accreditation bodies, and in the world of politics.

➜ Herewith we have a raster useful for checking and comparing different academic programs of political science (in Europe).
➜ Depending on the location of the academic institution around the globe some syllabi must be understood within this specific frame.
➜ United States as the location of the academic institution may give more weight to its specific history and global imperialism.
➜ It is self-evident that for example Arab countries, especially Islamic countries have their own specific syllabi.
➜ Some countries have a very specific geographical, cultural, religious, and historic frame, which replaces some of the classical Western topics, but not all.

Reduction of the political fields to its core pillars

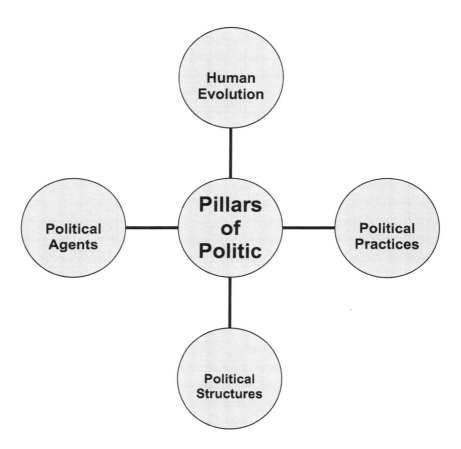

2. Human Evolution and Politics

2.1. Political Thoughts

We have selected some quotes from four authors (experts of our time) that discuss historic political ideas since Plato up to the modern time. Our interest is not the history of political ideas in general, but much more values and dynamic evolutionary components that appear directly or indirectly in historic political ideas. Those readers that are interested in a deeper understanding of the origin authors and their history may consult the corresponding literature.

The evolutionary dynamics

"We cannot shrug our shoulders in resignation and assume that fate, chance, or a dominant elite will shape things no matter what we think." [56]

→ Fate and chance are not dynamic forces that bring the psychical-spiritual evolution forward.

→ Trusting in the force 'faith' that will make the right way for an individual or humans in general is magic thinking that rejects personal and collective responsibility.

→ The elites are with its characteristics not a dynamic force that brings the psychical-spiritual evolution forward.

→ If the entire elite would consist of wise men (and women) having achieved a very high archetypal level of psychical-spiritual development, then the elite could bring the psychical-spiritual evolution forward.

→ What people think matters and the right way of thinking (balanced with all other sub-systems of the mind) is an indispensable factor that brings the psychical-spiritual evolution forward. But if the result of people's thinking is scrap because their mind is distorted and dehumanized or simply not well formed (shaped), then it expresses stupidity and stupidity leads to regression and extreme destructivity.

---

[56] Haddock, p. 9

☝ We have a strong impression that today a huge majority of the people and of politicians does absolutely not contribute to the psychical-spiritual evolution.

"If things go wrong for us, or those in authority make unreasonable or odious demands on our time and resources, in the last resort we have a responsibility to raise our voices." [57]

→ There are a lot of people in a society that are never satisfied; for them something always goes wrong. But what goes wrong for the ones, goes right for the others. Therefore we should consider here only 'mega-parameters' such as high rate of unemployment, extreme poverty and exploitation of labor, disrespect for human rights, contamination, destruction of the eco-systems, destruction of the democratic values, and so on.

→ 'Unreasonable or odious demands on our time and resources' is very relative. But if hundred thousands or millions go for demonstration, then something goes wrong. As governments usually react with force and punishments, the government is unmasked as the unable agents for the political business.

→ There must be a legal right and a moral obligation that citizens have to take responsibility and to raise their voices in such cases. This is a democratic value and duty, and the governments should learn to communicate with the citizens in the right way. On the other side, there are a lot of very stupid people that abuse this kind of 'voice of the people'.

☝ We have a strong impression that today a huge majority of the people and of politicians does not take responsibility if any kind of 'unreasonable or odious' abuse, exploitation, or existential matters damages the people and their lives.

"The nation was not simply there as a fact of national life, but had to be nurtured, cultivated, brought to fruition. The significance of politics was that it focused attention on common bonds which nature, history and culture had forged over centuries." [58]

→ Political duty: the nation has to be nurtured, cultivated, and brought to fruition.

---

[57] Haddock, p. 9
[58] Haddock, p. 68

→ Politics must preserve nature, history and culture that are forged over centuries.

☞ Nurtured: This positive claim has converted into a critical reality: Chemicals and pharmaceutics in all kind of food, the polluted and contaminated air and soil, and so on.

☞ Cultivated: This positive claim has converted into a critical reality: falseness, cheating, lies, deceit, fabricated information, brainwashing, manipulation, individualism, and so on.

☞ Bringing to fruition: This positive claim has converted into a critical reality: realization of a dehumanized world, self-alienated humans, tremendous lack of human values, and so on.

"Moral arguments are notoriously difficult to resolve, even among groups that share fundamental ideas." [59]

→ There is a basic moral that focus on criteria such as stealing, damaging, destroying, hurting, and killing. Such moral arguments are not difficult to resolve.

→ There is a moral that focus on criteria such as belief, attitude, culture, and religion. Such moral arguments can be understood as a private matter.

→ There is a moral based on eternally valid principles such as the Archetypes of the Soul, the natural requirements to form and shape the mind and soul, and nature as a complex organism that provides humanity with everything for needs and wants.

→ There is a first practical and fundamental question and decision for each individual: Do you want to destroy and to eliminate yourself (and everything that is part of your life) or to live and to develop yourself with all your mental and spiritual potentials?

→ In the perspective of humanity there is also a first practical and fundamental question and decision: Do you want to destroy and to eliminate other folks, other countries, the entire humanity and the planet with the consequence that the psychical-spiritual evolution of humanity is eliminated and the planet destroyed?

In the future perspective we have a moral problem that up to today never existed in the history of mankind: If we suppose that humanity will reach 10-12 billion people within 50-70 years, we must calculate with 80% stupid people that only produce waste, sewage, contamination, pollution, and eliminate the raw resources for living in the farer future.

---

[59] Haddock, p. 88

They do not develop (and use) their mind and soul, partly because they can't and partly because they don't want. They all want to eat meat. For that the 7 billion people today have 17 billion domestic animals (animal breeding). All of them drink, eat and defecate in much larger quantities than humans. Cattle consume enormous amounts of fresh water and food grown by mankind and lost for mankind. Animal breeding as well as agriculture and fishery operate with pesticide and pharmaceutics destroying all food chains and eco-systems. Unimaginable amounts of waste, sewage, chemicals and pharmaceutics go to the eco-systems and come back to humans on the everyday plate. [60]

With that the irreversible destruction of the planet with all its natural creations is guaranteed. Such a development of the planet will hit back and eliminate the entire humanity. Now, think a bit and you will become aware of the biggest critical moral problem that has never existed before! It's about saving the planet for the archetypal human evolution.

- Moral arguments are notoriously difficult to resolve because people have a distorted and rotten mind and soul, and are not interested in morals at all; or their morals are a result of their neurotic and insane mind.
- Moral arguments are notoriously difficult to resolve because people believe in archaic and distorted religion and because they are not interested in forming, shaping and using their mental potentials.
- There are billions of people, also academics and politicians, people of all religions and cultures, which reject and negate the mega-problems of humanity, and especially that there little time to start resolving these problems before they become unmanageable.

"Our primary consideration must be that we pursue the course of conduct that is likely to make our lives go better; and they are unlikely to go better if we deny ourselves the possibility of thinking hard and imaginatively about the choices we have to make." [61]

→ It's an elemental goal of governments and politics that the lives of the citizens 'go better'. But the GDP is a very narrow parameter that doesn't say much about these 'better lives'.
→ We need a new perspective of the 'good life': There is no collective future if for the ones (a small minority) the lives go better and for the others (a huge majority) the lives get worse.

---

[60] http://english.pravda.ru/business/companies/12-09-2012/122148-food_crisis-0/
[61] Haddock, p. 88

➜ It is not simply about 'deny ourselves the possibility of thinking hard'. It's about affirming and acting as a result of affirmation. It's also not simply about visualizing (becoming aware of) the choices we have to make.

➜ The 'better life' from America's perspective: "The U.S. consumes half the world's GDP, despite the fact that there is only 4.5 percent of the population living there. In other words, they eat ten times as much as compared to the citizens of all other countries. And they eat at the expense of China, Russia, India, Brazil - all other countries." [62] Is this really a 'better life'?

❧ A huge majority of people doesn't think at all; some think little and in a very narrow frame; and those who think extensively and profoundly are excluded from society.

❧ A huge part of those who don't think or think little are forced to do so due to economic reasons (e.g. poverty), lack of public education, a public education that does not teach the ways and necessity of 'thinking', and all the influences from the media and the consumer market that already have destroyed and dehumanized the brains of billions of people.

❧ For most people a 'better life' is related to living standard, work, and leisure. But life doesn't go better with a sick, neurotic, extremely narcissistic, perverse, psychotic and psychopathic mind and a never satisfiable mouth. It is not possible to live human values without an all-sided balanced forming and shaping of the psychical and spiritual parts ('sub-systems') of the mind.

❧ If the Western politicians in office, the heads of state, the ministers, and the lawmakers would have thought hard since 1945 and would think hard today, the world could be a 'humane paradise'.

"We will not help ourselves if we suppress views that we regard as inconvenient or disagreeable." [63]

➜ We have already discussed the defense mechanisms. To ignore, reject, negate, and suppress what is 'inconvenient' or 'disagreeable' is a global pest. It expresses a weak mind, a weak and insecure person, and a miserable character.

➜ Defense mechanisms do have a positive function to protect inner balance. But it also has a very destructive aspect if the defense serves the ego, the lies, and the rejection of the psychical-spiritual development.

---

[62] http://english.pravda.ru/russia/politics/21-09-2012/122236-russia_apec-0/
[63] Haddock, p. 88

- 99% of the people on earth (talking here about adolescents and adults) suppress views that are inconvenient or disagreeable.
- All dogmatic religions train (brainwash) people to use their defense mechanisms in order to maintain their sick and insane religious concept and to negate the individuals' responsibility for making a living, for holistic growing, and for the archetypal inner fulfillment.
- Most politicians train (brainwash) people to use their defense mechanisms in order to maintain their sick and insane ideological concept and to negate the individuals' responsibility for making a living, for holistic growing, and for the archetypal inner fulfillment.
- Most politicians suppress views that are 'inconvenient' or 'disagreeable' in order to maintain and increase their reputation, to climb up the ladder of their career, and to increase their power.

"Typically, bureaucracies bring last year's conventional wisdom to tackle this year's problems." [64]

→ Bureaucracy doesn't work with 'wisdom'. Bureaucracy also doesn't work with profound, creative, intuitive, and pioneering 'thinking'.
→ Bureaucracy works with figures, administration and control of facts and figures, and organizing the system with regulations and norms.
→ Bureaucracy doesn't see humans and society as vivid organisms that should be in a process of permanent learning and creating a balance.
→ Bureaucracy is clumsy, inert, dull, stubborn, compulsive, and bossy.
→ Bureaucracy has lost the ability to deal with human's matter in an appropriate and reasonable way.
→ Bureaucracy expresses the mind and soul, the attitudes and abilities to perform, and the character of people working in its institutions.

- A bureaucracy with an extremely rigid, highly inflated, and over-dimensioned apparatus paralyzes the psychical-spiritual and social (collective) evolution.
- A bureaucracy that tries to regulate and control everything with thousands of adjustments paralyzes the psychical-spiritual and social (collective) evolution.
- Bureaucracy is not a system with a permanent feedback control that would allow for immediately reacting to new arising critical phenomena in any society.

---

[64] Haddock, p. 131

"Are governments obliged to recognize and support faith-based schools irrespective of the practical tenets of the faith-based schools irrespective of the practical tenets of the faith in question? Clearly lines have to be drawn, but it is difficult to specify limits that will be acceptable to all cultures." [65]

What do we have to understand with the term 'faith-based'? We suppose it's about religions, the beliefs of the 6 big (or most important, Buddhism included) religions on earth. We could add some more religions, statistically of minor importance, even Scientology, the Mormons, and so on.

What is the difference between 'sect' and 'accredited' religion? What does female genital mutilation have to do with God and any belief (dogma)? Nothing! What does circumcision have to do with God and any belief (dogma)? Nothing! What does sexual (self-) excitement and satisfaction have to do with God? Nothing! Do we need for a (true, genuine) religion and for public education such pseudo-religious', insane, perverse and heavily abusive practices (of babies and young girls or boys)? Do such practices later in the future of the victims have any positive influence in the archetypal psychical-spiritual development? Not at all! Does God have any interest in a genital control of humans? This is not 'faith-based', but originates from a very sick masculine mind!

All religions contain different modules about dogmas, general beliefs, the right way of living, and the history of their teaching with its protagonists (prophets, Messiahs) in the past. Our critical approach about Christianity (see chapter 4.5.) shows us: Religion is not simply religion and a belief or faith does not guarantee its authenticity and correctness.

- Fact is: all the big and most important religions with more than 5 billion followers were completely unable to lead humanity forward on the path of the archetypal psychical-spiritual evolution. They all have lost the Archetypes of the Soul.
- Fact is: all the big and most important religions with more than 5 billion followers were completely unable to respect and preserve the planet with its eco-systems as our home and resource for making a living.
- Fact is: all the big and most important religions with more than 5 billion followers were completely unable to create worldwide economically balanced societies, to protect humanity from wars (warmongers), and to educate people for making a living aimed at inner fulfillment.
- Fact is: all the big and most important religions with more than 5 billion followers are responsible for all the misery and suffering on earth, the

---

[65] Haddock, p. 150-151

deicide and programmed doom of humanity because they are archaic religions and because they all ignore what makes a human with mind and soul and with the inner archetypal processes.

🖎 Fact is: all the big and most important religions with more than 5 billion followers have a complete incapacity to learn, to adapt new knowledge about the mind and soul, and to revise their old-fashioned archaic understanding of humans and of God. Apart of the Archetypes of the Soul, there is nothing that is 'infallible'.

🖎 Fact is: all the big and most important religions with more than 5 billion followers promise paradise in the other world simply by obeying the norms and rules, and by believing in their dogmas and teaching. This is a very cheap masculine dictatorship that is based on a rational submission: "Copy it and obey and you get your place in paradise". Or for the economic and political science: "Copy it and obey and you get your well paid place in the system".

🖎 Fact is: the core principle of archaic religions is the same as we have in the car industry: The car industry sells great living, style, superiority, strong personality, great character, importance, reputation, attention, emotional comfort, freedom, to be 'right', safety, joy, power, family values (with happiness), and so on. A buyer of a car gets all these human values included with the car. But 95% of the car owners have not elaborated (through personal development) a tiny part of these values.

🖎 Fact is: all the big and most important religions with more than 5 billion followers are anti-evolutionary in all senses. Does humanity really need such religious concepts in their public schools? Isn't it time today for an all-embracing new enlightenment?

🖎 Another big problem is that even a majority of politicians is imprisoned in such archaic religions. Also in that sense they are anti-evolutionary. Also politicians need an all-embracing new enlightenment.

🖎 A religion that is not actively rooted in 'spiritual intelligence' is non-evolutionary and from its core thoroughly destructive. The same can be said of the world of politics.

"Nothing does more to give a ruler a reputation than embarking on great undertakings and doing remarkable things. Above all a ruler should make every effort to ensure that whatever he does it gains him a reputation as a great man, a person who excels. Rulers are also admired when they know how to be true allies and genuine enemies: That is, when, without any reservations, they demonstrate themselves to be loyal supporters or opponents of others." [66]

---

[66] Wootton, p. 45

→ Politicians spend a lot of time from their starting point (entering into the field of politics), going up the ladder of a political career to be recognized, to gain a reputation, and to get the necessary votes.

→ Politicians must travel a lot, chat a lot, give speeches everywhere spinning them with ideological marketing slogans, and so on: much of their time is filled with that.

→ Politicians must fabricate and forge their speeches and messages to the citizens in order to be welcome and supported.

→ Politicians are permanently under pressure to give people what they want, to improve their reputation with mega-projects, grandiose declarations, or canting adaptations.

→ Politicians are forced by the stupidity of the masses to see the world in black-white or always from the positive side, and to declare that "we are on the right side". People need declared enemies in order to avoid seeing their inner enemy. The corresponding activities of politicians are time consuming.

→ Politicians are permanently confronted with competitors from their own party and from other parties. Therefore they must be vigilant, they must fight, they must defame their competitors, and they must develop strategies to win.

→ Politicians are periodically confronted with figures, facts, new incidents and events, money matters, unpredicted developments, and so on.

→ Politicians are used to react (mostly too late) and rarely to act, practically and proactively never ready for any pioneering new perspective for the entire society.

→ Politicians that are not actively rooted in the 'spiritual intelligence' are non-evolutionary and from its core seen in the long term thoroughly destructive.

☞ There is no business that could have success with such a time use.

☞ The time use for non-essential work is horrendous.

☞ All these activities are 100% non-evolutionary.

☞ Competition in the political world has a positive side and an evil side.

"No one supposed that everyone would benefit equally from an unfettered capitalism. But it was held that the society as a whole would be better off in absolute terms. It is the kind of doctrine that can look very impressive at times of significant economic growth. But any interruption of that growth can lead to questioning of the basis of distribution within a society. Questions of 'justice' or 'fairness' begin to seem more pressing than productivity and growth." [67]

→ Finally some evolutionary signs are appearing. The general fact is: productivity and growth have nothing to do with an archetypal evolution. The question is: How can politicians create a balance between living standards and 'humane factors' or 'human values'?

→ An archetypal psychical-spiritual evolution can never be created without creating a balance between living standard (economic and environmental conditions) and the mind and soul of people, in permanent development towards both quality and efficiency.

→ The parameter 'GDP' is a cheat and in that sense irrelevant for discussing growth. In any case as nowadays economic growth is paid for with public debt, debt of corporations, and debt of the consumers (also in international trade), the calculation gives us a wrong picture about real economic growth. Growth here is not reached by the performance of producers <u>and</u> consumers. History teaches us that such a development always leads to wars.

→ If we add to all the already mentioned different debts of a nation the costs of the negative externalities (nationally and globally) with their long term effects, we will see how much politicians distort the reality and how much a folk lives at the expense of 10-20 years or even 200 and more future generations. Herewith the reputation of politicians takes on a very dark side.

"If just and an unjust man both had the freedom to do whatever they liked, then they would both behave unjustly because everyone naturally desires 'to outdo others and get more and more' … every man believes that injustice is far more profitable to himself that justice." [68]

→ Thia kind of statement simply doesn't make sense as it suggests a natural law showing (maybe) an instinctive pattern of reaction.

→ The characteristics 'just and unjust' are the result of biographical experiences, from family education, and in general of the way a mind is formed (shaped) especially from exposure to mass media and the consumer environment.

→ The 'conscience' may be of a basic disposition, but it is never a fully prepared 'code' for justice.

→ 'To outdo others and get more and more' is not simply a natural desire. It is the result of experiences and education. It is also a dynamic that arises through the fact that humans are not equal: some have low potentials, some are lazy, some are stupid, some are infantile for their entire life –

[67] Haddock, p. 90
[68] Boucher & Kelly, p. 38

and others have enormous potential and want to transform their potential into something real.

→ 'Every man believes that injustice is far more profitable to himself than justice': In a society where the world of business and politics is build up on a house of card and on economic trickery, justice does not have a chance of winning.

"The best or ideal constitution is one in which political power is distributed, not simply in accordance with the principle of equity or proportional equality but also in accordance with the correct standard of virtue or goodness." [69]

☙ 'Virtue or goodness' are a basket case in the world of business and politics.
☙ 'Virtue and goodness' are never rewarded, but always abused by others.

"…warfare is inconsistent with distinctively human nature: it reflects the animalistic side of our existence." [70]

→ 'The distinctive human nature' doesn't exist as already a fetus is being formed and shaped (also contaminated) through the mother's emotional state, thinking, interaction, and environment (food included). The entire environment already influences (shapes) this so called 'human nature'.
→ Warfare is not simply an animalistic side of men. It may have been an animalistic pattern during the first phase of human's evolution and especially a reaction of fear.
→ Warfare is either a defense reaction to protect an area or country of a folk or its motives lie in ignoble motives.

☙ The motives for most wars since 600 years and of all wars since 120 years are thoroughly evil, first financed and then provoked and heated up by Christian, Jewish-Zionist interests and political imperialism and by the 'invisible hand'.

"The development of technology opens the way for human emancipation by offering the prospect of material abundance, but its immediate effect is the furthering of the dehumanization of man." [71]

---

[69] Boucher & Kelly, p. 91
[70] Boucher & Kelly, p. 105
[71] Boucher & Kelly, p. 464

We have extensively and profoundly explored the processes of dehumanization. Today the state of collective dehumanization is globally dramatic. [72]

- The development of technology has destroyed all human values.
- The development of technology has brought humanity at the abyss.
- The development of technology has brought more wars than ever before.
- The development of technology has resulted in 4-5 billion people living in poverty and absolute poverty.
- The development of technology has brought us more regicide than before.
- The development of technology has brought us unstoppable deicide.
- The development of technology has destroyed all healthy parts of European countries and the United States.
- The development of technology has destroyed democracy.
- The development of technology has distorted political activities.
- The development of technology has destroyed human's mind and soul.

Article 7 of the Universal Declaration of Human Rights: "All are equal before the law and are entitled without any discrimination to equal protection of the law." Law is equated with the expression of the general will of the entire community. 'All are equal before the law' is the principle under which all people are subject to the same laws of justice.

- Laws are made by the lawmakers. In many countries a majority of lawmakers represent the interest of the establishment, the elites, and the capitalistic and imperialistic or religious interests. Therefore many laws are not an expression of the general will of the entire community.
- Lawmakers are humans; a majority has a distorted mind with a very low psychological and spiritual development. Lawmakers are influenced by, lobbyists, pressure groups, financial matters, the mass media, and personal career interests. Systemic corruption favors the interest of selected entities.
- Many laws have a space of interpretation and in that sense depend on the judges and the customs of a region or country. 'All are equal before the law' ignores the fact that the same law in different countries has a different scale of punishment.

---

[72] Schellhammer. Trilogy on Economics. And: Deicide. 2012

🖐 The use of the scale of punishment depends on the interpretation of an infraction of a law (e.g. motivation), also depends on psychological expertise, on the manifoldness of words and its interpretation, and on the personality of the judge (character) and his hidden ideological or religious disposition.

🖐 Considering the actual and upcoming state of humanity, the world, and the planet, something is going very wrong with the entire system of justice (laws) and even with the constitution of many nations.

🖐 For an estimated 10-12 years there has been a development in the introduction of new laws in the United States, Canada, and Europe that prepares the foundation for a dictatorship and fascism, wars included. Governmental power is extended and 'privacy' of people is already much reduced. 'All are equal before the law' becomes herewith a Chimera.

🖐 The systems of law in practically all countries do not protect the genuine human values, the genuine human needs, the indispensable development of mind and soul of people, and the Archetypes of the Soul. The collective psychical-spiritual evolution is ignored, neglected, and even denied. The planet with all its vivid and non-vivid resources has no voice to be protected by law and be used globally in a sustainable and protective manner.

Summary of political statements:

→ Most statements are prejudgments, express superficial views or a narrow view.

→ Some statements have had a very high value in the historic context, but are irrelevant today.

→ Some mentioned human values and facts about humans and society or politics have today a very high value and importance, but are fully ignored and suppressed or already destroyed.

→ There is very little about the mental and spiritual potential (and development) for human's evolution.

→ The understanding of a 'human' is thoroughly very archaic and much reduced; absolutely unusable for political management.

→ The political human (politicians, agents in the governments) is not explored and reflected as a human and professional.

→ The fact that humans can and must be educated by developing all mental and spiritual potentials is fully ignored.

→ The fact that politicians, including the rulers, must be personally and professionally educated by developing all mental and spiritual potentials plus the professional knowledge and skills is ignored.

→ The entire system of laws in all countries around the globe has not been able to protect people, humanity, the world and the planet with all its vivid and non vivid 'things' from human made disasters, injustice and wars.

→ The evil influence of archaic religions and the interaction between politics and religion are ignored, not perceived or not acknowledged.

→ The fact that humans create themselves most of their own suffering and misery, of their failure and evil doing, is ignored.

→ The destructive potential of neurosis, narcissism, mental disorder, amoral character, and absence of virtue, absence of the truth and the attitudes to love, perversion, psychosis, and psychopathy is thoroughly ignored or unknown.

→ The Western world and many other countries live at the expenses of the future 10 generations. The people living in 500-1000 years will still have to pay for some very serious damages from today. There is no political or ideological thought (concern) about this perspective.

→ The world is on a path of deicide, of the destruction of the planet and humanity as a whole. There is no consideration about laws and jurisdiction that punishes its agents or sets rules for governance.

2.2. Philosophical Ideas

(Extracts from Schellhammer: 'Evolutionary Human Education'. 2012, p. 77-99, German edition).

Kmal

"Recognize yourself", is the Delphic dictum.

- Do politicians practice self-knowledge?
- How do politicians practice self-knowledge?
- What knowledge do politicians have about themselves?
- How distorted and disfigured is the self-image politicians have?
- Do students studying political science practice self-knowledge?

- A huge majority of politicians have a very low level of self-knowledge, a very distorted self-image, and overestimate the quality of their self-being.

Socrates (470-399BC) the Ancient Greek philosopher searched for answers about the question of life: What is virtue? What is conscience? He adhered to self-contemplation and self- knowledge.

Virtues are: [73]

- Morality
- Goodness
- Righteousness
- Ethical principles
- Uprightness
- Rectitude
- Efficacious quality
- Prudence
- Justice
- Fortitude
- Temperance
- Faith
- Hope
- Charity
- Beauty of the soul
- Harmony of the whole man

---

[73] http://www.thefreedictionary.com/virtue

- Intrinsic value like gold

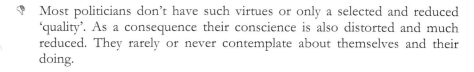

- Most politicians don't have such virtues or only a selected and reduced 'quality'. As a consequence their conscience is also distorted and much reduced. They rarely or never contemplate about themselves and their doing.

Plato (428-348 BC) another pivotal ancient Greek philosopher founded in 385 BC his 'academy', which prevailed for 900 years. He had a clear concept of the human psychological-spiritual development, which leads up to the level of supreme enlightenment and wisdom, to highest completion. Life-themes became more prevalent: moral aims of humans, virtue, truth, harmony, the good life, education, personal development, maturity and much more. Plato rooted the life-goals in the 'world of imagination'. The body, as a mortal shell of the human, is the source of lust and quest (power). Rational forces are: recognition, learning, ego (the I) and rationalism. The soul itself is immortal. The soul is divine. Within the soul there is transcendence and divinity. The goal of life is harmonization of these three forces, which leads us to 'the art of living' as moral behavior. This holy formation of human development implies the balanced order of all forces. Justice, honor, courage, prudence and wisdom is developed in the same way. The harmony of the soul is the ideal for the formation of states. The ideal state has the same order structure.

- Most politicians have achieved no or only a low level of psychical-spiritual development.
- There is rarely a politician that has reached the highest level of enlightenment and wisdom, harmony, and maturity.
- A majority of politicians don't have much truth; they have replaced the truth with lies, deceit, cheating, and falseness.
- Most politicians believe in religious myths, fairy tales, falsifications, distortions, fantasies; and they have an insane understanding of humans, God, and J.C.
- Their mental and behavioral forces are not in a balanced order and not rooted in their genuine inner (spiritual) source of life.
- Most politicians don't give a shit for justice, honesty, honor, bravery, sober-mindedness, and the harmony of the soul.
- Students of political science are never or rarely confronted with an education aiming to acquire and build such qualities and character traits.

Similarly with business.

Also Aristotle (384-322 BC) taught about human development, first at Plato's Academy, and later in his own 'school', the 'Lyceum'. Here we also find the moral improvement of human action, a virtue doctrine and ideas about the happiness of the people and of politics. Happiness results from benefits of morally valuable action that is guided by reasonable actions. Finding 'the right center', i.e. internally and externally balanced life without extremes, is the principle of action. The education is done by experiences leading to insight, by implementing and doing. Repressed emotions are a source of suffering and therefore of particular importance. They can be relieved by music, theater and art.

- Most politicians do not know what blessedness and felicitousness is. They have no interest or ambition to create such human qualities for politics and the folk.
- Politicians do not make any effort to find the right midway, the balanced center, not inside (in their mind and soul) and not outside in the real world.
- Most politicians have an enormous amount of suppressed emotions, which leads to fights and cantankerous behavior in politics and society.
- Students of political science do not learn anything about such qualities of attitudes, soul, and behavior; but they already have a lot of suppressed emotions.

Epicurus (341-271 BC) founded another school, called 'Garden of Epicurus'. He taught people the liberation from superstition, gave instructions for a happy and good life. His teaching is marked by individualism and atheism. The pleasure-reluctance-mechanism is the source of all behavior. These forces can and should lead a person with reason. The goal is a positive end result of pleasure and reluctance. That means: peace of soul, freedom from desires, modesty, absence of irrational fears and superfluous desires. He understood his ethics in this interest.

- There are not many politicians that have peace in their mind and soul. Most politicians are not free from avidity, humility, irrational fears, and stupid wants.
- Students of political science are not shaped through teaching to adapt attitudes of humility; they are already missing peace in their mind and soul.

The Stoic school (from 300 BC) is considered the fourth school of classical Greek antiquity. Zeno of Citium (340-262 BC) is considered the founder of the Stoic school. Practical life-counseling for the people was the defining engagement, consisting of instructions and lessons on leading the 'right life'. The focus is on the actions based on the principle of rationality. Man finds happiness in: dispassion, serenity, inner independence and asceticism. The rationality stands above the feelings.

- Politicians do not act based on reason. Their understanding of the 'right life' is full of neurosis, narcissism, falseness, psychopathy or psychosis.
- Politicians do not have inner freedom and they are also externally chained to and by the 'invisible hand' behind the curtain.
- Many politicians are unable to constructively deal with their emotions. They use the political stage to discharge their emotions by playing an emotional theatre.
- The 'right life' in the understanding of the Western politicians is increasing GDP and consumption or materialistic living standards, their personal wealth, and their power, image or reputation.
- Students of political science do not learn anything about the varieties of a 'right life'. They don't get knowledge about 'inner freedom'.

The philosophical schools of antiquity taught and practiced all the methods of psychical training such as meditation, concentration exercises, rules for living (discipline, loyalty, obedience, self-control) and methods of psychical guidance.

Even in the Roman Empire – with for example Cicero, Virgil, Horace, Ovid – we find public education as philosophy, poetry and rhetoric.

- Most probably there are not many politicians that meditate (with the right rules) regularly or even daily.
- A majority of politicians do not know what meditation is; and if they meditate, then their 'technique' is most probably stupid and inefficient.
- Faithfulness is not a practice in Western politics; it is replaced by fooling, deceiving, cheating, or breaking international laws, rules and contracts.
- Is there any study program of political science where the students learn to correctly meditate? No! And 'faithfulness' is also rather a foreign word.

In parallel, the teachings of the early Christian Gnosticism (as mystic and as cognition) have to be mentioned (Manichaeans). From prehistory to the Middle Ages the Church and philosophers contributed to education for society. Mentioned here are three outstanding figures which have dealt with self-knowledge, human education and leadership.

- Politicians today have lost any humane concept and understanding for a humanistic guidance of the citizens.
- Political science speaks at the best of 'management', but this is not understood as the traditional understanding of 'guiding' people (a folk).

Augustine (354-430 AD), sets self-knowledge at the beginning and at the center of all life. Not only personal introspection covered the content. The path of self-knowledge leads to us, through analysis of the lived life, simultaneously after or behind the sensuous and rational insight to God. Knowing yourself means knowing God. Human depravity and desire for self-indulgence is much rooted in lack of ability to love, which is itself an expression of a lack of self-knowledge, thought, insight, awareness and truth. Only the man with capacity to love can find true happiness.

- A huge majority has never elaborated their biography; they anyway don't know how to do such work.
- As politicians do not practice self-knowledge (or only in a very narrow way), they also can't know what 'God' is.
- Most politicians do not have much ability to love. And 'love' as an attitude or quality of human's way of living; they all totally lack love-attitudes.
- As a logical consequence, politicians are unhappy people; or their understanding of 'true happiness' is superficial, emotional, and ego-centered.
- But, the values of love are not a category to be considered, respected, protected, or practiced in the world of politics.
- Students of political science never do learn anything about love and self-knowledge and therefore they have no substantial idea what 'true happiness' means.

Thomas von Aquin (1224-1274) taught of the pre-existent soul which is the real man. Man is body, life, mind and spirit (reason) in one. Intellect, rationality and faith in God are the three pillars of the human formation. The virtue-theory contains: wisdom, courage, prudence, justice, faith, hope and love.

Moral behavior consists on one hand of these virtues and the implementation of rationality. On the other hand highest morality is dependent on grace. In the discovery of God lies the greatest bliss. The mystical union with God will at the end of one's life be the highest value of being. The ultimate fulfillment of man and his happiness will be laid in the afterlife.

- Morality is a difficult term with extensive connotations. Based on the common sense of morality, or highest possible state of morality, the moral does not depend on God; it depends on the Archetypal Processes of the Soul an individual has achieved. Morality and God is a political tool to deceive people, the folk, and the entire world.
- Genuine morality requires a lot of psychical-spiritual work to be done. There are not many politicians that do such work, or have done it before their career.
- Mercy and morality have however rarely a significant place in the political world.
- The 'unio mystica' is one of the highest Archetypes of the Soul and there is around the globe no politician that has fulfilled this transformation.
- There is no king, no queen, and no aristocrat in the political or economic world that has fulfilled this supreme archetypal process.
- Students of political science do not learn anything about such inner processes and supreme values.

There is no subject in any syllabi of political science that shapes students to become an integer personality (moral character/person).

Meister Eckhart (1260-1327) sees the salvation of the people essentially in discovery. Discovery is based primarily on intuition, on introspection and the inner sources. Faith, hope and love are central virtues. That which God is, can ultimately only be manifested through the human being. Introspection ultimately leads to God. Bonaventura and Bernhard of Clairvaux are other mystics of that time, who taught and themselves practiced the introspection of the divine truths as the last and highest aim of man.

- There is a knowledge that starts with perception (eyes, ears). The perception of most politicians is narrow, projective, and directed towards the external facades.
- There is a knowledge that one can get through inner archetypal processes, through meditation and dreams. Most politicians ignore this source of knowledge.

- As politicians do not or rarely do practice inner experiences and do not elaborate the inner archetypal processes. They have no idea what God is and therefore whatever they believe, they are far away from God.
- Politicians and politics in general are not focused on 'highest aims of humans'. Their aims are focused on use of power, on dominance, exploitation, and increase of wealth or reputation for themselves.
- The highest aims of humans are not a subject in any syllabi of political science. Therefore this is not something that students have to think about.

Only a few centuries later begins the time when great thinkers freed the question of man from the theological-metaphysical systems. The courage to explore with rationality the question of man's being, breaks the chains of dogmatism and opens the way to emancipation. But is this emancipation not again an ideology and illusion? Let's touch on the history of philosophical thoughts about man:

Descartes (1596-1650) intends to place ethics on a scientific basis and hopes herewith to re-educate the people: from the fool to the clever, from the coward to the brave, from a sentient being to the emotionally controlled being. The control of external nature should lead to the domination of the inner nature. Human formation is herewith embedded in the relationship with God. Given that ultimately, only the relationship with God makes us happy.

- Nothing new for 400 years: Dummies must become bright people. Cowards must become brave. Emotionally labile people must learn to control their emotion (by understanding). Dominating (or better: creating) the external world must lead to the forming of the inner world. The understanding of humans is rooted in (in words of today) the inner spiritual source of life. There is nothing about this in the political world and nothing in the science of politics. On the contrary, today politicians want dummies, emotionally labile people, people full of preoccupations and fear, and rooted in the prepared stream of collective opinions and especially in the sham of Christian belief.

Leibnitz (1646-1716) makes the individual become the crystallization point of thinking. Meditations are self-reflections of the thinking man. Only symbolic insight can make possible the insight of God. Reason makes faith possible and is not in its contrast. Here we find for the first time (?) the concept of the unconscious.

- If meditation is self-reflection of a thinking man, then politicians are not 'thinking men' as they do not meditate in order to reflect on themselves.

- A majority of politicians do not think with reason and do not act with reason.
- Do students of political science learn how to think with reason?

Kant (1724-1804) outlines a new image of man in which he explains the capability of reason. He calls on the people to create through the ethical state of nature a compulsory-free virtue of legislation. The human being is rooted in evil and must overcome this state by applying reason. The biggest question of all, 'What is man?' is provided by the three fundamental questions of philosophy, called: What can I know? What should I do? What may I hope? Also a practical aspect can be found: in the 'big world' a person's behavior must be 'world-wise' and needs for that, knowledge of humanity. It is the combination of reason and free will that regulate the happiness.

- We don't think that humans are 'de natura' evil. This is the insane Christian belief. But the archaic parents, public schools, religions, social life, consumption society, and the politicians create the 'evil human'.
- Free will depends a lot on morality and the content of the unconscious. As most politicians are overcharged with unconscious complexes and unsolved matters from the past, they don't have (psychologically) much free will. Therefore they are unhappy (in a spiritual sense) and act based on unhappiness.
- A majority of politicians are not sophisticated and they all have a very low, archaic, and distorted concept of knowledge about humans.
- Students of political science are not sophisticated and they all have no idea how their biography has shaped them; they are their biography. There is not such subject in the syllabi of political science.

Hegel (1770-1831) advocates that the motives of moral action must be strengthened. Politically oriented, religious public education creates free people. The alienation of man within society shall be brought to new life by recovering the context of moral action. The man is in his external nature an archaic deficient being. The distinction of man from the animal nature has to be found by looking inward. Its possibilities and limits of variability in space and time characterize the human condition. Philosophy should not know God, but man: his personality, his moral position, his place in the family and role as a citizen.

Indeed, what makes us different from animals is to be found inside. But what do we find in the inside of politicians, especially as politicians disrespect human's inside?

- Mixing political education with religious education leads to constructing and using nuclear bombs! This is because 90% of Christian teaching is a sham.
- The archaic nature of politicians has created the state of humanity and the planet with the doom we can expect in 35-40 years. And behind their doing is much religious psychosis.
- Most students of political science do not have much idea about the insanity of Christianity (it's not a subject of the political syllabi). Therefore they copy their fathers and forefathers politico-religious patterns like their professors do to. No thought, no progress, no evolution.

Many philosophers and poets from the Enlightenment period and then in modern times can be understood also as educators. Many names would have to be mentioned. We can only highlight a few keywords here from the last 200 years:

Schopenhauer (1788-1860) considers the human impulse-oriented, in which case the 'will' receives the decisive function. Intuition leads to the inner experience of this driving force, which is oriented in a nature-like state of economic and sexual exploitation. Bliss is obtained by giving up any aspirations. Man is 'the beast which can beat'.

- Drive and will are constitutive for humans. The will of a politician collides with the will of others. Suppressed drive must be compensated with power and fight-satisfaction. Here we are on the political stage of conflict: drive collides with drive!
- The politicians are the humans that can beat. We can see the verbal (sometimes also the physical) birching everyday on the political stage. Their suppressed sexual drive and longing for love or redemption (a spiritual drive) forces them to do so.

Kierkegaard (1813-1855) claimed that being a human is a free decision, which can also be denied. Those who set the sensual pleasure above the ethical principle make themselves un-free. With that the foundation for self-liberation, self-determination and being oneself is also withdrawn.

- Sensual pleasure may happen in hidden political rooms. More importantly: Political power pleasure is in most cases a compensation for immense deficit of sensual pleasure (and an expression of a state of inferiority).

🖑 Everywhere on this earth we can identify economic exploitation. That's why politicians have sold their power and country to the supreme masters of economics. The reason is that politicians do not operate with ethical principles. They can't after all live themselves and can't free themselves.

🖑 Does the science of politics shape and prepare the students for the fights on the political stage? As they 'copy and paste' to get the grade, they automatically internalize the patterns of political communication and operations.

Marx (1818-1883) was a time-critical committed intellectual. Realization of philosophy meant to him the design of the social reality according to the laws of reason. His critique of philosophy is an expression of his commitment: to change the world and not just interpret it. The ideal of human emancipation is understood socially. Man is a creature of nature that realizes itself through work. Alienation from work and the working conditions have to be reflected as action-oriented. The human being impacts on nature, changes it, and this in turn again alters the human being.

🖑 Politicians indeed are changing the world, since 30-40 years but much to the worse. They shape the nature, contaminating all ecosystems and destroying much of the planet; including most resources. This on the other side shapes and changes humans: much to the worse: dehumanizing and degenerating.

🖑 Politicians are (self-) alienated from the job they do. They have not correctly interpreted their position and power, their responsibility for the evolution of humanity.

🖑 The state of humanity and the planet shows how politicians are inside in their mind and soul, and how they are as a personality.

🖑 Students of standard political science are not introduced into the principle that says: "The way they are (will be), is and will be expressed in their (actions) ways of doing their job."

Nietzsche (1844-1900) analyzed how to reshuffle the necessity and paths of humans, the illusory-world and illusion. He sets clear counter-accents: God is an illusion of the weak, a myth and a symbol of values without perspective. Man is called to live by his own will, and to give meaning to himself and to life. The evil is the best power of the people. Man is 'the sick animal'.

🖑 A majority of politicians live in an illusory world. Some have in their mind a constructed world, full of ideological elements but lacking much in completeness whilst others are trapped in false and distorted religious teaching and beliefs.

- If humans are the 'sick animal', then the politicians also are sick animals. We can transform it: a rat is an animal, can be a sick animal. Therefore politicians (and mainly all humans) are sick rats. Is there a way out?
- If we add the component 'the evil is the best force of humans', then we can put it together as politics is always about power and about who gets more power: the sick and evil rats are on the political stage. Sounds like a basket case!
- Does the political science identify the 'evil' in the political world? Do they teach an alternative to this 'evil'? No!

Scheler (1874-1928) considered the 'position of man in the cosmos' (1966). The basics of human life are irrational feelings and impulses. Body and soul are one. Not only physiological differences between humans and animals make humans human. It is the Spirit, which makes man what distinguishes him from the animal. Spirit is outside our dimensions and trans-temporal. Spirit is intelligence and ability to choose. Spirit enables the display of ideas, the abstraction of concreteness. Man has the ability to let himself go from the environmental relationship (as opposed to the animal) and to recognize by freeing the drive-pressure of things (the life) in their 'own nature'. Spirit allows 'pure knowledge'. Insofar Spirit is an ascetic principle. Within this realization lies the experience of God, and 'God-realization'. Man and deification are reciprocal, interdependent processes.

- To identify the position of humans in the cosmos can become very psychotic. Or it can be humbling and very respectful towards nature, the world of animals, and humanity. A majority of politicians and masters of economics is on the psychotic path.
- Indeed we observe in the political world the dominance of chaotic irrational emotions. There is not much intelligence, reason or Spirit.
- The majority of those politicians that believe have experiences of God, experience a bubble that is not sustainable. The realization of God is not a matter for politicians and there may only be a few ones that have such deep inner experiences through contemplation and inner archetypal processes.
- Students of political science want party life and much fun; they also like irrational emotions. Therefore they don't get any insight into 'realization of God' as a perspective for a political career.

Marcuse (1898-1979) understood revolution as liberation of the human instinct nature. He outlined the 'one-dimensional man' (1968). His philosophical treatises are social-critical and cultural-critical studies. The practice lies at the beginning of the theory; translated: the life of human being lies before the theory of personality. The true interest of the individual is real freedom. This is not to be found in hedonism. The reality of happiness is freedom as lived self-determination.

- What is the true interest of politicians? Is it really freedom for people, their folk? Not really! If the neo-capitalistic world is fully focused on consumption, on unlimited wants of people, then this world is a hedonistic world. Hedonism destroys freedom!
- The public debt of most Western nations makes the governments, the ministers and the law makers slaves to whoever holds the debt.
- There are 6-8 mega media corporations in the hands of a few people extensively brainwashing and manipulating the people with false and fabricated information in order to shape a collective mainstream of opinions. With that this self-determination and freedom is gone.
- The practice stays at the beginning of the theory: On the one side the practice is characterized by lies, cheating, falseness, fabrications, and a tremendous lack of moral attitudes and behavior. There are no syllabi in the political science that explores these practices in order to create theories and overcome them.

We could conclude here: the real life comes before ideological disputes. How much time do politicians spend on ideological disputes? How much time do they spend for understanding the real life of people?

Gehlen (1904-1976) designed a human image under the term 'deficient being' (1971). Man is helpless, he not only lives; he has to lead his life. From this he justified institutions that have to support the process of upbringing and education. Man is a product of tradition and zeitgeist. Insofar he is a cultural being. Pluralist ethics as an instance of social regulation allows for a reorientation towards biological, psychological and social forces (1969).

- The people as well the politicians are a product of tradition and zeitgeist. The political tradition of the Western coalition is amorality and triggering wars, exploitation of their own and other peoples and over-exploitation of all resources, regicide and deicide. Herein we identify the true face of politicians.
- The students of political science do not explore the true faces of politicians and absolutely never the practices of regicide and deicide.

Horkheimer (1895-1973) sees man caught between those who enjoy possession (have) and those who abstain and suffer as a result. Philosophical and psychological activities about the 'authoritarian personality', about the 'authority and family' as well as about the society mark an image of man in the sight of 'critical theory'. His philosophy is 'philosophy of life'.

- Today we have around the globe an extreme imbalance in terms of economics, money and wealth: 1% has a lot and 80% have practically nothing. This is a result of policies. And again we see here the moral character and the attitudes of the majority of politicians (in the Western countries).
- As more than 5 billion people suffer and live on less than $300 per month and a majority with less than $50 per month, we must conclude that not much has changed in political attitudes for hundreds of years.
- Authority serves itself. More than 5 billion people do not have time to contemplate about a positive life philosophy. They must fight for their daily needs.
- What is the 'positive life philosophy' a student of political science learns in the holy academic rooms? It is the absence of human values.

Adorno (1903-1969) sees the clarification of the unconscious as an act of enlightenment. The lack of consequences of thinking has driven the people into a 'delusional hubris'. The 'Education for maturity' (1973) is central to the 'practical engagement'.

- Everywhere in America and Europe we identify delusional self-overestimation, on the political stage as well as in a majority of the people. People don't think, or think but without considering the consequences. The picture about the world shows us that a huge majority of politicians are not any better: They don't contemplate the consequences of their thinking and actions.
- The unconscious mind of people is full of sorrow, fear, embarrassing experiences, painful events, suppressed desires, suffering, conflicts, problems, lies, cheating, guilt, anger and hate, absence of love and care, and unanswered questions; politicians are not free from such an unconscious burden. Education is only built up on such an inner life.
- Political science does not teach about the unconscious mind and its ways of operating. Emancipation and maturity is not achievable by ignoring the unconscious burden. The theatre that politicians play is not much more than an expression of their inner complexes, the inventory of the unconscious mind. Students of political science do not get an

understanding of these psychological, spiritual, educational, and human worlds.

These are some small extracts with emphasis on the aspects of the education of human beings. These philosophers - along with many other philosophical issues - researched the fundamental questions about human being and the 'good life'. For some, the central idea of ancient Greece was elementary: "Self-knowledge is the beginning of wisdom" and the basis for a happy and good life.

Again and again, the Socratic 'Daimonion' - the divine element of the Spirit in man as the primary objective of the ethical and personal responsibility - stood at the center of philosophical efforts. To form innate morality and practice inner dialogue with God is the core theme of human formation of all metaphysically oriented philosophers up to the positions in the new philosophical anthropology (Rothacker 1966; Landmann 1969). Other philosophers are based more on empiricism (English empiricism) and distance themselves from Platonic-Aristotelian metaphysics. The focus is on the right of sensory experience. Space-time categories have priority. Since the mid 19th century we find social conditions as part of the human improving as well as the possibilities for self-development.

🖑 Where has all this valuable and priceless philosophical and ethical thinking led us today? A huge majority of politicians (and of the people) do not give a shit about this legacy of 2500 years of cultural history.

Over and over again the 'spirit' appears in the human images of the great philosophers, as the main characteristic of being human. But what is 'spirit'? Many accents have been set, including: intelligence (thinking) and reason, creative force of the universe, God's power, creative power in man, in the unity of body and soul and in the unity of body-soul-God, the unity creating power in man, a normative principle (because of cosmic and/or divine order) and strength in the human being that frees him from the dimension of space and time.

🖑 A huge majority of politicians have lost the respect for the divine creation.
🖑 Any kind of divine dimension is excluded from the science of politics. But there are academic institutions that are rooted in religious belief and from there they teach an understanding of for example 'catholic' perspectives in politics.

This 'spirit', however understood, places man in a plan of creation, where he can not be interpreted as a random product of evolution (Monod, 1971). Such interpretations receive an additional horizon if they taught for example, that man is bound by memory and by his unconscious to that what he lived, thought and experienced. Or, from another point of view: The man unfolds himself in the interplay of culture (which he creates) and inner psychical reality. The social conditions and the molded psychical powers are the determinants of any development-opportunities. The biography and life take active part in determining what man is and can become (evolve into).

- Politicians (and a majority of people) have lost the integrity of the creation. They play at being the creators of the creation.
- Humanity is shaped and programmed by the media, the political propaganda, and the economic conditions, not from an inner genuine psychical-spiritual coding.

The question is obvious: Is there a conclusive final human-picture? Can one create a 'whole' from all the psychological, pedagogical and philosophical fragmentations? Is the question "What is a human being and his human race?" (Pestalozzi) perhaps purely a play of words? Can cognitive processes ever break away from the individual psychical powers and their interrelated ways of functioning, which in turn are embedded in historicity? Various philosophers answer these questions differently. Some are inside-oriented, others outside-oriented.

The truth is to be found inside or truth is found by thinking performance, or: the social reality is the truth. That makes it difficult, to define 'knowledge'. The matter gets even more problematic when asked if philosophy has to be without purpose or action-oriented. Technocratic understanding stands next to 'pure science'. Who can really bear the responsibility of their own definition, not only with words committed to paper?

- The reality of society is the truth: most humans as well as most politicians have lost their soul. There is no inner freedom!

With Scheler (1928), Portmann (1956), Plessner (1965) and Gehlen (1969), Philosophical Anthropology has become an autonomous philosophy, which deals with the 'nature of man'. Lately there is also talk of 'psychological anthropology' (Gadamer/Vogler 1973, vol.5). As far as philosophical topics are dealt with, this is rather 'philosophical anthropology', and as far as knowledge of psychology and psychoanalysis are the subject of discussion, we assign this to psychology.

🖙 Philosophical Anthropology means contemplating about humans, based on facts of soul and mind, and also about the facts of the external world that they have created and continuously create: A soulless world! A soulless world of politics and governance.

Finding evidence of man and his ways, in the context of historicity, is the task of philosophical anthropology. Empirical research stands next to interpretation of sense (meaning). The increasing newly ideologisation by methodological reduction with simultaneous abstraction of questions of meaning is rejected. Those who ask about themselves are looking always for meaning and to interpret themselves and their life. Life is always to be understand hermeneutically (e.g. Habermas 1973).

Purposelessness and relevance of actions characterize the position. The tendency derives an educational postulate of this new science from the facts held by all systems of thought: Man is in need of education and capable of formation, from birth on and throughout his entire life.

🖙 In essence 'Hermeneutic' means: exploring and contemplating about the meaning of whatsoever. Students of political science do not learn these methods of social science.

We want to separate this understanding of education compared to that of humanism, which is characterized by hedonism or eudemonism, sometimes mixed with a kind of 'spirit' and 'transcendence'. Basic human needs as the starting point and goal of existence is a reduction of the human image to the present and moment. It lacks the 'intelligence of the spirit' and it disregards the fact that human life always includes crises, conflicts, problems and difficulties.

Life always includes suffering. From the perspective of wisdom one has to say: There is no comprehensive psycho-spiritual evolution without inner suffering. There is no system of thought with which one can get rid of suffering. We consider this problem an important basic topic of philosophical anthropology.

🖙 The psychical-spiritual evolution is not a matter of politics, not even a frame with future perspectives for humanity as a whole

A manageable life-near philosophical image of man must make it possible to understand in a larger context the behavior and well-being of man, his thinking and his life. Also difficult life issues should be covered with it. Let us keep in mind a few basic questions:

Why does man suppress his psychical daily life? Why do humans live physically and psychologically unhealthy and self-defeating, even though they are aware of this? Why does the human being repeatedly subject himself to formalized religious, political and social rituals? Why do people intentionally cause other people psychological and physical suffering up to torture and murder?

Why does the human being wage war? Why do people live sexual perversions, which are far away from love and natural instinct? Why is man always looking for God and contact with the afterlife, even though God and the afterlife have never been 'proven'? Which forces drive a person, to kill himself? Why does man seek the game? Why do people intentionally fail to respect common laws, they drew up themselves? How do mental disorders such as anxiety, compulsions, depression, abandonment and 'inner voices' develop? Where do dreams and pictures of imagination come from? In other words: How can the intelligent information from inner images be explained? Why people need their 'home'? Why has the psycho-spiritual evolution been 'forgotten', and today has no meaning to most people?

🖙 Students of political science are never confronted with such questions.
🖙 Politicians have no time to contemplate about such questions.

Many thinkers have investigated the fundamental human questions, certainly before the ancient Greeks. We have omitted some; worth mentioning: Plotin, Anselm, Bacon, Hobbes, Pascal, Spinoza, Hume, Fichte, Husserl, Steiner, Heidegger, Plessner, James, Portmann, Sartre, Popper and Habermas, and even this list is only a small selection from the range of noted and worthy philosophers.

🖙 Their priceless work serves for intellectual discussions but without grasping the meaning and importance for today and tomorrow.
🖙 Politics and economics have destroyed all the precious findings and thought in order to get world governance and unlimited wealth.

On the margin of philosophy, many esoteric movements and secret orders have dealt with the education and formation of man. To be mentioned here: Freemasons, Rosicrucians, Quakers, Gnostics, anthroposophists and mystical schools of all kinds. All operated (and operate) within their own systems of self-awareness, of self-development and of philosophical and/or religious education of the human being (Doucet 1980, Miers 1980).

🖎 Whatever the concepts of these institutions contain, that may be of relevance to politicians, there is no space for such considerations in power positions and economics as a whole.

Secret teachings and secret orders have a tradition that goes back to the days of ancient Greece. It is not possible here to give a brief outline. Only a few hints may clarify that there have been and still are other organizations that are engaged in significant 'public education', be it in terms of the general philosophy of life, be it in terms of esotericism and personality development (character education, self-knowledge, creating awareness, spiritual growth, inner transformation for unity, etc.).

🖎 Politicians on a career path will lose their spiritual growth, if there is something like that, and they will form a character and a knowledge that makes them fit for political fights. This is called 'political acculturation'.

Gnostic theosophical orders, holy-grail-communities and cabbalistic schools of all sorts have formed millions of people since Plotin (204-270) with their teachings, cults and rites. Then there are the Freemasons with all their various groupings, the Rosicrucians, the Illuminati, the Gnostic-neo-Platonic Hermeticism, the Pansophic currents of Jewish mysticism, Alchemy, the Knights Templar and some other occult societies with mixtures of Christian teachings, as well as Buddhism and magical practices. The 'mystery of human being' as the object of cognition and create in need of education is at the center of their teachings and practices. The primary objective is finally also for all the self-development and self-actualization of man. The extent to which, the personal and collective unconsciousness was already the subject of the practice, can be seen for example with alchemy, which had predecessors going back to Pythagoras (Jung 1972, Frick 1978, I, II, II, 1980 Lennhoff/Posner)

🖎 The 'mystery of human being' is something unknown to the majority of politicians and also people in general. There are millions that say they found it. But what they have found is nothing more than a bubble of filled with delusions.

🖎 Politics is not built up on philosophical contemplation and the 'truth'. The world of politics disrespects and ignores all the historically identified human values.

2400 years of human values from Philosophy

Morality, goodness, righteousness, ethical principles, uprightness, rectitude, efficacious quality, prudence, justice, fortitude, temperance, faith, hope, charity, beauty of the soul, harmony of the whole man, intrinsic value like gold, wisdom, maturity, honesty, honor, bravery, sober-mindedness, harmony of the soul, blessedness, felicitousness, balanced center, free from avidity, humility, peace, acting based on reason, the 'right life', inner freedom, discipline, fidelity, self-control, faithfulness, self-knowledge as a condition to approach God, true happiness, considerateness, love, hope, intuition, contemplation, inner sources, self-reflection, reason, knowledge, self-awareness, will, self-liberation, Spirit, and more.

→ Politics does not take all the manifold findings of these wise pioneers seriously (not today and not in the past).
→ Economics does not take all the manifold findings of these pioneers seriously (not today and not in the past).
→ Religion does not take all the manifold findings of these pioneers seriously (not today and not in the past).
→ Science of politics and economics does not take all the manifold findings of these pioneers seriously (not today and not in the past).
→ Public education does not take all the manifold findings of these pioneers seriously (not today and not in the past).
→ The Western world has lost most of the humane values built up by many pioneering experts, scientists, and individuals over time. It has stopped evolving!

2.3. Psychological Ideas

(The following part is based on paragraphs from the book 'Evolutionary Human Education', p. 104-117, German edition)

Now, from here on we want to enter into the world of Psychology. Psychology explores and describes the mind. The mind is formed, (shaped) by family, upbringing, education, environment, and social pressure. The mind is the source and 'engine', in a certain way also simply the tool of most of what people think and do. Our purpose is to find out what the world of politics has learnt and adapted from the study of Psychology and Psychoanalysis.

The history of psychoanalysis, psychotherapy and psychological counseling begins in the 19th century with research into the unconscious. In the 20th century then follows the application of scientific methods in the context of independent departments of psychology that developed gradually and adopted clearer shapes. For example, the first psychological laboratory was founded by Wundt (1832-1920) in Leipzig. Until then, philosophy and pedagogy engaged almost exclusively and intellectually with the 'inner life'. Psychology was therefore part of philosophy.

The practice of psychoanalysis and psychotherapy has its precursor in antiquity. On the one hand, the philosophical schools have to be mentioned. On the other hand, the worshipping practices must be mentioned: Healing through dream-incubation, by magic rites and alternative medical care (Kerényi 1971). The philosophy of the four temperaments for example goes back to Knigge (1752-1796) and the antiquity. It was significantly understood as the education of mankind. Without a doubt, the Christian church's practices have since then developed their own methods of self-help, counseling, self-knowledge and psycho-catharsis. Exorcisms were practices that Charcot tried to tap into via hypnosis for new findings. The confession can be understood as a practice of psycho-catharsis. Religious practice is in addition to the classical pedagogy as a forerunner of today's psychotherapy and psychoanalytical counseling. Other precursors are found in the Gnostic, in mysticism and secret orders such as Rosicrucian and Freemasons.

🖑 In the antic world psychological knowledge had an intrinsic claim for education. Self-knowledge, self-explorations, psycho-catharsis, and guidance of people (practically, philosophically, and spiritually or religiously) played an essential role. Human's need for such support was self-evident and indispensable. But today the politicians do not operate with that purpose in mind.

🖐 Students of political science do not learn anything about self-knowledge, self-explorations, psycho-catharsis, and the guidance of people.

The systematic exploration of the unconscious began in the circle of Charcot (1825-1895), whereby a history dating back to Mesmer (1794-1815) would have to be looked into. Ellenberger (1973, I, II) thoroughly documented that Janet (1859-1947) had already operated extensive research on the neuroses, the unconscious mind, the psychic energy, the psychological analysis, the complexes ('idées fixes'), and their pathological expressions (e.g. hysteria). In 1913 at an international congress of Medicine in London, Janet claimed the methods of psychotherapy, report, resistance dissolution and cathartic treatment of neurosis as his discoveries. He strongly criticized the interpretation of dreams by Freud.

Theories and therapies of all major research institutions around the Salpetriere and Nancy were based on the clinical pictures from psychiatry. Dessoir, the author of a now-famous book about 'The Double Ego', can also be added to this circle. In his book he introduced the concept of upper-consciousness-unconsciousness and explained that dreams give access to the unconscious mind. The story of the systematic exploration of the unconscious began hereby. At the first 'International Congress on experimental and therapeutic hypnotism' under the honorary presidency of Charcot (8-12.08.1889) there were also names present such as Freud, Janet, Forel and James (see: Ellenberger 1973; Helmchen/Linden/Rüger 1982).

🖐 Scientists discovered and explored the unconscious mind. They acknowledged the importance of this part of the mind. On the one hand we could say that today politicians have absolutely no knowledge about the unconscious mind and its ways of operating. But on the other hand it seems today that on the top levels of power they know perfectly well how to abuse the knowledge about the unconscious mind.

🖐 Students of political science today do not learn anything about the unconscious mind and its ways of operating. They have no idea how important this knowledge is for people in political power.

Freud (1856-1939) took a lot of ideas from his stay with Charcot in Paris. He also rejected some (e.g. hypnosis) and experienced self-confirmation in others. The theoretical work of Freud can be grouped into four main parts: personality model (ego, id, superego, and resistance), method of psychoanalysis, study of neurosis, and (later) analysis of culture and religion.

The repression of sexuality and its destructive effect (on mind, body, culture, and politics) may have been a central socially critical education issue addressed also to the 'healthy' people. Religion as a 'childhood neurosis' was a theme that was not addressed primarily to psychiatry, but to the whole target-field of Christianity and Judaism. Freud then tried to protect his theory of psychoanalysis for the future with a secret society (in the sense of a lodge). His impulse-oriented concept was met with fierce resistance and at the same time with simultaneous international interest.

- Knowledge about the suppression of sexual desire and its destructive effects are not a visible matter for doing politics. But the science of politics would be the right place for exploring this field. They do not.
- Infantile neurosis is not only a matter of Christianity and Judaism, but as well for the institutions of politics and governance.
- Suppression of sexual desire as well as infantile neurosis is a hidden part of the everyday political business — totally ignored in its destructive effects of doing politics.
- Political science in general (as far as we could explore) does not teach anything about such sexual phenomena.

Adler (1870-1937), a member of the Psychological Society of Freud, with his theories about the human psyche was vehemently rejected by Freud. His studies circled around topics that may be indicated by a few key words: power and inferiority, compensation and pursuit of superiority, thinking and social factors as important factors in the Noseology of neuroses. Adler left this circle in 1911. He founded his own society.

- Holding power and inferiority, striving for compensation and supremacy can explain many aspects of political behavior (politicians, members of political parties, lawmakers, prime ministers, and also heads of state). There is no 'spirit' in the political world that wants to explore these realities.
- Political science in general (as far as we could explore) do not teach anything about such psychological realities in the world of politics.

Also Jung (1875-1961) expressed serious doubts about the theory of sexuality. Freud and Jung broke off their relationship in 1913. Jung developed his own work: the collective unconscious with the archetypes, the Individuation process, the complexes and the psychic energy, the type theory with the Anima-Animus aspects, persona-mask, introversion-extraversion and psychic functions, and later religious-psychological issues. Jung turned more and more away from his actual psychiatric research.

His main works have hardly got anything directly to do with psychiatry, psychopathology and psychotherapy. The 'numinous', i.e. mysterious depths of the human soul with its symbolic form of expression have a humanistic, Gnostic and metaphysical dimension. For Jung, this dimension was essential for the understanding of man.

- Politicians have an archaic understanding of humans and are not interested in exploring and contemplating about the 'inner world' of humans or the inner world of themselves.
- Entering into the world of the unconscious, the complexes, the 'anima' (or 'animus') dynamics, and the masks is something that the world of politicians is totally rejecting.
- A deeper examination of the psychical functions would lead to the demand of a personal psychical-spiritual development that politicians do not want to practice.
- The numinous inner world, or the inner source of life and the Archetypes of the Soul, experienced in dreams, would completely change political life. That's why politicians reject understanding themselves and humans in such dimensions.
- Political science answers here that this is not about politics, political institutions and political power, and scientifically anyway not measurable. Trying to integrate such topics into a syllabus would be a basked case.

Reich (1897-1957), after discussions with the Freudian school and the expulsion from the International Psychoanalytic Association from Vienna emigrated to the USA, and dealt with his own concepts of psychotherapy: character-armoring, social causes of neurosis, character analysis, orgon (psychic energy/bioenergy), character analysis, emotions and psychological reactions, technique of psychoanalysis, etc. His extensive pioneering work with Lowen created a new line of development in psychoanalysis.

- The armored character of politicians is a taboo and can't be revealed as an immense critical human factor in political processes (e.g. communication, negotiation, mediation).
- Character analysis (of politicians) would lead to too many cases with frightening results.
- Emotions and psychical reactions we only see through the result of political decisions and their use of power. The hidden emotional world dominates a majority of politicians' activities, much more than the rational-choice theory wishes.

❧ Analyzing the use of power of the Western political leaders would reveal an outrageous satanic world, which obviously can't be a subject in the program of political science.

❧ Students of political science would be enormously challenged if they would have to explore the armored character and all the suppressed emotions. Thank God, they don't have to look into this world!

In this period of development of psychoanalysis the Gestalt psychology of the Berlin School is added: Wertheimer (1880-1943), Koffka (1886 - 1941), Koehler (1887-1967) and Lewin (1890-1947). Gestalt psychology teaches that the origin of the psychical is always present in the form of 'Gestalt' (organisms) and not as 'elements'. Entireties are organized according to certain laws. They are dynamic and not mechanical. This fundamental concept of psychical space or field can be carried over as a formal model also for thinking, needs, learning, development, memory and behavior.

❧ Most politicians are absolutely not aware how their behavior depends on the network of their perceiving-thinking-feeling-learning-inner needs and (uncontrolled) development.

❧ Politicians don't operate by considering the totality of (unity) of a field of their actions. They have a mechanic understanding of their doing and of the fields of their responsibility. But humans and life form a dynamic and vivid unity.

❧ The youth today, including students from political science have a very short minded perception and thinking. They simply can't think in networks or dynamic models, especially in human matters: How do the academic institutions answer to this? There is here and there a subject that refers to systemic theories; finally after 100 years of developed psychoanalysis.

With the political developments in Germany from 1932 psychoanalysis in Europe experienced a rupture. Many analysts emigrated. The beginning of the Neo-Freudianism starts in the U.S.A. and after the Second World War in Germany. It is hard to divide the development into homogeneous groups. The contributions of many psychoanalysts are based on completely different topics and interests. Social psychological views, society-critical approaches and philosophical foundations for a new psycho-analysis are just a few related keywords. Individual contributions to the so-called 'neo-psychoanalysis' - away from the classical pathology cases of hysteria and schizophrenia toward narcissism and daily life – were primarily delivered by Horney, Sullivan, Kohut, Sandler and Schultz-Hencke. We highlight a few examples:

Mrs. Horney (1885-1952) desexualized Freud's theory and realized that many forms of neurosis was neither caused in childhood nor by drive disruptures, but simply as a result of life problems and life conflicts such as illness, misfortunes, unemployment, money worries and job problems.

Sullivan (1892-1948) developed an interpersonal theory of personality with the 'self-system', analyzed fear as a core emotional factor of the neurosis and designed a 'Lifespan Psychology' as an alternative to Freud's phase concept (anal-oral-phallic). Sullivan's commitment to a 'better society' reflected his hopes for the positive possibilities of the people.

Erikson (1902-1994) advanced the understanding with his model of the psycho-social stages of developmental processes. His theory of personality based on eight stages of ego development, ranging up to an advanced adulthood.

Fromm (1900-1980) extended the theoretical foundations of psychoanalysis with studies about love, the good and evil, narcissism, human freedom and a 'new society'. His humanity in contrast to Freud is rather optimistic.

- How do politicians deal with the conflicts, problems, sorrows and difficulties people have in their everyday life? They ignore this world!
- The world of politics has learnt nothing about love, the good and evil, narcissism, and a path to freedom.
- Politicians fear a policy that would lead to a new society. And the masters of economics would punish them very hard as they sometimes do with the use of the mass media.
- Do students of political science learn anything about the conflicts, problems, sorrows and difficulties people have in their everyday life? No!

In Switzerland Boss (1903-1990) developed the analysis of existence. The experiential approach related in space and time plays an important role therein. Existence and development of the world disclosure receive a central psychical importance. The path to one's own self, to psycho-spiritual wholeness is the course of psychoanalysis. Love plays a main function in the application of psychoanalytical technique.

Boss categorically rejects the notion of the unconscious. He puts psychotherapy on a new basis: philosophical understanding which allows people a fairer meaning against the drive-oriented based approaches of the social sciences. From the American Psychological Association, he received the 'Great Therapist Award' with which his approach – based on the philosopher Heidegger, gained international recognition.

Szondi (1893-1986) extended the analysis of the ego and the analysis of drive with his 'destiny-analysis'. He analyzed with a meticulous system the relationship between genetics (pedigree) and psychical reality. He developed a categorization of ambitions and needs, which would serve as an explanation of psycho-pathological symptoms. He created the concept of the 'familial unconscious', in which the whole of the ancestral claims are included. His psychoanalytical practice creates new forms of work.

✤ There is a saying since the time of Sigmund Freud: The criticalities (complexes) of (in) the unconscious are transferred to the next generation, and this during at least four generations without significant changes. This is a perspective to help understand the politicians: they operate based on the unconscious complexes of their forefathers!

✤ It's even worse: The mind of the politician's forefathers is a hidden active world in their present political life, in their communication and decisions, even in the way they use political power.

✤ Considering such extensive and crucial realities of doing politics it would be very exciting for the students of political science; but the door is closed for such revelations.

Psychoanalysis in the United States has lost the 'culture of psychoanalysis in Europe'. The result was the development of a 'well appointed psychoanalytic profession' (Russell Jacoby 1990). Still today medically oriented psychoanalysts raise the claim that they are the only ones who have the right to call themselves a psychoanalyst with the right of exercising psychoanalysis. But the history of psychotherapy from about 1920 on became detached from this claim. Nevertheless, it was argued - and still is disputed – about the so-called 'laity-analysis' of non-medical psychoanalysts. Outside of the orthodox psychoanalysts there are the 'wild psychoanalysts' and the 'laity-psychoanalysts', back then as today.

✤ There is something similar on the political stage: On the one side there are the 'orthodox' politicians and on the other side the 'wild' politicians. It's a terrible simplification, but it uncovers ways of thinking and explains many political fights.

✤ How do students of political science form their position? They do not learn anything about 'orthodox' or 'wild' positions.

Mitscherlich, Adorno, Sartre, Jaspers and Holzkamp – just to name a few - opened in the 60's and 70's extended discussions about the question of man or of psychology and the study of neuroses of psychoanalysis and psychotherapy. Socio-critical considerations close the circle again to Freud's commitment for culture and society.

- Politicians don't like critical contemplations about society because it would lead back directly to their character, personality, ways of operating, actions and attitudes.
- A majority of political syllabi prefer to offer just ideas, thoughts or theories than delve into critical explorations of modern society.

Parallel to the neo-psychoanalysis – and with the other concepts of psychology – developed in the USA and later in Europe, a new movement away from the depth psychology: Humanism in psychology. Rogers (1902-1987) assumed from the idea that in every human being there are 'immense resources' that help to change his life and to become himself. At the center of his personality theory is the concept of 'self'. The attitudes and feelings that a person has about oneself, faces the ideal-self. Self-actualization and self-development are at the focus of his interest. To that he developed a special form of therapy, now known as 'client-centered conversational psychotherapy'.

With Rogers self-realization takes on a large importance. However, this concept can be given little theoretical value, just as with his concept of personality ('self'). Fear, resistance analysis, sexuality (drive-dynamics), guilt and depression take little part in his range of interests. Rogers's commitment shifted to the so-called 'encounter groups'. Openness, honesty, compassion and actualization of the 'here and now' are characteristic of his method. The philosophical orientation is in humanism, partly probably also in religion.

- Today in neo-capitalistic economics and politics, humanism is 'passé'.
- Client-centered (folk-centered) politics or policies have disappeared over the past 30 years.
- Openness, honesty, and empathy are poison for political career success. No realistic politician can be naïve enough to practice openness and honesty!
- Concepts of openness, honesty, and empathy are not a matter that is studied. Students of politics must just copy (memorize) and later paste (exam).

Maslow (1908-1970) is regarded as the main representative of humanistic psychology. He sees this approach as a viable alternative to the orthodoxy of Freudianism. The transcendence and the transpersonal obtain a fundamental importance in the understanding of man and his suffering. In the center is a new way of life, not just a cure for a suffering. However, he has not the (psychiatric) sick people in his vision, but the 'normal-healthy' people with disabilities for self-realization.

Contact points to James (1842-1910) and Dewey (1859-1952) can be recognized here. They believe in love, the good in people and in the possibility of a new world, influenced by this psycho-transcendental humanism. The satisfaction of basic needs is essential to do so. His model of the self-realized person is marked by this hope and love.

The Gestalt-therapy by Perls (1893-1970) fits into this psychological development line, whereas psychoanalytic elements and ideas of Existentialism are incorporated here. The gain of sensory perception and the body-awareness are exercise elements of psychotherapy for that direction.

- In the world of politics there is no place for love, the good in humans, and the options for examining new paths and a new world.
- A new way of living and doing politics would be something akin to a healing process. But there is no demand in the political world for such therapy.
- The satisfaction of the genuine inner needs is of highest importance for a balanced human living in relative harmony. Many politicians certainly have a 90% lack of satisfied genuine inner needs. They are therefore unbalanced!
- The young students do not know what genuine inner needs are. There is no subject that explores this world. How can they, then in the future understand themselves and others, or even satisfy these inner needs?

Frankl (1905-1997) belongs to the second Vienna generation. His extensive work is praised as 'overcoming the psychoanalytic nihilism', as 'restoration of God in the soul', as '... fullfilled of ardent humanism'. His sense (meaning) oriented 'Logotherapy' is considered as the 'Third Viennese School' along with Adler and Freud. Frankl wrote more than 25 books that have been translated into 14 languages and have found wide acceptance, especially in America. Nevertheless, they found no place in the textbooks on personality theory. The question of meaning of life in general and metaphysical questions about man and life are frames and centering forces in his psychoanalysis and study of neuroses.

The religious element in man, and the question of meaning of life already found their basis in James, e.g. in his study of human nature (The Varieties of Religious Experience, 1901/1902), an approach that was then not met with interest by Freud. This range also includes Graf Dürckheim (1896). His 'spiritual goods' are based on the holistic-psychology, Gestalt psychology, Jung's work and especially Master Eckhart. He described the religious abyss as a major cause for the 'Non-Wholeness'. We find in Frankl and Graf Dürckheim central connections to humanistic psychology. Its roots are to be located with James (1842-1910), who held in contrast to behaviorism, introspection as an essential path to the analysis of consciousness. From that field the current 'transpersonal psychology' was developed (Assagioli, Grof, Tart, etc.).

- The religious dimension, in its most extensive meaning 'the inner source of life', is indeed a matter of psychology and not primarily of religion. I name this 'spiritual intelligence'. In the world of politics there is a complete lack of this, the highest intelligent source of human life.
- The search for meaning is even a matter of everyday life. Humans are 'de natura' oriented on meaning (of life, of existence, of purpose). Politicians are oriented on power, authority, regulations, prescription, laws, and so on.
- The 'religious bottomless pit' we understand as being disconnected from this inner source of life. The entire world of politics and political science is in that sense religiously and spiritually bottomless; from the inner source of life, means disconnected from the inner Spirit.

Today's relaxation techniques, hypnosis and imagination originated in psychiatry, also already in the 19th century, partly from the same field of Charcot, Bernheim and Liébault. Schultz (JH), Langen and others, as well as in France Chertok built on this tradition, and developed the methods of suggestion, hypnosis and relaxation - as part of the psycho-analytic practice - that are not only of concern in psychiatry. Also in America hypnosis as psychotherapy is taken up again (see Erickson MH). Mental training, imagination, and autogenic training have been introduced throughout Europe in popular education.

- In the Western world there is a common acknowledgement of stress (= distress). Stress is everywhere, nearly permanent, and omnipresent. Stress is around people and stress is inside of people. Also politicians are under continuous stress. Stress reduces and distorts the capacity of perception and thinking, peace of mind, ability to contemplate; and increases aggression, mal-behavior, and psychical disorder.

☞ Nearly 50% of the world population lives in big towns and cities; in the future it will be 75%. Today 50% of people live under environmental stress and in the future it will be 75%. In the long term such stressful existence dehumanizes humans. Politicians don't give a flying fuck about this key issue of human existence.

Is this direction 'neo-psychoanalysis' or a completely new development in the theory and practice of psychoanalysis? Janet said in 1919: "The decline of hypnosis in the history of psychotherapy is an instantaneous accident ... hypnotic suggestion will come again" (Chertok 1973). In fact, today this tradition has found a revival in medical practice and especially in the sector of the practical life counseling, psycho-esotericism and the natural healing practice. The 'Neuro-Linguistic Programming' (NLP) builds upon it (Grinder / Bandler 1991, Bandler / MacDonald 1991).

☞ Hypnosis and hypnotic suggestions, suggestive communication in general, are used in propaganda and marketing. Neuro-linguistic-programming (NLP) has become a tool for mass media, economics (sales), and politics. The idea is: What is good for psychotherapy is also useful for brainwashing, manipulating and creating the mainstream of opinions or attitudes. The world of politics and religion is full of this practice.
☞ The programs of political science ignore this kind of (subtle) guiding, leading, dominating, and shaping of the masses.

Parallel to the development of psychoanalysis, the neo-humanistic psychology and psychoanalysis the shaped behaviorism increasingly became a challenge for psychoanalysis: Watson (1878-1958), Hull (1884-1952), Skinner (1904-1990) and Eysenck (1916) dealt with the psychic powers and their learning processes as well as with a general theory of personality. They created diverse scientific methods. The factor-analytical (nomothetic) personality theory and the laws of learning are the main results. They laid the foundation and performed scientifically pioneering work in the areas of experimental psychology, educational psychology, social psychology and the psychology of perception. The behavior therapy emerged as a self-contained new concept, independent and aloof from the psychoanalytic theories and techniques. Basically the behavioral therapy focuses on clearly operationalized therapy targets in the area of behavior, thinking and emotions. This relearning happens in many variants, for example: Deconditioning, model learning, self-defense-training, aversion therapy, systematic desensibilization, etc. The applications tap into the broad field of mental illness and deviance, including addiction and delinquency.

The psychology of behaviorism, as for example understood by Watson, should belong to the past: "Psychology is a completely objective experimental branch of natural science which needs as little introspection as chemistry and physics." (1913) But with behaviorism - that includes Pavlov too (1849-1936) - approaches and research-methods have been developed that have no doubt continued to occupy a central place in psychological research - concepts among many others for gaining knowledge and theory.

(NLP: a way of programming the brain by means of words (and all senses) and its connotations – meaning – aiming to change built up structures.)

🎺 Psychology of learning, of perceiving and (re-) conditioning of behavior has become a tool in both economics and politics. Humans are reduced to mechanical beings that can be analyzed, measured, and with that influenced by manipulations via 'rational behavior' and stealth influences.

🎺 Politics and economics operate by re-conditioning, learning by copying, directing by attractiveness, manipulating by aversive stimuli, and systematic redirecting or annulling sensual experiences.

🎺 Why doesn't it get into the heads of the responsible people in political science that such psychological 'tools' operate everywhere in the fields of politics?

🎺 Students of political science and of economic science must know that they are permanently influenced by re-conditioning, learning by copying, directing by attractiveness, manipulated by aversive stimuli, and by systematic redirecting or annulling sensual experiences. When they get their Bachelors degree they are re-programmed and ready for a political (or economic) career.

Clinical psychology is understood among others as a connection to Piaget's clinical method in developmental psychology as an applied science (Baumann 1979). With its scientific aspect it belongs to the set of behaviorism. The 'clinical psychologist' works in socio-educational institutions, homes for children and young people in welfare centers, in hospitals, in psychiatric hospitals and geriatrics; additionally also in private practices.

Clinical psychology deals with mental and psycho-social responses in terms of disease, difficulty and disorders. Clinical work is: prevention, treatment, consultation, analysis, social pedagogical education and diagnostics. The philosophical-anthropological orientation is centered in humanism: "Similar to psychotherapy [in clinical psychology] the individual should actually be brought to the conflict-free development of his personality." (Schraml/Baumann, 1975, I, 716)

The clinical psychologist can use the whole methodical spectrum of education, counseling, psychoanalysis, behavioral therapy, milieu therapy, group analytical psychotherapy, children psychotherapy, marriage counseling, conversational psychotherapy, relaxation and hypnosis and psychagogic methods. The clinical psychologist is not a doctor, and neither a psychiatrist. Clinical psychology is a technological attempt of professionalizing psychologists alongside medical psychoanalysis. (Petermann/Schmook 1977, I, II; Baumann/Berbalk/Seidenstücker 1978).

🖎 A personality development free of conflicts (problems, difficulties) we consider as impossible and not even desirable. But it is indispensable to teach people (in the family and in public schools) how to deal with conflicts in an efficient and constructive way.

🖎 Checking media sources from around the globe (not the 100% Western media) everyday, we see that the entire Western policy is gearing up towards more conflicts, problems, up until another war.

🖎 Already the concepts of political parties include the dynamic (fault) of creating more and more conflicts, confrontations, and even hate.

🖎 Considering the status of public education and the result (when the youths start their own life), we must conclude that the ministers of education don't have much insight into the importance of education. They operate in an alienated way – totally ignoring real educational needs geared to preparing the youths for mastering life and managing their development with responsibility.

🖎 Most conflicts (if not all) in the political world start with the conflicts the political agents have in their life and unconscious mind. This is so important that all students of political science should know about it and contemplate their own external and internal (unconscious) conflicts. But they don't learn anything about it.

160 years of human values from the Science of Psychology

Self-knowledge, self-explorations, psycho-catharsis, and guidance of people, spirituality, knowledge about the unconscious, knowledge about the suppression of sexual desire, knowledge about power and inferiority and striving for compensation and supremacy, contemplating about the 'inner world', character analysis, understanding the vivid psychical organism (field, totality), respecting the phases of development, care for development, love, self-being, understanding needs and unconscious networks (family, collective), understanding society with psychological categories, humanism, the self-ideal and the true self, openness, honesty, participation, empathy, the humane potentials for a new world, inner meaning of life, introspection, Spirit, meditation, contemplation, balance between intellect and emotion or spirituality, learning, and more.

➜ Politics does not take all the manifold findings of these pioneers seriously (nor did do so in the past).
➜ Economics does not take all the manifold findings of these pioneers seriously (nor did do so in the past).
➜ Religion does not take all the manifold findings of these pioneers seriously (nor did do so in the past).
➜ The "science" of politics and economics does not take all the manifold findings of these pioneers seriously (nor did do so in the past).
➜ Public education does not take all the manifold findings of these pioneers seriously (nor did do so in the past).
➜ The Western world has lost most of the rich humane values that have been historically built up by many pioneering experts, scientists, and individuals!

2.4. Educational Ideas

(The following part is oriented on paragraphs from the book 'Evolutionary Human Education', p. 133-145, German edition)

Until the 18th century, pedagogy was a part of philosophy: pedagogy was seen as practical philosophy. Then the period of actual pedagogy began. All the famous teachers in the following time up until today have also dealt with public education, i.e. in human development. Some of them refer to Plato or Aristotle. In Plato's 'Politeia' one can find the [probably] first educational theory. In this regard are: virtue, competent thinking and acting, liberation and inner freedom, and professional skills (for making money). Raising awareness is indeed the core of Plato's human formation. The medieval concept of education is interpreted theologically and receives in Meister Eckhart (1260-1327) the highest spiritual expression in the form of 'mystical union'. Far from such depths is the educational concept of the Enlightenment. Reason and true virtue are at this time the contents of education (Wehnes 1991).

Throughout the whole history of Christianity, education and human development have been key tasks. The philosophy of the Middle Ages found in the ecclesiastical practices their essential active pedagogic expression. The Christian churches are therefore referred to as the key educational institutions of the Occident, at least until the 18th century. We want to highlight briefly some aspects of the human development of the history (Knoop / Schwab 1992; Horney others 1970; Böhm 1980; Scheuerl 1985).

Comenius (1592-1670) is considered the first great theoretician of a systematic and comprehensive pedagogy, including the education of adults and the elderly. Man is capable of learning, in need to learn and deserves as a 'creature of God and a member of the universal human community' to be adequately treated or formed.

- Without entering into the divine and Darwinian dimension of human's creation, we can say that a human being is a wonderful and amazing creation with outstanding potential. But for a majority of politicians and economists, human beings are nothing more than rats.
- Those politicians and masters or servants of economics that understand humans as 'rats' fail to see that given that they are also humans, they are also 'rats', maybe just 'upper class rats'.

- Indeed, most of these people in politics and economics do not value the creation of humans and of the planet with all its potentials.
- The history of wars and the imperialistic Western politics (also with wars) show us that the people in power do not understand humans as a universal human community. Other folks, cultures, religions, politics are always of 'lower human class' with minor quality or simply the evil and the foe.
- Studying 'the Western human' as a species of lowest moral qualities, of inability to respectfully live with the planet, of absence of soul and inner Spirit, of absolutely ignoring the truth and with that the Archetypes of the Soul, would give the students a completely different perspective.

Rousseau (1712-1778) interpreted the human caught between society and individual possibilities. "Everything is good as it leaves the hands of the author of things, everything degenerates in the hands of man.". Freedom,

equality and emancipation were the aims of his idea of a 'new man'. His cultural criticism circles around the problem of 'cerebralization', alienation through rationalization and automation of life.

- Freedom is never unlimited and requires responsibility. Equality doesn't exist, it is a myth. And emancipation without inner holistic psychical and spiritual growth leads to dehumanization and a collective mess. The actual problems of nations and the world show us this mess that politicians (and capitalistic economics) have created.
- It is unclear if 'everything is good' (at the beginning). But what is clear: That everything in the hands of politicians degenerates and will lead humanity to a doomed future.
- The problem about 'everything is good at the beginning' starts with the procreation: with the prenatal time, with mother and father (at that time), the parental relationship and the ways of living and shaping (education) a child during the first three years. Analyzing politicians should surely include this perspective that will lead to some dramatic and very neurotic acknowledgements.
- The Western human is dehumanized and degenerated from over-intellectualization, self-alienation and through rationalization and technological management of humans and society, of humans' life in general.
- The study programs of political science – probably of all social sciences – shape their students towards dehumanization, degeneration, intellectualization, and self-alienation.

Humboldt (1767-1835), marks the beginning of a comprehensive theory of education. Education becomes for him in his time of turmoil extremely important. Education leads to self-confidence, to achieve mutually harmoniously formed individuality and self-expression. It is separated into general education, people education and training. Dominating is the central idea of 'universal human and universal harmonic formation'.

- Disruption was already a matter of philosophical and educational concern in the 17th and 18th century. Today it's even worse: most societies and a majority of humans are rotten to the core, and now heading towards the abyss. This is the result of a political legacy centuries in the making that operates today at a high speed and with full power ahead.
- Today in the best case we have 0.0001% of humans that have an all-sided balanced (harmonic) individuality and self-development. Is there such a human in the world of politics? Possibly, but in the best case only a few.
- Students of Western standard political science will adapt this archaic political legacy and apply it in their future professional career, just perpetuating failed political theories.

Herbart (1776-1841) taught about the morality as the highest good of human development. He is considered 'the last philosopher among teachers and the last teacher among philosophers'. Issues of public life are viewed from an educational perspective. His human formation is centered on the concept of decency - as 'the pinnacle of character education' - with ethics as the defining goal and psychology (Greek origin meaning study 'ology' of the soul 'psyche') as the ways and means for that purpose.

- Politicians have completely forgotten that morality is the highest good of humans' education, of human life in general.
- Political concerns about public matters exclude the human values, the humans in general, and especially morality. Ethics has lost its place on the political stage and psychology has become a tool for deceit, cheating, falseness, and brainwashing.
- Forming a moral and spiritual character is not a subject or aim of political science.

Froebel established (1782-1852) the 'General German educational Institution' and dealt with 'human education' (1826). The human being should experience himself connected with the cosmos and with God. Mankind has to find the way back to itself, where everyone will discover their 'higher purpose in life'. 'Life agreement' with nature, with mankind and with God is to be understood as a model of human nature.

- Go and tell the Western rulers that they must connect with the cosmos and with God! They will slap you (verbally) in the face.
- Go and tell the politicians that they should first find themselves, find in their soul their inner 'mission' (dedication, purpose of life), and be unified with nature, with mankind and with God. Politicians will put you in a psychiatric home!
- Students of political science (and economics) should demand that their professors and teachers or heads of faculty should first find themselves, find in their soul their inner 'mission' (dedication, purpose of life), and become unified with nature, with mankind and with God.

Pestalozzi (1746-1827) is known around the world for his teaching about 'head, hand and heart-education'. The 'modern public education' has until today received remaining inspirations. He understood education as the 'fulfillment of the own destiny' and integrated people, family and Fatherland. He was never exclusively a children educator. He was also a theorist of the people education. A key sentence from him is: 'Life educates'. Purpose for general education is the rise of the internal forces of human nature. Vocational training is therefore subordinate to the human formation.

- Education must aim for the fulfillment of one's own (divine) purpose. Life shapes. What can we conclude by observing the activities of politicians? There is rarely any kind of (divine) fulfillment, but a lot of distortion and self-alienation.
- Inner forces of politicians' nature are for example the content (complexes) in the unconscious mind, deficient ability to love, amorality, greed, and falseness.
- The archetypal processes leading to fulfillment are completely excluded from political science.

Schleiermacher (1768-1834) founded pedagogy as action of science (theory and practice) with historical and ethical responsibility. The model was the maturity of each individual in the state. Education and state have a common interest based on the maintenance of the state. The human formation is therefore in dialectical relation to the interests of society, dialectically faced by morality and instinctual nature, immateriality and reality, as well as reason and our individual nature.

- Education and a society have a common interest: maintenance (perpetuation) of the state. De facto we experience an increase or perpetuation of power, an increase of bellicose activities, an increase of regulations; and everything is about money and increase of money.

Education is a tool for the accommodation of a consumer lifestyle. Human education in the corresponding departments has gone down the drain.

🖐 Human (public) education and family education has become a basket case: the agents of education are today the media, the Internet, the mobile phones, the corporations, and so on. Human education from its traditional understanding has lost its potentials and genuine aims.

🖐 Political science does not place the human factors as an indispensable part in their syllabi, not even a small part.

Dilthey (1833-1911) saw education as 'formation of all mental functions'. He designed a teleology of mental life, a doctrine of psychical functions and methods of understanding (hermeneutics). He understands the soul's life as a holistic structure, nestled in the historical cultural fields. By all historicity of human life, the life of the soul is given independently. Herein educational philosophy and human formation (education) are based.

🖐 The claim is here: All psychical forces must be understood, formed, shaped, and developed (up to the highest potentials), always taking into consideration environmental factors. Which forces of politicians are predominantly formed and which forces are neglected or distorted? The answer is disastrous!

🖐 Which forces of the students of political science are predominantly formed and which forces are neglected or distorted? The answer may frighten the students.

Natorp (1854-1924) dealt with the 'social popular culture and the culture of personality'. He was close to the workers-, family- and women's-movement. Public education tasks took a significant space. As a neo-Kantian, he saw the goals of human formation in the enforcement of the law of reason. Based on that are ethics and virtue theory. The human being as part of the community has to be educated towards rational-activity and truth. Drive, will and reason are put into a context of meaning and value.

🖐 How much of ethics, virtues, and reason can we identify in the world of political activities? Not much!

🖐 How much of reasonable activities and truth can we identify in the world of political activities? Not much!

🖐 Do politicians integrate their aims and do they put their aims into a frame of meaning and human values? Not much!

🖐 How much of reasonable (relevant and useful) subjects and political truth can we identify in the syllabi of political science? Not much!

Kerschensteiner (1854-1932) contributed significantly to labour-education as well as to the theory and practice of civic education. The conception of man is practically oriented: "The character develops through action" is his basic axiom of education. Training he sees as 'gateway to the human formation'.

- ✎ Character is developed (shaped) through activities: How does a political career develop starting as a member of a political party, later going up the ladder from a local position to a provincial position, and finally becoming a member of the central government? Self-alienation, rigidity, amorality, increasing greed for power, cantankerousness, stubbornness, and more and more trickery will shape his character.
- ✎ In a parliament we have 100, 250, 500 or more lawmakers. They are all shaped through their previous activities (learning, behavior). What kind of character traits do they all have in common? The answer will shock you!
- ✎ How does political science shape the character of their students? Some simply focus on getting their Bachelor degree. Others already know: don't be critical towards the study program, the professors, or the ideology and political practices of the USA and EU in general.

Spranger (1882-1963) was particularly engaged on the issue of education in the interplay between spirit-soul-culture and in public education ('general knowledge'). He also developed a cultural education and humanity' oriented psychology. In addition, he developed the three-step approach: Basic education – training – general knowledge. Not the free development of personality is the ultimate goal, but to take the 'best values' of the social whole and return our own best values. The adults he sees in a constant process of change ('stages of life'). Permanent learning and the continuous growth is implicitly seen as natural.

- ✎ What are the 'best values' one can get from the political stages? What are the best values one can get from social life? What are the best values one can get from the social communities in the Internet? If these values are miserable, then in general one does not give back to the society something better. Politicians are responsible also for the 'best values'!
- ✎ Permanent learning for life, mind and soul is a requirement from the human nature. This understanding goes beyond professional learning. It includes the archetypal psychical-spiritual development as a life long process. But politicians in general do not reach a significantly higher level of psychical-spiritual development during their life.
- ✎ On the political stages and also in the classrooms of political science there is no interplay between Spirit-Soul-Culture.

Montessori (1870-1952) is known for her 'Pedagogy from the child's perspective'. She has in her commitment made sharp criticism of all adults as originators of wars, famine, injustice, misery, and as the inventors of the atomic bomb. The adult is to be changed; he has to become in his self-development more mobile and to develop new forms of his own life. Not only the child is dependent on adults, the adult is dependent on the child too.

- With arrogance, brutality, and rigidity public education ignores the individual disposition of the children and pupils forcing and breaking their mind and soul with rules, regulations, and continuously giving grades.
- Politicians are the cause and people responsible for wars, hunger, injustice, misery, and the nuclear bomb arsenals. Who will bring them to justice?
- Politicians are adults and adults are responsible for permanent learning, also and especially for their inner archetypal growing process. But most politicians and a huge majority of people don't care about such inner development.
- Children depend on adults, future children as well, also the future generation and the people in 100, 200 and many more years are dependent on the adults on the political stage of today. Today they all fail terribly in their responsibility!

Litt (1880-1962) conceived his pedagogy fundamentally on philosophical considerations. He sets man as educational topic in the dimension of spirit and being. He understood realization of sense on the one hand in the context of metaphysical ideas, and on the other hand in relation to work and career. Here humane development takes place.

- Spirit and existence today are reduced to the factor of consumption, money, and power, reputation and narcissistic satisfaction.
- Realization of meaning, better of 'archetypal meaning' or of 'human values', extensively disappeared on this planet.

Flitner (1889-1990) was very close to the popular education (adult education movement). Lifestyle, cultural traditions and forms of education are faced with the theory. For him education is always to be understood in the larger context of Western intellectual and cultural history. Questions of meaning and values belong just as much to the understanding of the education as philosophical thoughts do.

With the emphasis on the particular responsibility of educators and adult teachers he wants to understand the education and training as an independent science, particularly emphasizing the social and humanistic practical relevance. The adult is in need of education until the end of his life.

- Real life (lifestyle, culture, education) comes before theories. The politicians could learn here that resolving the factual problems comes before ideology.
- Governance includes guiding people and that requires educational operations. Politicians don't guide, they do what they want with all means until one millimeter before the breaking point. Often they miss this limit and everything in society gets into a mess (e.g. unrest) or erupts in war.
- Educators, teachers, and professors (including those from political science) have an exceptional responsibility; and we add here the politicians in office. Everywhere there is absence of such responsibility and with that increase of failure.

The first turning point in the history of education since the 18th century first becomes apparent in the 20th century. Flitner (1889-1990), Nohl (1879-1960), Weniger (1894-1961), Roth (1906-1983) and others in the first half of this century contributed significantly to human development. Historic-hermeneutic reflections, thoughts on education-philosophy and culture- and value-pedagogy were guidelines in the employment of human-development. The education and 'education of man' attains scientific character, first hermeneutic-pragmatic, then gradually empirical.

- All the pioneering work from countless scientists of education is forgotten; or serves here and there as a sterile topic of a syllabus. A lot may be useless and outdated today. But there is also a lot about humans and human values that the world of politics has put in the oven.

An in-depth analysis of the educational processes based on the insights of depth psychology has not been made (with few exceptions; Aichhorn eg 1878-1949). 'The structure of the person' by Lersch, 'The layers of personality' by Rothacker and 'Basics of theory of character' by Klages (1872-1956) are considered as the personality theories of pedagogy. For the human education of pedagogy these teachings were considered as cataclysmic. Some basic concepts and findings are still recognizable in everyday speech, such as choleric, melancholic, sanguine, phlegmatic, the 'lifestyles' of Spranger (the religious, social, economic, aesthetic, theoretical man and the man of power) and the constitution types of Kretschmer. The scientific personality psychology emerged from the Characterology.

🖑 Finally, psychology of personality has become a science. Personality is the result of education and processes of shaping through social interactions and environment. Today the term 'personality' has a respectful meaning. But political science doesn't see the importance of forming 'personalities' or of analyzing political personalities.

A second re-orientation - to some extent the scientific revolution in education – starts around 1955-1960 (we're talking mainly about German-speaking countries). The pedagogy becomes a systematic empirical science. Enormous pioneering work, the minting of the new notion of science was contributed by Roth, Roehrs, Klafki, Brezinka, Mollenhauer and Blankertz. The research on teaching, on curriculum and school reform was gradually developed. In didactics, education is understood twofold: on the one hand the material and on the other hand the human. Dealings with the world, object awareness and understanding of sense characterize this new understanding of education in didactics. Adult education becomes clarified as the 'education permanente'. The German Education Council (1970) called for government responsibility for adult education; unsuccessfully, noted Mattl (1991, 529).

🖑 The science of education has understood that teaching is only one side; the other side is the method of teaching (didactic) and this becomes now highly important in order to be much more efficient. Academic teaching in general and most teaching in political science are taught like archaic times.

🖑 From didactics politicians could learn how to inform the citizens, how to make understandable their politics and policies, and how to form a political citizen that contributes to a balanced development in society. But nowadays more and more politicians treat the citizens like the rulers in archaic times.

While in psychology and psychoanalysis from the end of the 19th century enormous theoretical pioneering work was done, pedagogy until the mid 20th century did not yet see profound pioneering theoretical upheaval, except from the 'progressive education' (about 1900-1914, 1920-1930). Pedagogy gradually shaped its scientific identity from spiritual hermeneutical science towards empirical science. Enormous achievements we see also in practical teacher training and public schooling as well as in the establishment of adult education and educational counseling. Pioneering work was done in the broad field of social pedagogy, in home schooling for children and adolescents as well as in social education. The home schooling provided the educators just the same challenge as the institutional psychiatry did to the psychiatrists (see e.g. Montessori), at the turn of the century.

☞ Where is the pioneering spirit and where are the great performances for a humane society and world on the political stage and in the classrooms of political science? Huge sad emptiness!

Another reform development in this century, in the period 1960-1980, expanded the educational interests with comprehensive school reform programs, curriculum theories and a new understanding of science. The search for a new understanding of education takes up considerable space (Roth 1991). Humanistic concerns and commitment provoke temporarily significant discussions. Educators argue for an ethically better individual and social life. Emancipation and freedom of ideology and dogmatism as well as technical-practical skills characterize the educational development of this new era.

☞ There have been pioneers in the educational fields that explored scientifically the path for an ethically better individual and social life. In the fields of politics the 'good life' is measured by the GDP and with the allocation of goods, especially for the wants. There are no political pioneers on the political stage exploring and being active for a real democracy.

☞ Does the political science scientifically explore the aims and paths for an ethically better individual and social life? No!

From about mid-1975, the entire field of pedagogy and adult education becomes deeply explored and widely expanded. Science, theoretical commitment, based on Habermas (rationalist interest in knowledge), Albert (ethics and critical rationality) and Topitsch (ideology-freedom) belong to the introduction of many studies. The 'Frankfurt School' (Adorno, Horkheimer, Habermas) and positivism (Popper) significantly influenced the pedagogy¡s search for identity and their new view of the theory and practice in the formation of man. The linguistic formulations however cut themselves off from the everyday reality of what 'personality-development' is, that a new type of alienation in the practice of education is creatd. Perhaps this is only a theoretical distancing to grasp the cognitive interest more objectively and operationally.

☞ It would be interesting to analyze the verbal expressions (formulations) of the language of politicians. What would we discover? Empty words, aggressive expressions, lies, distortion of realities, and empty promises.

☞ At least here we discover the engagement for a new identity of the science of education. But there is rarely a subject in the syllabi of political science that shows a specific search for a new identity. Only now here and there they start searching for a new identity where education and psychology already started in the seventies of the last century.

The unconscious, the dream-life and the concept of drive of psychoanalysis have not yet found all encompassing inclusion in the theory of education. Pedagogic professors and teachers of all school types could not make up their minds to an own 'training analysis' (or shall we say 'educational analysis') (Habermas 1973, 262 f, 290 note). Concepts of psychological-spiritual unfolding, in the sense of Jung or Fromm are still far from the idea of education. Some teachers of the younger generation had learned enough about religious 'formation of conscience', metaphysical 'questions of meaning' and Christian 'virtues'. Curriculum research and school reform programs are in the focus of 'modern teachers', with some exceptions of course (Oser, 1976; Brezinka 1978). A turning point in direction of 'education in values' and formation of conscience is today recognized again (Oser/Althof 1994; Oser/Althof/Garz 1986).

Human-development at the beginning of the first century was understood as public education. The older terms 'popular education and education of society' came from the pedagogy. They capture the full range of adult education. In the 19th century education was operated by the labor movement, the churches and the middle class (so-called 'bourgeois-liberal National Education'). In the twenties in Germany the term 'free public education' was introduced.

- ☙ In the political world there is still nothing that acknowledges the need and gives weight to programs for political reforms and for shaping a new humane Western society, e.g. for more real democracy and more genuine meaning of life.
- ☙ Some subjects in the manifold syllabi first show an interest in a theoretical progress. But the rational-choice theory is anyway a faulty construction and behaviorism is nothing more than a very limited, preponderantly superficial approach to political behavior.

Only after 1945 was the term 'adult-education' introduced. In the 20th century the popular education in political, ecclesiastical, Christian charitable and educational institutions as well as at university institutes was developed. Today we find adult education in terms of teaching practices in many organizations and groups in society: communities, churches, private organizations (individuals and companies), party political institutions and alternative movements (e.g. women centers).

🖎 Offers for the general education of the public (and adult) education have grown enormously in the north of Europe. But political subjects are rather seldom. The interest in knowledge about politics is strongly retarded due to the distrust that has increased in the 30 years with politics. Distrust from the citizens is the 'feedback' for politicians! But they ignore it and only answer with exercises of power!

If we consider the adult education as something historically pre-given, we can identify the following subsystems: 1) fields of practice (facilities); 2) carriers; 3) stakeholders (business, churches, political parties, etc.); 4) the state education system; 5) professionals; 6) participants; 7) didactic; 8) contents; 9) facilities such as libraries, museums, etc.; 10) associations; 11) institutions of vocational training to adult-education; 12) Science teaching and research; 13) Jurisdiction.

This diversity inevitably raises the question of what characteristics hold together the structure of 'adult education'. There are different organizational structures, a versatile catalogue of tasks and matters that may be associated with various fields of science. On the other hand we have here not only structures and processes of organization diversity, but also diverse personality-structures from participants. These personality-structures can again be seen in complex environmental structures, e.g. micro-, meso-, exo- and macro-systems (according to Bronfenbrenner 1989). Our educational concept about adult education will have to include these networks.

🖎 Indeed from around 1970 until the year 2000 the science of education and also the private institutions for adult education developed a great élan for pioneering innovations in the faculty and in the society; except for example in Spain where the syllabi in education is still today not much different from what was taught in Germany and Switzerland during the years 1970-1975. The cause may lay in the politics and politicians that are not interested in top-educated adults.

Organizationally, the adult education and popular education is assigned in educational science and pedagogy. But this assignment is not unopposed. Kade suggests here, to establish a 'comprehensive educational science' (Kade, in: Krueger/Rauschenbach 1994, 159).

Adult education opens up along with vocational and general education and training: political education, life education, formation of culture, spiritual education, education to maturity and emancipation, crisis intervention, life-counseling, philosophical education and guidance of the people to differentiated awareness and ethical behavior.

A subdivision into educational, psychological, subject-specific, religious, spiritual, cultural, practical living and philosophical education is virtually impossible (Tietgens 1981). Adult education is a field of action insofar as science is an interaction-logical discipline ('agogic'). The problem of science-classification is therefore not solved. Because: "(There is) no constitutionally or historically inherent science of adult education." (Tietgens in: Mader 1991, 47)

🖎 The values that form the main stream of adult education in Northern Europe have a human oriented focus, but are preponderantly oriented on vocational further education. It reflects a rational understanding of human education and human life providing knowledge and skills for professional development and success or satisfaction in personal life. There is not much of such innovative spirit in the political fields and science.

(The following part is oriented on a paragraph in the book 'Evolutionary Human Education', p. 147, German edition)

Adult Education generally means: Transferring of knowledge and insights, intentional educational process, self-education towards completion, aid to learning, rational action for the purpose of ability-improvement, without making an effort on ideological or political thinking and behavior (at least at the community colleges). This includes a very wide range of targets: communication of knowledge, solidarity, character development, responsibility skills, life-counseling, creativity, sense of purpose, peace, non-violence, virtues, morality, orientation of life and more.

🖎 Reading about the development in the science of education and in the private adult education until the beginning of the 21st Century provides us with a picture of pioneering spirit, élan, creativity, activity and commitment for a variety of human values. We cannot however find such a development in political (and economic) science.

(The following part is oriented on a paragraph in the book 'Evolutionary Human Education', p. 165, German edition)

Andragogy is according to our first definition: personality-psychological, life-psychological and life-practical, philosophical and spiritual formation. The (science of) Andragogy focuses on the formation of personality (the adult person) and the fundamental questions of human-being. We define Andragogy from the humans being, i.e. from his psychical and spiritual wholeness.

Andragogy, according to this definition, is not understood in its core-perception as vocational education in terms of professional training and development.

🖑 The concern of adult education (Andragogy) is identified: psychological, practical (for living), philosophical, and spiritual aims. The basic questions of the meaning of human life are in the center of its justification and motives. There is really no such spirit on the stage of politics, absolutely nothing in the economic world, and nothing or not much in the political science. We can't see here any evolution that focuses on such aims and human values or meaning of life in order to make the society and the practical politics better off in terms of peace, justice, a healthy planet, and a safe world.

400 years of human values from the Science of Education

Need for learning and ability to learn, humans are part of the universal 'body' of humanity, morality, the truth, the divine aspect of humans, freedom, equality, emancipation, the 'new man', genuine self-realization, authenticity, individuality and self-development, harmonic education, shaping character, the inner connection with the cosmos and with God, the higher meaning of life, fulfillment of the genuine (inner) being, love and truthfulness, individual nature, forming the psychical functions, teleology of the soul (aim-oriented soul), social culture, virtues, will, vocational education, the best values as orientation, meaning of life phases, self-forming (-shaping), interdependences between humans, interaction between Spirit-Soul-Culture, realization of meaning, lifelong learning and self-forming, pioneering spirit of education, all-embracing education, and more.

→ Politics did not in the past and do not today take seriously all the manifold findings of these pioneers.
→ Economics did not in the past and do not today take seriously all the manifold findings of these pioneers.
→ Religion did not in the past and do not today take seriously all the manifold findings of these pioneers.
→ The science of politics and economics did not in the past and do not today take seriously all the manifold findings of these pioneers.
→ Public education did not in the past and do not today take seriously all the manifold findings of these pioneers.
→ The Western world has lost most of the humane values built up historically by many pioneering experts, scientists, and individuals!

2.5. Mind and Soul of Politicians

What is a 'human'?

Today we determine a 'human' with the entire mind (psyche, inner life) as a whole. We call it 'the psychical-spiritual organism' as the mind contains several systems (sub-systems') operating each other in interactions.

Many non-physical functions determine a human being:

- The conscious (the content of the 'inner screen')
- The intelligence: the ability to think and learn
- The memory
- The 'I' (self) as the control and decision making instance
- The defense and projection mechanisms
- The feelings (emotions): the whole spectrum from love to hate
- The capacity to love
- The genuine psychical needs
- The unconscious
- The inner psychical pole of the opposite gender
- The 'spiritual intelligence', called also the 'inner Spirit' creating dream messages and forming results from meditation
- The ability of visualization (imagination, contemplation, meditation)

Additionally to the mind we have to relate these mental functions with:

1) The behavior: Behavior is always a result of how the mind is working.

2) The individual psychical energy: thoughts and emotions form psychical energy being active in the physical body, influencing physical and mental functions, and radiating towards the external world.

3) The collective psychical energy: the stored sum of the individual energy radiating towards outside and being around us like the air.

➜ What is a human being without these psychical functions? He is a pure human biomass. In other words: these inner psychical and spiritual functions make humans different from animals. And all humans have these psychical and spiritual potentials.

→ Without doubt we can say: These functions are formed since prenatal time. These functions must be formed / shaped during the entire life. A human without such forming processes has no chance to become a human that is able to live in a humane and efficient way.

→ Obvious is also: all these functions can be formed or deformed in countless ways and filled with countless 'content'. The combination of formed functions or parts of functions are countless, nearly unlimited.

→ The innermost entity of a human is the disposition consisting of these mental, psychical and spiritual functions with an immense manifold potential that must be formed for the world and for the human itself. There are many examples proving that this disposition is primarily or existentially non-biological. Talking about the 'soul', the inner Spirit, and the mental energy we enter in this dimension of the reality.

The mutual influences of the singular psychical forces are manifold; some examples are given (you can add more):

- Feelings influence thinking
- Needs drive perception and actions
- Perception is influenced by wishes
- The unconscious acts on feelings and on thinking
- The capacity for love forms feelings and thoughts
- Dreams activate moods
- Psycho-dynamism is formed by thoughts and experiences
- Actions are produced by different inner psychical forces
- What we have in our consciousness, influences our self-being
- Suppression and oppression make our psychical energy tense

All these functions can be formed in countless ways, with constructive and destructive results.

The inner Spirit is the anchor and the most powerful 'spiritual intelligence' that all humans have in their mind. The principles (dynamic characteristics) of this inner Spirit give us the normative orientation for education and life in general.

In a certain way we can make some logical or comprehensible and self-evident systemic and practical conclusions:

- All functions have to be formed (trained, shaped) and this is a natural need of every human being.
- The forming of a function must be in an adequate relation to the other functions.

- The most valuable aim of forming these functions is an all-sided balanced state of all functions.
- Suppressing and neglecting singular functions always has a destructive effect.
- The inner Spirit is informative, corrective, educative, supportive, and normative.
- The most essential and primary meaning of life is forming the psychical-spiritual organism as a whole.
- Love is as essential as intelligence for living and realizing the meaning of life. Love is much more than an emotion. It is also a spiritual function.
- Ideals, values, attitudes, and norms must be in an appropriate network with these functions.
- Everything that is over-excessive and over-dominant by ignoring other functions is destructive.
- The unconscious world is more powerful than the conscious mind and Ego (Self or 'I').
- An unelaborated unconscious mind means disequilibrium and is always destructive.
- An unelaborated collective unconscious produces wars and world destruction.
- Real life today demands extensive forming (shaping, educating) processes of all psychical functions.
- Ignoring authentic and genuine development (growth) and living ends in illness and destructivity.
- The qualities (efficiency) and values of all the functions must be higher than external values (interests).
- There is no peace, no happiness, no (relative) harmony, and no fulfillment by lack of a balanced formation process.
- The state of humanity and the earth is an expression of the results of wrong human formation.
- Giving priority to fun, assets, wealth, reputation, prestige, and power destroys humanity.

The single psychical forces can be put together into 'sub-systems':

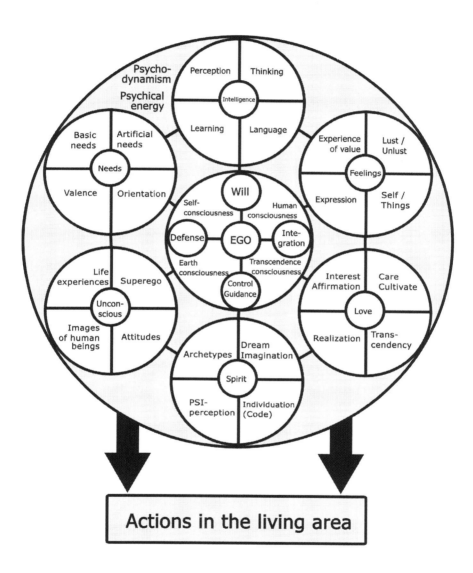

We also can find an understanding by common sense principles of a system. We can understand a human on the one side by its biological organism and on the other side by its mental (psychological) organism. Both organisms consist in varied subsystems, and some subsystems consist in sub-sub-systems. Certainly, we can make different models of a system of the mind (psyche); but it's not relevant here.

The relevant systemic principles are easy to comprehend:

- The system 'body' is in interdependence with the system of the mind.
- If one sub-system of the body doesn't work well, then criticalities arise.
- The system 'mind' is in interdependence with the system of the body.
- If one sub-system of the mind doesn't work well, then criticalities arise.
- A criticality on the body-system can produce criticalities in the mind system
- A criticality on the mind-system can produce criticalities in the body system
- The entire system can work well, but its functioning depends on the person.
- If a person doesn't control and maintain both systems, criticalities arise.
- Behavior is the result of the state of the mind, its ways of functioning.
- The result of behavior we see in the personal, social and natural environment.
- Criticalities in personal and social life and in the environment are an expression (a result) of criticalities in the mind (seldom simply in the body).
- Obviously also the social, political, and natural environment can create criticalities for humans mind, body, and existence. In this case the mind must learn how to adapt with such challenging criticalities, especially how to be flexible in one's ways of living (or behavior) in such a case.

A trivial example: Stupid people produce everywhere stupid criticalities.
In an academic way: A badly (unbalanced) formed mind produces criticalities.

→ We conclude that politicians (or politics, governance) don't need an ideology or a dogmatic (fundamentalist) religion for their governmental system and their policy. They simply need to accept and respect the natural requirements of the body, of the mind, of the necessary knowledge and skills (for behavior, ways of living), of the nature (planet), of the society, and of some given external (natural and social/humane) criticalities.
→ A logical conclusion for politicians, lawmakers, ministers, and heads of state is: The less and worse and the more self-alienated the mind of

humans (and their knowledge and skills/behavior) is shaped, formed, educated and trained, the more politicians need to implement rigid regulations in their society.

→ Seen from the other perspective: The less politicians, lawmakers, ministers, and heads of state accept and respect these simple and natural principles of the body and the mind of humans in the structure of their governmental apparatus and in their policies (politics), the more criticalities arise in the body, mind, and behavior of people, and also in the nature (planet) and social environment (society as a whole).

Based on this dynamic structure of the mind and soul we can analyze the mind and soul of politicians (as well as of anybody). Our first thesis is in this context:

→ All activities of politicians are rooted in the ways their mind and soul is formed (shaped).
→ The knowledge politicians have about the system of mind and soul and its potentials is the starting point of their political ideas, their politics and policies.

Let's explore the single sub-systems of the mind in the context of the political agents without going into scientific discussions about the manifoldness and complexity of these single functions:

1) The conscious

The conscious is something like a 'screen' we have in our mind. What a human perceives with his eyes enters into and shows on the screen. But perception is always partly subjective and partly selected. For example, if 5 people see the same car accident, they will all report a picture with different elements or shapes of aspects. One may describe 20 elements, another only 15 or 10 elements, etcetera. Most reports will be also in some details different, in sizes or colors, or whatever. The same happens if 5 women see the same man in a specific situation; or if 5 men see the same woman in a specific situation. We could mention thousands of patterns, and always we will have different results in a report from 5, 10 or 100 people.

Starting from here we can generalize: everything that people perceive gets a subjective picture in their inner screen that in most cases is not 100% identical to the reality they have observed. In the extreme case we could have 100 reports from 100 different people with 100 different results.

Reporting, verbally or written, another function comes into action: the language and with that the repertoire a person has about specific fields or in general.

Simultaneously most people tend to mix description with interpretation and emotion. From here it's a short moment or distance to add a moral component or an attitude (opinion) to the elements in the inner picture (screen).

The more complex an external reality is the more people will have a different inner picture on their inner screen. People tend then to add elements from similar experiences in the past or from knowledge they have at disposal in their mind. Such a picture becomes very fast a creative touch.

Quality of perception
Clear, precise, awaken
Differentiated
Deep going
Manifold, all-embracing
In clear order
Precisely classified
Flexible, mobile
Far-reaching
Objective
Considerate
Responsible
Value-experience
Deliberately, purposeful
With field-competences
Assimilating, integrating
In a more broaden field
Revealing, unfolding
Free of prejudgment
With time perspective
Analyzing

Conclusion: An external reality is in most cases partly and often significantly different in the inner screen that people have after having seen this reality.

➜ A politician is never free from such selective and 'creative' mechanisms.
➜ If 100 or 250-500 politicians (e.g. lawmakers) talk about the same external reality, they are all talking based on the picture they have on their inner

screen. In that sense they do not talk about the corresponding external reality.

🖛 On the political stage the inner picture the agents have about the topics they discuss is the first step towards misunderstanding, misinterpretation, strong arguments, and in the end it leads to ugly fights.

2) The intelligence

The ability to think contains many components. A basic intelligence is indispensable. Thinking can be analytical, theoretical, causal, prospective, hermeneutical, creative, intuitive, meditative, all embracing, categorizing, and even critical or short-sighted; and it can include the time dimension (past-present-future), or dimensions of interrelations, chain-reactions, or of meaning.

Certain knowledge, certain learning processes, a language repertoire (words), and a memory are indispensable to efficiently think.

We must compose it with the perception and the inner screen: Thinking is always about something a human has on his inner screen.

Elements in the inner screen also can be a thought, a fantasy, a dream, and a result of meditation, a matter from the past and therefore coming from the memory or unconscious mind.

Thesis-1: Nothing works without the mind

Everything starts with the mind, with thinking and all the supportive functions. Stupid, but true: there is no philosophy, no religion, no ideology, no politics and no thinking without the functions of the mind.

Thesis-2: The entire formed mind

All the functions of the mind are formed since prenatal time from people, from learning, environment, and so on; also from the way a person deals with the result of the formed state of the mind and its functions.

Thesis-3: The ego-operational functions

The main control functions / management functions are the 'intelligent functions' making 'thinking' happen, such as:

- Perception
- Defense mechanisms
- Integration mechanisms
- Giving meaning
- Giving words
- Thinking, judging, analyzing, etc.
- Interpreting
- Concluding
- Decision making
- Evaluation/ control of the action

Thesis-4: Realities

a) There is an objective reality:

- There are physical and 'inner' realities
- Humans perceive realities with different senses
- Partly we see realities directly or through tools
- Partly we don't see realities for many reasons
- Partly realities are consciously hidden (avoided to see)

b) What we perceive and identify is a subjective reality (in the mind)

c) What we form in the mind about the perceived reality, is an elaborated subjective reality, based on the elaboration pattern we have formed (descriptive, normative, emotionally rejecting, interpreting, and so on)

d) What we conclude from the formed / elaborated reality is a subjective reality, e.g. life philosophy, attitudes, opinion, necessary actions

Thesis-5: Subjective influences

Our 'reality' is also formed by subjective influences:

- Biography
- Culture
- Social environment
- Learning
- Media/political-/religion-elaborated
- Subjective state of "personality"
- Living conditions
- Desire, needs, deficits

- The way we see and deal with realities is adapted

We can identify qualities and activities of the intelligence. The network of intelligence depends on many qualities:

- Perception
- Manipulation of perception
- Mechanisms of rejection
- Giving words
- Linked associations
- Emotional components
- Giving meaning
- Interpretation
- Questioning
- Ways of thinking
- Critical thinking
- Looking behind the façades
- Giving values
- Judgments
- Learning
- Time frame (past, present, future)
- Network of causes-effects
- Conclusions
- Action

Using intelligence for life, business, work, and study means:

Basic steps:

- Recognizing (to perceive)
- Identifying
- Giving words
- Interpreting
- Valuing
- Categorizing
- Judging (pre-judging)
- Concluding
- Acting

Qualitative step: Analyzing

- The elements of the perceived reality

- The complex interrelations of the inner and external realities
- Qualities of the scene with its elements
- The context of the past
- The perspective of the future
- The individual motive factors
- The causes and circumstances
- 'Weight' by multiplying by 1m or 1bn or 5bn
- Importance and urgency
- Desired and non desired effects
- Efficiency in relation to the aim(s)
- Analysis of risks and lateral effects
- Present and future (long term) consequences
- Active defense mechanisms and the truth
- The hidden realities (conscious and unconscious)
- Critical analysis of patterns of interpretation
- The use of words, terms and symbols with their fields of meaning
- The ways of rational and emotional argumentation
- The ways of description of the scenery and its elements

Management step: actions and consequences

- Decision making process and taking a decision
- Determining aims and purpose of (re-) action
- Ways of communicating, informing (transferring information)
- Ways of introducing, implementing action
- Controlling conditions of an action and its effects
- Managing and controlling action
- Balancing with attitudes, values, belief, norms
- Management of supportive lateral actions
- Controlling the strategy of a determined process
- Identifying direct and lateral interactions of the action
- Long term consequences of actions (personal, collective)
- Analysis of the result of a new action and again: learning

There are several thinking processes that constitute quality and efficiency:

- Identifying similarities/analogies
- Abstracting from space and time
- Breaking into pieces and recomposing
- Combining and comparing
- Understanding interrelations
- Identifying causes

198

- Giving meaning
- Relating with values
- Aim oriented elaboration
- Conclusions
- Classifications (categories)

Facts and patterns of interpretation and managing realities is an active network: Humans do not simply have facts in the mind to manage life. Humans have patterns of interpretation to act and react.

'Patterns of interpretation' means:

- Stereotype ways of view and ways of interpretation
- Interpretation is based on experiences
- Patterns are stable and invariable to feel secure
- Built up patterns through biography (education, copied)
- Used for everything in life
- Form one's self-identity and "position"

Importance of patterns of interpretation:

- People act on the meaning they give to facts
- Patterns determine what people consider as true and correct
- Patterns are learnt, can be revised, reflected and improved
- Patterns are part of the daily routine knowledge
- Patterns contain plausibility giving certainty
- Patterns from the past form the present patterns
- Patterns are linked with emotions
- The interpreted world is a simplified world
- Subjective theories form part of patterns
- Uniqueness are generalized through patterns
- Patterns also reflect the spirit of the society (zeitgeist)
- Behind superficiality is always the biography
- Interpretations tend to be simplifications, to make acting easy
- Prejudgments and opinions form part of patterns
- Patterns filter the perception of realities
- Patterns are relatively stable
- Changing patterns is difficult because they are based on the biography
- Patterns select and accentuate
- Changing patterns destabilize self-identity
- Patterns from the early childhood are especially strong
- Correcting ideology, dogmatism and norms are difficult

- Reorganizing interpreted realities is strenuous
- Simple patterns make life easier and reduce inner dissonance
- Patterns of interpretation often result from social pressure
- New patterns arise from new experiences of one's own acting
- Fundamental crisis in life (about meaning of life) demands correction

→ A politician has a certain capacity and preference in the way he (she) is thinking. Politicians are never free from such selected thinking.

→ If 100 or 250-500 politicians (e.g. lawmakers) think (and then talk) about the same external reality, they are all talking based on the picture they have on their inner screen and the way they have made their thoughts about it. In that sense they do not talk about the corresponding external reality.

✎ On the political stage the way the agents think or have their thoughts about the topics they discuss depend on the second step from the way of their thinking. Logically, as these ways of thinking differ much between politicians, and therefore their talking leads towards misunderstanding, misinterpretation, strong arguments, and in the end to ugly fights.

3) The defense and projection mechanisms

Already during the perception process people tend to select what they see. The more something is uncomfortable (embarrassing) or challenging to the conscience or the ego, the more people tend to reject such a part of the perceived reality. At the same time people easily project their positive attitude, a want or wish, a dream, or a longing. They also tend to project their own weak and evil aspects in order to feel (to be) better or to construct an 'enemy'. People especially, also tend to register either those aspects that conform to their values, ideals, attitudes and norms or those aspects that confirm their values, ideals, attitudes and norms.

Defense and projection mechanisms depend a lot on the biography (learnt mechanisms through experiences) and mostly also on their favored peer group or social environment. The focus can be a political ideology or a religion or a life philosophy or simply friendship.

Defense Mechanisms
Ignoring
Selecting
Lying
Hiding

Suppressing
Projecting
Distorting
Turning into the opposite
Deceiving
Cheating
Disfiguration
Displacing
Simplifying
Minimizing
Exaggerating
Deviating
Detracting
Intriguing
Denying
Falsifying
Replacing
Compensating
Provoking
Devaluating
Overvaluing
Giving opposite value
Making noise
Putting rumors in the air
Looking away
Perverting
Instrumentalizing
Embellishing
Demonizing
Magic interpretation
Discrediting
Dogmatizing
Ideologizing
Indoctrinating
Trivializing
Ridiculizing
Radicalizing
Reshaping
Putting curtains of fume
Polarizing
Annulling
Playing indignation
Putting down

Defense and projection already operate in the process of perception, continue during the intellectual elaboration, and even when the result appears (by speaking about) it can be victim again of a defense or projection.

→ Defense and projection mechanisms are omnipresent also by politicians, and especially when a group of politicians with different 'ideologies' discuss together a matter of concern.

→ If 100 or 250-500 politicians (e.g. lawmakers or members of a party) think and then talk) about the same external reality, they unavoidably become victim of defense and projection mechanisms that operate mostly unconsciously.

☞ On the political stage these defense and projection mechanisms create increased misunderstanding, misinterpretation, strong arguments, and in the end lead to ugly fights.

4) The feelings (emotions): the whole spectrum from love to hate

Feelings are like a music instrument. There are the positive feelings such as good mood, excitement, joy, happiness, wellbeing, trust, security, satisfaction, and fulfillment. And there are the negative feelings such as bad mood, sadness, boredom, emptiness, aggression, disgust, fear, anxiety, and hate. Feelings always contain a message and have a cause to be. The quality of a feeling can be intensive or superficial and is experienced over a short or long period of time.

Causes can lie in the way of thinking and valuing, in existential or social matters or factors, and also in suppressed complexes. Positive and negative feelings can be a result of performance or in the absence of satisfaction of genuine inner needs. For a majority of people feelings depend a lot on consumption, social acceptance, life standard and money. Strong deep positive feelings are always a result of performances and created psychical-spiritual growth. Strong and deep negative feelings can lie in all kind of serious illnesses and traumas, but also in the absence of existential needs for mind, body and soul.

Feelings (emotions) are an important psychical function with a very high spiritual value (or absence of spiritual value).

→ The world of politics is full of aggressive behavior, false communication, destructive attitudes, and emptiness of soul, hate, and hostile attitudes. All these people have enormous psychical and spiritual deficits; or they suffer in their unconscious mind from unsolved past experiences that can even go as far back as prenatal time.

→ If 100 or 250-500 politicians (e.g. lawmakers or members of a party) are together disputing over matters, we have to consider that they all have certain feelings, preponderantly negative feelings, hostile feelings up to hate and desire for going to war.

🖐 There has never been any real motive to build up nuclear bombs, an arsenal of 5000 and more nuclear weapons. There have never been serious reasons to go to war since 1945. But Western politicians have never stopped triggering wars since the Vietnam War to today with the same imperialistic expansion plans, accelerated since 1991.

🖐 War shows the true face, the conflictive mind, the over-charged unconscious, the wrong thinking, and the inner evil world of those people in office that have decided for war. They are all unable to build up positive feelings with a spiritual quality. Their mind is destroyed, malformed, rotten and therefore very dangerous for the collective.

🖐 Logically these people in power radically ignore the feelings of their folk and they especially fight against spiritual qualities that create positive fulfillment (in that sense also feelings). These people do everything that destroys all positive feelings, except those that arise as short bubbles from consumption. Most politicians are totally unfulfilled and distorted in their soul.

5) The capacity to love

Love is much more than a feeling. Love includes attitudes and ways of behavior such as respect, care, interest, understanding, cooperation, participation, support, promotion, protection, sharing, accepting, developing, patience, fidelity, faith, flexibility, and so on. Love in that sense is directed towards the beloved people and friends, towards the world of animals and nature, in general towards the entire creation. But the first call of love is to love oneself, to one's inner life and potentials to be developed.

Love wants to develop life, to grow holistically, to live well balanced, to bond in Spirit, to realize transcendence (meaning, values), to build up joy in life, to express itself in the life areas.

Self-love is active: interested, dedicated, to promote, to protect, to develop, to strengthen, to activate, to guide, to use, to accept, to educate, to form, to take seriously, to take responsibility, to act competently, to treat with care.

Weaknesses are an inevitable part of the human being. But if one doesn't work on them, then self-fulfillment of one's potentials and of one's real life cannot be built up.

Love without intelligence ends in chaos and becomes self-destructive. Intelligence without love destroys mankind and the planet.

Love and the truth are very delicate matters. Both must be protected from all kind of human and environmental factors that suffocate, destroy or abuse them.

Abilities to love are expressed in:

- Having an active interest in the psychical-spiritual life of human beings.
- Giving importance to one's own psychical-spiritual life and to consciously form it.
- Valuing one's own sensuality, to care for it creatively.
- Valuing one's own real resources and to use it for the psychical-spiritual life.
- Searching for the high values of the human being in dreams and contemplations.
- Discovering spirituality in one's own inside and in other people too.
- Being vigilant of the destructive forces of the unconscious and of thoughts.
- Not rejecting (suppressing) the desires, but being more open to live them in a creative way.
- Respecting the healthy needs of the body and consciously taking care of them.
- Regularly and actively experiencing nature and valuing it.
- Caring for the values of living together (family, relationship) and to protect them.

To love being on this earth means:

- Value your physical being, your psychological being, your talents, your special character, and your spiritual potentials
- Value everything life offers you to live and to realize yourself, including all the little things that can make you enjoy life
- Value all possibilities to learn for your development, for your work, for creating a home, living with a partner, relationships and a family
- Value what your society can give you: a frame for your life, infrastructures, a cultural identity, and much more

- Value the history of your country and culture with all the countless efforts made during centuries by all kind of pioneers for a better and more comfortable life

The quality of ability to love:

- Extended perception of the psychical and real world
- Acceptance of oneself, of others and of nature
- Spontaneity and authenticity in relationships
- A good and clear focus on problems
- Flexible way of dealing with conflicts
- Flexible distance and yearning for privacy
- Autonomy and resistance against external influences
- Deep understanding of emotional expressions
- High frequency of experiences about genuine human values
- Psychical and spiritual openness for relations between people
- Democratic and partnership-like structure of character
- Strong and manifold creativity to express love

→ The world of politics is thoroughly a world with lack of love. All these people in charge have enormous psychical and spiritual deficits (deficiencies) that lead to being unable to love. The state of humanity and the planet extensively shows us this complete inability to love the creation.

→ If 100 or 250-500 politicians (e.g. lawmakers or members of a party) are together disputing matters, then the attitudes of love have no say.

☞ In the entire political and government structures the power of love is practically absent. This means that also in the soul of the political agents, love is absent. And all the candidates that want to bring the power of love in the management of a state and folk will be forced to resign or to throw away such attitudes if they want to go up the political career ladder towards the central government.

☞ Love and the truth have long ago lost their place on the political stage!

☞ How can the politicians lead a folk with the absence of love attitudes?

6) The genuine psychical needs

Genuine psychical-spiritual human needs are:

- True love
- Honesty

- Authentic expression
- Emotional safety (protection)
- Respect
- Autonomy
- Authentic self-confidence
- Authentic self-esteem
- A positive authentic self-identity
- Freedom from inside to live
- Growing (development)
- Care
- Having a good father
- Having a good mother
- Being taken seriously
- Complete fulfillment
- Substantial transcendental experiences
- A spiritual rootedness
- A spiritual orientation
- Spiritual experiences
- Fulfillment of all longing
- Sex with love and tenderness
- A positive working unconscious
- Marriage
- Exploring the personal world
- Developing and living talents
- Understanding one's own (inner) being
- A constructive dynamic meaning of life
- A positive understanding of suffering
- Hope in personal life and future oriented
- Satisfaction of desires and special wishes
- Joy of life
- Peace and justice
- Harmony with one's self

- The majority of politicians, especially members of parliaments, ministers and head of states don't care about such genuine inner needs of their folk.
- Political science does not teach such topics of highest importance in the management of society.

Genuine educational and social human needs are:

- Education (from family)

- Education (school)
- Education (professional perspectives)
- Education (personal, life)
- Support in managing life and growing
- Physical safety (protection)
- Sharing life with a partner of the opposite sex
- Living in peace with others
- Having one's own family
- Physical nearness (relationship)
- Fairness
- Social attention
- Democratic rules
- Work (working)
- Being adequately paid for work
- Stability in life
- A positive social environment
- Social celebrations
- Knowledge about human life
- Playing, games, fun, entertainment, pleasure
- Humor
- Cooperation
- Justice

- All these topics are constitutive for efficiently mastering life, for satisfaction and happiness, for security and sustainability, and for personal fulfillment; but are mostly ignored.
- Many of these topics are not managed by politics with a focus on such aims. Politicians understand such topics or aims as a private matter or as a matter of behavioral 'regulations'.
- Estimated 80% of the world population experience in much of the topics on this list a dramatic deficit or even total absence. This shows us the attitudes of the responsible politicians.

Genuine physical needs are:

- A healthy natural environment
- A healthy living environment
- Healthy food and drinking water
- A humane shelter (home)
- Experiencing nature
- Experiencing the world of animals
- Sport (physical) activities

- Performing something special

☞ Poverty, contamination, and the big cities show us how much politicians respect such needs and how they care for them.

7) The unconscious mind

The unconscious mind is first of all something like a 'storeroom' where everything that people feel embarrassing, or that hurts, or that is too difficult to mange is 'outsourced' from the defense mechanisms.

Not clarified and unresolved difficult life experiences ('complexes') operate as unconscious units and interfere with one's mind functions, being and daily life.

By the effects produced (on physical and mental health, in social patterns, in behavior, and the human made environment) we can identify the elements of this unconscious 'storeroom'.

An authentic (genuine) self-realization is not possible without conscious reflection of one's own defense mechanisms and from there with the elaboration of the content of this 'storeroom', called 'the unconscious mind'.

- Complexes: e.g. painful and unresolved experiences and conflicts
- Specific uncomfortable experiences that have got to do with sexual drive
- Experiencing deficits of general basic psychical needs
- Feelings of inferiority and devaluation of one's own being and life
- Overloaded affective confining bonds from father or mother
- Tense conflictive interest in oneself and in others
- Cramped unilateral bonds on drives; wish and rejection at the same time
- Images about an 'I'- ideal; including one-sided positive perception
- Secret wishes in all possible directions (not allowed, not fulfilled)
- Emotional bonds through fear of punishment and therefore fear of life
- Unresolved feelings of guilt, subjective (imaginary) and objective
- In general not living pleasant (interesting) sensual experiences
- Defense mechanism to hold content from the unconscious at a distance
- 'I'- aspects, not recognized, or rejected (critical shadows, masks, etc.)
- Severe and unbalanced norms, demands, attitudes, belief, ideals
- Difficult child-parent-relations with an ambivalence of rejecting and binding
- Dogmatic religious images and practices transferred as the real truth

In summary we can say: The unconscious mind is the reservoir of suppressed, ignored, forgotten, and unsolved life experiences. Characteristic is: Pain, Embarrassment, Hurt, Humiliation, Punishment, Disagreeable moments, Sadness, Suffering, Harassment, Insecurity, Fear, and Failure.

Signs of existing unconscious complexes are:

Jealousy
Physical tension
Nervousness
Headache
Tendency to be possessive
Claustrophobia
Phobia

Inappropriate Panic
Inappropriate Anxiety
Depression
Sleeplessness
Cantankerousness
Addiction
Compulsion
Imperiousness

Megalomaniac
Over-controlling
Obesity
Always tardy (unpunctual)
Exaggerated greed
Inappropriate fear
Exaggerated Narcissism
Inappropriate emotional reaction
Dyslexia
Lack of retentiveness
Hate
Suicide (attempt)
Unable to be caring
Unable to have strong feelings
Always low voice
Long term sexual disturbance
Mobbing and sadistic behavior
Criminal behavior
Chronic untruthfulness and

Tendency to distort realities
Revengefulness
Always being late repeated
Extreme lack of concentration
Stubbornness
Superstition
Rigid ways of living (extreme rules)
Symbiotic tendency (relationship)
Oppressive towards others
Chronic liar
Hyper sensibility
Stress without external reason
Heavy ups and downs
Amorality
Belief in impossible terrestrial matters
Complete lack of respect
Tyrannical behavior
Constipation
Magic praying
SM-Sexual behavior
Homosexuality
Tendency to distort realities
Revengefulness
Scheming behavior
Chronic rejecting critical matters
Impersonal sexuality (with others)
Abnormal lack of empathy
Impulsiveness
Perfectionism in human matters
Chronic Aggression
Not justified Suspicion
Unable to truly love
Loss of contact with reality
Compulsion to wash or to clean

insincerity

Complete loss of insight	Strong irrational projections
Inadequate antisocial behavior	Strong regressive behavior
Rejecting sexual satisfaction	Tendency to minimize serious matters
Perverting realities	Exaggerated Egocentricity
Theatrical (showily) behavior	Infantile behavior towards parents
Not justified strong libido-ties	Permanent hunger (not satisfiable)
Inappropriate guilt or self-reproach	Very low self-esteem, self-confidence

The content of the unconscious mind is energetically loaded (more or less 'sleeping') and always reloaded if in present moments something happens that is on the level of meaning identical or similar to an existing complex.

The content of the unconscious also operates as a kind of coding that influences the other mental sub-systems and functions in the everyday life.

Dreams, meditation, regressive meditation, and hypnosis give us access to the content of the unconscious mind. Through this way the content can be elaborated, cleaned up, and freed from the negative energetically loaded complexes ('unities').

The unconscious mind also contains positive complexes ('unities'); but in most cases these inner 'sources' are of lower energy than the critical complexes.

Above that the unconscious mind operates in a very intelligent and logical way, is also a source of creativity and potentials, and tends to find a healthy balance (in its content). But the positive potentials are losing power through the way of modern and archaic living in general that permanently react in defense, in the rejection of the values of the inner Spirit, of love and the truth.

→ All politicians do have such a 'storeroom', an unconscious mind full of critical complexes. This is their 'inner hell'.

☞ Apart from some individuals all politicians reject the existence of this inner reality; they simply ignore it and try to hold its energetic power rationally under control.

- A majority of political behavior, decisions and conflicts are influenced by the content (the complexes) in the unconscious mind that politicians have.
- Political science as well as the science of economics fears terribly the unconscious mind. But they use and abuse the unconscious mind of the folks. They know perfectly (in that sense) that this world dominates nearly all humans.
- Worldwide it is an intentional political (and religious) strategy that all the folks are not allowed to discover this unconscious world, and that they all must be over-charged with critical content in their unconscious mind (lack of love and care, a lot of fear and sorrow, sadness, inner suffering, existential problems, being tied to stupid and archaic parents, etc.). They must suffer and struggle, chained to unconscious complexes in order to never be able to find the truth (and to depend on others).
- Local, provincial, and national political disputes and fights, as well as international relations always operate independently from the unconscious complexes the agents have. The winner is always this unconscious mind.
- The success of all archaic religions and also of all infantile spirituality (or esoteric) is based on the use and abuse of the unconscious mind of the people, making them dependent on a sick belief that God or a prophet or a Messiah or an ideology will free them from their inner unconscious chains (inner suffering and longing).

8) The inner psychical pole of the opposite gender

Men and women are different in their innermost being. There are natural male and female psychical-spiritual qualities.

Spirit
Structure
Projects
Management
Orgastic sex
Principles
Exploration
Beget life
Analytical thinking
Rational power

Life
Care for
Nourish
Protect
Look after
Sensitivity
Receive
Romantic sex
Intuitive thinking
To give life
Emotional power

➔ Male characteristics are also: mathematical reasoning, formality, and abstraction.

➔ Female characteristics are also: connectedness, informality, and care for details.

Thesis for the man: If a man cannot form his masculine principles in a balance and orientation with feminine principles, so he is a destructive man and not a really developed man.

Thesis for the woman: If a woman cannot form her feminine principles in a balance and orientation with masculine principles, so she is a destructive woman and not a really developed woman.

- The world of politics from members of parliaments to ministers and heads of states is dominated by men. And they all have not formed a cooperative inner male-female balance.
- A genuinely not formed or a disfigured inner psychical-spiritual pole of the opposite gender is intrinsically destructive. This destructive factor is absolutely dominant in politics, economics, and religion; it is also totally dominant in the science of politics and economics, and in the technical sciences.
- Most women in leader and management positions are forced to ignore their psychical-spiritual femininity and to copy male patterns. In that sense they have 'amputated' both their breasts and vagina.

🖐 The new laws in many countries that allow homosexuals to use the term 'marriage' for their same sex relationship and its legal state show us how perverted the politicians have become in mind and soul. They have lost the meaning of what it is to be a man and a woman, a father and a mother.

🖐 Students of political science and of economics are forced to copy male patterns and to ignore female patterns. Therefore this misery will never end until the academic institutions extend their understanding of mankind, of society, and of male and female natures.

9) The 'spiritual intelligence' and the dreams

The 'Spirit' is the force that creates our dreams intelligently composing meditations; and is also the source of intuition and inspiration.

- The Spirit is an informative, educative, organizing and guiding force.
- The Spirit is the principle of acting in the soul.
- The Spirit is animating, stimulating, and benevolent.
- The Spirit is the source of wisdom.

Therefore, the Spirit is not a human creation, not a product of culture, but a spiritual psychical function in each psyche (soul, mind) of each person.

The Spirit as the force creating dreams has some specific characteristics. For example:

- The Spirit knows how and for what purpose he/she transfers messages to the person.
- The Spirit knows the 'Code program' of the psychical-spiritual growth process.
- The Spirit organizes the elaboration of the inventory in the unconscious mind.
- The Spirit knows the paths and steps to a well-balanced being and life.
- The Spirit is the source for information about God and transcendence.
- The Spirit identifies solutions where people can't find a solution with intelligence.
- The Spirit is the source of each religion, of all religious and spiritual teaching.

The most explosive fact for religions, economics, politics, education, and all the kings and queens, the rulers and leaders, the aristocrats and elites is:

→ The inner Spirit is the highest authority and stands above all religions and dogmatic teaching!

→ The spiritual consciousness of most people is still on an archaic level! Most people avoid getting in touch with the Spirit in their soul.

→ Do people have to make their God responsible for everything and ask him for help as a substitute for dream interpretation?

→ God (religion, dogmatism) is for most people a substitute for self-knowledge and self-education! Instead of dealing with dreams people prefer to ask God to solve everything.

We can conclude:

- Rational intelligence without spiritual intelligence can never solve the state of humanity.
- Rational intelligence without spiritual intelligence destroys humanity and the world.
- Spiritual intelligence without rational intelligence can't manage life and the world.
- Rational intelligence with spiritual intelligence promotes humanity and the world.
- All religions are far away from a balance between rational and spiritual intelligence.
- The entire history of humanity is dominated by excessive focus on rational intelligence.
- Spiritual intelligence has never had a significant place in the entire history of humanity.
- The archaic Age of humanity is characterized by excluding spiritual intelligence.
- The new evolutionary Age of humanity must begin now and globally or humanity is lost.

☞ Most politicians do not know anything about this spiritual intelligence. They do not learn to understand the world of dreams and to interpret their dreams. They also do not meditate or contemplate; or if they do, then it's most probably the wrong way.

We need to give here additionally an insight into the way this 'spiritual intelligence' is operating. It's in the world of dreams aided by the methods of meditation.

Everybody dreams and human beings have always taken dreams as important. Just as there are people who don't care about their thinking and never reflect upon their thoughts, there are also people who take dreams as unimportant and never reflect on them. But indeed, dreams are the most valuable source of life!

Some theories of dreams may be unilateral, but all theories have in common that various typical images and symbols in dreams, human beings or animals, facts or actions, inform us about the reality of the person dreaming. All concepts of dream interpretation are based on the notion that dreams are not accidental appearances. We can draw conclusions from dreams of the person, who is dreaming, and his life.

It is generally well known, that in the olden days 'great dreams' were messages from God. It is not only an opinion of the people from archaic times, when many people presume, that there are messages hidden in dreams. Dream theories are based on the idea, that the messages are useful: they inform, counsel, warn and help, where thinking no longer has access. This clearly means: An intelligent force organizes the dream elements to a valuable construction, to a 'message for the ego'. We call this psychical force 'the inner Spirit'.
You would like to understand someone: What does he mean? Why does he speak like he does? What forces him to live as he does? The more you know about the psychical life, the more you will recognize. The more a person knows this reality, the more this person has starting material, to understand other people. Dream interpretation is also based on knowledge about the psychical life and the real external life: The more you know about the psychical life and the life of human beings in general, the more differentiated your dream interpretation becomes.

Human beings have manifold ways of communicating something. One can speak very loud or markedly soft, because the other doesn't want to listen. Or one can give a hint, because it seems impossible to focus directly on the matter, while the other person is being defensive. Sometimes we speak in allegories, draw a comparison or exaggerate something, so that the other person becomes attentive. We all know the difficult matter: Human beings want to know the truth and at the same time don't want to see it. Furthermore there are messages that inform, warn, explain, foresee. We value and judge; we inform and interpret according to manifold points of view.

The force that creates dreams also uses all those daily varieties in forming a message. The more one works with one's dreams, the more one experiences how this Inner Spirit 'speaks'. The language of dreams is as varied as the use of language in real life, in literature, in art and painting. Everyone can notice that this intelligent force obviously knows more than the ego can. The Spirit can also inform about himself or about the spiritual world (transcendence). The only truthful source that can give the human being an orientation in his life, his psychical and spiritual existence and development, is the Spirit. This spiritual force is the 'architect' of dreams.

Dreams help us in all aspects of life for a good, happy and meaningful life. Dreams show us the path to the deepest inner being, to the essential psychical-spiritual being.
Dreams help us to educate all psychical forces.
Dreams help us with an orientation in the external reality.

→ Dreams are the door to the psychical and spiritual universe!
→ Dreams are the tool for the psychical-spiritual development!
→ Dreams are powerful for finding the right political solutions!
→ Dreams are a very powerful source for managing humanity!
→ By using our 'spiritual intelligence' humanity has a good future!

🕈 Dream theory and interpretation do not form part of any religion.
🕈 Dream theory and interpretation do not form part of public education.
🕈 Dream theory and interpretation do not form part of academic education.
🕈 Dream interpretation does not form part of a relationship or family life.
🕈 Dream interpretation does not form part of the work of politicians.
🕈 Dream interpretation does not form part of the political decision-making.
🕈 Dream interpretation does not form part of political theories and thoughts.
🕈 Everywhere around the globe 'spiritual intelligence' is ignored.

10) Meditation: imagination, contemplation

About meditation we can summarize:

During inner visualization the same spiritual intelligent force is in play as in dreams. With imagination one can relax oneself, find new strength, prepare paths to solutions for problems, free the mind, understand others, find meaning to life, elaborate dreams, recognize causes of suffering and difficulties, work through the unconscious mind, etc.

Imagination is the form of meditation, with which we can explore and form a whole new psychical and real life.

Contemplation focuses on symbols and Archetypes. Archetypes reflect general patterns of the psychical forces, the processes of transformation of the psychical life, of the essential life themes, of sense (meaning) and values and also of the transcendental reality. General symbols reflect the concrete basic themes of existence that concern all of us. Contemplation creates access to the 'mystery' of being human.

Meditating correctly means:

1. Determining what you want to reach: Knowledge, changes, strengthening.
2. Determining the images and symbols with which one will work.
3. Following the image course accurately, controlling passively or actively.
4. Feeling the meaning. Interpreting the result like a dream.
5. Formulating consequences for your life and evaluating them after having realized them.

→ Meditation is the method to clean up the unconscious mind.
→ Meditation is the method to promote psychical-spiritual growth.
→ Meditation is the method to create a stable inner balance.
→ Meditation is the method to find solutions for all kind of concerns.
→ Contemplation is the method to explore the deepest meaning of life.
→ Contemplation is the method to explore the meaning of whatsoever.
→ Contemplation is the path towards the mystery of mankind and God.
→ Contemplation roots human life in the innermost source of life.

❦ Contemplation does not form part of any religion.
❦ Contemplation does not form part of public education.
❦ Contemplation does not form part of academic education.
❦ Contemplation does not form part in a relationship or family life.
❦ Contemplation does not form part of the work of politicians.
❦ Contemplation does not form part of the political decision-making.
❦ Contemplation does not form part of political theories and thought.
❦ Everywhere around the globe 'spiritual intelligence' is ignored.
❦ A huge majority if not 95% of humanity have lost the inner source of life.

11) The psychical individual and cosmic energy

We all have in our physical body a non-physical energy:

→ a psycho-energetic body
→ psychical energy
→ mental energy
→ bio-energy
→ orgon-energy
→ para-psychical energy
→ fluidum
→ astral-body
→ prana

This energetic body is formed through:

→ perception
→ thinking
→ feeling
→ emotions
→ imaginations
→ inner conflicts
→ stress
→ judgments
→ valuations
→ norms
→ and all the suppressed experiences

▪ Our past is also with us as a complex code with its own energy. The energetic body is formed from the past and present, the conscious and unconscious mind and living.
▪ All people radiate their energy and influence the energetic body of other people.
▪ The energy that people radiate forms (pollute, poison) the energetic environment that is the energy our soul needs to be connected.
▪ There is also a divine energy that is radiated from the cosmic source of all life. The already totally polluted energy that people radiate does not allow anymore that this cosmic energy can reach all humans' soul.

If this inner energy is not cleaned, strengthened, centered, balanced, harmonized, etc. then such a state produces manifold reactions:

→ permanent hunger (for whatever)
→ headache
→ tensions

→ stomach pain
→ depression
→ anxiety
→ sleeplessness
→ compulsions
→ addictions
→ madness

We cannot exclude that many serious illnesses (e.g. tumors) are also a result of a complete chaotic, tense, broken, and conflictive inner and external energy. In other words:

The energetic body is in its critical state:

→ in disharmony
→ not strengthened
→ not centered
→ not a clearly demarcated (and in that sense closed in itself)
→ not formed as a unity of its parts
→ full of mental and emotional pollution
→ compressed in itself by hundreds of different energetic elements from life and from what's going on in the conscious and unconscious mind

❦ Most of the political world is unaware of this psychical and cosmic energy.
❦ The science of psychology does not explore this world of energy.
❦ The science and practices of medicine is unaware of this energy.
❦ The archaic religions are not connected with this energetic cosmic source.
❦ The toxic mental energy everywhere dooms humanity in hopelessness.
❦ The toxic mental energy everywhere makes the entire humanity mad.
❦ There is never a political solution to solve and clean up this dark energy.

12) The 'I' (self, ego), the will, and the behavior

Will and control leads to action together with several components: Knowledge, skills, energy, motive, decision, strategy, aim, rules, norms, attitudes, tools, and methods. But behavior and decision-making can't be isolated from all the psychical and spiritual sub-systems and functions. Determining forces forming behavior are:

▪ Energetic state determines behavior
▪ Feelings determine behavior

- The will determines behavior
- Defense mechanisms determine behavior
- Psychical needs determine behavior
- Perception determines behavior
- Biography determines behavior
- Complexes determine behavior
- Learning determines behavior
- The 'I'- control determines behavior
- Meditation determines behavior
- Mental-training determines behavior
- Thinking determines behavior
- Judging determines behavior
- Norms determine behavior
- Values determine behavior
- Belief determines behavior
- Attitudes determine behavior
- Belief determines behavior
- Opinions determine behavior
- Suppressing determines behavior
- Dream messages determine behavior
- Love ability determines behavior
- Personal ethic determines behavior
- Personal ideals determine behavior
- Ignorance determines behavior
- Interpretation determines behavior
- Knowledge determines behavior
- Personal aims determine behavior
- Personal interests determine behavior
- Experiences of values determine behavior
- Environment determines behavior
- Economic factors determine behavior
- Social contexts determine behavior
- The state of the mind as a whole determines behavior
- Physical health determines behavior (and mind)
- Legal and physical power determine behavior

→ On the one side the 'I' operates in relation to the content in the inner 'screen' and to the way of all psychical sub-systems with its single factors is formed.
→ On the other side the 'I' operates in relation to the state of the body and the external world with its manifold human and objective factors and conditions.

- All political concepts, ideas, and ideologies (also religions) are pre-determined from these internal and external worlds. In that sense nothing is 'infallible' or 'perfect'.
- The majority of politicians (and religious incumbents) behave very big-headedly as if they are an exclusive species. But they are all like everybody simply pre-determined from and by the internal and external worlds.
- The worst of all is that most politicians (and religious incumbents) have a very chaotic and unbalanced mind. They are all driven especially by the content of their unconscious mind.
- Most politicians (and religious incumbents) think that their rational (or rational-religious) decisions are the crown of what makes politics (and belief). But ignoring the 'spiritual intelligence' is already one of the wheels that run for deicide.

2.6. Human Evolution with Politics

There are a lot of politicians that want a new world; some are of good faith. Others are on the path of global governance. Expressed differently: Spirit, love, and self-fulfillment are the indispensable conditions for solving the problems of humanity and the earth. The other path is dictatorship (or oligarchy) and using all the media for creating a collective mainstream of opinion.

➜ The collective nightmares about humanity and the world are horrifying!
➜ The irreversible breaking point for humanity and the earth is very near!
➜ Many politicians see the huge problems of mankind and want changes!
➜ Evolutionary solutions must start with collective self-knowledge!
➜ Spirituality and religions must integrate the vivid archetypes of the soul!
➜ A new global Spirit for global peace is necessary for human evolution!
➜ Dreams & the inner Spirit are the most valuable source of human life!
➜ The ultimate solution for humanity and the world is Global Individuation!

Renewing the world and resolving the global problems can't simply start with technological measures or with political and economic power concentration. No army will be able to manage the world in an evolutionary way. Everything must start with education, with individual and collective psychical and spiritual forming (educating) of humans. This process is called 'Individuation'.

Individuation has a strong focus on humanity and the earth:

- Openness to learn and readiness for changes in the personal and collective interest.
- Flexible integration of life realities respecting social networks and conditions.
- Living with social skills, life techniques, responsibility for health and the environment.
- Forming an efficient self-management for life issues, also in matters of health.
- Liberation from the generation-destiny for an evolutionary future.
- Establishing a harmony between the inner and external life to reduce egoism.
- Consciousness about the inner world and the network of external realities.

- Understanding humanity as a community on a collective spiritual path.
- Solidarity with the human community in all human basic needs.
- Respecting human beings in the spiritual view of the collective evolution.
- Self-control within inner and external world for constructive interactions.
- Cleaning the subconscious for inner peace and peace in the world.
- Dissolution and balance of contradictory inner forces for peace on earth.
- Relevant knowledge about the complexity of inner and external life.
- Many-sided consciousness about mankind and the state of the world.
- Differentiated perception of one's reality as well as the reality of others.
- Strengthening life energy, using it aim-oriented for a better life and world.
- Living consciously with responsibility and love for humanity and the world.

A Global Individuation that follows the path of the archetypal processes of the soul is the sole solution for humanity and the earth!

→ Individuation is the ultimate understanding of human beings and life on this earth for politics.

→ Individuation includes the spiritual understanding of human beings and meaning of life for all religions.

→ Individuation is the indispensable psychical-spiritual path for all officials in all religions and every concept of Spirituality.

→ Individuation is the collective path of salvation! A concept that can be lived in all cultural expressions.

Not many years are left to collectively start Global Individuation. If 500 million people follow this path, then the world will see that this is the only chance to save humanity and the earth. Another 20 years will follow to entirely renew the world. Then the global evolution of humanity will lead into a good future for the following generations.

The alternative is to continue living and doing politics like today, and then humanity and the earth will be lost forever.

Another approach is given through the archetypal human values: [74]

- A life with love, truth, honesty, happiness and truthfulness.
- Authentic satisfaction and fulfillment of the genuine inner needs.

---

[74] More extensive elaboration in: Schellhammer Deicide, p. 304-305

- Understanding oneself, one's behavior and life, and other people.
- Efficiency with knowledge and skills to deal with life.
- Being free of biographical burdens and unconscious complexes.
- Authentic, integral, self-realized and strong personalities.
- Ideals, norms, values, and rules that are constructive towards life.
- Capability to understand and constructively manage feelings.
- Living sexual needs and longing for affection with love.
- Solving difficulties, crises, problems and conflicts for peace.
- Outstanding self-management that provides a strong self-confidence.
- Correctly interpreting dreams and meditating provides best development.
- Preparing a happy relationship and family life with education.
- Elaborating quality of life with thorough and networked thinking.
- Living the meaning of the Archetype 'Marriage', leads to fulfillment.
- Meaning of life, anchored within, centered in the inner Spirit.
- Environment and business world for the soul of people.
- An all-encompassing positive life philosophy for living and growing.

These positive human values are founded in the Archetypes:

- The complete acceptance of the inner life and the dedication towards it.
- The discovery and formation of psychical forces and functions.
- The formation of the genuine inner self through conscious formation.
- The integration of the inner Spirit as a guiding power (dreams, meditation).
- Carrying out the process of 'dying and rebirth' (inner catharsis and renewal).
- The development of the unification with the inner opposite gender pole.
- Integrating the spiritual principles in ethics, behavior and meaning of life.
- Bringing the inner and outer world into a balance, anchored within.
- Achieving the fulfillment of wholeness and completeness (= Individuation).

- Today 95% of all humans on this planet are 'archaic' human beings. The 'archaic human being' is characterized by the negation of the psychical life, by neglecting the psychical organism as well as suppressing love and Spirit. At the same time this kind of human being is more or less completely tied to the unconscious psychical life.

- The consequences are disruption (inner conflicts) and decomposition, lack of inner freedom, and infantile dependencies. Such an unformed and wrongly formed psychical life is expressed in greed, envy, hate and destruction, exploitation, violence, unscrupulousness, ignorance, arrogance, belief and dogmas as well as in ideologies, despotism and egocentrism.

The essential characteristics of an 'archaic human being' are:

- Ignoring the psyche as the genuine life; therefore no holistic development.
- Rejecting the inner Spirit and the performance potential of the power of love.
- Pushed from suppressed burdens and in the tendency of projecting strongly.
- Not living with dreams, imagination, contemplation, and introspection.
- Only partially conscious forming of the psychical forces – if at all.
- Defense from and suppression of all uncomfortable, weak and different realities.
- To a large extent an unconscious way of living without being aware of the psychical life.
- Personal and life culture are rooted in ideologies, dogmas and fundamentalism.
- Extensively being fixated on material goods, events (fun), and external securities.
- Undifferentiated unilateral experiencing of love, lust and sensuality.
- Performances with increase of gain and the extreme have highest value.

- ✥ If a society is created by archaic human beings, notably by archaic politicians, then one can see the result around the globe.

The intrinsic aim of the soul is the evolutionary human being. The essential characteristics are:

- Accepting the psychical life and a conscious forming of all psychical forces.
- Liberation from inner burdens of the biography and becoming free from projecting dynamics.
- Elaborated images in the unconscious constructively and progressively promoting life.
- Continuous inner orientation through dream interpretation, imagination and contemplation.
- Integration and elaboration of all the uncomfortable, weak and different 'things' in life.
- Creating relationships, politics and economy (etc.) from the understanding of Individuation.
- Dealing with nature and the world of animals, and the environment with Spirit and love.
- Differentiated development and use of the power of love and the Spirit.

- High flexibility and inner freedom towards material goods and external values.
- Psychical-spiritual performances, characterized by love and Spirit have highest values.

👍 If a society is created by evolutionary human beings, then one can see the result in the environment.

👎 But politics and economics understand humans as only a human biomass with physical needs and wants.

It's obvious that a human being would be unable to live without formed psychical functions. Unformed functions would mean a pure instinctive way of living. This would also mean: Level 'quality zero' of the psychical functions. On the other end would be the top quality; let's say, the level 'quality hundred'; or we determine a scale of 0-100 points expressing the sum of the levels of qualities of all psychical functions. Quality means also: efficiency in real life.

Some psychical functions (such as thinking and learning) have instrumental purposes. Others (such as love and moral) influence more directly in the existential and factual (spiritual) quality of human life. All functions are formed by family, social environment, education, media, and personal performances (learning, working). The entire biography of a person determines the general forming processes. In that context a person is not responsible for his state as long as he can't freely operate with these areas of influences.

Fact is: a weak ego and will, with strong and rigid uncontrolled defense mechanisms (including projections), inappropriate norms, attitudes, values (etc.), a very low level of thinking and judging, a complete lack of dealing with dream messages or imagination and intuition, uncontrolled and extreme emotions, an over-loaded personal unconscious (biography), and a strong lack of abilities to deal with their own and other genders, with life and issues, political and religious matters, etc., means: a very low level of constructive and evolutionary qualities of the psychical functions.

As a consequence, these functions as a whole are not able to constructively and evolutionary deal with all or most life issues, including consumer behavior and management of economic matters.

The simple conclusion is: human beings need a complex education (forming) of all these psychical functions to make them able to constructively and evolutionary deal with all their life issues.

🏵 A very low level of qualities of the psychical functions produces enormous damages in the life of a person, in the family life, in the social and political life, in the economic life, in the world of nature and animals, and in earth matters.

Certain combinations of low level of quality of some psychical functions produce psychical disturbances such as neurosis, narcissism, dogmatic and fundamentalist thinking, psychopathic character, depression, anxiety, phobia, rigidity, hallucinations, obsession, paranoia, psychotic reactions, illimitableness, arrogant and ignorant attitudes, magic thinking and living, and other disturbances. Above that, certain combinations of low level of quality of some specific psychical functions produce psycho-somatic reactions and critical behavior such as addictions and compulsion, exaggerated greed, envy, hate, dogmatic and fundamentalist behavior, megalomania, perverse and amoral (criminal) behavior.

We also have to distinguish between low level of forming, with wrong forming, imbalanced forming, and lack of forming. Low level of forming, wrong forming, imbalanced forming, and lack of forming can be understood as a grade of quality of 'efficiency for managing life'. The critical result can be individual, social, collective on the one side and local, national, and global on the other side depending on the interdependences and culmination of singular effects. An individual critical result has no global importance, not even a national importance.

But if hundreds of millions of humans have a low level of forming, wrong forming, imbalanced forming, and lack of forming, then it becomes of national importance. With billions of people having a low level of forming, wrong forming, imbalanced forming, and lack of forming, then it becomes of global importance.

🏵 The collective lack of efficiency for constructive and evolutionary living destroys humanity and the earth.

From another point of view a single individual or a small group of people with low level of forming, wrong forming, imbalanced forming, and lack of forming become of high regional, national or global importance, if this person or group gets economic or political power (instruments) in their hands. The consequences are fatal.

2.7. The Archetypes of the Soul

Archetypal principles of the soul for human's evolution are of highest importance also for politics:

1) Accepting and turning to the whole inner life

- Not accepting leads to tension, lies, distortion, aggression, etc.
- Not accepting consumes a lot of psychical energy for suppressing
- Not accepting leads to wrong decisions, wrong solutions
- Accepting produces inner peace and genuine self-confidence
- Accepting is an expression of love (self-love) and care
- Accepting gives strength for a realistic dealing with humans

2) Discovering and forming all inner forces

- Not discovering leads to 'shadows' following oneself permanently
- Not discovering leads to ignoring these realities by other people
- Not discovering means completely devaluing human's inner life
- Discovering is an expression of love, of accepting one's being
- Discovering leads to realistic knowledge and correct interpretation
- Discovering is the first step that leads to a balanced soul-management

3) Developing the true Self by conscious forming

- Not developing means remaining in an archaic state of being with regressions
- Not developing leads to inner chaos, imbalance, psychopathological growth
- Not developing leads to ignoring or neglecting one's inner potentials
- Developing is an expression of evolution and a dynamic of human's behavior
- Developing is an expression of love and care, of responsibility in oneself
- Developing is the calling from life and psyche to become genuine and strong

4) Integrating the inner Spirit as guidance (Dreams)

- Not working with the inner Spirit enormously reduces the understanding of humans

- Not working with the inner Spirit hinders the access to the unconscious world
- Not working with the inner Spirit paralyzes the growth towards holistic growth
- Working with the inner Spirit facilitates the all-sided balanced development
- Working with the inner Spirit activates the genuine spiritual power for solutions
- Working with the inner Spirit anchors human life in the Archetypes of the Soul

5) Proceedings of dying and becoming new

- One cannot become new as long as everything (psychical subsystems) remains unchanged
- One cannot become new without re-forming or changing inefficient psychical functions
- One cannot become new without identifying and elaborating the unconscious coding
- Becoming new gives enormous relief, strength, power of self-control, inner peace
- Becoming new produces a breakthrough in forming and living one's inner potentials
- Becoming new means also becoming genuine, truthful, just, authentic, and constructive

6) Unification with the inner opposite gender pole

- Not forming this unification leads to the endless stupid war between man and woman
- Not forming this unification makes a man either rigid or stubborn, or a blind tyrant
- Not forming this unification makes a woman an emotional chaos or a hysteric witch
- Forming this unification leads to a creative, constructive and complementary relationship
- Forming this unification makes a man to become a real man and a woman a real woman
- Forming this unification is a psychical-spiritual process creating totality and completeness

7) Integration of the spiritual principles

- Ignoring the spiritual principles always creates imbalance, wars, exploitation, destruction
- Ignoring the spiritual principles makes man into a rational animal with highly criminal energy
- Ignoring the spiritual principles leads to lies, deceit, falseness, distortion, crimes, wars
- Integrating the spiritual principles creates harmony, balance, justice, peace, strong love
- Integrating the spiritual principles allows solving the problems of humanity and the planet
- Integrating the spiritual principles leads to fulfillment and with that towards God and Paradise

8) Balance between external and internal life

- People live the way they are formed in their soul, mind, inner life
- The state of humanity and the planet shows how people are rotten to the core
- Not forming inner life (psyche) leads to an imbalance of the world
- Living within the Archetypes of the Soul leads to a world according to these Archetypes
- Optimal inner balance and developed psychical functions make external life efficient
- The new formed inner qualities of people will be transformed in the external life

9) Fulfillment of the completeness and wholeness

- No fulfillment of the completeness and wholeness of people leads to wars and the doom
- No fulfillment of the completeness and wholeness must be compensated with dogmas
- No fulfillment of the completeness and wholeness must be compensated with dictatorship
- Fulfillment of the completeness and wholeness is the highest meaning of human's life
- Fulfillment of the completeness and wholeness creates the vivid paradise on earth
- Fulfillment of the completeness and wholeness leads to be in God and in Paradise

The psychical-spiritual process characterized by these nine Archetypes of the Soul is the royal path towards the aim of highest personal fulfillment. People with responsibility in any field of society and human life around the globe, especially politicians, can and shall fulfill this process, also called 'Individuation'. The collective importance of these archetypal principles also for politicians, masters of economics, and the incumbents of religions is obvious.

Conclusions: Those experts of politics and agents in the political world that reject these archetypal principles have in their mind the evil coding that leads to the elimination of humanity and the destruction of the planet, and in the end to deicide.

→ Politics must become evolutionary – worldwide – because it determines human life and the evolution of mankind!

During a higher phase of psychical-spiritual development, a 'man of God' or 'woman of God' experiences very special dreams related to highest archetypal processes:

1) God and his manifoldness.
2) God's alliance with him/her.
3) Becoming a specific destination of service in God (e.g. priest, religious leader, supreme teacher).
4) The transcendental world of the souls.
5) Denomination as a representative of a messiah or prophet (member of a council).
6) Authorization from the inner Spirit to develop further the religious (spiritual) teaching and practices.
7) Getting a mission from God as a prophet or Messiah.
8) Power of attorney from God: Highest Judge of all Souls.

There are since millenniums the supreme Archetypes (eternally infallible symbols) that express the power and destination of a King, an emperor, and a (highest) religious leader. These symbols and supreme Archetypes of the Soul are, here briefly interpreted:

- Orb: God's Dominion over the World
- Crown: Royal Authority, Christ, the King of Kings
- Royal Scepter: Power, Dominion of a Monarch
- Scepter and Crown: Christ, Authority, King
- Pair of Balance: Justice, Jurisdiction, Spiritual Jurisdiction
- Owl: Pure Spirit, Wisdom

- Eagle (with open wings): Power above the World
- Circle-Cross-Mandala: Highest Fulfillment in God
- Sun: God, the Ultimate Source of Life
- King of the Holy Grail: Highest Transcendental Mission

In the history of mankind, the inner Spirit in the soul of some wise men (and women), spiritual kings, has created (has made vivid) these Archetypes in their inner life (soul).

There have been a few men since millenniums in varied places on this earth that have performed (made vivid) all the Archetypes of the Soul in their inner life, including all highest Archetypes of God and they all got the mission from God to bring forward the psychical-spiritual evolution and they were committed in God.

❦ Religions have stolen the transcendental archetypal experiences these wise men, spiritual kings in their soul, had performed and received (experienced) in dreams. All Popes and Cardinals have stolen their archetypal experiences. Terrestrial Emperors and Kings have stolen their archetypal experiences.

❦ Politicians, supreme rulers of folks, aristocrats and the elites in the capitalistic economy have stolen their experienced inner archetypal processes, have copied the archetypal pictures (from dreams these wise individuals had), but never performed such inner transformations produced and guided by the inner Spirit. This is the systemic failure of economics, politics, religion, public education, and society in general.

❦ All that these thieves do is to support their fake (stolen) legitimacy with magnificent buildings, with historic paintings and other works of art of immense value, with 'holy' robes, with immense military and financial power, and with fake impressive ceremonies. And the stolen supreme Archetypes of the Soul they hang on their walls and buildings or have stuck them on their flags and emblems. They think that what they have stolen are the appropriate substitutes for the lost vivid supreme Archetypes of the Soul. They have all dethroned the spiritual kings, and God and his Spirit, expressed in these supreme Archetypes of the Soul. Finally, in the inner roots and final aims of these people is nothing short of DEICIDE.

If politicians continue as usual they get a what they deserve:

A life without love and Spirit is characterized by ego-centrism, narcissism, self-satisfaction and arrogance. Where there is no love, there is emptiness, sadness, pain, rejection of life, anxiety, greed, lack of Spirit and ultimately no balance. Narrow-mindedness, naivety, ignorance, blindness and showing off are incredibly dangerous for an individual and for the whole society.

What is a human being without love and Spirit? It is a biological organism. Don't be surprised if world-leaders in politics, military, industry, trade, economy, religions and sects also see the people as an organism to be raised for their (own) interests.

- Everybody must become a mental slave. Everybody must live a life pushed by their drive and by fear, coded by their non purged unconscious, and must live a life without peace, love and Spirit. They must live life-lies.

What is a human being that doesn't follow the path to self-knowledge and self-fulfillment? Such a person lives in chaos and unconsciousness. Nothing can be further away from the Spirit than a human being which lives beyond the process of self-fulfillment. Without Spirit the path is an endless meander. The market offers over 10,000 meanders!

A majority of politicians form part of this type of human: [75]

- Most politicians know themselves on a level of 3-5 %; the rest they avoid to see; logically they are all driven by their chaotic inner mind.
- Most politicians don't think about the tomorrow of their folks and the inner network of their own thinking and acting.
- Most politicians believe that they have the right picture in their inner screen; it's manipulated from their own mental functions.
- Most politicians believe that they are totally right with the way they think, interpret, judge, and take consequences.
- Most politicians have no idea about their nagging unconscious inner world – their true being that pushes them ahead, daily.
- Most politicians believe it is enough what they learnt about humans and the development of the society; but that is only blind obstinacy.
- Most politicians cannot distinguish between infatuated appearance and realities; and they don't see how they filter out most human factors.

---

[75] Schellhammer. Economics I, p.20-21

- Most politicians cheat themselves spiritually, religiously, ideologically, or practically and project their own evil parts on 'foes'.
- Most politicians don't want to learn for love, Spirit, happiness, peace, and justice; they exclude these human values from their policies.
- Most politicians don't have the knowledge and skills for their self-fulfillment and at the same time they have lost the reality of the people.

If we put all these mental realities of the politicians together in one picture, and envision that they lead humans, folks, nations and humanity, then we get a very frightening global perspective for the coming decades.

2.8. People and the Mind

(Reading this chapter you must have read chapter 2.5., 2.6., and 2.7. We start our explorations with a short reminder about the topic.)

We discuss here people and their state of the mind. Two questions must be clarified: 1) What do we mean by 'people'? And 2) How can we have the necessary knowledge to answer questions about the people?

1) The word 'people' relates in general to the entire humanity. Therefore the word 'people' includes babies, adolescents, adults, elderly people, and very old people. 'People' also includes all kind of races or cultural folks: Europeans, Swiss, Americans, Africans, Chinese, Indians, Russians, Latin Americans, Australians, the Vietnamese, etc. We focus in general on adults. We stress out the unchangeable existential fact:

➜ All humans around the globe do have a mind and soul with a variety of dispositions and potentials.

2) The knowledge we have, encompasses life experiences, books, information from the media, and so on. We also conclude from the state of humanity and the planet about people's behavior and from there about people's mind. The level of education and standard of living (or economic conditions) can also give us some insight into the mind of people. The fact that probably all public schools on earth do not teach their children and pupils about the sub-systems of the mind and how to shape and manage these functions for efficiently mastering life and finding fulfillment is also an indicator about the state of the mind of people. Last but not least we can get some insight of the people's mind by having an eye on their religious beliefs and culture.

We will mostly use the word 'a majority' or 'in general' without giving age or national specification, and especially letting open any figure – until the final conclusions of this elaboration here. In general we must say:

➜ Humans are not all equal. There are immense differences in 'qualities' referring to the mind's functions, the behavior, and the ways of living.

Apart from the human body there is only one characteristic that absolutely all humans around the globe do have: the mind and soul with a variety of dispositions and potentials. Even if we would assume that every soul that incarnates on this earth already has a specific dynamic character, strength and maturity, it does not exclude the fact that every human has a mind and soul with its characteristic sub-systems. 'Soul' refers here to the psychical energy and to an energetic body all humans have. 'Soul' also refers to the 'spiritual intelligence'. Denying the existence of this psychical (and cosmic) energy and soul is simply an expression of much reduced content in the 'inner screen' (consciousness).

➜ It is absolutely clear that the mind of all people can be shaped (formed) in millions of ways and combinations.

The result of these explorations has immense consequences for politicians, governance, for public relations, for education and religion, for the science of politics, and for a roadmap aiming to solve the immense problems of humanity and the planet.

The mind and soul

Many mental functions (sub-systems of the mind) determine a human being:

- The conscious (the content of the 'inner screen')
- The intelligence: the ability to think and learn
- The memory
- The 'I' (self) as the control and decision making instance
- The defense and projection mechanisms
- The feelings (emotions): the whole spectrum from love to hate
- The capacity to love
- The genuine psychical needs
- The unconscious
- The inner psychical pole of the opposite gender
- The 'spiritual intelligence', called also the 'inner Spirit' creating dream messages and forming results of meditation
- The ability of visualization (imagination, contemplation, meditation)

The people:

🖎 Most people take it as self-evident that the realities they have in their inner screen does entirely or highly match with the previously perceived external reality. But it is not; this inner picture about an external reality is mostly reduced and distorted.

237

- Most people talk before they think, and either they do not think or they think in a very narrow way and frame. The ability to think in interrelations, chains, and time perspective or cause-result interrelation is very low or nearly absent.

- The capacity of the memory is immense, but people in general forget most of what they learnt or experienced. A huge majority of people are constantly focused on the present moment ignoring the content of their memory that could help a lot in understanding and managing present situations.

- The 'I' as the control and decision making center is not reflected, not free, thoroughly focused on self-interest, and driven by the content of the unconscious. The 'I' understood as the self-image is far away from the corresponding reality. People are not what they believe to be.

- People do not know what defense and projection mechanisms are. But these mechanisms are thoroughly active and distort practically everything of importance that people perceive (with all senses). People tend to reject, ignore or negate everything that could challenge them in whichever way.

- Most people can't control their feelings. Feelings come and go and the people can't see the meaning (message) of positive and negative feelings. Most people are unable to have deep positive feelings, but they always like indulge in very mad and evil feelings.

- The capacity to love is around the globe at a very archaic and emotional level. The huge majority of people don't know that to love requires some strong attitudes. Most people want to get love and ignore that they must learn to love. Love is strongly related to another person and to sex, practically never to the creation.

- Most people can't identify more than 3-4 genuine inner needs (if ever); but there are more than 50 genuine inner needs. In that sense people are permanently in a huge deficit of satisfaction of genuine inner needs.

- The huge majority of people do not have any idea about the unconscious mind, about its content and ways of operating. Apart from some individuals, all people are 'victim' and controlled from the content of their unconscious mind. They don't know that they could become free from the influences of the energetically loaded complexes in the unconscious. People suffer a lot from these 'irrational' (uncontrollable) influences.

- The majority of people have no idea about the reality of the inner psychical pole of the opposite gender. In that sense they can never create a balance between natural (psychical) male and female qualities. Many problems in a relationship between man and woman can't be correctly understood and solved.

- The 'spiritual intelligence', also called the 'inner Spirit' creating dream messages is unknown to a majority of people. Dogmatic religion or atheism is the choice. Sure is, that a huge amount of books and services about dreams and dream interpretation offered in the Internet is pure rubbish.
- The majority of people never do meditate. And the minority uses some strange methods that simply serve to relax, or they are rather self-brainwashing or do not promote psychical-spiritual development. Meditation without using 'spiritual intelligence' has no power.

General conclusions:

→ We estimate that up to 95% of the mental potentials of the entire humanity are unused, distorted, weak, inefficient, and even destroyed.
→ We identify a complete failure of public education and everywhere a horrifying lack of knowledge about the psychical-spiritual inner life.
→ We identify also for a huge majority of people that the functions of their mind are inhibited, blocked to learning, undifferentiated, unconscious (being unaware), disordered, chaotic, not or badly controlled, unbalanced, unpredictable, destructive, one-sided, suppressed, and in defense.

Additionally to the mind we have to relate these mental functions with:

1) The behavior: Behavior is always a result of the kind the mind is working.

2) The individual psychical energy: Thoughts and emotions form psychical energy being active in the physical body, influencing physical and mental functions, and radiating towards the external world.

3) The collective psychical energy: The stored sum of the individual energy radiating towards outside and being around us like the air.

- We identify an unbelievable stubbornness in the world of politics and state administration, but also in the world of the people. Not even with nuclear bombs could we make them clear these up. All the functions of their mind must be formed for a holistic development and for constructively mastering life.
- There are a lot of people that know very well about this mental energy. The entire world of animals operates with this energy. The simplest experience is telepathy between humans, between animals, and also between humans and animals. But it seems that nobody wants to know

more about it and to explore this energy for a better life and for understanding humans in general.

🖑 The collective psychical energy around us (like air) has stored the entire history. Every unsolved matter from the past (e.g. hate, guilt) will hit humanity in the future. Humanity can't evade from this collective energetic world.

Now we want to give some more examples to make clear the consequences of ignoring to correctly shape and form the mind of humans.

1) The conscious (the 'inner screen')

The conscious is something like a screen we have in our mind. What a human perceives with his eyes enters into the screen. But perception is always partly subjective and partly selected.

🖑 As perception of people is 3-6 hours per day directed towards the television and an additional hour towards newspapers and magazines or hours towards realities in the Internet, a huge majority of people are completely poisoned from the highly fabricated and unreal (superficial) realities given on TV programs and through all other media.

Everything that people perceive gets a subjective picture in their inner screen that is not 100% identical to the reality they have observed. In the extreme case we could have 100 reports from different people and 1000 different results about one single perceived event.

🖑 An example is the marketing people are confronted with everywhere, not only in the media but also on streets, buildings or in shop windows 24/7. All the needs and wants are stimulated, and products are interpreted as satisfaction or fulfillment (of inner deficits or frustration with life).

Reporting, verbally or written, another function comes into action: the language and with that the repertoire a person has about specific fields or in general.

🖑 Most probably some billions of people have a word pool that is extremely limited and encompasses preponderantly general daily objects and matters. A majority does not have the right words to express what they see or feel about themselves and others.

Simultaneously most people tend to mix description with interpretation and emotion. From here it's a short distance to add a moral component to the elements in the inner picture.

🐦 The ways of interpretation of people depends on their education, their needs and wants. Religion plays an immense role and includes superstition or simply magic thinking (interpretation). The result is mostly alienation from the perceived reality. What people can't get, they very often load with a negative value and this is another distortion of perceived realities.

The more complex an external reality is the more people will have a different inner picture on their inner screen. People tend then to add elements from similar experiences in the past or from knowledge they have at their disposal. Such a picture becomes very quickly a creative touch.

🐦 Most people see elements, but not the complexity of an event or product. They never see for example the whole chain from raw resources for a product, the production, the collateral effects, and the final implications once the product is thrown away into the rubbish bin. People buy things without thinking of possible alternatives that could be more reasonable than the good they buy.

2) The intelligence

The ability to think contains many components. A basic intelligence is indispensable. Thinking can be analytical, theoretical, causal, prospective, hermeneutical, creative, intuitive, meditative, all embracing, categorizing, and even critical or short-sited; and it can include the time dimension (past-present-future), or dimensions of interrelations, chain-reactions, or of meaning.

Certain knowledge, certain learning processes, a language repertoire (words), and a memory are indispensable to efficiently think.

🐦 The majority of people don't know what 'analytical thinking' means. They can't think in terms of theories. They don't think in causal and future oriented perspectives.
🐦 A majority ignores intuitive reaction, have in the best case a thin bit of (useful) creative thinking.
🐦 People can't think in a hermeneutic way; they don't search with contemplation for the meaning and the context of a statement, text or fact.

- Critical thinking of most people is rather limited to their anger and general disgust. People's critical thinking is absent in matters of religion.
- The learning processes of most people begin to reduce with the adult age, especially above the age of 35-38.
- A huge majority of people can't think in an efficient way; and their thinking is much reduced and alienated from reality.

3) The defense and projection mechanisms

Already in a process of perception people tend to select what they see. The more something is uncomfortable (embarrassing) or challenging conscience or the ego, the more people tend to reject such a part of the perceived reality. At the same time people easily project their positive attitude, a want or wish, a dream, or a longing. They also tend to project their own weak and evil aspects in order to feel (to be) better or to construct an 'enemy'. Especially people also tend to register those aspects that conform to their values, ideals, attitudes and norms or those aspects that confirm their values, ideals, attitudes and norms.

Defense mechanisms are for example:

- Ignoring
- Selecting
- Lying
- Suppressing
- Projecting
- Distorting
- Turning into the opposite
- Deceiving
- Disfiguration
- Displacing
- Simplifying
- Minimizing
- Exaggerating
- Deviating
- Falsifying
- Replacing
- Devaluating
- Overvaluing

- Here we are with the most critical psychical function: What people don't like, that offers a challenge or a risk or imbalance of their self-image or

242

inner world, they simply ignore, negate, or at best distort. And this starts already with the perception.

- ☙ The majority of people have in their inner screen a big part of life very reduced and distorted.
- ☙ People tend to focus on what they like, on what increases pleasure, and especially on what confirms their knowledge, attitudes, and images about the external reality.
- ☙ If people don't have already a frame in their brain about a perceived reality, they tend to ignore this reality or shape the perceived reality in a way they can deal with.

<u>4) The feelings (emotions): the whole spectrum from love to hate</u>

Feelings are like a music instrument. There are the positive feelings such as good mood, excitement, joy, happiness, wellbeing, trust, security, satisfaction, and fulfillment.

And there are the negative feelings such as bad mood, sadness, boredom, emptiness, aggression, disgust, fear, anxiety, and hate. Feelings always contain a message and have a cause to be. The quality of a feeling can be intensive or superficial and is experienced during a short or long time.

- ☙ A majority of people can't understand properly the feelings they have.
- ☙ Feelings can very fast dominate judgment, decisions, and behavior.
- ☙ Feelings can dominate an entire mind and even block all other functions.
- ☙ The majority does not contemplate and think about the meaning of the feelings they have.
- ☙ Most people can't differentiate between superficial feelings and feelings of deep spiritual value.
- ☙ The majority of people loses very fast, control over their feelings, heats them up unlimitedly and finally loses their rational mind.
- ☙ Most people never learned how to deal with strong feelings, the positive and critical ones.
- ☙ Most people fool themselves by producing superficial feelings through eating, drinking, drugs, all kind of compensations (consumption), and even through visualization (creating fantasies).

5) The capacity to love

Love is much more than a feeling. Love includes attitudes and ways of behavior such as respect, care, interest, understanding, cooperation, participation, support, promotion, protection, sharing, accepting, developing, patience, fidelity, faith, flexibility, etc. Love in that sense is directed towards the beloved people and friends, towards the world of animals and the nature, in general towards the entire creation. But the first call of love is to love oneself, for one's inner life and potentials to be developed.

- The huge majority of people confuse strong positive feelings towards a person with true love.
- Most people are not aware that love always starts with self-love: interest, explorations, care and dedication for their own inner being.
- People don't know that love sometimes is strenuous, requires abdication, forgiveness, accepting weaknesses and mistakes or even failure.
- Practically all people have no idea that love is directed towards the entire creation, the world of nature and animals, the world of different cultures, and the everyday life, the general human values and the archetypal values.
- A majority of people say to their beloved: "I love you", but they have no idea about their own inner life and the inner life of the addressed other person.
- People don't know that love must be protected and that most people try to steal or destroy the love (and happiness) other people live.
- Most people don't know that love requires to explore and develop one's inner life and potentials, and to live their potentials.

6) The genuine psychical needs

Genuine psychical-spiritual human needs are for example:

- True love
- Honesty
- Authentic expression
- Emotional safety (protection)
- Respect
- Autonomy
- Authentic self-confidence

The satisfaction of genuine psychical needs is constitutive for efficiently mastering life, for satisfaction and happiness, for security and sustainability, and for personal fulfillment.

- As most people don't have a clear understanding of their genuine inner (psychical and spiritual) needs, they all ignore this world and automatically compensate with dogmas, ideologies, or consumption.
- True love, honesty, and trust are a basket case on this earth. These values have gone down the drain worldwide. And nobody gives a shit.
- Nobody would move his ass to protect and promote the genuine inner needs and the all-embracing human values.
- In the modern world authentic expressions or self-realization have become a myth or a narcissistic self-expression (self-culture) and in the poor countries people anyway have no chance for such a 'luxurious' way of living. They must run for food and healthy drinking water or for some dollars for their daily costs; or they suffer from disease and misery.

7) The unconscious mind

The unconscious mind is first of all something like a 'storeroom' where everything that people feel embarrassing, or that hurts, or that is too difficult to mange is 'outsourced' from the defense mechanisms.

Not clarified and unresolved difficult life experiences ('complexes') operate as unconscious units and interfere with one's mind functions, being and daily life.

By the effects (on physical and mental health, in social patterns, in behavior, and the human made environment) we can identify the elements if this unconscious 'storeroom'.

An authentic (genuine) self-realization is not possible without conscious reflection of one's own defense mechanisms and from there the content of this 'storeroom', called 'the unconscious mind'.

- For most people the unconscious world is unknown or is simply a black box they never would want to open.
- Most people don't like to clarify their problems, conflicts, weaknesses or difficulties. They all ignore, trivialize, or compensate with consumption or a specific behavior.
- Nearly all people have no idea how they are driven and controlled by their unconscious. They all think they can rationally deal with it and with their life. But they all pay the price in the future – or their children or the following generations will pay the price.
- The self-realization people claim to live is a Fata Morgana as long as they don't explore and elaborate their inner world.

- The unconscious complexes always force the person to repeat the conflictive component until it's solved. But most people prefer to even die than to solve this critical matter.

8) The inner psychical pole of the opposite gender

Men and women are different in their innermost being. There are natural male and female psychical-spiritual qualities.

→ If a man cannot form his masculine principles in a balance and orientation with feminine principles, so he is a destructive man and not a really developed man.

→ If a woman cannot form her feminine principles in a balance and orientation with masculine principles, so she is a destructive woman and not a really developed woman.

- Most men do not understand that a woman is really very different in the way her mind is working. Men think they are superior to women.
- Most women unconsciously try to reduce the male power, to make impotent the males functions.
- In the modern world the trust between a man and a woman (in a relationship, marriage) is on average maximum 65% and rarely 100%.
- An undeveloped woman is embarrassing and very uncomfortable to live with; and an undeveloped man is very nasty and useless. The world is full of such men and women.
- Men and women around the globe have lost the meaning of marriage; they have 'sold' this Archetype with a wrong understanding of tolerance to homosexual relationships. Herewith they killed one of the most valuable Archetypes of the Soul.

9) The 'spiritual intelligence' and the dreams

The 'Spirit' is the force that creates our dreams intelligently composing meditations; and is also the source of intuition and inspiration.

- The Spirit is an informative, educative, organizing and guiding force.
- The Spirit is the principle of acting in the soul.
- The Spirit is animating, stimulating, and benevolent.
- The Spirit is the source of wisdom.

- On the one side there are a lot of people having a very sick understanding of this 'spiritual intelligence' or of the 'Spirit'. On the other side a majority of humans have no idea that such s force does exist in their mind (or soul).
- The huge majority of people do not deal with the dreams they have at night. They have no idea about the priceless value of their dreams.
- People can have 10 or more nightmares but they still reject asking the questions, about the meaning of such dreams.
- The potential of 'spiritual intelligence' is immense, but people reject this valuable source and prefer to deal with life in their stupid and ignorant ways.
- The fact that Christianity does not teach any dream theory and dream interpretation proves that their teaching is completely disconnected from the Spirit and from God. A majority of people like that very much.

10) Meditation: imagination, contemplation

About meditation we can surmise:

During inner visualization the same spiritual intelligent force is in play as in dreams. With imagination one can relax oneself, find new strength, prepare paths of solutions for problems, free the mind, understand others, find meaning to life, elaborate dreams, recognize causes of suffering and difficulties, work through the unconscious mind, etc.

- People are not much interested in actively solving their problems, in learning how to deal with life matters, in finding an inner meaning, in understanding others, in finding out the causes of illnesses or inner suffering.
- Therefore a huge majority of people are not interested in meditation. Or they use meditative methods that avoid any confrontation with the inner Spirit and inner conflicts. People are unbelievably lazy. They reject to be responsible for their life.

11) The psychical individual and cosmic energy

- Our past is also with us as a complex code with its energy. The energetic body is formed from the past and present, the conscious and unconscious mind and living.
- All people radiate their energy and influence the energetic body of other people.

- The energy that people radiate forms (pollute, poison) the energetic environment that is the energy our soul needs to be connected.

- Most people don't know that their thoughts, their negative emotions and their unconscious complexes form psychical energy. They are not aware that they radiate a poisoning energy in their environment.

- The huge majority of people deny the cosmic energy with its sources in the cosmic source of life (can be named 'God'). Therefore they are not aware how far away they are from God and how much they are disconnected from this source.

- The huge majority of people have enormous guilt in front of God as they deny or reject to be responsible for their psychical-spiritual development. Their solution is to ignore this guilt, the God and its energetic source for humans' soul, and they compensate with suffering or consumption, or fights or going to war 'in the name of J.C. and God'.

- Another compensatory behavior is to pray. Trillions of prayers have been sent to the heaven for thousands of years, and God or J.C. or any Prophet or Holy individual has not helped. They can't help. It's simply a magic superstition. Humans get help through their spiritual intelligence. People don't want to see that! That's why they all become (or remain) infantile and irresponsible for themselves and for the planet. That's why they all get more and more dehumanized and mad. Herein lays the source of evil.

12) The 'I' (self, ego), the will, and the behavior

Will and control leads to action together with several components: Knowledge, skills, energy, motive, decision, strategy, aim, rules, norms, attitudes, tools, and methods. But behavior and decision-making can't be isolated from all the psychical and spiritual sub-systems and functions. Determining forces forming behavior are:

On the one side the 'I' operates in relation to the content on the inner 'screen' and to the way all psychical sub-systems with its single factors is formed.

On the other side the 'I' operates in relation to the state of the body and the external world with its manifold human and objective factors and conditions.

- The majority of people think they decide about everything based on their thoughts and their free will. But they are wrong with this view. The 'I' has converted into something like the private 'Holy Grail', their narcissistic self, their stubborn self, their ecstatic self, and their psychotic self.

- The huge majority doesn't have a well working 'I'. They live highly in an unconscious way driven by external and internal factors. Or they create a bubble of an 'I' that one day will surely explode.
- The huge majority of people around the globe are totally lazy in matters of learning and caring for their personal development. They don't even want to be responsible for their life. They even wish to be paid for being forced to live on this earth. They are sheep, blinded, stupid, naïve, and need an authority that dictates how to live.

Human Evolution with Humans

Renewing the world and resolving the global problems can't simply start with technological measures or with political and economic power concentration. No army will be able to manage the world in an evolutionary way. Everything must start with education, with and individual and collective psychical and spiritual forming of humans. This process is called 'Individuation'.

- Individuation is the ultimate understanding of human beings and life on this earth for politics.
- Individuation includes the spiritual understanding of human beings and meaning of life for all religions.
- Individuation is the indispensable psychical-spiritual path for all officials in all religions and every concept of Spirituality.
- Individuation is the collective path to salvation! A concept that can be lived in all cultural expressions.

- A huge majority of humans on earth are too lazy, to narcissistic, too arrogant, and blabber mouths to have an interest in Individuation or any kind of serious inner development.

Today 95% of all humans on this planet are 'archaic' human beings. The 'archaic human being' is characterized by the negation of the psychical life, by neglecting the psychical organism as well as suppressing love and Spirit. At the same time this kind of human being is more or less completely tied to the unconscious psychical life.

- A majority of people are not open to learning, not interested in a conscious way of living, not interested in being balanced and developed, and not interested in finding the genuine inner meaning of life.

The consequences are disruption (inner conflicts) and decomposition, lack of inner freedom, and infantile dependencies. Such an unformed and wrongly formed psychical life is expressed in greed, envy, hate, destruction, exploitation, violence, unscrupulousness, ignorance, arrogance, belief and dogmas as well as in ideologies, despotism and egocentrism.

The Archetypes of the Soul

1) Accepting and turning to the whole inner life
2) Discovering and forming all inner forces
3) Developing the true Self by conscious forming
4) Integrating the inner Spirit as guidance (Dreams)
5) Proceedings of dying and becoming new
6) Unification with the inner opposite gender pole
7) Integration of the spiritual principles
8) Balance between external and internal life
9) Fulfillment of the completeness and wholeness

- Apart from some individuals, the entire humanity is not aware of the Archetypes of the Soul and its importance for the psychical-spiritual development and fulfillment.
- Christianity and probably all religions do not teach these Archetypes of the Soul. It would unmask the entire dogmatic teaching and all the cheating, deceit and lies of religion.
- Politics and governance do not focus on these Archetypes of the Soul. It would unmask the entire ideological scrap and all the cheating, deceit and lies in the world of politics.

During a higher phase of psychical-spiritual development, a 'man of God' or 'woman of God' has also experienced very special dreams related to highest archetypal processes:

1. God and his manifoldness.
2. God's alliance with him.
3. Becoming a specific destination of service in God (e.g. priest, religious leader, supreme teacher).
4. The transcendental world of the souls.
5. Denomination as a representative of a messiah or prophet (member of a council).
6. Authorization from the inner Spirit to develop further these religious (spiritual) teaching and practices.
7. Getting a mission from God as a prophet or Messiah.
8. Power of attorney from God: Highest Judge of all Souls.

- ❧ Humanity has completely lost these supreme Archetypes of the Soul. They all have no idea that such values reflect inner processes and must be made vivid through immense hard inner work.
- ❧ Christianity and probably all religions have completely lost these supreme Archetypes of the Soul. They all have no idea that such values reflect inner processes and must be made vivid through immense hard inner work.
- ❧ Religions and politics abuse these supreme values for their power legitimization and for cheating and deceiving humanity.

I, the author, I have fulfilled all these Archetypes and I have documented everything for humanity like never before any prophet or wise man (or woman) has documented. A hundred governments, two hundred mass media and some millions of people have been informed about this work repeatedly during many years. But not one human, not any authority in any religion and political institution or media has been interested in knowing more about it. It proves the archaic and very evil state of most humans, of politics, economics, and religion.

The evil man and the evil woman

- A vivid, chaotic, emotional, energetic biomass
- A highly bred, self-alienated, mad being
- A bragger, impostor, bluffer, gambler
- A lying, false and brutal creature unable to love
- A destroyer, breaker, spoiler, embitterer, hater
- An waster, only taking and stealing being
- A suppressing, displacing, falsifying, decomposing, distorting person
- An obsessed, religious-psychotic driven person
- A slave, exploited, abused, misused, violated, raped person
- An exploiting, enslaving, desecrating, oppressing rapist
- A babbler and talker poisoning the environment
- A devil, a beast, a thoroughly evil being
- A bellicose, a warlike, predacious, killing beast
- A lunacy obsessed figure, a global mass killer
- A destroyer of nature, the species, the climate and the planet
- A liar, dispraiser and destroyer of psychical-spiritual values
- An unreasonable, unscrupulous, violent, relentless creature
- An indifferent, irresponsible, dull inferior human
- An insane, tricky, inhumane being
- A human poisoning trust, hope, love, Spirit, the truth
- A deicide, a killer of the truth, a destroyer of the Spirit, a hater of love

- A frightening nightmare in the name of J.C.
- An absolute sad and hopeless case for God and the Spirit

The guilt

- Most people want lies, falseness, perversion, illusion, a mentally ill religion and psychopaths.
- Most people are hypocrites, cowards, narcissists, neurotics, materialists and mentally ill people.
- Most people are self-opinionated, greedy, stubborn, egotistic, ignorant, arrogant, false and too lazy to learn.
- Most people are too cowardly to question the authority of politics, religion, media, economy and education.
- Most people have unscrupulously exploited, enslaved, and killed billions of people and used lies to lead wars.
- Most people have driven the planet and humanity to the abyss with their greed and arrogance.
- Most people themselves have chosen and elected the mentally ill and megalomaniac leaders in politics and religion.
- Most people have not learnt anything from history; in return they now have the concealed dictatorship, the police state.
- Most people blindly believed their politicians out of laziness; now they are both victim and offender in their own world.
- Most people don't want the truth or the inner values, nor the inner Spirit, and neither true love.
- Most people disdained the Archetypes of the Soul and with that ultimately also themselves and humanity as a whole.
- Most people talk without thinking, but self-realization and psychical-spiritual development are rejected.
- Most people want a good life, but they all accept that billions of people are exploited for their good life.
- Most people provoked the financial crisis themselves, because they all wanted to possess goods without first working hard for them.
- Most people have sold all human values and natural resources for the soul, to monsters.

Destroyed gift to be on this earth

Many people on earth don't stand up for and don't bother (means: give a shit) about the human values such as love, care, hope, trust, truth, reliability, faith, faithfulness, justice, balance, honesty, fairness, joy of life, happiness, inner fulfillment, protection, emotional security, respect for human's weaknesses and inner suffering, attitudes in the interest of protection of the nature and the world of animals and the values of the Archetypes of the Soul. Their only reason for being on this earth is to abuse resources, produce waste and sewage, contamination and mental poison, hate, cheat, distort, lie, behave arrogantly, aggressively, commit violence, fights and wars.

➜ Not standing up for the human values and the Archetypes of the Soul has immense destructive individual and collective consequences.

Such consequences are: Unemployment, economic inferno, public debt, poverty, misery, riots, wars, contamination, pollution, climate change, inhuman mega-cities, slums, collateral damages of car traffic, industrial accidents, increase of sea level, drought, floods, tornados and hurricanes, nuclear waste, waste, sewage, dirty water, industrial food and meat, famine, destroyed fish resources, exploitation, damaged eco-systems, illnesses, mental disease, behavior disorder, epidemic plagues, melting of glaciers, elimination of species, destruction of environment, crimes, mafia, corruption, lack of health care, analphabetism, lack of drinking water, decrease of agricultural land and forests, chemicals and pharmaceutics and heavy metals in the food chain and already in human's body, lies, cheating, distortion, brainwashing, manipulations, billions of humans radiating toxic mental energy, and so on.

➜ To be on this earth is a great gift. The planet is a wonderful and very valuable creation, and is the home of all humans today and in the (far) future. All people have a soul and their goal is to develop this soul with learning, growing and living. Humanity is just at the beginning of a cosmic evolutionary project.

The shocking human reality

- It is outrageous how disfigured, deformed and crippled people are as human beings.
- People need to recognize that they have their eyes closed almost everywhere.
- It destroys people's illusion to accept that their church is a perverse house of lies.

- It is embarrassing, how people with their religion only compensate their internal deficits.
- It is disadvantageous for people to admit, that they suffer a deep emptiness inside.
- To recognize how the priests only play theatre is a huge frustration.
- All monkeys laugh at how people behind their face are nothing more than stubborn.
- It is extremely precarious to see how rotten to the core a huge majority of people are inside.
- People's ego will not allow them to admit that they are merely stubborn and not in the right.
- It's a shame to see how a majority of people pathologically defend their faith.
- Nothing can be as horrible as enlightenment about the lunacy of religion.
- It is a shock, when people see how the Bible is an insane piece of patchwork.
- People think that the faith that has been taught for 2.500 years can never be wrong.
- It's sad how people live ignorant, full of prejudices and illusions.
- People's self-styled religious image crumbles as soon as they look in the mirror.
- It is embarrassing to see how people are hypocrites, cowards and quitters.
- People could go crazy when they see the real spiritual truth.
- It is disgraceful, how naive people defend archaic and dogmatic beliefs.
- No one must know how much of a soulless man you are, not even you.
- It's nasty, how authoritarian and stupid people impose their lazy belief on others.
- It is unbearable to see how obsessed by faith, most people deny themselves.
- It is terrible to see how naive and gullible a majority of people give trust.
- People need to recognize that they have blindly subjected themselves to religious authorities.
- For most people it is inconvenient to have to stand up for themselves and their true inner being.
- Most people will experience an earthquake within themselves, when they see how religion has cheated them.
- It is a shame how most people neither live nor promote the Archetypes of the Soul.
- The prospect that the Pope never represents God and Christ is unbelievable to some people.
- It cannot be that the reincarnated Christ is different from what the Church teaches.

- People make a fool of themselves to admit that they believe in religious fantasies.
- People think it cannot be that 2.4 billion Christians have lost themselves in the wrong belief.
- It is shameful to see how delusional people promote religious falsehood.
- People's ego is deeply offended when they realize how spiritually they are incompetent and ignorant.
- People's whole belief system breaks down, when they see the truth.
- People have to be ashamed until their grave, how mindless, stupid and lazy they believe.
- All the devils roll on the floor laughing, at how people have sold their soul to religion.

Belief and ideas

- Humans are lazy, lazy to think, sluggish, superficial, don't want to learn.
- Humans want easy, fast, simple and direct solutions for their 'salvation'.
- Humans are submissive to authority, easily deceivable and easily enslaved.
- Humans are like blind sheep, driven herd animals and followers.
- Humans are cowardly and fearfully paralysed by social pressure.
- Humans believe in 'holy lies' because they themselves lie, live in lies.
- Humans believe in archaic nonsense, because they themselves are archaic.
- Humans want to belong otherwise they are alone and excluded.
- Humans do not want to take responsibility for the truth.
- Humans need a belief in dogma or ideology to live their quarrelsomeness.
- Humans cannot give up their ideas and belief, because they are stubborn.
- Humans live their sick cantankerousness with their belief and opinions.
- Humans are scared of the shock that the truth can release.
- Humans have such a small ego, that they refurbish it with belief.
- Humans think they are better with their belief than non-believers.
- Humans are scared of life and therefore cling to their belief and ideas.
- Humans themselves play a false, deceitful, deceiving game in life.
- Humans are psychically on the stage of development of a small child.
- Humans can live their own, open or concealed arrogance with their ideas.
- Humans choose illusions over the strong facts of life and humane being.
- Humans hope for the redemption of their complexes with belief.
- Humans compensate their human weaknesses with beliefs or consumption.
- Humans have enormous concealed guilt, partly real and partly self suggested.
- Humans increase their extremely low and bad self-value with their beliefs.
- Humans expect help from God and J.C. instead of helping themselves.
- Humans compensate their weak, instable self-confidence with their belief.

- Humans flee from themselves and their own inferiority with their belief.
- Humans think that with belief they can tame their 'unworthy' lust.
- Humans see their life as unworthy and low; create balance with belief.
- Humans cannot live themselves and need the 'mother church'.
- Humans have not been loved and hope to receive the love of God.
- Humans have experienced suffering and experience relief through belief.
- Humans strengthen their own imperiousness and their tyrannical personality.
- Humans don't have a genuine self-identity and find it in a community.
- Humans conceal with their low psychical-spiritual development with belief.
- Humans do not have any substantial self-enlightenment and do not want any.
- Humans do not want to see, how their own parents are completely archaic.
- Humans suppress their hate of their father, mother and life with their belief.
- Humans are sickened by themselves, their own body and flee into belief.
- Humans have an increased feeling of triumph, being in the 'true' belief.
- Humans are submissive and masochistically bonded in their drive to religion.
- Humans are orally unsaved and nurture themselves through fixation on ideas.
- Humans don't have substantial knowledge to question themselves or others.
- Humans are scared, to look at themselves in the inner mirror.
- Humans are scared, to recognize the devilish lies of the church and politics.
- Humans fear to recognize how they are deceived by politics and religion.
- Humans loose their ground, when they recognize 'infallible truth' as a lie.

The welcome archaic people

- Politicians of the Christian-oriented party need their naive, blind followers.
- Politicians in general want this type of human being, so that they can do what they want.
- The military needs this type of human being, as a soldier, as submissive cannon fodder.
- The military can declare their military action as act of God, and 'in the name of God'.
- The industry needs this type of human being, to make maximum profit.
- If the Pope and the Bible lie, Christians believe the lies, so also politicians can lie.
- The big media have it easy with their games of deceit and distortion.

- Brainwashing, manipulation and propaganda only functions with this type of human being.
- Most of the billionaires base their wealth and their power on this type of human being.
- If the people are focused on the suffering of Jesus Christ, then they bear a lot of suffering.
- If the people are fixed on the after life and the relieving Paradise, then they accept poverty.
- If the people believe in the authorities of the Church, then they protest very little against state powers.
- If the people are psychically and spiritually weak and submissive, then the politicians are strong.
- If religion can deceive people without being detected, then those in power can as well.
- If people have their soul at the mercy of the Church, then they give their life at the mercy of those in power.
- If people let themselves be exploited by the Church, they let themselves be exploited by the state.

The politicians and the folks

We have now on the one side these archaic politicians and religious incumbents with a completely repressed and chaotic inner life. They have no idea about the Archetypes of the Soul and the supreme Archetypes. They lead and govern humanity.

We have on the one side these archaic folks, a huge majority very undeveloped, totally distorted and self-alienated. We have estimated 90% of humanity that lives with limited or very scarce financial resources; 50% of them in serious and extreme poverty, suffering daily from hunger, lack of water, disease, and a miserable life in general.

Therefore we posit that there are around 90-95% of humans on earth that are rooted in an archaic understanding of humans, of mind and soul. An estimated 5 billion people run for salvation in religions that are not rooted in the Archetypes of the Soul, but much more in countless fabrications, fairy tales, myths, superstitions, and distortions about God and Paradise, and the meaning of life on earth in general.

- 75-85% of the world population lives or must live like rats and they are treated from political, economical and religious authorities like rats.

- 90-95% of the world population lives in a very unconscious way, ignoring their real soul and inner life. We can say these people live in a very 'stupid', in a very ego-centered, blinded, stubborn, naïve, inefficient and therefore totally destructive way.
- The 5% on the top of society (economically and politically) are preponderantly heavy neurotics, psychopaths, and many of them driven by a religious psychosis, however having a mind and soul that is totally distorted.

→ All this is the result of politics, religion, economics, and public education!
→ Politicians, religious incumbents, the masters of economics, and the people responsible in public education that are in this rat race, on the hamster wheel, don't come forward and can't get out.
→ The huge majority of people are also running in the rat race, on the hamster wheel. They will never find the Archetypes of the Soul and therefore never find their complete inner fulfillment.

What is the picture that politicians have about humans? Do they know what makes a person a human being? It's his psychical-spiritual inner life, in a few words with the following aspects:

A huge majority of humans in the Western world have been deformed, malformed, and dehumanized in their inner being and ways of living. There are signs everywhere about the result:

- An inferior, unreasonable human of minor value
- An unidentified animal without instinct
- A blind, brainwashed human biomass
- A conceited bigmouth without truthfulness
- A being full of lies, self-lies and life-lies
- A deformed, distorted, disfigured human being
- A crushed, chained and suppressed being
- An artificial, superficial vivid object
- A very weak, adulterated copied product
- A greedy, ravenous, insatiable monster
- An uninformed, ignorant, dull, primitive creature
- A naive, gullible and easy seducible sloth
- An archaic, perverse, psychopathic driven creature
- An inner weak beast, strengthened only by external things
- An inflated narcissist with a completely disfigured ego
- A follower, copycat, stereotype of the collective
- An animalistic being with a completely rotten inner core

- A hypocritical, pitiable, embarrassing figure of fun
- A cushy, lazy, indolent, fastidious human biomass
- A very low-thinking, even unable to think pre-hominid
- A boring, bossy person too lazy to learn
- An ego-driven, blind "I do what I want"-machine

The Western society has created masses of much distorted humans; aspects can be seen everywhere:

- A vivid, chaotic, emotional, energetic biomass
- A highly bred, self-alienated, mad being
- A bragger, impostor, bluffer, gambler
- A lying, false and brutal creature unable to love
- A destroyer, breaker, spoiler, embitterer, hater
- An thief, only taking and stealing being
- A suppressing, displacing, falsifying, decomposing, distorting person
- An obsessed, religious-psychotic driven person
- A slave, exploited, abused, misused, violated, raped person
- An exploiting, enslaving, desecrating, oppressing rapist
- A babbler and talker poisoning the environment
- A devil, a beast, a thoroughly evil being
- A bellicose, warlike, predacious, killing beast
- A lunacy obsessed figure, a global mass killer
- A destroyer of nature, the species, the climate and the planet
- A liar, dispraiser and destroyer of psychical-spiritual values
- An unreasonable, unscrupulous, violent, relentless creature
- An indifferent, irresponsible, dull inferior human
- An insane, tricky, inhumane being
- A human poisoning trust, hope, love, Spirit, the truth
- A deicide, a killer of the truth, a destroyer of the Spirit, a hater of love
- A frightening nightmare in the name of J.C.
- An absolute sad and hopeless case for God and the Spirit

➔ This chaotic and archaic state of humans is extensively due to an inappropriate public education, the economic imbalance, and the glorified Western 'living standard'.

The gift to be on earth is thoroughly ignored:

To be on this earth is a great gift. The planet is a wonderful and very valuable creation, and is the home of all humans today and in the (far) future. All people have a soul and their goal is to develop this soul with learning, growing and living. Humanity is just at the beginning of a cosmic evolutionary project. Do humans consider this gift? Do politicians consider this gift?

Many people on earth don't stand up for and don't bother (means: give a shit) about the human values such as love, care, hope, trust, truth, reliability, faith, faithfulness, justice, balance, honesty, fairness, joy of life, happiness, inner fulfillment, protection, emotional security, respect for human's weaknesses and inner suffering, attitudes in the interest of protection of the nature and the world of animals and the values of the Archetypes of the Soul. Their sole reason of being on this earth is abuse of resources, waste and sewage, contamination and mental poison, hate, cheating, distortion, lies, arrogance, aggression, violence, fights and wars.

→ All people don't think that the 'good' doesn't grow and doesn't become strong itself.

The guilt of people is disastrous:

- People want lies, falseness, perversion, illusion, a mentally ill religion and psychopaths.
- People are hypocrites, cowards, narcissists, neurotics, materialists and mentally ill or deformed.
- People are self-opinionated, greedy, stubborn, egoistic, ignorant, arrogant, false and too lazy to learn.
- People are too cowardly to question the authority of the politics, religion, media, economy and education.
- People (Christians) have throughout history unscrupulously exploited, enslaved, and killed billions of people and used lies to start wars.
- People (in the Western world) have driven the planet and humanity to the abyss with their greed and arrogance.
- People have chosen and elected too many mentally ill and megalomaniac leaders in politics and religion.
- People have not learnt anything from history; in return they now have the concealed dictatorship, the police state (in America and Europe; & the rest?).
- People don't want the truth or the inner values, nor the inner Spirit, and neither true love.

- People disdained the Archetypes of the Soul and with that ultimately also themselves and humanity as a whole.
- People talk without thinking, but self-realization and psychical-spiritual development are all rejected.
- People want a good life, but they all accept that billions of people are exploited for this good life.
- People provoked the financial crisis themselves, because they all wanted to have goods without first working hard for them.
- People have sold all human values and natural resources for the soul to the economic monsters.
- If people continue to live like they do up to now the contamination will eliminate humanity in 35-40 years.

Guilt calls for learning:

- People have made terrible mistakes; but they can profoundly learn from it.
- People have missed chances to take the right decisions for a proper development.
- People have ignored and neglected the most important human values.
- People have forgotten the immeasurable values of their cultural and social history.
- People have lost themselves by running for superficial and egoistic purposes.
- People have lost themselves in a dark labyrinth of political and religious fights.
- People have missed chances to do politics and business with the inner Spirit for humans.
- People have played with lies, cheating, deceit, distortion, delusion and empty promises.
- People have forgotten that they only have one earth and that they must care for it.
- People have ignored that all humans on earth are a divine creation to be formed.
- People have not seen that they destroy their society with centralized rigid regulations.

Others are guilty:

People cannot blame the politicians and the leaders in the industry, economy (banks, the world of finances), media, public education, governmental administration and religion for the dire state of humanity and the planet.

People can not lay the blame on the 'Illuminati' or hidden megalomaniacs driven by unlimited sick greed and a religious psychosis for the economical disaster, the human made catastrophes, the wars, the soaring implementation of the 'One World Order', the destruction of environment and the eco-systems, etc. People cannot blame the rich and superrich and the most powerful leaders for their suffering and misery. People, with their stupid, ignorant, lazy and superficial way of living and thinking, make the rich richer and richer, and unlimitedly powerful! Most humans of all ages starting with from the age of 12 – well educated or not, rich or poor – are extensively guilty for all the immense local, national, and global problems – and for their own misery and suffering.

- People must change their view, their thinking, their ways of living and their attitudes.
- People must find new faith in themselves, in their inner Spirit, in their inner potentials.
- People must become creative, innovative and pioneering for new solutions.
- People must decisively give an effort much stronger than ever before in the history.
- People must aspire to new goals with faith, strength, endurance and perseverance.
- People must cooperate, talk, discuss without taboos and take decisions together.
- People must listen to each other with respect, trust, openness and understanding.
- People must work together for a new holistic and a sustainable development of societies.
- People must go through a catharsis and complete renewal for the sake of future generations.
- People must solve the immense global problems with their soul and not with wars.
- People must unify humanity for a cooperative, balanced, peaceful and equitable path.

→ And politicians must promote them with the right education! It would reduce by 50-65% the very critical humane problems politicians have to manage and try to solve.

Considering the state of humanity and the planet it's absolutely disastrous and frightening. It's probably the biggest nightmare in the cosmos. We have to be aware that in 35-40 years 10 billion archaically shaped people will live on earth.

Humanity is lost in a dark labyrinth. The entire creation is at risk. There will never be a solution for humanity and the planet without Global Individuation and the supreme Archetypes of the Soul as the highest authority of humanity.

Technology will never solve these problems. The biggest war will not solve anything, except it may lead to a collective catharsis that prepares the path for the supreme Archetypes of the Soul.

- Estimated 75-80% of the world population produces during their entire life only negative things: waste, sewage, destruction of the environment and the eco-systems, over-exploiting all resources, and poisoning the social environment with toxic mental energy.
- Is this disastrous concept and ways of living a humane life the meaning of human life, the plan of creation, the mission of all religions, the duties of politicians, and the purpose of spirituality on earth? Is this all that politicians are able to do in leading folks and the entire humanity?
- It's a cosmic disgrace in front of the source of all creations! As it leads collectively to the all-embracing deicide, it's also the worst guilt of all these humans in the face of God.

Becoming a human

The entire history of philosophy, psychology, and education tells us that everything starts with self-knowledge, that everybody is self-responsible for his/her development, and that a human is a 'divine' creature with enormous potentials. Therefore let's focus again on the core question: What makes a person a human being? It's his psychical-spiritual inner life, in a few words with the following aspects:

→ Perceiving: e.g. also looking behind the façades and giving meaning
→ Thinking: e.g. analyzing, interpreting, evaluating, judging, real conclusions
→ Intelligence: e.g. dealing with all kind of components and understanding
→ Feelings: e.g. all possible positive and negative states, each with a meaning
→ Psychical needs: e.g. being accepted, autonomy, security, friendship, love
→ Spiritual needs: e.g. values, meaning of life, spiritual longing and understanding
→ The force of love: e.g. self-love, love for a partner, kids, others, nature, animals
→ Dreams and visualization: e.g. the messages given by the inner Spirit
→ Self-Identity: e.g. living talents & disposition, psychical-spiritual development

→ The opposite gender pole: e.g. the extensive manifoldness of gender qualities

→ The unconscious: e.g. the biography, conflicts, complexes, norms, creative source

→ The psychical organism: e.g. the drive to become an all-sided balanced whole

→ Sexual desire: intimately experiencing the varied messages of tenderness and actions

→ Communication as a way of resolving life issues and living in peace and cooperation

All these psychical and spiritual aspects of the psyche (soul, inner life) have to be formed in an all-sided balanced way for success in life, for happiness, for genuine joy of life, for fulfillment, and for a constructive way of living.

→ Without these forming processes no Archetypal forming processes are possible! Without this forming process no salvation and no redemption is possible. Without these forming processes a human being stays in inner oppositions, inner disruption, in defense of the realities, and in a high level of unconsciousness.

If a human does not consciously form these aspects with aims, then he is and will remain an archaic human; simply a human biomass with a congruent low value.

Ignoring the inner life not only destroys humanity and the earth, but it also makes a person dependent on authorities (Churches, institutions, personalities) for spiritual fulfillment and life in general.

→ Rejecting all the Archetypes of the Soul and all the supreme Archetypes is deicide! Rejecting all these Archetypes show humanity's true face!

All Archetypes of the Soul and also the supreme Archetypes of the Soul are simple, self-evident, comprehensible, even logical on the functional level, and plausible in their meaning. There is no reasonable argument that they do not exist or that they are irrelevant, or even that they can be ignored without any loss or damage for humans, for human's life, or for the entire humanity and the planet.

2.9. Limits of Living Standard

Description and Definition

Let's start with some classical definition we can find on the Internet:

1) "A level of subsistence or material welfare of a community, class, or person.
A term describing the amount of goods and services that an average family or individual views as necessary." [76]

➜ The standard of living is here 100% focused on material goods and services.

2) "Economics: a level of subsistence or material welfare of a community, class, or person. Standard of living - a level of material comfort in terms of goods and services available to someone or some group; 'they enjoyed the highest standard of living in the country"; the lower the standard of living the easier it is to introduce an autocratic production system'." [77]

➜ The standard of living is here 100% focused on material goods and services.
➜ The interpretation (or importance) is extended to the level of living standard and the risks of a low living standard in a country.

3) "The amount of goods and services that a person can buy with the money that he earns, i. e. the real value of his income. This depends on the value of goods and services produced per head of the population and living standards can increase only if output and productivity rise. Source: European Union." [78]

➜ The standard of living is here 100% focused on material goods and services, measured by the GDP.
➜ The rise of output and productivity determines the rise of living standard; or: living standard is determined by the productivity and its output.

---

[76] http://dictionary.reference.com/browse/standard+of+living

[77] http://www.thefreedictionary.com/standard+of+living

[78] dictionary.org/definitions/living+standard?cx=partner-pub-0939450753529744%3Av0qd01-tdlq&cof=FORID%3A9&ie=UTF-8&q=living+standard&sa=Search#906

➜ From the same source we interpret: The politics of the European Union is fixated on the GDP as the unique significant factor that creates or improves life standard.

4) "The level of wealth, comfort, material goods and necessities available to a certain socioeconomic class in a certain geographic area. The standard of living includes factors such as income, quality and availability of employment, class disparity, poverty rate, quality and affordability of housing, hours of work required to purchase necessities, gross domestic product, inflation rate, number of vacation days per year, affordable (or free) access to quality healthcare, quality and availability of education, life expectancy, incidence of disease, cost of goods and services, infrastructure, national economic growth, economic and political stability, political and religious freedom, environmental quality, climate and safety. The standard of living is closely related to quality of life…" [79]

➜ The standard of living goes here much further as the above mentioned definitions that are limited to wealth, goods, and services.
➜ The GDP only forms one variable in a very extensive group of variables that characterize living standard.

We have here some variables that are primarily not material or economical, but obviously it's always also about availability and partly about services which both include financial resources:

- Comfort (has a wide immaterial connotation)
- Quality of employment
- Class disparity
- Quality of housing
- Number of vacation days per year
- Quality healthcare
- Quality education
- Life expectancy
- Political freedom
- Religious freedom
- Environmental quality
- Climate
- Safety

---

[79] http://www.investopedia.com/terms/s/standard-of-living.asp

5) "...The standard of living is often used to compare geographic areas, such as the standard of living in the United States versus Canada, or the standard of living in St. Louis versus New York. The standard of living can also be used to compare distinct points in time. For example, compared with a century ago, the standard of living in the United States has improved greatly. The same amount of work buys an increased quantity of goods, and items that were once luxuries, such as refrigerators and automobiles, are now widely available. As well, leisure time and life expectancy have increased, and annual hours worked have decreased." [80]

→ Critically we can ask: Which of these increased and available variables are really relevant for a high living standard? And: If some variables are relevant for a high living standard, are they also relevant for all countries around the globe?
→ An increased quantity of goods could include a critical quality, e.g. in the case of industrial food.
→ An increased leisure time does not guarantee an increase of personal life quality.

6) Wikipedia presents the list above in the paragraph 4). We mention here the following statements: "...Standard of living is generally measured by standards such as real (i.e. inflation adjusted) income per person and poverty rate. Other measures such as access and quality of health care, income growth inequality, disposable Energy (people's disposable income's ability to buy energy) and educational standards are also used. ... It is the ease by which people living in a time or place are able to satisfy their needs and/or wants...

→ What are the indispensable needs for making a humble satisfying life?
→ What do people want? They want as much as possible of what the market is offering. Is this reasonable? Does this want have anything to do with human's life or with an excellent life standard?

"...The idea of a 'standard' may be contrasted with the quality of life, which takes into account not only the material standard of living, but also other more intangible aspects that make up human life, such as leisure, safety, cultural resources, social life, physical health, environmental quality issues, etc. More complex means of measuring well-being must be employed to make such judgments, and these are very often political, thus controversial..."

→ We must contrast 'living standard' with 'quality of life'.
→ We cannot take into account only the material standard of living.

[80] http://www.investopedia.com/terms/s/standard-of-living.asp

→ Standard of living also has immaterial psychological and social qualities.
→ Life standard must include human values that are in its core spiritual.
→ Standard of living must include environmental quality issues.

"…Standards of living are perhaps inherently subjective. … Countries with a very small, very rich upper class and a very large, very poor lower class may have a high mean level of income, even though the majority of people have a low 'standard of living'. This mirrors the problem of poverty measurement, which also tends towards the relative. This illustrates how distribution of income can disguise the actual standard of living…" [81]

→ The parameter of (material) living standard (GDP) expresses an average, but an average does not reflect the picture of a country.
→ The parameter of (material) living standard (GDP) always disguises the actual standard of living.

What is a human life without love, care, trust, reliability, truth, faith, fairness, inner happiness, peace, justice, social safety, self-esteem, beauty from the soul, authenticity, genuineness, honesty, benevolence, grace, creativity, joy, pleasure, living inner potentials, performance, etc.?

It means emptiness, coldness, superficiality, sadness, fear, depression, distrust, forsakenness, insecurity, cheat, deceit, lies, hostility, reduction to material satisfaction and satisfaction through all kind of perversion, absence of human values, etc.; in the end it is the hell on earth.

There is also another dimension of human values, or human 'qualities'. Some critical examples can explain what 'human values' could also be:

- The perception of a person is much reduced.
- The knowledge of a person is on an infantile level.
- People have no idea what defense mechanisms are.
- People don't realize that they always project a lot.
- A person can't think about more than one short idea.
- The way a person interprets something is mostly wrong.
- A person is permanently dominated from feelings.
- People don't understand and can't manage their feelings.
- In the inner life there are always opposite forces.
- The unconscious mind is very over-loaded by complexes.
- A person has no idea about genuine inner needs.
- In a relationship between man and woman there is no love.

[81] http://en.wikipedia.org/wiki/Standard_of_living

- A person has no self-esteem and no self-confidence.
- All people have dreams every night, but nobody understands them.
- People take what they see or what others say for granted.
- The huge majority of people don't know about spiritual intelligence.
- People do not learn from life and never learn from others.
- People reject to be responsible for their life.
- Most people are absolutely not free in their inner life.
- Most people can't listen to what others say.
- People distort everything already before talking or acting.
- People never do experience inner fulfillment.
- The huge majority of people are totally brainwashed.
- Most people don't have the knowledge and skills to master life.
- Most people are stubborn and absolutely inflexible.
- People are unable to deal with inner tension.
- People can't constructively deal with conflicts and problems.
- Most people simply copy everything from others.
- People are unable to make reasonable judgments.
- Most people have very little power of endurance.
- The majority of people want to be another person (self-hate).
- Most people are unable to balance opinions, attitudes, and norms.
- Most people are lazy and don't even want to know themselves.
- Everybody talks before thinking without considering the effects.
- People don't accept what life requires for a humane life.
- Most people are naïve, credulous, and subversive to authority.
- Most people want to have lots, but not willing to work for it.
- The majority of people are chaotic in their mental functions.
- Most people are quarrelsome, avaricious, greedy, and envious.
- Most people can't think critically and creatively or intuitively.
- 95% of inner potentials people have are ignored, not developed.

- Sick! Insane! Valueless! Inefficient! Useless! Destructive! Hate for life!
- What is the value of such dimensions of human values or human 'qualities' if up to 80% of humanity is characterized by such 'qualities'?
- What is the 'human value' of 80% of humans if they destroy the planet with their ways of living, thinking and following a distorted and fabricated religion?

A first psycho-analytical approach to understand a human is: "Tell me the three most important and superior wishes you have for your life." This is what 2000 clients (age 25-50) during the last 30 years told me. I summarize the top answers:

- A luxurious car
- A lot of money
- To be loved
- My own successful business
- To have my own home
- To have a car
- Becoming a CEO
- To play golf
- Being admired
- Always a good sleep
- Sex
- Complying with the Bible's requirement
- A comfortable job
- To get appreciation
- Never have to work
- A family and children
- Physical health
- A lot of fun
- A pension instead of working
- God will give my destiny
- Always long holidays
- An easy going life
- A life without problems
- To be respected
- Living the will of God
- That J.C. will save me
- A lot of friends
- And so on

Not one person mentioned something that is related to get well shaped psychical functions, efficient skills for making life, becoming a strong personality, finding inner fulfillment, understanding the meaning of human life, living an authentic life, forming and living my inner potentials, always learning and acquiring a lot of knowledge.

👍 An estimated 10% of all answers were focused on some general genuine human values such as 'living love' and finding 'inner peace' (harmony)!

Conclusions:

→ Coming to earth is not for free. From conception to death there are costs.
→ Human values are also not for free. They must be built up and protected.
→ The first and most important human value is 'being on this earth'.
→ The second most important human value is the individual person itself.
→ Values such as love, truth and self-confidence are a result of performance.
→ A person cannot have self-esteem without inner qualities and performances.
→ Humans can't live human without well-formed psychical functions.
→ Inner freedom is the result of hard work, also of spiritual contemplation.
→ Running away from one's inner life results in losing human values.
→ Holistic psychical-spiritual development is the top-principle of human life.

We must find an understanding of this dire situation: [82]

- 1.3 billion people earn less than $1 per day.
- 1.4 billion people dispose of less that $1.25 per day.
- 3 billion people struggle to survive on $2 per day.
- As many as 2.8 billion people on the planet struggle to survive on less than $2 a day. [83]
- 80% of the earth population (5.6bn) lives from less than $10 per day (= $300 per month).
- The richest 20% of the world population cover 76.6% of worldwide private consumption.
- The poorest 35% cover 1.5% of the consumption volume.
- The richest 10% cover 59% of all consumption; and the poorest 10% only 0.5%.

The interpretation of such data we found in different sources is a bit critical. On the one side it is not clear if there are 1.3 billion people earning less that $1 per day and another 1.4 billion people that earn between $1-1.25, and 3 billion people that earn between $1.25 and $2 per day. However we get a huge majority of people that earn less than $10 per day, which is in the best case a wage for surviving with the satisfaction of the absolute basic needs. All these people that earn less than $2 per day don't have a realistic chance to live human values, to shape themselves for psychical-spiritual efficiency and 'qualities'. A general conclusion is that minimum 5 billion people live far away from the level of the Western living standard measured by goods and service.

---

[82] Schellhammer. Economics III, p. 183
[83] http://www.worldwatch.org/node/810

We can conclude from this economic picture and from the above-mentioned lack of humane 'qualities', human values, and the Archetypes of the Soul:

➔ A good or even high living standard does not automatically stimulate and promote human's evolution and does not guarantee that the people care for their psychical-spiritual being and development to be efficient in their ways of living, to live genuine human values, and to give importance to the inner source of life and the core aims of human's life (as described above).

➔ A very low and even miserable living standard does not stimulate and promote human's evolution and does not allow that the people can care for their psychical-spiritual being and development to be efficient in their ways of living, to live genuine human values, and to give importance to the inner source of life and the core aims of human's life (as described above).

➔ The five or six most important (by size) religions do not stimulate and promote human's evolution and do not motivate that the people care for their psychical-spiritual being and development to be efficient in their ways of living, to live genuine human values, and to give importance to the inner source of life and the core aims of human's life (as described above). All these religions are dogmatic and fundamentalist, which excludes the forming of the psychical-spiritual function of humans' mind.

➔ All relevant political systems, ideologies and structures do not stimulate and promote itself human's evolution and do not motivate that the people care for their psychical-spiritual being and development to be efficient in their ways of living, to live genuine human values, and to give importance to the inner source of life and the core aims of human's life (as described above). There is no political ideology or approach that focuses on the psychical-spiritual organism and its development as a whole.

➔ All kind of economic systems and structures do not stimulate and promote human's evolution and do not motivate that the people care for their psychical-spiritual being and development to be efficient in their ways of living, to live genuine human values, and to give importance to the inner source of life and the core aims of human's life (as described above). The capitalistic economic systems aim to exploit every non-vivid and vivid thing in order to concentrate power with money and wealth on a selected group.

→ All systems of public and academic education do not stimulate and promote automatically human's evolution and do not motivate that the people care for their psychical-spiritual being and development to be efficient in their ways of living, to live genuine human values, and to give importance to the inner source of life and the core aims of human's life (as described above). By the given rules of accreditation the most important parts of the mind and soul and also essential knowledge and skills for mastering life are excluded from public and academic education.

Herewith the evolution of humanity has become a basket case. Humanity does not have 50, 100 or 200 years to find a new evolutionary path that includes the psychical-spiritual being and development to be efficient in ways of living, in living genuine human values, and by giving importance to the inner source of life and the core aims of human's life (as described above).

Humanity is like the people on a monstrous ship that is heavily damaged and at risk of sinking within 35-40 years. The momentum of all causal relevant factors (parameters) does not allow for simply giving a new order for a new direction in humanity's path. It is never possible to renew archaic dogmatic and fundamentalist religion. It is never possible to change the economic structures just like that. It is not possible to provide within 10-30 years the entire humanity with a Western standard of living.

The rigid structures of accredited governmental education can't be transformed into a pioneering and future oriented concept that includes the relevant human values and the Archetypes of the Soul. The media around the globe, owned by a very small group of very rich people, have gigantic power in shaping human's mind, soul, and behavior. They dehumanize, degenerate, and operate in absolutely evil ways to exploit and direct the entire humanity into a main stream of their economic, political or religious interest.
There is no chance to re-direct the satanic doing of the supreme masters into an evolutionary perspective that includes the Archetypes of the Soul. Deicide is their insane obsession with religious roots that go back around 3000 years. Ministers of departments and even heads of states in the entire Western world, India and the Arab world included are nothing more than the paid protagonists of these supreme masters.

In general there is nothing bad with a good life standard for the entire humanity. We even agree that a certain level of life standard is indispensable for human's evolution and is an essential frame that people can care for their psychical-spiritual being and development to be efficient in their ways of living, to live genuine human values, and to give importance to the inner source of life and the core aims of human's life (as described above).

Nevertheless, very delicate and even explosive questions arise:

- Is it necessary that all the children and the youth have a mobile phone?
- Is it necessary that most children and the youth have Internet connection?
- Is it appropriate and a real need that everybody has a car or can get a car?
- Is it reasonable that a billion people yearly travel around the globe?
- Do all the societies really need the big corporations?
- Do we really need the extensive unlimited globalization of trade?
- Does humanity need these 5000-8000 nuclear bombs around the globe?
- Is there a meaning of 60-100 million victims of car traffic accidents?
- Is it really a benefit if everybody can use electricity as much as they like?
- Does a society need that much media as most of it is pre-fabricated?
- Do we need everywhere lighted signage during the entire night?
- Does humanity really need 50,000 products in the mega-supermarkets?
- Is it meaningful that every blabber-mouth can expose his mental scrap?
- Do the people really need 250 TV channels to be entertained or informed?
- Is it constructive that people everywhere, are bombarded by marketing?
- Do we need Goldman Sachs; should banks be decomposed to small units?
- Why should skiing be allowed as it produces much natural damages?
- Do all people really need all the imported food and flower etc.?
- What is the point of betting, lottery, and all kind of speculative games?
- Why are sects bad though the sectarian Catholic Church is everywhere?
- Why can corporations contaminate air and environment, but smokers not?
- Is it appropriate that people get insurance for every small loss and damage?
- What is the serious need for high-speed trains with 250-400 km speed?
- Does it make life better when people buy every year new clothes and shoes?
- What is the benefit of reading a newspaper that consists in 80% rubbish?
- Can people become happy when they daily watch 3-6 hours television?
- What is meaning of life by getting a pension payment during 20-35 years?
- Why are stupid people with a bad character allowed to drive a car?
- Why do the youth from (18-25) have a right to possess and drive a car?
- Is there any spiritual benefit that people only work 35-38 hours per week?
- Does everybody need a printer (for the computer or other device) at home?
- Why do people get a consumer loan for goods that they don't really need?

- Why are extremely overweight people not punished, but wrong parking is?
- Do all governments need palatial buildings and high quality furniture?
- Do the banks and centers of corporations need palatial buildings?
- What is the meaning of wearing a suit and tie for normal employees?
- Is it efficient to standardize everything from cucumbers to premises?
- Why is a bank allowed to make money with the money in our account?
- Why are in the fields of governments people having worked for big banks?
- Why is it allowed producing goods that most people throw away very soon afterwards?
- Does a society need a centralized government that regulates everything?
- Do people really need a credit card to pay for the small shopping of everyday?
- Is there a mortgage model that is 100% safe for debtors and lenders?
- Why do people that are good-for-nothing get an unemployment payment?
- Why are stupid and penniless people allowed to procreate a baby?
- Why can homosexuals abuse the Archetype 'marriage' for their neurosis?
- Do we need a law that procreating a baby needs preparative education?
- Why are the youth exposed to all evil, all dangerous seductions and lure?
- This list can be endless!

Most of these questions and topics are of high collective importance. But no political party or politician would dare to take such very hot potatoes in his hands. Why?

To get a minimum level of standard of living (in economic terms) that allows to shape (form, educate) the mind and soul of people politicians will have a big challenge, especially in the developing countries. Most developing countries have their locations (cities) where such a living standard is at least in a small sector given, but a huge majority of the people can't participate on it; they live in absolute or serious poverty. Changes in these countries may require a roadmap of 20-30 years.

In contra the politicians in the industrialized countries must answer the questions:

➜ How much more and how much higher standard of living (in economic terms) can we afford and do humans need?

Sure is that the Western countries have plenty of opportunities and potentials to extend the understanding of living with human values and a human related environment. Although also industrialized countries have noticeable poverty, the extreme poverty could be solved with the right measures within 5-7 years. Poverty in Western countries has in most cases a very different picture compared with developing countries; such populations live in conditions that allow a certain 'education' in human values, mental functions, and personal development as described above.

The bigger challenge is to set a limit and to find a balance in the standard of living. Other challenges are contamination, the banking system, the public debt, the media, the lobbyists, the big corporations, the warmongers, the standardization of practically everything, and a reconstruction of governmental systems that allow a (decentralized) real democracy, free from the dominance of the financial supreme masters operating with 'invisible hands'.

3. Humanity, the Planet and Political Failure

This is an extract from the Chapter 3 in Economics III[84], added with a short Chapter about facts and the problems of unemployment. The topics here are elaborated in the perspective of political activities and responsibility.

3.1. Hunger, Food and Water

Hunger

- Today 4-5 billion people don't have enough healthy food and drinking water.
- An estimated 2.3-3 billion people are malnourished, under-fed or starving.
- An estimated 1,000,000,000 people are undernourished.
- Nearly 30% of all children in developing countries are undernourished.
- High food prices and lower incomes put poor households at an additional risk of not providing expectant mothers, infants, and children with adequate nutrition.
- Between 2 and 3.5 billion people have micronutrient deficiency (not enough vitamins and minerals).

- All the lawmakers, ministers and head of states being responsible in allocating food and healthy water for their folk – part of these 4-5 billion people don't have enough healthy food and drinking water – have terribly failed in the organization and allocation of the necessary food and water.
- It is logically also their responsibility to organize enough work and a wage for the people that allow them to buy the necessary food (and water).
- These politicians additionally responsible for the future and health of their young generation.

Comparative examples:

- 1.2 billion people suffer from obesity (excess of fats and salt, often accompanied by deficiency of vitamins and minerals).

---

[84] Schellhammer: Economics III; and: Deicide. 2012

- In the United Kingdom 30-40% of all foods are never eaten.
- Overall, £20 billion ($38 billion) worth of food is thrown away each year.
- In the USA 40-50% of all food ready for harvest never even gets eaten.

- This short picture shows us how sick and decadent people become when they live in a society with opulent food offers and in general in an environment of a high life standard.
- People have lost the importance and value of food. They have lost the indispensable respect for food as a basic need for all humans around the globe.
- Obesity is the result of problems in life and especially of a high burdened unconscious mind full of pain, unsolved problems, ignored spiritual values and absence of love and care. It's the hungry monster in the unconscious mind.

Water

- Lack of drinking water or healthy drinking water affects 3.3 billion people.
- Half of the world's hospital beds are filled with people suffering from water related illnesses.
- People with no access to safe drinking water: 1,400,000,000.
- At least 4.000 children die every day from water-related diseases.
- Glaciers and snow cover expected to decline, reducing water availability in countries supplied by melting water. These big water reservoirs will be gone in 20 years.
- The United Nations estimates that nearly 900 million people live without clean water.
- Up to 250 million people across Africa could face water shortages by 2020
- In northern China, the water table is dropping one meter per year due to over-pumping.
- 90% of the developing world's waste water is still discharged untreated into local rivers and streams.

- All the lawmakers, ministers and head of states can't manage their resorts with a future perspective. They ignore the suffering of people. They can't even think in the network of the financial consequences for their country.
- All the lawmakers, ministers and head of states have lost their responsibility and especially any natural conscience or basic moral attitude.

- All the lawmakers, ministers and head of states, responsible for this issue, have a very narrow perception and a complete disregard for the eco-system of water and nature.
- The view politicians have ends with the length of their noose. They must have an very ego-centered attitude in their professional activities.

Humane Implications

Not to have healthy food and drinking water means for 3-4 billion people:

- No pleasure
- No joy
- No health
- No mental health
- No strength
- No wellness
- Feel ashamed
- Can't be proud
- Can not promote social health
- Can not find a feeling for quality
- Makes drinking for survival important
- Can't find respect for water
- Can't properly wash themselves and their clothes
- High risk for aggressions
- Can't contribute to society with whatever
- Are not efficient manpower
- Completely resigned
- Can not benefit from their education (if they have / had)
- Always occupied and worried to find food and water
- Always occupied with health concerns
- Have a very bad body feeling
- To enjoy and 'celebrate' sex and love is not possible
- Can't develop the force of love (for / with a partner)
- Can't educate their children in a appropriate way
- Are permanently frustrated
- Can't communicate critically about any spiritual/religious truth
- Can't benefit from the inner spiritual source of life
- Contribute enormously to environmental pollution (sewage)
- Have a low esteem of humans (being a human)
- Are running for each cent to get however and from wherever

- 🖐 Don't trust anybody
- 🖐 Inner restlessness: nervousness, lack of concentration

We can conclude that alone lack of food and healthy drinking water destroys all human values, creates illnesses, and reduces the victims to pure human biomass (or 'rats') that try to survive however, but surely thoroughly inhumane and totally undignified.

Around half of the world population must live an inhumane and undignified life whereas 15% of the world population has more than plenty of food and healthy drinking water.

If a surgeon makes a grossly negligent mistake, he gets a fine or lands in a prison. If a car driver parks on a wrong place, he gets a fine. If two people have a fight and one kills the other, the murder gets 10-25 years prison (or even more). In some states a murder can even get death penalty. But these lawmakers, ministers and head of states are 'untouchable' although they are responsible for millions of victims. For how long should these lawmakers, ministers and head of states – all together responsible for allocating food and water for 3-4 billion people – being put in prison?

Is there any of these lawmakers, ministers and head of state that suffer from hunger and lack of water or dirty drinking water?

3.2. Poverty and Misery

Global Poverty

- The UN estimates that 2.6 billion people live without proper sanitation.
- Today the sewage of 2.5-3.5 billion people goes to the soil, seas and oceans.
- 4-5 billion people live under poor and extreme poor conditions.
- 50% of all children on the earth (2.2 billion) live in poverty.
- Over 1 billon people have no housing.
- 640,000,000 children have no housing or live in slums.
- 2 billion people don't have access to electricity.
- 4 billion people have insufficient education.
- 1 billion people are analphabets or can't read or write properly.

Poverty in a country can have many reasons from natural catastrophes to economic crises and political disasters or corruption. However, the lawmakers, ministers, heads of state, kings or aristocrats they all are responsible for long term poverty.

- Insufficient education creates poverty. Poverty reproduces poverty. Collateral effects are manifold from illnesses, crimes, lack of housing and electricity or sanitation. This is the result of lawmakers, ministers and heads of states.
- 4-5 billion people live under poor and extreme poor conditions simply because politicians are incompetent and irresponsible to manage their job.
- It seems that there are a majority of lawmakers, ministers and head of states that can't think properly, have a reduced perception, can't find a complex picture about their society and folk.
- If today the sewage of 2.6 billion people goes to the nature, the waterways and seas or oceans, then mainly these politicians are the culprits. In the end the entire humanity will have elements of this contamination on their plate, especially in 30-40 years when humanity will count more than 10 billion humans.
- Should this be the result of a religion or any kind of magic culture, then this religion and culture is not a penny worth, lacks completely of human values and shows an all-round disrespect for the creation.

- Most of the poor and all extremely poor people can't buy books. They can't concentrate on psychical-spiritual development. Nobody teaches them how to explore themselves. Doing this they would need to have some specific knowledge and methods, but they don't have access to these resources.
- Not offering the necessary education to the folk for mastering life and properly doing any kind of work (for a wage), is a capital sin and must be punished. The best punishment would be that the responsible people in political office must live for the rest of their life in extreme poverty.

Economical Conditions

- 1.3 billion people earn less than US$1 per day.
- 1.4 billion people dispose of less that $1.25 per day.
- 3 billion people struggle to survive on US$ 2 per day.
- As many as 2.8 billion people on the planet struggle to survive on less than $2 a day.
- Nearly 50% of the earth population lives from less than $2.50 per day (=$75 per month).
- 80% of the earth population (5.6bn) lives from less than $10 per day (= $300 per month).
- 1-1.2 billion people live in comfortable economic conditions.
- 200,000,000 people live in very comfortable or luxurious economic conditions.
- 3.4 billion people disposes of 1% of the world's wealth.
- The richest 20% of the world population cover 76.6% of the worldwide private consumption.
- The poorest 35% cover 1.5% of the consumption volume.
- The richest 10% cover 59% of all consumption; and the poorest 10% only 0.5%.

The most important conclusion of our interest is here: 5.5 billion people don't have any knowledge and methods to explore themselves, to learn about inner life, to understand their spiritual intelligence or their unconscious mind. They don't learn how to manage life and to solve problems and conflicts. Their mind is operating on a very low and highly inefficient way. Part of this population can't spend money on books or seminars. Another group brings the money to insane (Christian) Churches. And the rest struggles to survive daily counting the pennies they have.

- Poverty is preponderantly an economic matter that lawmakers, ministers and heads of states could and should solve at least to enable people economically and educationally for a modest living. They don't!
- Considering the high number of poor and extreme poor people we must conclude that the responsible people in office only have cynical attitudes for their folk.
- The distribution of goods and services for needs is globally extremely imbalanced; most of the poor can't even think of special 'wants'.
- We have here a systemic fault in the structure and kind of governance. Also religion plays an important role, which only shows their sick and fabricated belief in order that the incumbents get a slice of the economic cake.
- We cannot thoroughly accuse that the richest 20% of the world population cover 76.6% of the worldwide private consumption. The problem is first of all a matter of the local politics and religion (of poor areas, countries).
- The fact that the richest 20% of the world population cover 76.6% of the worldwide private consumption leads to the question how it came to that. To find the right answers we must go back to colonialism, the First World War and the Second World War and from there, to today's globalization.

Wealth and Countries

- The world's wealthiest countries (approximately 1 billion people) accounted for $36.6 trillion dollars (76%).
- The world's billionaires — just 497 people (approximately 0.000008% of the world's population) — were worth $3.5 trillion (over 7% of world GDP).
- Low income countries (2.4 billion people) accounted for just $1.6 trillion of GDP (3.3%)
- Middle income countries (3 billion people) made up the rest of GDP at just over $10 trillion (20.7%).

HNWIs

- Globally, HNWIs' financial wealth grew 9.7% in 2010to reach $42.7 trillion.
- The population of HNWIs in Asia-Pacific, at 3.3 million individuals, is now the second largest in the world behind North America.
- Europe's HNWI wealth totaled $10.2 trillion after growing 7.2% in 2010, while Asia-Pacific HNWI wealth was $10.8 trillion, up 12.1%.

- North American HNWI wealth hit $11.6 trillion in 2010, up 9.1%.
- Latin America saw another modest gain (6.2%) in its HNWI population in 2010 and HNWI wealth rose 9.2%.
- (2010) the world's HNWIs were still concentrated in the U.S., Japan, and Germany.

The Wealth-X research company said in a report (17 September, 2012): "The number of people with at least $30 million in their pockets grew to 187,380 (total wealth $25.8 trillion) – a sum bigger than the combined size of the U.S. and Chinese economies. At the same time billionaires became even richer. Their number grew 9.4 percent to 2,160 people with the combined wealth of $6.2 trillion, according to the Singapore-based firm that provides intelligence on the ultra-rich to banks, fundraisers and luxury retailers." [85]

It is too simple if some people claim that there must be a limit for wages, bonuses, and wealth. This will not solve the global economic imbalance. More important is the question: How did and do the rich and HNWI make so much money? And: What do they do with so much money?

The top-CEO of – for example – Goldman Sachs is not the owner of this bank. Therefore he is a top-paid executor of orders from the owners. The same we can say for every bank. Who are the owners (the main shareholders) and what is their religion? This is the core question.

- The ways (private) banks operate on the global stage is characterized by total absence of ethics and moral attitudes. They abuse every possible change to multiply their money.
- If there are a few individuals that become very rich, then there are always other people that lose money and people that fall into poverty.
- Blankfein, CEO Goldmann Sachs, says: "I am just a banker doing God's work." [86] This is the Jewish-Zionist World Governance (Dominance), the worst and most satanic development in the history of humanity with roots that are around 3000 years old (Genesis I, verse 28).
- It seems that there is no European politician that sees how these Jewish-Zionist masters of economics on the stage behind the curtains destroy Europe, European societies (throwing the folks into poverty) and the entire world.

Poverty in Industrialized Countries

[85] http://rt.com/business/news/report-wealth-trillion-325/
[86] http://blogs.wsj.com/marketbeat/2009/11/09/goldman-sachs-blankfein-on-banking-doing-gods-work/

- Currently 3.7 million children are living in poverty across Britain overall.
- Out of the 22% (13 million British people), 5.8 million suffer from 'deep poverty' this means they earn less than 40% of the median income.
- In the countries of the European Union, the rate of poverty varies between 10% and 23%.
- Countries with the highest poor population: France, Germany, Italy, Poland, Spain, and the UK.
- 11.5 million Germans live in poverty (population: 82 million).
- Roughly 100 million people in the EU live below the poverty level or are in danger of doing so.
- In 2009 14.6 per cent of the population of Switzerland was in danger of becoming impoverished, which means around 1,140,000 people out of a total population of 7,800,000. 6.7% of the Swiss population is affected by strong material deprivation.
- About 9 million people live in poverty in Spain (population: 45 million), many without legal support or access to information to enable them to assert their rights. New report says 25% of Spain's population lives below poverty line.
- In the United States 2012, over 50 million people live below the poverty line; one in five children in the United States live in poverty. (44 million in 2010).
- 3.5% of U.S. households experience hunger. Some people in these households frequently skip meals or eat too little, sometimes going without food for a whole day. 9.6 million people, including 3 million children, live in these homes.
- In the U.S., households with incomes below the poverty line: 14.3%.
- New official data has revealed; "more than eight million Italians, constituting almost 14% of the country's population, live in relative poverty. From among the same number, more than 3 million, over 5% of the whole population, live in 'absolute poverty'; every one out of five Italian households lives under the poverty line.

- These developments are the result of the mentioned banking world. The supreme masters of economics already have taken away the power of all head of states and their ministers.
- A few years ago probably all politicians did not understand what was going on in the banking world. They were all naïve and incompetent in economic matters. They have all fallen into the trap of the Goldman Sachs type banking activities.

It would not be surprising if today most politicians still do not understand what happens on this economic stage. They have not learnt the lesson or they look helplessly or cowardly away.

Humane Consequences of Poverty

How do people living in poverty feel? How is their daily life of not-well-being? Let's look at this:

- Helpless, powerless, hopeless, desperate, passive, distrusting
- Very low self-esteem, no genuine self-identity, no self-realization
- Fighting for food, drinking water, and some cash every single day
- Fear of violence, disease, illnesses, lack of food and water
- Unable to think analytically about their situation
- Running after every dollar just to be able to buy something necessary
- Resigned and consumed with fatalistic attitudes
- Turning towards criminality to get some cash
- Life experiences full of misery, suffering, misfortune, sadness
- Unable to understand and communicate for solutions
- Easily suggestible for radicalism, fatalistic and dogmatic religion
- Increasing readiness for aggression, unrest, riots, and revolution

Poverty has immense humane and social consequences with long-term effects:

- Poverty makes homeless; homeless people feel lost
- Poverty creates sadness, despair, frustration, aggression, crimes etc.
- Can not develop themselves and grow for a positive self-identity
- Can not find constructive personal expressions and life style
- Can not develop constructive personal motivation for projects
- Can not form any positive life aim
- Have a low esteem of humans (being a human)
- Do not feel wellness, joy, zest for life, no personal pride
- Have high risk of illnesses, infections, disease, etc.
- High risk of aggressions, crimes, addictions, accidents, etc.
- Can not live intimate moments with a partner safely
- Can not relax and recover in a safe way
- Can not experience or promote social health
- Can not give the family members a family-identity
- Can not celebrate personal / family events
- Can not contribute to a social life / to society

- Have a permanent fear of being unprotected
- Can be more easily exploited and abused; don't trust anybody
- No orderly washing, cooking, eating, sleeping, spending personal time
- Personal psychical-spiritual development is impossible
- Responsibility and contributions for society is impossible
- Are unable to constructively master life and to solve their life problems
- Feel ashamed, inferior, weak, vulnerable, depressed
- Can't wash themselves and their clothes properly
- 'Safe sex' is not possible
- To enjoy and 'celebrate' sex as an expression of love is not possible
- Can't develop the force of love (for / with a partner)
- Can't educate their children in an appropriate manner
- Can't contribute to a better local community
- Their aspiration: at least a dirty, stinking hut is better than nothing
- Can't communicate critically about any spiritual/religious truth
- Can't benefit from the inner unconscious source of life
- Contribute enormously to environmental pollution (sewage)

This is the result of tens of thousands of incompetent and ignorant politicians, members of parties, lawmakers, ministers, and head of states in the European Union as well as in the United States and elsewhere.

- Most lawmakers, ministers, and head of states in the European Union as well as in the United States and elsewhere entirely ignore the human values, the real life of the citizens, and the state of the whole humanity and the planet. They all have lost their responsibility.
- Democracy has converted into a perverse hidden satanic dictatorship. The big media, also in the hands of the same economic rulers, fabricate their 'information' in a way that does not show the real effects and its insane roadmap. The entire humanity is cheated, deceived, exploited, dehumanized and enslaved.
- When politicians, especially lawmakers or heads of states, address the people, then we see a theatre full of lies, empty words, and show. That's outrageous!

3.3. Agricultural Land, Forest, Oceans

Agriculture

- 500 million small farmers suffer from hunger partly because their right to land (and water) is violated.
- Industrial agriculture has destroyed around 200 million small farmer businesses.
- India: the average landholding fell from 2.6 hectares in 1960 to 1.4 hectares in 2000.
- Crop yields decrease by up to 30% in Central and South Asia.
- Wheat, grain, corn, rice, cocoa, fruit juices, sugar, staples, meat, and coffee are now the new fields for speculators (banks). The consequence: 15-40% price increase.
- 70 to 90% of the available water is used by the agriculture industry.
- 25-35% of all plant and animal species at increased risk of extinction if temperatures rise between 1.5 and 2.5 C. This will also affect agricultural production.

- That's the work of the internationally operating corporations, backed from the economic masters. And there is no lawmaker, minister or head of state that has stopped or can stop such development.
- The globalization, once celebrated as the savior of the world and provider of a high living standard, is today unmasked as the 'invisible hand' of the Zionist programs controlled by some special private banks to exploit and dominate the entire humanity.
- The dogs bodies of these banks are everywhere in public banks, in special positions close to the governments (e.g. as advisor or director of a sub-department). This 'friendship networks' starts at Harvard and Co and continues with a position in one of these banks to later being 'elected' for special tasks in the political apparatus (e.g. European Central Bank, President of Italy, etc.). This is systemic corruption everywhere.
- A majority of lawmaker, ministers or heads of state have converted into puppets, well paid and with perfectly orchestrated reputations to be used (abused) by the television channels and newspapers. And most of the uninformed folks with a narrow and selected content in their inner screen are moved full of respect and hope for salvation.

Arable Land Loss

- About 2 billion hectares of soil, equivalent to 15% of the Earth's land area (an area larger than the United States and Mexico combined) have been degraded through human activities.
- It takes approximately 500 years to replace 25 millimeters (1 inch) of topsoil lost to erosion. The minimal soil depth for agricultural production is 150 millimeters. From this perspective, productive fertile soil is a non-renewable, endangered ecosystem.
- Up to 30 million hectares of (agricultural) land (the size of Italy) is lost each year due to environmental degradation, industrialization and urbanization.
- The average landholding fell from 2.6 hectares in 1960 to 1.4 hectares in 2000.
- Worldwide, soil erosion has caused abandonment of 4.3 million km2 of arable land during the last four decades.
- UN: Food and agricultural organization, 75 billion tons of soil, the equivalent of nearly 10 million hectares of arable land, is lost p.a.
- Climate change is a major factor in damages to agriculture land.
- Over the past 40 years, approximately 30% of the world's cropland has become unproductive.

- We will have every 12-14 years one billion more people on earth. The end of the population growth can't be foreseen. At the same time the arable land decreases and the quality of the soil as well decrease due to contamination (chemicals).
- We could conclude that lawmakers and ministers or head of states do not understand that people need food and most of the food production depends on arable land with healthy soil.
- It seems that a huge majority of politicians, especially lawmakers, are not informed about this extremely dangerous development. Some head of states understood the criticality and rented for 100 years or bought (have stolen by means of corruption) arable land in Africa. The history of colonization gets a new picture.

Oceans: Fish and Sea Fruit

- Fishing resources are rapidly decreasing because of excessive exploitation.
- One billion people in the world depend on fish for their principal source of protein.
- The seas and oceans are extremely exploited; fishing resources are destroyed.

- Fishes and sea fruits are 'eating' unimaginable chemical and drug cocktails of residue.
- 1 billion people will lose access to fish for (principal source of protein)

- Politicians, lawmakers and heads of state do not understand that fish and sea fruit are an essential and necessary part of nutrition that people need.
- These responsible people in politics can't think in complex networks. They don't see that contamination of the seas and oceans leads to contaminated fish and sea fruit that people will eat and also the following generations will need to eat fish and sea fruit; and in the end all the people will be contaminated – also these blinded politicians.
- We also realize that despite of ten thousands of regulations for the citizens and society, the governments of EU and US are unable or disinterested to stop the over-exploitation of fish resources.

Exploitation of Raw Resources

In February 2011, at the World Economic Forum in Davos (Switzerland), the UN Secretary-General Ban Ki-Moon stated that "the world is committing collective global suicide by consuming resources without replenishing them and warned that we are running out of the most important resource of all: Time."

- A strong word from an international authority that makes clear: Politicians, lawmakers, ministers, and heads of state are incompetent, irresponsible, ignorant, abettors of collective global suicide by consuming resources without replenishing them.
- The owners of the big corporations that are the active part of this collective global suicide (as they are the exploiters in the interest of maximized profit) must be impeached and punished with a minimum of 20 years prison. It's not possible as everywhere are self-interested coward politicians.
- Most corporate groups don't care about environmental destruction or contamination. The 3,000 most important corporate groups produce environmental damages of nearly $2 trillion each year (UN report); other sources say $3-5 trillion.
- Lawmakers create more and more laws to limit the freedom of people, the freedom of doing business, and to reduce the citizens' privacy. There must be a toilet for handicapped people on all premises. Countless regulations inhibit pioneering business. But these corporations can damage without consequences the entire planet, its resources, and in the end the health of people. Perverse politicians!

🖐 The monstrous greedy apparatus of politics is not better than these corporations: for every little movement of something they require a tax. These lawmakers, ministers and heads of state have never enough money for their duties, their sick megalomania and warmonger drive, and hidden personal interests. They are not better than the Goldman Sachs and Co: the same amoral behavior, the same radical attitudes, the same cynicism, and the same unlimited exploitation by all means.

The owners (top shareholders) and the CEOs of these 3,000 most important corporate groups must be morally seen as criminals. They must be punished and these corporations must pay for the damages they produce every year.

Facts due to Over-Exploitation

- Most of the bees around the world are sick and billions are dying every year. Bees pollinate over 90 types of vegetables, fruits and grain.
- Most resources are exorbitantly overexploited and within 40 years will be destroyed.
- Carbon dioxide (CO_2) emissions per year approximately, in tons: 183,000,000,000
- Desertification per year (hectares): more than 12,000,000
- Forest loss per year approximately: 7-10,000,000 (hectares)
- Species that become extinct per year: more than 100,000
- Days until end of oil: 15,000 days = 42 years (if consumed at current rates).

🖐 We have here again some examples; hundreds more could be mentioned. It shows the same basic incapacity and character of politicians: amoral, passive, ignorant, evading from responsibility, lazy-minded, unwilling to learn, and always trivializing the seriousness of criticalities. A doctor would be fired from the hospital. Children would have to repeat a school year if they fail is learning and performance. And an individual that would directly produce such damages would end in a prison. But politicians can't be made responsible for their failure.

🖐 The political decisions and activities are preponderantly re-active. Politicians are unable to consider future developments and the consequences for humanity and the planet. They totally lack pioneering thinking and spiritual values. In the future such kind of people can't be allowed to get any responsible position in the political apparatus. Such politicians are not even good enough for cleaning streets and pavement (footways).

3.4. Health and Health Care

Health Care Overview

- More than one billion (1.5 billion) people are overweight
- 2.3 billion adults will be overweight by 2015
- In the European Union over 30 million are undernourished
- More than a billion people suffer from diarrheal diseases
- Huge illnesses caused by dirty water and malnutrition
- Hunger causes a variety of illnesses and millions of deaths
- Alcohol is a major cause of serious illnesses
- Chemical products and fine dust everywhere influence health
- Health care expenditure per day: $7,300,000,000
- 1 billion have no access to health services and another 4 billion only to poor health services.
- Every year 1.5 million children die due to illnesses caused by dirty water.
- Every year 11 million children under the age of 5 die, half of them due to malnutrition.
- Over 9.5 million people die each year due to infectious diseases – nearly all live in developing countries.
- In the European Union more than 30 million people are undernourished, especially people in hospitals and nursing homes, but also 5-15 % of the population in general.
- Germany: Every year around 600,000 hospital patients get infected with dangerous germs. Up to 40,000 patients die every year as a direct result of insufficient hygiene in hospitals.
- Medicare fraud costs Americans $60 billion each year.
- Approximately 46 million Americans do not currently have any health insurance at all. Approximately 41% of working age Americans either have medical bill problems or are currently paying off medical debt.

- The picture as a whole shows clearly: Politicians don't care about the consequences of living standard (opulent or deficient), lack of education (for mastering life), healthy environment, fulfilling ways of living, and economic balance.
- There are plenty of possibilities to reduce within 5 years all factors that produce health care costs. Minimum 50% of this expenditure could be saved. But most politicians are already reduced in their mind capacity, dehumanized, and robots of the rigid political apparatus.

🖎 It is breathtaking how such people with miserable and amoral character, emptiness of soul, low mind qualities, highly skilled as blabbermouths, and highest egomania are allowed to sit on a political chair and to use a pencil and paper that the citizens have to pay. The indispensable use of electricity, probably with a volume of the production capacity of a nuclear power station, also the citizens have to pay.

Obesity

- 50.1% of adults across the 27 EU nations are overweight or obese based on the BMI (body mass index) values.
- 2010: more than 72 million adults in the USA suffer from obesity which has turned the condition into a major public health threat.
- Money spent due to obesity in the USA per month: estimated $80,000,000 and per year approximately $1,000,000,000; on weight loss programs: $35,000,000 per month.
- 🖎 A high living standard as well as a very low living standard promotes obesity. Another main cause of obesity is the monstrous content of the unconscious mind that permanently must be tranquilized with eating. It seems that politicians have no idea about how the mind is constructed and how it works.

Chemical products

- Around 100,000 chemical products are used in Europe. More than 700 carcinogenic elements are present everywhere in the environment of everyday life. They can be found in food, water, soil, air, furniture, electrical devices, computers, carpets, cars, paintings and clothes. Heavy metals in high concentration can also be found in animal bowels, fish and seafood.
- Poisonous substances can be found in food, in the soil, in the air, in the sea, and then in the body of humans.
- About one in three people in the UK will get cancer due to contamination.
- One of four German people in the future will die due to cancer.
- The animals we eat are given large amounts of antibiotics and this not just when they are sick: healthy animals can be fed antibiotics every day because it makes them grow bigger and faster. As a result, people are getting sicker and sick people are taking longer to get well. The day will come that antibiotics will be over – thanks to chicken farms.
- The sewage that goes into the sea is full of traces of medicines. When eating fish we take in these chemical elements into our bodies. What will be the result for pregnant women and children in the future?

- 11 million Canadians go to hospital every year due to food poisoning (especially from chicken).

🖐 In matters of health and contamination most politicians, especially ministers and heads of state play the 'blind cow'. And the citizens pay the price. This is 'political action' or 'political responsibility'.

🖐 For each single item politicians declare that the contamination is on a very low and riskless level. Unfortunately politicians also here are unable to think in complex networks: Nobody can predict the effects of the cocktail of toxic elements people eat or respire every day. But this risk is 100% real and very explosive.

Results of Living Standard

- 1,200,000 suicides per year around the globe; that is 1,200,000 human beings!
- Abortions worldwide: more than 40 million per year.
- Over one in 5 Americans has a personality disorder due to alcohol or drug abuse.
- In Europe people spend €11 billion on ice cream, €50 billion on cigarettes, and €105 billion on alcohol.
- Alcohol is a major cause of serious illnesses and early deaths. Exaggerated consumption of alcohol plays a serious role in traffic accidents, crimes, traffic violations, home and working place accidents, arsons, etc.
- Stress, work stress, time pressure and traffic jams result in people constantly being tense. Blood pressure, blood sugar and serum lipid levels increase with stress. Stress promotes cardiovascular diseases such as arteriosclerosis, high blood pressure, heart attacks and strokes.

🖐 Politicians talk a lot about living standard and economic growth. Every month they make an emotional theatre when the GDP is low, at zero, or decreasing. But they don't know anything about the damages in mind and soul their growth madness implies through the ways of living stimulated by consumption.

🖐 The way lawmakers, ministers, and heads of state deal with the problems of 'health, health care, and contamination' reveals their attitudes that are not much different from the banking world practices (betting, casino, toxic papers, speculations, Ponzi schemes, derivatives, profit greed, abusing people's naivety, credulity, and lack of knowledge, etc.).

Nobody shall identify that diseases of the respiratory system are in the most part a result of completely different carcinogenic sources (and not from smoking):

- Pollution (fine dust)
- Contamination
- Chemicals everywhere in daily life
- Heating
- Oil refineries
- Chemical factories
- Coal mining industry
- Gold mining industry
- Other mines sourcing for raw material (operating with chemicals)
- Chemical substances in goods
- Chemicals in food and drinks
- Asbestos
- Agriculture industry (chemicals such as pesticides and fertilizers)
- Fine dust emissions from cars (diesel, break pads, tires, tarmac)
- Fine dust and chemical emissions from airplanes
- Fine dust from pavement (car traffic)
- Fine dust from mines and surface mining
- Chemical emissions from the auto industry
- Chemical emissions from the chemical and paint industry
- Pesticides in the agriculture and cotton industry, etc.
- Carcinogenic toxic elements (to promote addiction) added to tobacco

- The visible damages today of contamination are a result of emissions from the last 30-40 years. With every billion more people on earth the sum of all contaminations will immensely increase. It's practically a mathematical calculation that tells us what will happen in the coming decades: hundreds of millions (or even some billions) of people will die due to the complex contamination. That means: The responsible politicians, lawmakers, and heads of state commit already, today a creeping genocide. In the end these people can't be identified as the culprits.

- Contamination damages health and the mind; the mind capacities become reduced – are already 30-50% reduced by a majority of people today. This is what politicians and the masters of economics want: people must suffer, must be occupied, and must become a reduced mind capacity. The benefit: politicians and the masters of economics can do what they want in the interest of multiplying money (for themselves) and the manifold ego-interests.

❧ As contamination also heavily damages and even destroys the eco-systems and with that the entire planet, all these responsible politicians commit decide and herewith they can be identified as the collaborators of the economic deicide – the Jewish-Zionist madness.

The creation of the scapegoat

- The smoker is at fault.
- The smoker is the bad person.
- The smoker makes others ill.
- The smoker is a danger for society.
- The smoker kills other people ("passive smokers").
- One has to beware of smokers.
- One has to denounce smokers (when they smoke in prohibited places).
- One has to always give severe punishment, if there is a lack of obedience.

❧ These false and cowardly politicians created the anti-smoking law in order to hide the million times worse and much more dangerous contamination.

❧ It's an absolute perverse crime how politicians dramatize and shock the people with 'smoker-lungs' and at the same time they trivialize any risk of local and global contamination. This is the true face we find everywhere in political activities.

Mental Disorder and Disease

Mental health problems are costing Scotland £10.7 billion a year… The report said almost one in six working people in Scotland have poor mental health, such as depression or anxiety…. They also estimated employers lose £439 million a year through absence caused by mental health issues; 20% more than in 2004-05. The total loss rises to £2 billion a year if other factors, such as staff attending work but being less productive because of hidden problems, are included.

Dementia: The total estimated worldwide costs of dementia will exceed 1% of global GDP in 2010, at $604 billion. About 70% of the costs occur in Western Europe and North America. The report revealed that the number of people with dementia will double by 2030, and more than triple by 2050.

Increasingly psychical disorders are the reason for absences at the work place. Thus, the psychical state of workers produces damages to the economy in the billions.

According to statistics from Germany, in 2006, depression caused damages worth €26.7 billion to the economy.

The consumption of antidepressants has tripled in the last 10 years in Spain... The spending on antidepressants represents 47% of the pharmaceutical spending on mental health in Spain.

In the European Union, the most common disorders are anxiety disorders and depression. By 2020 it is expected to be the number one illness in the developed world. "Social anxiety disorder is the most common anxiety disorder and the third most common mental disorder in the U.S., after depression and alcohol dependence."

The WHO has determined that 58,000 people commit suicide every year in the European Union. "In the last 45 years suicide rates have increased by 60% worldwide ... one death every 40 seconds."

People that keep on working with depression instead of seeking treatment cause damages of €9 billion. A person suffering from depression at the workplace performs half an hour to two hours less than a healthy colleague. €5.2 billion is the sum of the direct costs of treatment. On top of that there is the cost from the incapacity to work. The total sum for the economy amounts to €15.2 billion up to €22 billion. Every year depression drives around 14,000 people to commit suicide.

One in 100 adolescents between the age of 14 and 18 falls into the grip of anorexia, while 2.4% develop bulimia. Other figures are: Chronic anxiety (6.0%), diabetes (5.9%), depression (5.3%) and asthma (4.3%). All these problems, except for diabetes, have a higher presence in women than in men.

According to data released by the United Nations, three out of every 100 Spaniards is a cocaine addict, making Spain the most addicted country in Europe...19% of all European cocaine addicts are in Spain.

In 2008, with over $14 billion in sales, antipsychotics became the single top-selling therapeutic class of prescription drugs in the United States, surpassing drugs used to treat high cholesterol and acid reflux.

Once upon a time, antipsychotics were reserved for a relatively small number of patients with hard-core psychiatric diagnoses – primarily schizophrenia and bipolar disorder – to treat such symptoms as delusions, hallucinations, or formal thought disorder. Today, it seems, everyone is taking antipsychotics. Parents are told that their unruly kids are in fact bipolar, and in need of anti-psychotics, while old people with dementia are dosed, in large numbers, with drugs once reserved largely for schizophrenics. Americans with symptoms ranging from chronic depression to anxiety to insomnia are now being prescribed anti-psychotics at rates that seem to indicate a national mass psychosis.

Most people around the globe are highly affected from mental disorder (disease) and from deformed or degenerated psychical functions:

- Depression
- Social phobia
- Chronic anxiety
- Stuttering
- Sleeping disorder
- Alcoholism
- Headache and migraine
- Speech disorder
- Personality disorder
- Behavior disorder
- Learning difficulties
- Family disruption
- Squalidness (waywardness)
- Aggressive behavior, violence
- Addictions (drugs, medicine, gambling, etc.)
- Morbid (psychopathic) relationships
- Neuroticism
- Narcissism
- Psychopathy
- Psychosis
- Perversion
- Sadism
- Emotional stress
- Megalomania
- Aberration
- Schizophrenia
- Religious psychosis

🖐 The psychiatric and psychotherapeutic madness to therapy by giving drugs (ignoring the real problems) has converted into a new lifestyle: Solve all problems with drugs! But it doesn't solve anything; it makes everything worse in human's life course. Politicians like this (people will be lifelong followed from their problems and continuously become reduced in mind capacity) and even promote it strategically.

🖐 Another aspect shows us the adoration of the capitalistic lifestyle together with the worship of an unlimited increase of living standard. The collective mental state is sign enough that something is going totally wrong here. But politicians have 'rose-colored' classes. Even worse: A huge majority of politicians hate the truth, the genuine human values, and the inner psychical-spiritual potentials and its holistic (archetypal) development.

3.5. Contamination, Waste, Sewage

Oceans and Water Supply

According to a new report by the World Bank, urban rubbish generation is set to increase twofold over the next 15 years … Household waste is set to soar from its current 1.3 billion tons to 2.2 billion by 2025, while the annual cost of managing this mountain of rubbish will rise from $205 billion to $375 billion … The challenges are going to be enormous, on a scale, if not greater than, the challenges we are currently facing with climate change. It's a relatively silent problem that is growing daily … The rubbish problem not only can be compared to climate change, but is also contributing to it. Greenhouse gas emissions from rubbish disposal, estimated at 5% of total emissions, must also be reduced, the report says. Methane from landfill sites accounts for 12% of total global methane emissions.

🖙 Politicians like 'relatively silent problems'. They don't have to take action despite of these growing daily. Problems are annoying and would require to learn, to clearly inform the citizens, and to find pioneering solutions. But nothing much or nothing relevant is 'pioneering' in the political fields.

Oceans: Sewage and garbage (plastic), poisoning chemical elements, cesium, pesticide, heavy metal and mercury, oil pest, chemicals for agriculture, etc.

🖙 Lawmakers, ministers, and heads of state must go back to primary (or secondary) school: If today hundreds of thousands of millions of tons of sewage, waste, chemicals, pharmaceutics, and toxic metals go to the oceans, how many tons will be in the oceans in 10, 20, 30, and 40 years? Don't forget to multiply the increase by the billions of more people every 12-14 years that will live on earth!

Oceans, seas, lakes, rivers, streams and groundwater are contaminated by remains of consumed medicaments: 50-90% go to the sewage, medicaments in urine and feces, also from showering: pain killer, antibiotics, hormones, tranquilizers, cholesterol reducers, medicaments for epilepsy and cancer, birth control pills, and other drugs.

Soaps, shampoos, cosmetics and perfumes contain chemicals that disappear down the drain, and go to the water in the nature: elements from cosmetics, perfumes and hair products. Fishes and sea fruits are eating this chemical soup.

Farmers give veterinary drugs to their animals, including large amounts of antibiotics. Drug-contaminated sewage sludge is sold as farm fertilizer. Later, these chemicals disappear down the drain and go to the water in the nature. Fishes and sea fruits are eating this chemical soup.

Already today and much more in the future, people around the globe have the chemical cocktail in the fish or sea fruits on their plate.

🖐 Let's hope that all politicians and people in political offices will now be aware of the chemicals, pharmaceutics, and nano-elements of plastic in the fish they have weekly on their plate. They will not due to the defense mechanisms and their stubbornness! Stubbornness is a power fight strategy.

The artificial female sexual hormones in the anti-baby pill have lasting effects beyond the sewage plant treatment facilities, turning male fish into females.

A teaspoon of fully concentrated Estradiol is enough to cause the male trout in a river section of ten meters deep, twenty meters wide and ten kilometers long, to turn into females.

Apart from hormones from the pill, fish also absorb painkillers, antibiotics and cell poisons from cancer treatments. Even medicines to treat cholesterol levels are now readily found in pike fish.

Even at low doses, the drug residues in water stop cells from reproducing.

Fish are experiencing reproductive problems as a result of chemical contamination.

Beyond having their sperm damaged, some fish are actually changing sexes due to chemical and medicament elements.

🖐 Maybe we should shock and can awaken the male politicians with a horror scenario: in 100 years 50% of the Western men will have inactive sperms. Half of the other 50% will have damaged sperms and procreate deformed humans (one leg, only 2 fingers, 3 legs, 50% reduced brain volume, organ failures, etc.).

In the middle of the equatorial Pacific Ocean sharks, tuna and other top-of-the-food fish are half the size and their population is 80% smaller in numbers than they were 50 years ago. More than 100 different pharmaceutical compounds have been detected around the world, affecting fish and wildlife everywhere.

India's rivers are full of dangerous pharmaceuticals. One Indian River where 90 different pharmaceutical companies dump their waste tested positive for over 21 active drug ingredients. Immeasurable amounts of sewage go to the nature, the soil, the water streams, and the oceans. It is estimated that 75% of India's surface water is now contaminated by human and agricultural waste.

At least 46 million Americans are drinking water contaminated with trace amounts of pharmaceuticals. All kinds of drugs are being found in the bodies of fish near major U.S. cities.

Researchers found drugs for high cholesterol, allergies, high blood pressure, bipolar disorder and depression in the livers and tissue of fish.

Antidepressants, blood pressure and diabetes medications, anticonvulsants, oral contraceptives, hormone replacement therapy drugs, chemotherapy drugs, antibiotics, heart medications and even codeine are all showing up in the water supplies of American Cities.

🖋 In the future people will not need to buy pharmaceutics anymore. They will get them for free with every fish based meal. Also politicians will get free everything they need for any illness or disease with their fish based meals.

Sea-life faces extinction, unprecedented in history, because of waste.

Carbon is being absorbed by the ocean at an alarming rate.

Groundwater pollution is essentially permanent. Water recycles extremely slowly underground, too slowly to flush out or dilute toxic chemicals. Water that enters an aquifer remains there for an average of 1,400 years, compared to only 16 days for rivers.

90% of the developing world's waste-water, is still discharged untreated into local rivers and streams.

Approximately 150 billion tiny pieces with an average weight of 1.8 milligrams, that is approximately 500 tons of tiny plastic pieces from waste, are currently swimming in the Mediterranean Sea. They serve as food for plankton and therefore for the fish and can easily land on our plates at the dinner table.

🖝 It is beyond imagination how the lawmakers, ministers and heads of state ignore this time bomb. Either they perfectly know about this immense problem but ignore it - this would make them into criminals, and culprits to the creeping genocide. Or they don't know it because they don't have time to search for such information or they don't get such information from their experts and advisors. In that case the entire political apparatus is blocking everything that promotes human evolution with human values. What for do we need such a costly apparatus?

Livestock

Less and less medicine is working to combat illnesses. Antibiotics resistance will become a global problem. The responsibility lies in the massive use of medicines in the industrial livestock farming. There are enough loopholes for producers with highly criminal intentions.

Around the globe every year millions of tones of antibiotics are being used. Herewith industrial livestock farming is one of the most important markets for the pharmaceutical industry.

In Germany, nothing related to livestock husbandry is under control. Organized crime dominates. Global corporations don't care what happens to their animals. They see them in monetary values. It is all about the profit, 15% profit that needs to be retrieved. It doesn't matter how this is achieved.

🖝 The problem could easily be solved: All people on this globe eat 65% less meat. A politician that would advice his folk to do so would lose his job and probably ruined from the masters of the big food corporations.
🖝 There is no other solution. But also the people would react with rage and totally reject such a solution. Therefore the people must be forced to reduce their consumption by reducing their wages by 50%. And those who protect must be put in a re-educational camp in the North of China to be conditioned by being happy to eat just rice and some drinking water.

Illustration of Contamination

As most politicians and most people are not informed about the dramatic state and development of contamination, we will give here a few examples. Some examples have a strange chemical character. Don't bother, simply interpret it as 'contaminating element'. But breath deeply before you read the following list! Prepare a whiskey with ice or a chocolate bar!

- 60% of the most hazardous liquid waste in the United States – 34 billion liters of solvents, heavy metals, and radioactive materials – is injected into deep groundwater via thousands of injection wells...
- 2.6-3 billion people have no access to sanitation; no local sewage treatment!
- Lack of toilets and sanitation facilities costs India nearly $54 billion a year.
- About 200 million tons of human waste is discharged into waterways yearly.
- Toxic chemicals released by industries into the air, land, water: 650,000,000 tons of sewage, 60,000 tons of mercury, 36,000 tons of phosphates is dumped into the Mediterranean each year.
- 7,000,000 of tons of plastic debris, industrial chemicals, agricultural waste, petroleum, etc., end up in the oceans every year.
- 250 billion of small plastic pieces are swimming in the oceans; and 500 tons swim in the Mediterranean Sea.
- 46,000 pieces of plastic debris swim in each square kilometer of ocean.
- Medicine residues go through the toilette into the water circles and via fish back into the human food chain.
- Global emission of carbon dioxide will increase until 2030 by 40% up to 40,000,000,000 tons (2006: 29,000,000,000 tons).
- The increase, a half-billion extra tons of carbon pumped into the air, was almost certainly the largest absolute jump in any year since the Industrial Revolution.
- Acidification of the oceans is a major threat to marine life and humanity's food supply. It affects marine life and in turn it affects the number of fish.
- The beautiful island in the Maldives that's been reduced to a pile of rubbish: Three-quarters of a million tourists flock to the pristine, white beaches every year. The Maldives dumps upwards of 330 tons of rubbish on the island every day. Each visitor generates 3.5kg of waste per day. Clouds of pungent, toxic smoke rising from open fires, piles of filth made up of plastic bottles, crisp packets and consumer detritus ... environmental damage ... large amounts of asbestos, lead and other toxic metals have been dumped into the lagoons ... sending soot and carbon

dioxide billowing into the air … The freighters are now ferrying debris to India instead!

- There is the rubbish that comes from the land, delivered by run-off, storm water drains and the wind-blown rubbish that people leave behind. There is also ocean-based debris; it includes fishing lines and nets, offshore oil and gas rig/platform debris, waste from merchant ships, ferries and cruise liners and garbage from recreational and tourist vessels. Every day, ships jettison 5,500,000 million pieces of rubbish into the sea.

- An estimated 14 billion pounds of trash, much of it plastic is dumped in the world's oceans yearly.

- Today, Americans generate 10,500,000 tons of plastic waste a year but recycle only 1 or 2 % of it.

- Electricity generation in the United States: "The United States 400-plus coal-fired power plants emit more toxins into the air than any other single source … Half of all Americans live within 30 miles of a coal-burning power plant, which in addition to mercury, emit more than 361,000 tons of other toxins including vanadium, barium, zinc, lead, chromium, arsenic, nickel, hydrogen fluoride, hydrochloric acid, ammonia and selenium."

- The worldwide fishing industry dumps an estimated 150,000 tons of plastic into the ocean each year, including packaging, plastic nets, lines, and buoys.

- A plastic milk jug takes 1 million years to decompose. A plastic cup can take 50 - 80 years to decompose.

- The traffic emissions: Many tons of oil drops of vehicles go every day into nature (soil and drinking water): rate of cancer, asthma, depressions, stress, and simple tickle in one's throat, etc., is increasing.

- Fine dust from cars, industry, oil heating, trains, chemical industry, oil industry, coal and gold mining, etc., produces immense illnesses (respiratory tract) and cancer, millions of times more than smoking.

- The chemical industry, working 24 hours daily, let into the air thousands of tons of poisonous emissions.

- Toxic chemicals released by industries into our air, land, and water in January 2011: 870,000 tons.

- Carbon dioxide (CO_2) released in January 2011: 2,000,000,000 tons.

- An estimated 90 tons of gold has been sold in 2010. The dark side: scrupulous exploitation, environmental damages and serious violation of human rights. Gigantic areas of land and exorbitant amounts of water are needed to exploit gold. The extensive contamination is horrifying. Cyanide is used to separate gold from rocks. Cyanide is highly poisonous and deadly. One gram of gold is found in 5 tons of rocks.

- 190,000 tons of asbestos, produced in Canada, are shipped to India, Pakistan, Indonesia, Thailand and Vietnam despite global bans of asbestos. Asbestos is a toxic mineral that causes lung cancer. Asbestos is responsible for 90,000 deaths per year worldwide.

- With over 20 million tones of nitric oxide every year the shipping industry outnumbers the air traffic industry tenfold; with 12 million tons of sulphur dioxide even by one hundred. Carbon dioxide stays in the atmosphere for up to one hundred years. Sulphur dioxide contributes massively to the contamination of the air close to the coasts, especially around areas with harbors.
- Russia has a long list of environmental problems. The total amount of hazardous waste stockpiled in the country is over 30 billion tons. Reversing the environmental damage is a large and complicated topic.
- Pollutants come from cleaning products, furniture, cars, building materials, and the much-debated odorless radon gas.
- The accelerated problem of air pollution is determined not only by the increase of the carbon dioxide in the atmosphere but the phenomenon is closely connected with deforestation as well. Trees absorb the carbon dioxide from the atmosphere and in turn release oxygen but with the reduction of the wooded areas like forests and jungles this causes new issues.
- Ships and cruise ships are major water pollutants that are responsible for the deaths of about 65,000 people every year. Calculate for 50 years ahead!
- Power plants that generate the electricity which we rely on everywhere in our society cause about three and half thousand lung cancer cases and over thirty-five thousand heart attacks and this is just in the United States on a yearly basis.
- The chemicals in the water evaporate and fall back on the ground in the form of acid rains.
- There are 74 different kinds of pesticides that have been found in groundwater, which is used today as potential drinking water.
- Toddlers born to expectant mothers exposed to a common chemical found in insecticides show a slower brain development, a new US study says. Pyrethroid insecticides, including PBO and Permethrin, are commonly used in many homes.
- Space debris: There are now more than 370,000 pieces of junk compared with 1,100 satellites in low-Earth orbit (LEO), between 490 and 620 miles above the planet.
- US estimations calculate $40-100 billion for environmental and economical damages from the oil-spill in the Gulf of Mexico.
- Dioxin is present everywhere in the environment. Dioxin is ultra-poisonous. Improper recycling of electronic scrap produces enormous environmental damages.

- The 3,000 most important enterprises produce environmental damages ('lateral effects') of approximately €2 billion (unknown if per day or month or year).
- Each year, approximately 500 billion to 1 trillion plastic bags are consumed worldwide. That's over one million bags per minute. Billions of them end up as litter each year. The Worldwatch Institute estimates that in the U.S. alone, an estimated 12,000,000 barrels of non-renewable petroleum oil are required to produce the 100 billion bags consumed annually. That's over $500,000,000 the country could be saving to put towards clean, green energy. These plastic bags can take from 400 to 1,000 years to decompose but their chemicals residues remain for years after that.
- Ink found in printers produces fine dust that gets breathed in, which can produce illnesses as well as cancer.
- Billions of batteries in electronic products and cars, which are not correctly disposed of produce contamination that leads to severe health risks and cancer.
- In clothes and shoes there are chemical dyestuff that partly lead to allergies and in some cases even lead to cancer; e.g. colored bras whose dyes get transferred to the skin of the breast.
- If we take a global average life expectancy of 50 years then within 50 years 7 billion people will die. 7 billion corpses that need to be disposed of; staggering figures in the future. Already today, dead bodies contain a high concentration of chemical and medicinal substances. More and more people also have artificial components in their body.
- Biphenyl A: The hormonal effects of biphenyl A is suspected, among other things, to create erection and ejaculation problems, to create infertility, damage the development of the brain and trigger breast cancer. Biphenyl A is found in baby bottles made of polycarbonate, on paper receipts, baby pacifiers, tickets and invoices. Biphenyl A is absorbed through the mouth and skin contact.
- The sperm quality of men in industrialized countries is continually decreasing. Over 500 hormones related substances are responsible for this. These substances are found in a huge variety of products such plastic, insecticide, pesticide, medicines, flame retardants (chemicals), UV-filters in cosmetic products and sun creams.
- Most of the bees around the world are sick and billions are dying every year. Billions of bees have completely died off around the world. The entire human food chain is in danger given that 80% of all edible plants are dependent on bees. Bees pollinate over 90 types of vegetables, fruits and grain. The damage to harvests as a result of dying bees can easily be in the hundreds of billions, if not over a trillion (dollars, Euros).

- The loss of species is increasing at an alarming rate. The reasons are: construction, urbanization, deforestation, overfishing, climate change and invasive species. The diversity of species on our planet provides the basis of the fundamental elements of our ecosystem such as food, drinking water, medicine, wood, etc. Humanity must expect serious consequences in the coming 20-30 years.

Wikipedia: "Smog is also caused by large amounts of coal burning, which creates a mixture of smoke and sulfur dioxide. World coal consumption was about 6,743,786,000 short tons in 2006 and is expected to increase 48% to 9.98 billion short tons by 2030. China produced 2.38 billion tons in 2006. India produced about 447.3 million tons in 2006. 68.7% of China's electricity comes from coal. The USA consumes about 14% of the worlds total, using 90% of it for generation of electricity."

Bio aerosols and Contamination

Bio aerosols are airborne particles that are biological in origin. Bio aerosols are transported by the wind around the globe; with the climate change today – unpredictable 'trips'.

Bio aerosols can be formed from nearly any process that involves biological materials and generates enough energy to separate small particles from the larger substance, such as wind, water, air, or mechanical movement.

Plants, soil, water, and animals (including humans) all serve as sources of bio aerosols, and bio aerosols are subsequently present in most places where any of these sources live.

Bio aerosols have a direct effect on our world on a daily basis, causing many health and welfare effects.

The health hazards associated with bio aerosols can range from more mild reactions such as allergies, to much more severe reactions, such as death caused by airborne pathogens.

Welfare effects range from crop and livestock damage to lost tourism dollars and beyond.

While all bio aerosols are biological in origin by definition, an important attribute is whether the bio aerosols are living. Based on this attribute, bio aerosols are categorized into:

Two very important classifications: viable and non-viable. Non-viable bio aerosols are not currently alive and, therefore, cannot multiply; aerosolized pollen, animal dander and saliva, and insect excreta are all forms of non-viable bio aerosols.

In contrast, viable bio aerosols are living organisms that demonstrate microbiological activity and have the potential to multiply. These include airborne bacteria, fungi, and viruses, of which bacteria and fungal spores are the two most prevalent bio aerosols present.

Individual bio aerosols particles can range in size from approximately 0.02 to 100 micrometers in diameter, depending on the type and source. However, they also frequently agglomerate in clusters, thereby forming larger particles.

Important properties characterizing bio aerosols are size, viability, infectivity, allergenicity, toxicity, and pharmacological activity.

For bio aerosols to be infectious or pathogenic (cause disease), it must be viable. However, non-viable bio aerosols can still cause allergies or toxic reactions.

Bio aerosols can produce a wide range of health effects. Recall from earlier that for a bio aerosol to be infectious (pathogenic), it must be viable. However, non-viable bio aerosols can still cause allergies or airborne biological matter can affect toxic reactions - allergy sufferers. People with compromised respiratory systems, such as those with asthma and emphysema, can suffer respiratory sensitization attacks caused by bio aerosols as well.

On a daily level, countless people are afflicted with allergies or respiratory sensitization reactions, such as asthma, caused by interactions with fungi, pollen, and dander.

Sources of pathogenic bio aerosols include humans, animal houses, wastewater treatment plants, and bio solids storage units.

Pollen particles not only contain the actual pollen allergens inside, but also carry harmful substances of all kinds (e.g. pollution, fine dust, toxic particles) on their surface.

Indoor air quality: The central air system distributes them to the entire structure, spreading the pathogens incredibly effectively and exposing numerous people as a result. Therefore, the threat of pathogenic bio aerosols is especially potent in indoor scenarios (houses, working places, airplanes).

Phthalates

Phthalates (...) or phthalate esters, which are esters of phthalic acid and are mainly used as plasticizers (substances added to plastics to increase their flexibility, transparency, durability, and longevity). They are used primarily to soften polyvinyl chloride (PVC ...Phthalates are being phased out of many products in the United States, Canada, and European Union over health concerns.

But production just gets moved to India, China and other Asian countries. The end product such as packaging for food then simply gets re-imported. The corporations are effectively 'forced' to save costs.

Serious health effects related to Phthalates are: "Organ system toxicity (non-reproductive), Endocrine system, Reproduction and fertility, Birth or developmental effects, Persistent and bio-accumulative, Brain and nervous system, Immune system (including sensitization and allergies)."

"Phthalates are used in many products, including: automotive components, building materials, vinyl flooring furniture, pool liners and garden hoses cosmetics, perfume and nail polish footwear, outdoor clothing and rain wear inflatable products medical devices such as intravenous and feeding tubing, catheters, blood bags, anesthetic and dialysis equipment printing inks solvents such as adhesives, lacquers and varnishes sporting goods toys wires and cabling—in many machines and appliances and as insulation for transmission cables and fiber optics."

"Most dangerous are the Phthalates. They make the packaging soft and smooth (elastic). But they actuate also like hormones. As a consequence men become infertile. Furthermore these toxics can be found in crèmes, fruits, milk, oil, sauces, finished products and also in film packaging of meat and fruits."

Effects according to numerous studies

- There is an association between phthalate exposure and endocrine disruption leading to development of breast cancer.

- High doses have been shown to change hormone levels and cause birth defects.
- Exposure during pregnancy results in decreased anogenital distance among baby boys.
- Boys born to mothers with the highest levels of phthalates were 7 times more likely to have a shortened anogenital distance.
- There may be a link between the obesity epidemic and endocrine disruption and metabolic interference.
- Has showed statistically significant correlations with abnormal obesity and insulin resistance.
- Large amounts of specific phthalates fed to rodents have been shown to damage their liver and testes.
- Initial rodent studies also indicated hepato-carcinogenicity.
- Found a link between allergies in children and the phthalates.
- Found an association between phthalates in the home and asthma, especially in children.
- Found that prenatal phthalate exposure was related to low birth weight in infants.
- Low birth weight is the leading cause of death in children under 5 years of age and increases the risk of cardiovascular and metabolic disease in adulthood.
- Statistically significant correlation between urine phthalate concentrations in children and symptoms of ADHD.

Nuclear Waste

The ideology and vision of nuclear power stations is a horrendous lie. Nuclear energy is the most expensive energy that has ever existed. The state even subsidizes the industry with various indirect contributions (tax contributions!). Nuclear energy is the result of the obsession with economic growth. Then you have the tens of thousands of tons of nuclear waste around the globe, which contains a lethal danger and entails billions (of dollars) in maintenance and storage costs. The coming generations will have to pay for today's electricity for thousands of years. Anyone that accepts this is absolutely stupid, evil and devilish! There are no end storage places that are safe; and they will never exist. Possessed by delusion the representatives talk about a "minor risk". Every body already knows this "minor risk", we saw it with Chernobyl and more recently again with Fukushima (Japan). Billions of people can get sick and die in such a nuclear accident. Not to mention the immense contamination of land, seas and oceans. Even entire continents could become poisoned for hundreds of years, including the entire drinking water and agricultural land. Not even the devil could want such a 'minor risk', only those people in the industry that earn billions with this.

- 9 states discharged on 15 locations in the North Atlantic: 115,000t in 223,000 barrels with nuclear waste; now leaking (concentration of plutonium 238).
- Nuclear waste is extremely hazardous for both environment and humans.
- Nuclear waste – many thousands of tons – must be stored for 1,000,000 years.
- Nuclear waste storage must be controlled, protected and administered for 1,000,000 years and will always carry a permanent risk.
- Nobody knows if the nuclear waste storage packaging is safe for 1,000,000 years.
- Repackaging nuclear waste in the future will have to be paid for by future generations. It will be very expensive.
- Nuclear electricity is the most expensive energy humanity has every produced.
- Sweden has stored 9,000 tons of nuclear waste. Hundreds of thousands of tons are stored around the world.
- Nuclear storage always has a permanent risk.
- Nuclear waste – many hundred thousands of tons – must be stored, controlled, protected and administrated for 1,000,000 years.
- Storage, maintenance, repackaging, and recycling nuclear waste will cost the following generations billions of dollars each year, over and over again.

The main products of emissions

- Toxic chemicals
- Plastic debris
- Industrial chemicals
- Industrial waste
- Agricultural waste
- Agricultural chemicals
- Petroleum, oil
- Sewage
- Rubbish, garbage
- Household waste
- Nuclear waste
- Emission of carbon dioxide
- Residue of medicines

Other Chemicals in the Water

- Natural oestrogenes
- Synthetic oestrogenes
- Clofibric acid
- Phytooestrogene
- Benz(a)anthracen
- Benzo(a)pyren
- Benz(a)anthracen
- Benzylbutylphthalat
- Bisphenol
- Nonylphenol
- Nonylphenoldiethoxylat
- Endosulfan
- Dieldrin
- Chlordan
- Diethylhexylphthalat
- Dibutylphthalat
- Tributylzinn
- Dichloranilin
- Dichlordiphenyldichlorethylen
- Linuron
- Diuron
- And much more …

The unstoppable collective suicide of 7 billion, 8 billion, 9 billion, 10 billion!

Results of Contamination

- Millions of people die every year due to fine dust: cars, industry, heating with oil, all kind of mining.
- Hundreds of millions of people die due to chemical emissions from the industry.
- More than 3,000,000,000 people suffer from illnesses and disease due to pollution.
- Air, soil, sea, oceans, drinking water, nature and animals are dramatically contaminated.
- Chemical reactions in human bodies will reduce fertility or create handicapped babies.
- Dying in the future will be very painful due to chemical elements (combined multiple effects) in the body.

- What people don't see, doesn't exist. What politicians don't see, doesn't exist.
- People and also politicians don't see the complexity and manifoldness of contamination.

- Statistics about the actual damages (health, nature) of contamination are kept under lock and key.

Nuclear Power Stations

Seventy-six operating power stations in Japan, Taiwan, China, South Korea, India, Pakistan and the US are located in areas close to coastlines deemed vulnerable to tsunamis.

Of 442 nuclear power stations globally, more than one in 10 are situated in places deemed to be at high or extreme risk of earthquakes -- in Japan, the US, Taiwan, Armenia and Slovenia.

In every nuclear reactor in Germany there could be a meltdown. All the radioactive elements would be freed, destroying the environment completely in a radius of 400-500 kilometers.

Nuclear waste is very dangerous for the environment and humankind.

Every reactor has a limited lifespan. At the end, what remains are thousands of tons of contaminated material. Disassembling is done by hand. That is time consuming and very expensive.

The cost of storing nuclear waste is high: 1.8 million tones is the weight of all the nuclear power plants 'end material'. A third of it, around 600,000 tones, is contaminated radioactively; 10,000 tones so much that they have to go to a nuclear waste repository. This waste has to be stored safely over decades, some even hundreds and thousands (up to one million) of years.

The whole process of dismantling a nuclear power plant costs enormous amounts of money. The electricity consumer foots the bill, and as is often the case the state or better said the taxpayers.

In Germany the talk is of €3.2 billion until 2013 to dismantle one reactor. End storage several hundreds of millions of Euros more. Add all this together and for the 17 currently operating nuclear reactors we reach a figure of around €55 billion.

Restoration of old nuclear power stations, final storage of nuclear waste, relocation of unsafe nuclear waste storages, and maintenance of provisional and final nuclear storages will cost, for example for Germany, during the next two decades, at least €10 billion with highest probably two or three times more. This means: €20-30 billion (as experts calculated).

- Such costs are not on the electricity bills that citizens get today every month! Who will pay this in the future? The citizens with their taxes will have to pay such enormous costs.

- High consumption of electricity (also of petrol) brings a lot of profit and VAT-money to the political apparatus. That's why politicians are never interested in a solution.

Human Causes of Contamination

- Loss of human values
- Loss of genuine spirituality
- Unlimited capitalism
- Uncontrolled financial business
- Corruption
- Lobbyism
- Lack of adequate education
- Archaic religions imprisoning people in illusions
- Megalomania
- Narcissism
- Egoism
- Individualism
- Greed
- Loud-mouths
- Religious lunacy disrespecting human problems
- Unlimited consumption
- Fun oriented society and lifestyle
- Pure hedonism
- Unlimited consumption
- Brainwashed and manipulated (seduced) people
- Life lies
- Religious obsession
- Arrogance
- Ignorance

- Laziness
- Superstition
- Brainless ways of living
- Lack of leadership integrity
- Insensibility and indifference
- Lack of moral education
- Incompetent and irresponsible politicians

3.6. Transport Systems

Cars and Public Transport

People like cars. Most people want a car. Here we have a short picture about this 'wonder' vehicle:

- Road Traffic Accidents (RTAs) result in 1.2 million deaths and 50 million injured every year.
- Over the last 50 years more than 60 (other source: 100) million people died and 2.5 billion people were injured due to RTAs.
- WHO: The global annual cost of Road Traffic Accidents is almost 518 billion US dollars. Another source: The global annual cost of RTA is almost 230 billion dollars (2006).
- 10% of all hospital beds are occupied by RTA-victims.
- In 2008, 380,000 people died in Europe as a result of fine dust from road traffic; and millions more around the globe.
- Cars produced in January 2011: 4,500,000; for 2011 as a whole, expectations are 65-70,000,000 (as China enormously increases its car production).
- In 2007 an estimated 73 million cars were produced.

Traffic Pollution

- Exhaust gases, including fine dust (diesel)
- Fine dust from the abrasion of tires
- Fine dust from the abrasion of driving surfaces
- Fine dust from the disk brakes
- Traffic noise is also considered as an extremely unhealthy emission
- Train: Fecal fine dust, fine dust from rail abrasion and iron wheels.
- Aviation: Fine dust, gases and noise (civil, military, sport)
- Wrecks of cars and lorries or trucks, all kind of transport vehicles, also trains and airplanes leave behind dangerous metals and chemical elements.
- Oil tankers, pipelines, and oil derricks produce – especially catastrophic accidents – produce an incredible amount of destruction of the world of animals and nature, including sea and oceans. Contamination of soil and drinking water has dramatic long-term effects on nature and humans.

Other Toxic Examples

- In Germany 55% of the driven car-kilometers are due to holiday and leisure travelling.
- Special holiday pollution: A cruise ship produces the same amount of fine dust as 50,000 cars driving at 130 km/h.
- There is an enormous demand for petrol, diesel, ceresin, and oil; not only from private traffic; probably even more from military use.
- High-speed trains consume a lot of electricity and also produce fine dust.
- Traffic noise is also considered an extremely unhealthy emission.
- There are estimated 1.5-2 billion cars and other motor vehicles (eg. Lorries, vans, etc.) in use worldwide; all producing pollution, contamination, accidents, etc.
- In the air inside certain car models, traces of more than 100 different chemicals can be detected - some of them can cause cancer. Source: Degassing plastics and solvent-based adhesives and coatings. Carcinogenic substances in the interior of a car are not uncommon.
- The concentration of toxins from traffic congestions such as the cancer-causing benzene is about five times as high in the car as in nature. The concentration of toxins in the car also rises sharply when one is stuck in traffic.
- Traffic accidents produce more than one million fatalities and several millions of injured people every single year. There are additional costs and institutions working for: unemployment, handicapped people, loss of manpower, orphans, as well as separation and divorce due to dramatic changes in a family life as a consequence of car traffic accidents, etc.
- Within the next 20 years an estimated 1.5-2 billion cars will be produced around the globe! Conclusion: fantastic business for the owners of the factories in the production chain, for the CEOs and for some car dealers. But it is lethal for the planet and for the entire humanity!

Main Profiteers

- Car and car supplier industry
- Mining industry
- Oil industry
- Insurance companies
- Hospitals, clinics, doctors
- Lawyers
- Car dealers
- Repair and service industry

- We should not forget that the government of a country gets immense amounts of taxes (VAT, toll, fees) with each produced, sold, and used car. It's logical that a government is never ready to change anything in the traffic systems of society.
- But politicians must learn to govern, to control the big corporations (banks included), and to lead their folk with carrot and stick. But then the problem is, we need somebody that talks to the members of political parties, the lawmakers, the ministers and heads of state also with carrot and stick.

3.7. Climate Change

General Overview

The fact of Climate change is without doubt proven by thousands of scientists around the globe: this Climate Change is human made! All the catastrophes due to climate change, in the past, the present and the future will cause unimaginable damages, billions of victims, misery, suffering, poverty, and displacement of entire folks.

- Probable temperature rise between 1.8C and 4C; or: between 1.1C and 6.4C
- The past decade has been the hottest ever measured.
- Sea level most likely to rise by 28-43cm; probably up to 1.50 meters
- Arctic summer sea ice disappears in second half of century
- Increase in heat waves very likely
- Increase in tropical storm intensity likely

- The greed for money and power of the elite in politics and industry is the main cause. The ignorance of billions of people is the other part of the human cause.

The year 2010 is almost certain to rank in the top 3 warmest years since the beginning of instrumental climate records in 1850.

Warming will have many severe impacts, often mediated through water. Increasing global warming triggers an unstoppable chain reaction with unknown effects.

June 2010 was the warmest month on record worldwide, according to a report from the National Oceanic and Atmospheric Administration. Warmer-than-average conditions were present across nearly all continents, including much of the United States.

The US space agency NASA has reported the largest collapse of our Earth's upper atmosphere in history, and they don't know why.

We are destroying the climate balance and the balance of the eco-systems that are essential to the survival of our civilization, of our children and our following generations.

More greenhouse gases than ever before: Carbon dioxide, methane and nitrogen oxides are the gases that produce global warming. The more we emit into the atmosphere, the faster climate change develops. The most recent measurements from the global weather organization reveal absolute peak values. Researchers fear that, climate change has already taken on a momentum all of its own.

Irreversible destructions of the environment: the Gulf Stream, the glaciers in the Alps and the massive ice caps in Greenland and in Antarctic. Source: the human emitted greenhouse gases make the global average temperature rise.

As a result of the ice melting: The algal bloom in the Arctic comes earlier. This is a result of climate change, which brings the ice in the North Pole region to melt. This has heavy consequences for the food chain.

At that point huge parts of the planet, beset with over-population, droughts, soil erosion, freak storms, massive crop failures and rising sea levels, will be unfit for human existence.

In the past 25 years the water temperature of the 160 biggest fresh water basins has risen. Every decade the water temperature has risen by an average of 0.45 degrees Celsius, in many seas up to 1 degree. The biggest increase was registered in Northern Europe, followed by Siberia, Mongolia, Northern-China and South-east Europe around the Black Sea.

Minor temperature changes can already lead to an increase in algae growth. This can destroy the habitat of fish or lead to foreign unknown species reproducing, which in turn alters the natural ecosystem of the Oceans.

It is clear, that Asia and the Pacific regions are the ones most affected by the changes in climate. The heating of the planet and its consequences could result in masses of migration in the coming decades.

Arctic summer sea ice will disappear in the second half of century.

Since the Gulf of Mexico oil and methane gas leak our world has experienced its hottest temperatures in recorded history.

Methane gas emanating from the bottom of the Arctic Ocean is harmful to the climate.

20-30% of all plant and animal species are at increased risk of extinction if temperatures rise between 1.5-2.5°C.

The 15 nations (of the UN Security Council) warn that global warming can become a threat to global peace. Droughts could lead to food and water wars.

Ice Melting

- The melting of Arctic and Antarctic ice started in 1990. Glaciers are melting twice as fast as in 1999. Billions of people are affected!
- Today each year more ice is melting than the amount of ice that exists in the Alps.
- Glaciers are melting faster than expected and jeopardizing the demand of drinking water.
- The melting of the glaciers in the Himalayas will affect 70% of India's population dependent on agriculture.
- The Arctic summer sea ice will disappear in the second half of the century.
- Melting glaciers will initially increase flood risk and then strongly reduce water supplies.
- According to a new study global warming will result in the defrosting of 30-60 per cent of all permafrost by the year 2200. As a result around 190 billion tones of carbons emissions will go into the atmosphere. As the permafrost begins to thaw they rot and thus set free greenhouse gases especially the damaging carbon dioxide and methane gases.

Rise of Sea Level

- The global average sea level would probably rise by 28-43 cm by the end of the century; but is likely to rise by about 1.4 meters globally by 2100 as polar ice melts.
- Many islands and costal towns will be lost already at a global warming of 2°C.
- The increase in sea level by 100-150 cm by the year 2100 is more than certain.
- UK: Seas could be 1.5 meters higher by the end of the century.

The sea level in the Mediterranean has risen by between 1 and 1.5 millimeters each year since 1943, but this does not seem set to continue, because it now seems that the speed at which it rises is accelerating"... Since the start of the 21st century the level has already risen by 20 centimeters. During the next 30 years the rise in temperatures and in sea level will continue: estimated 20 cm per 10 year which means, for instance, more than 60 centimeters in 30 years (not only in the Mediterranean Sea).

☞ Scientists warn: The record droughts, fires, floods and mudslides continue to increase in severity and frequency. Weather extremes are more frequent and intense due to global warming. Does any politician listen to the experts?

Effects of Global Warming

- The global average sea level will rise by at least 20-30 cm within 20-30 years. During the next 30 years the rise in Mediterranean Sea level will be 2 cm per year.
- Heat waves, drought, fires, rainstorms, floods, tornados, hurricanes, tropical cyclones, become more frequent, more widespread and/or more intense.
- 300,000 deaths and 300 million people affected every year by global warming.
- Floods will affect 2 billion by 2050 due to climate change, deforestation, rising sea levels.
- 3.2 billion people will experience water shortages due to climate change.
- Areas around the Mediterranean and other subtropical regions: increase in wildfires and tropical storms.
- Water shortages, heat waves, tropical storms, hunger, and floods will be an ever-growing threat.
- The area of land vulnerable to flooding will increase by about 50% in the next 40 years.
- Heat waves, rainstorms, drought, tropical cyclones and surges in sea level are among the events expected to become more frequent, more widespread and/or more intense.
- Until 2100 up to 20-40% of the species (plants, animals) are endangered.
- Frequent drought and higher global temperatures could destroy until 2100 up to 70% of the Amazon rain forest. Enormous amounts of CO2 (carbon dioxide) will increase global warming.
- Since the Gulf of Mexico oil and methane gas leak, our world has experienced its hottest temperatures in recorded history.

- Climate change (global warming) and its consequences will produce an inter-regional movement of population of unknown extent, especially in Asia.

- When politicians see or hear such data, then they are frightened, terribly tremble, and bury their head in the sand.
- Hundred thousands of lobbyists knock at the door of the politicians and menace: "You don't touch this matter!" Politicians understand the threat (as many of them have children and a bank mortgage, and others want in the future a job in a corporation) and react: "Too big to be solved. The problem doesn't exist"

Costs of Climate Change

- Estimated yearly costs of climate change damages (worldwide): over €1 trillion.
- Heat waves with agricultural losses reached $15 billion.
- Climate change could cost the world up to 25% of its entire wealth.

- The citizens today already pay for the costs of the damages due to Climate Change.
- The following generations will pay for the costs of the damages due to Climate Change.
- The costs of these damages will explode to heaven, as the damages will lead to wars.

Thermohaline Circulation

2010: The latest satellite data establishes that the North Atlantic Current (also called the North Atlantic Drift) no longer exists and along with it the Norway Current. These two warm water currents are actually part of the same system that has several names depending on where in the Atlantic Ocean it is. The entire system is a key part of the planet's heat regulatory system; it is what keeps Ireland and the United Kingdom mostly ice free and the Scandinavian countries from being too cold; it is what keeps the entire world from another Ice Age. This Thermohaline Circulation System is now dead in certain places and dying in others.

The Thermohaline Circulatory System, where the warm water current flows through a much cooler, much larger, ocean, effects the upper atmosphere above the current as much as seven miles high. The lack of this normal effect in the eastern North Atlantic has disrupted the normal flow of the atmospheric Jet Stream this summer, causing unheard of high temperatures in Moscow (104F) and drought, and flooding in Central Europe, with high temperatures in much of Asia and massive flooding in China, Pakistan, and elsewhere in Asia.

Superstorms

- Superstorms are combined with the cataclysmic destruction of over one-third of Russia's crops due to historic fires and drought, the historic drought in China that is now feared could cripple their entire winter wheat crop.
- Superstorms have pounded Southern Africa leaving their agricultural sector in ruins.
- Superstorms have virtually destroyed Sri Lanka's ability to feed itself.
- Superstorms killed over 2,000 in Pakistan and destroyed its agriculture sector
- Suprstorms produced historic fires and drought in Ukraine and destroyed 20% of their crops, the record cold and snow hitting a European Continent after their worst flooding in decades.
- Superstorms hitting Brazil left nearly 700 dead.
- Superstorms produced catastrophic drought in Argentina.

The Coming Risks

- To all of this and more, the damage done in the past 24 months to our world's ability to feed its 7 billion human beings has been completely destroyed.
- 300,000 deaths and 300 million people are affected every year by global warming.
- Every year an average of over 400 million people are directly exposed to a flood.
- 200 million are to be displaced due to rising sea levels, heavier floods, and more intense droughts (other figures go up to 500 million).
- Floods will affect 2 billion by 2050 due to climate change, deforestation, rising sea levels.
- 3.2 billion people will experience water shortages due to climate change.
- An additional 600 million people are at risk of famine due to climate change.

- Most of the world's major river deltas are sinking, increasing the flood risk faced by hundreds of millions of people.
- Food speculations increase food prices by 10-40% yet in 2011, unaffordable for billions of people. Hunger will increase dramatically!

- There are heads of state that have a solution strategy of 'waiting until the problem solves itself'. Which problem? The unstoppable global population growth!

Eco-Systems

As a result of the thawing of permafrost enormous amounts of greenhouse gases are emitted into the atmosphere. Scientists warn insistently of the consequences.

Global warming will lead to the thawing of one to two thirds of the global permafrost by 2200. The atmosphere will have to take on 190 billion tones of carbon dioxide from this.

The permafrost areas in Canada and Russia for example, store large amounts of frozen plants. If they begin to thaw, then these plants rot and release greenhouse gases – especially the very damaging methane (CH_4), but also carbon dioxide (CO_2).

Depending on forecasted scenarios by 2100 only 18 – 45 of today's rainforests would still exist. The tropical forests in South America, South-east Asia and Africa are home to more than half the planet's animal and plant species. The combination of climate change and deforestation forces these species to adapt, migrate or die.

Around 41% of the oceans are badly damaged as a result of direct human intervention; only 3.7% of these waters are still untouched.

- Politicians can't think in 'eco-systems'. Their thinking is unilateral and ego-centered. They also have too much of papers every day on their desk. They have many calls every day. They have meetings. They always must talk everywhere. They must travel. There is no time for such strange thing such as 'eco-system'. They are imprisoned in their mind and political apparatus.

Costs of Climate Change

- Costs of extreme weather alone could reach 0.5 to 1% of world GDP in 40 years.
- Impacts of climate change will cost $75-100 billion per year in the developing world.
- The total cost of global warming will be 3.6% of GDP, if nothing is done.
- Hurricane damage, real estate losses, energy costs, water costs: $1.9 trillion per year.
- Floods will produce damages in the trillions of US dollars in the future.
- UN: $500 billion in costs for climate damages per year (in developing countries alone).
- Estimated yearly costs of climate change damages: over €1 trillion.
- Costs of $500 billion per year due to climate change only for developing countries.
- The costs of damage from extreme weather (storms, hurricanes, typhoons, floods, droughts, and heat waves) will increase rapidly at higher temperatures.
- A 5 or 10% increase in hurricane wind speed, linked to rising sea temperatures, is predicted to double annual damage costs, in the US.
- Heat waves with agricultural losses reached $15 billion will be commonplace in 30-40 years.
- Climate change could cost the world up to 25% of its entire wealth. Global gross domestic product (GDP) could be reduced by up to 20% due to the damages caused by rising temperatures, droughts, floods, water shortages and extreme weather events.
- In the UK, annual flood losses alone could increase from to 0.2 to 0.4 per cent of GDP once the increase in global temperatures reaches 3°C or 4°C.
- Fighting against climate change could cost the international community up to $20 billion per year.

It seems politicians never do use a calculator. They don't even know how to use it. But for sure, they have calculated how much of a pension payment they will get with each year they are in office.

Future Development of Climate Change

Thousands of scientists and thousands of dreams I experienced during the last 30 years draw a frightening picture about our future over the next 20-30 years:

- Rapid climate change will most probably result in a global catastrophe costing millions of lives in chaos, wars and natural disasters.

- A strong and fast increase of climate change could bring the planet to the edge of anarchy. Conflicts and warfare will define human life.
- Widespread flooding as a result of an increase in sea levels will create major upheaval for hundreds of millions of people.
- Dramatic shortages of water and energy supplies will become increasingly harder to overcome, plunging the world into global war.
- Over the past 50 years around 60% of the global ecosystems have been heavily damaged. Over 40% of the oceans are also significantly damaged due to human behavior. The damages increase exponentially every year. The additional combined damages between interacting ecosystems will produce combined damages of unknown dimensions. In 10-15 years around 95% of the global ecosystems humans depend on will be damaged.
- Most politicians are unable to think in exponential scales. They also can't combine and identify the interrelations of 'humans-planet-humanity-economy-politics'. They are good-for-nothing, not fit for purpose and must be fired. And a new science of politics must prepare a new category of political and economic leaders.
- Climate Change with is damages today and as expected in the future will destroy all visions and dreams of economic growth and a good living standard around the globe. At least politicians should think on their own future living standard and the one of their children.
- Lawmakers, ministers, and heads of state do not lose one second contemplating about their responsibility for the future, of the youth today and the future generations. They are in terms of moral criminality not a tiny bit better than their friends the banking fraudsters and the media elite whores.

3.8. Criminality and Corruption

Manifoldness of Crimes

- Organized crime threatens peace on earth, development and sovereignty of states.
- Organized crime is one of the biggest economies of the world.
- Organized crime use immense money, weapons, bribes, and corruption.
- Organized crime decomposes politics, blackmails politicians, and abuse the military.
- 140,000 people in Europe are abused by human trafficking, especially sexually; profit: $3 billion.
- In Russia 70 tons of hard drugs are consumed; Europe is the heroin supermarket.
- Corruption: $5 trillion, approx. 5% of the world's GDP.
- Around the globe 43% of companies are affected by economic crime (corruption).
- Up to 80% of international aid to Afghanistan is being lost in international and local corruption schemes.
- The revenue of organized crime worldwide is estimated at $2 trillion.
- Damage caused by cybercrime estimated at $100 billion annually; we estimate: $300 billion.
- Over 700,000 people around the globe are trafficked every year for sexual exploitation and forced labor.
- World spending on illegal drugs per year: more than US$300,000,000,000.
- Fossil fuel and nuclear energy industries receive direct / indirect subsidies over $300 billion.
- Bribery and price-fixing influencing public policy costs billions of dollars in lost revenues.
- Malicious computer use such as virus writing and hacking cost businesses globally more than $1 trillion each year.
- The respondents estimated that in 2008 businesses lost data worth a total of $4.6 billion and spent about $600 million cleaning up after breaches.
- The recent recession is only increasing the security risk for corporations, with 42% reporting that displaced workers were the biggest threat to sensitive information on the network.
- 47% of Chinese said they believed the US poses the biggest security threat to their data.
- The average company has $12 million worth of sensitive data residing abroad.

- Companies lost on average $4.6 million worth of intellectual property each year.
- At least one of every three women on earth has been beaten, coerced into sex or abused in some other way, usually by an intimate partner or family member.
- Two million girls between the ages of 5 and 15 are introduced into the commercial sex market each year.
- 6,000 people are executed every year; 95% in the following countries: China, Iran, Pakistan, Saudi Arabia, and USA. In total, 58 countries practice the death penalty.
- Pompously ultraconservative and nationalistic ideals about manliness promote readiness for violence.
- Fundamentalist attitudes (beliefs) promote readiness for violence

Governmental Corruption

Report from 'Transparency International' about Corruption in the European Union; some statements:

"A number of countries in southern Europe – Greece, Italy, Portugal and Spain – are shown to have serious deficits in public sector accountability and deep-rooted problems of inefficiency, malpractice and corruption, which are neither sufficiently controlled nor sanctioned…

Political parties, public administrations and the private sector are evaluated as the weakest players in the fight against corruption across Europe…

Greece, Italy, Portugal and Spain top the list of the Western European countries found to have serious deficits in their integrity systems…

Legal corruption goes beyond bribery and includes influence peddling, for example the excessive and undue influence of lobbyists in the European corridors of power. It skews decision-making to benefit the few at the expense of the many…

In Greece, Ireland, Italy, Romania and Spain, more than 80% of people believe political parties are corrupt or extremely corrupt…

19 of the 25 European countries assessed have yet to implement legislation to control lobbying and those that have often lack enforcement mechanisms and sanctions for non-compliance…

Only 3 national parliaments have appropriate and well-functioning integrity mechanisms for their MPs...

Causes of Crimes

- Humans create crime.
- The society creates crimes.
- Lifestyle and living standard create crime.
- Poverty and misery creates crimes.
- Inadequate sexual education creates crimes.
- Neurotic parents create crimes.
- Unlimited greed for money creates crimes.
- Early childhoods with difficult family environments create crimes.
- Lack of love and Spirit, care and understanding, creates crimes.
- Unemployment creates crimes.
- Social injustice creates crimes.
- Amoral politicians are a pattern for crimes copied by countless people.
- Amoral leaders in economy and industry are a pattern copied by others.
- Archaic religions create lies, cheat, deceit, and crimes.
- Lack of psychical-spiritual and ethical education creates crimes.

3.9. Re-armament, Military and Wars

War is on the horizon: "If You Can't Hear the Drums of War You Must Be Deaf" - Henry Kissinger

The last two decades humanity has suffered from many wars: Gulf War I and Gulf War II, Balkan Wars, Iraq War, Afghanistan War, Israel's Wars against Palestinian and Arab people and today the War against Libya and another brewing in Syria.

In not one of these wars was the capitalist coalition, especially not the European Union and the United States, threatened, attacked or in any way in a dimension of collective emergency state of war. All these wars were and are based on lies.

These wars produced millions of victims, injured and handicapped people, of orphans and widows. Hundreds of thousands of soldiers will suffer mentally during their entire life. Millions have been displaced and forced from their homes. Countrywide infrastructure and extensive environments have been totally destroyed. Most released figures are manipulated or distorted.

Perspectives That Form a Picture of War

In numerous countries around the world, USA and NATO soldiers are active since decades. They kill, they murder, they rape, they torture, they torment, they injure, they create handicapped and psychically ill people, they burn babies and women and men, they slaughter, they bomb homes of human beings, they destroy infrastructure, they destroy agricultural land, they destroy the functioning of the administrations and governments, they create hunger and thirst, they produce fear and terror or terrible nightmares, they produce untold agony and calamity, they create strife and sow hate for the coming 100 and more years.

The global military armament business is booming. Germany has a big part of the pie. According to the peace research institute SIPRI this third biggest weapons exporter holds an 11% portion of the global market. Only Russia and the USA export more weapons.

The defense business as a whole has increased by 24% in the past 5 years compared to the period between 2001 and 2005.

The biggest weapons producer between 2006 and 2010 was the USA, laying claim to around 30% of the global weapons industry.

According to a report, other official estimates point to a whopping 2,500,000 Iraqi fatalities as the result of the invasion, in addition to four million children that were left orphaned by the war. The Iraqi Interior Ministry has also released figures pointing to 800,000 individuals that had gone missing in the country by January 2008. Another source reports: Since 2003, over 1,300,000 Iraqi civilians have been killed and an estimated 4.7 million have been displaced as a result of the war. Other statistics speak about 2m - 2.5m Iraqi victims. Most of the infrastructure has been destroyed.

According to UN statistics, Afghanistan produced only 185 tons of opium before the 2001 US led occupation. Currently, however, the figure stands at 3,400 tons annually.

A Swedish think-tank reports the possession of over 20,500 nuclear weapons by eight nuclear states, including Israel, with 5,000 of them all ready for instant use.

By the end of November 2010 the number of private military contractors in the United States will surpass for the first time in history the combined number of US Military forces and police officials combined.

US Military: Lies of American Politicians and the Media to start riots, unrest, civil war, war or to intervene with no democratic and no transparent (proxy) activities:

- Vietnam (1964-1975)
- Grenada (1983)
- Panama (1989)
- Iraq (1991)
- Somalia (1993)
- Bosnia (1992-1995)
- Yugoslavia (1999)
- Afghanistan/Pakistan (2001)
- Iraq (2003)
- Venezuela - Ecuador (2008)
- Libya (2011)
- Syria/Yemen (2012)

People do not decide about war. Governments decide about war and go to war even if there is no threat for the country. Governments fabricate 'terrorism' and invent all kind of other reasons to go to war. Pre-emptive attack is also an invention. The true motives are on the hidden stage behind the curtains!

Costs of Wars

- June 2010: World military spending increased by 5.9% to hit a new record high of $1.53 trillion in 2009.
- Global military expenditure is increasing fast; money spent per year: $36,000,000,000 with increasing tendency.
- Global military expenditures in January 2011; i.e. during one month: $3,200,000,000.
- The USA has wasted $3,000 billion on wars that have no benefit whatsoever.
- Cost of Iraq War (2001-2010) plus war in Afghanistan: over $1,000,000,000,000.
- Iraq War victims: 1.4 million killed people; 4.7 million displaced; 5 million orphans; 1-2 million widows.
- The Afghan war costs the US taxpayers $300 million per day.
- The war in Afghanistan and in Iraq since 2003 costs the US citizens $3 trillion just for caring for the wounded from both of those two wars over the next thirty years.
- Washington plans to invest $92 billion to expand its nuclear arsenal in the next 10 years.

The US government has admitted selling $40 billion worth of private arms worldwide in 2009 with almost $7 billion of them going to the Middle East and Northern African countries.... The main recipients of the US arms in 2009 were Japan with $4.5 billion, Britain with $3.4 billion and Singapore with $5.5 billion purchases.

A total of $7.3 billion arms were sold to the Middle East and North African nations. Turkey and the United Arab Emirates with $1.50 and 1.09 billion purchases respectively, were among the major recipients of the US arms in these regions.

The US military spends $20.2 billion annually on air conditioning for the American troops stationed in war-torn Iraq and Afghanistan; including the costs to deliver the fuel to the most isolated places, escorting, command and control, and other support and infrastructure.

The Pentagon's demand for a budget of $300 million a day for the Afghan war will put a 'back-breaking burden' on US taxpayers ...

The world's military spending has increased to a record high of $1.6 trillion in 2010.... the top three arms investors are the US, China and Britain ... The Unites States, with extravagant military operations in Afghanistan and Iraq, increased the arms investment by 2.8% to $698 billion -- about six times as much as China which is the world's second-biggest spender followed by Britain, France and Russia.

The US Department of Defense (DoD) has wasted almost $50 billion over the past decade, an independent public policy think tank in the United States says. According to a report on the 2012 US defense budget, issued by the Center for Strategic and Budgetary Assessments (CSBA), Pentagon has put some $46 billion since 2001 into developing military systems that were never deployed in the combat fields, Reuters reported Monday. The think tank has suggested in his report that the Pentagon's efforts have produced no meaningful results as far as the modernization of the US military is concerned.

An article in July 2011 reports:

"The latest objective estimate for the wars in Iraq and Afghanistan, made public June 29, is between $3.7 trillion and $4.4 trillion. This doesn't even include the thousands of deaths and injuries among quasi-military contractors ... (not included) the "hidden" costs of the war that include enormous medical care expenses over the next 50 years for tens of thousands of badly wounded soldiers, other benefits, equipment replacement, and interest on war debts ... (the effective costs) will certainly top $5 trillion in real costs ... Defense Department expenses are only half the story. Double the Pentagon's $700 billion for a true estimate of the amount of money the U.S. spent on war-related issues last year. That's $1.4 trillion a year for the United States.... Washington's various other "national security" budgets. That of course includes the costs of Washington's 16 different intelligence services, the percentage of the annual national debt to pay for past war expenses, Homeland Security, nuclear weapons, additional annual spending requests for Iraq and Afghan wars, military retiree pay and healthcare for vets, NASA, FBI (for its war-related military work), etc. When it's all included it comes to $1,398 trillion for fiscal 2010."

US Wars and Aggression

America has intruded in the affairs of at least 50 countries of the world over 130 times during the last 121 years. We give an extract from the source:

While the US troops have intervened in the affairs of Panama eight times (1895, 1901-14, 1908, 1912, 1918-20, 1958, 1964 and 1989), they entered Nicaragua (1894, 1896, 1898, 1899, 1907, 1910, 1912-33), Honduras (1903, 1907, 1911, 1912, 1919, 1924-25, 1983-89) and China (1894-95, 1898-1900, 1911-14, 1922-27, 1927-34, 1948-49, 1958) some seven times each under one pretext or the other during this period under review.

The American forces sailed for Cuba (1898-1902, 1906-1909, 1912, 1917-33, 1961, 1962) six times, they went to Iran five times (1946, 1953, 1980, 1984, 1987-88), and they interfered on four different occasions in Haiti (1891,1914-34, 1987-94, 2004-05) Dominican Republic (1903-04,1914,1916-24,1963-66), Yugoslavia (1919,1946,1992-94,1991-93), Iraq (1958, 1963, 1990-91, 1991-93) and Philippines (1898-1910, 1948-54, 1989, 2002).

The US troops were dispatched thrice to Korea (1894-96, 1904-05, 1945-53), Libya (1981, 1986-89, 2011), Guatemala (1920, 1954, 1966-67), Yemen (2000, 2002, 2004) and Liberia (1990, 1997, 2003).

They were sent on foreign missions twice to nations like Chile (1891, 1964-73), Mexico (1913, 1914-18), Puerto Rico (1898, 1950), El-Salvador (1932, 1981-82), Germany (1948, 1961), Laos (1962, 1971-73), Somalia (1992-94, 2006) and Afghanistan (1998, 2001).

Apart from featuring prominently in World War I and II, the US combat forces have also been active at least once in countries like Argentina, Samoa, Russia, Guam, Turkey, Uruguay, Greece, Vietnam, Indonesia, Cambodia, Oman, Macedonia, Syria, Pakistan, Bolivia, Virgin Islands, Zaire (Congo), Saudi Arabia, Kuwait, Lebanon, Grenada, Angola, Sudan, Albania, Bosnia and Colombia.

Since the end of World War Two the United States has:

- Endeavored to overthrow more than 50 foreign governments, most of which were democratically elected.
- Grossly interfered in democratic elections in at least 30 countries.
- Waged war/military action, either directly or in conjunction with a proxy army, in some 30 countries.
- Attempted to assassinate more than 50 foreign leaders.

- Dropped bombs on the people of some 30 countries.
- Suppressed dozens of nationalist movements around the world.
- Has spent over $50 trillion on Israel.
- Has masterminded and dictated politics throughout the European Union.

- We observe here an endless series of cantankerousness, quarrelsomeness, bossiness, meddling in alien affairs, intrigues, harasser, troublemaker, hysterical theatre, greed of always having the superior say, compulsion to control and dictate, trying to take away any possible slice of a cake from somebody else, hurting and killing others as if these other people would be their inveterate foe, destroying everything that they can't possess, an extreme hyped up self-aggrandizement, and an attitude showing that they understand all other folks as 'underdogs', 'under-humans', or rats.

- People that show such signs in high concentration during a long time have a deep inner suffering, are extremely neurotic, are imprisoned in their own lies, are very avaricious and envious, are entirely disconnected from their inner source of life, have totally lost any commitment to the truth and the creation. Behind all this is a deep guilt and complete lack of ability to love. They all must have (had) a despotic father and despotic forefathers; and a mother that is thoroughly distorted in her mind, disgusting in her character, and fully unable to enjoy sensuality and sex (called a 'frozen witch').

- There is only one race or group of humans on earth that unify all these miserable and evil attitudes and behavior; and that's the Jewish-Zionist-Folk (not all Jews). We can identify all these characteristics since the foundation of Israel until today, having stolen the land of the Palestinians and Arabs.

- From here we must conclude that the United States are entirely controlled and even governed by these Jewish-Zionist élite. It makes clear that they still are obsessed from the mission their forefathers got some 3000 years ago. But they have failed and therefore God has revoked them the mission as they misunderstood it (and still misunderstand it today). This frustration is the engine of their behavior. They are fully on the path of deicide to hurt and punish God; and what better way than to destroy his creation.

- We can go back through the history until the time of the early Roman Imperium and we can identify everywhere these signs that hundreds of authors have reported during two millenniums. The biggest difficulty is that the supreme masters that trigger wars are never on the political or public stage.

- There are enough sings that allow posing the thesis that they have triggered the First World War and also the Second World War, and many wars during the last centuries. Both wars had the same prophase as we also have today: an extreme economic war destroying entire nations or governments. The proof of this thesis is a job for neutral political experts and scientists.

🖎 From this point of view the entire history of the Holocaust and Israel could have a new dimension, and Hitler and his SS-masters a new face.

US Army and NATO

In 1971, the United States stored 7,300 tactical weapons in Europe. Today they have 200 nuclear warheads in European countries without an all-out accord from Europe. Where are the remaining 7,100 tactical weapons now?

The US Military has more than 1,000 military bases in about 130 countries and another 6,000 bases in the United States and its territories. In total, there are more than 3,000,000 US personnel serving across the planet. Additionally they have an unknown number of so-called secret bases and other bases in the Middle East. There are still 268 bases in Germany, 124 in Japan, and 87 in South Korea. There are also bases in other European Countries.

Global NATO: The U.S. and NATO military alliance has expanded into a globally active 50-nation military network; Germany, Australia, Spain, France, Italy and Japan also on the new war-boat.

The North Atlantic Treaty Organization (NATO) has 24 military bases in Turkey alone.

The annual cost of US intelligence has been made public for the first time and it shows that the overall spending this year (2010) has surpassed $80 billion.

Figures released by the government demonstrate that $27 billion goes to military intelligence and $53.1 billion covers the CIA and some of the other 16 intelligence agencies. Official documents have shown that in 2007 spending was $43.5 billion and as such spending on intelligence has almost doubled since then.

By the end of November 2010 the number of private military contractors in the United States will surpass the combined number of US Military forces and police officials combined for the first time in history.

In the US, in any case of "state of emergency", the government can take over any goods and wealth, including fruits, vegetables or meat the citizens produce in their own garden; self-evidently without paying or compensating for it.

The US Government now says it has the right to assassinate any American citizen they deem a "terrorist". Under US law only the President can define who a "terrorist" is. Under US law the President's defining of an American as a "terrorist" is not only secret but cannot be reviewed by any court.

A study calculated the cost of the Iraq and Afghanistan wars, publicized as the "war against terror" could end up costing the American tax payers $6 trillion.

🖎 The United States are entirely controlled and even governed by the Jewish-Zionist élite; and as today the US controls Europe, which means behind the curtains are the Jewish-Zionist élite, certain private banks included.

🖎 All this evil doing that is light years away from an appropriate reaction to terrorist attacks, is not of European roots on the level of the modern folks and philosophical or social sciences since 1980.

🖎 Considering the Jewish-Zionist character and role as described above, we must conclude that most of Europe's nations are chained and controlled from the 'invisible Jewish-Zionist hands'. Europe, European politics and the European economy are fully in the hands of the mega-octopus with thousand vacuum arms.

🖎 Based on this thesis (or facts) we can get a much deeper understanding of the actual development of Europe and of the 'paralyzed' lawmakers, ministers, and heads of state in Europe in all European and global matters of mega-dimension.

Motives for Wars

- Need for water, food, and other resources
- Bankrupt financial situation of a country
- Lunacy of a religion; collective religious psychosis
- Dogmatism and fundamentalism of a religion
- Unsolved conflicts between countries from the past
- Sovereignty of stolen lands
- World greed for power
- Geopolitical strategic interests
- Radical ideologies

- Poverty, misery, famine
- Climate change: originator and victims
- Archaic understanding of humans and human life
- Financial interests of the arms industry
- Industrial profit and power interests
- Projection of the evil aspects of humans onto others
- Extreme high rate of unemployment
- Collapse of economy and industry
- Extreme distribution of wealth (financial power)
- Power conservation in unstable political situations
- Originator and victims of emissions
- Political megalomania and psychopathic leaders
- Governmental oppression and exploitation of a folk
- Regional injustice in most basic services
- Religious claims to have the only true God and belief
- Fundamentalist missions to lead humanity to God
- Brainwashed, manipulated, blinded and exploited folks
- Religious frustration and hate of God
- The planet in danger due to climate change / pollution
- A nation in danger due to overpopulation
- Humanity in danger due to overpopulation and emissions

- All motives for a new global war, WWIII are given today!
- The motives of big wars are pathogenic. Narcissism, neurosis and psychopathic, perverse lunacy, obsession and greed, lies and falseness are the source of area-wide murdering, but do not sufficiently explain a roadmap for a Third World War, the elimination of humanity, and the destruction of the planet.
- The madness of the 'One World Government' of the capitalist coalition, stirred up also by hidden rulers as well as by certain leaders in Christian (Evangelic) circles must have a roadmap to succeed.
- Triggering religious wars against Islam and the Muslim people is only a step on this roadmap (without religious interests) in order to maximize profit on a level of trillions of dollars.
- The neo-capitalistic economics as analyzed in the 'Trilogy on Economics', is the roadmap to destroy entire countries, entire governments, folks and cultures, and to trigger wars.
- Those who are thoroughly unhappy and entirely unfulfilled want to destroy the happiness of others. Those who can't love not even a tiny bit, want to destroy the love others have, even if this love is of low quality. Together with economic means it leads to war.

Trouble Spots

Definition 'trouble spot': A place of recurring trouble, riots, civil war, religious fights, political unrest, especially a country or region where fighting between opposing groups often happens. These places are today in 2012:

- Afghanistan
- Albania
- Algeria
- Angola
- Antarctic areas
- Arctic areas
- Armenia
- Bahrain
- Basque (Spain)
- Beirut (Lebanon)
- Bekaa Valley (Lebanon)
- Bosnia
- Burma (Myanmar)
- Cambodia
- Central Iraq
- Chechen (Russia)
- Chiapas (México)
- Colombia (drug war)
- Congo
- Côte d'Ivoire
- Cuba
- Cyprus
- Darfur (Sudan)
- Eastern Congo
- Egypt
- Falkland Islands
- Gaza Strip
- Georgia
- Gibraltar
- Golan Heights
- Guinea
- Iran
- Israel
- Jammu and Kashmir
- Kosovo
- Kuril Islands

- Lebanon
- Liberia
- Libyia
- Macedonia
- Mali (West Africa)
- Mindanao Island (Philippines)
- Nigeria
- North and South Korea
- Northern Ireland
- Northern Uganda
- Pakistan
- Rwanda
- Senkaku (Diagoa; China/Japan)
- Serbia
- Sierra Leone
- Somalia
- South Africa
- South Lebanon
- Southern Sudan
- South Vietnam
- Straits of Hormuz
- Syria
- Sudan
- Taiwan
- Tamil (Sri Lanka)
- Tibet
- Tunisia
- West Bank
- Western Sahara
- Yemen
- Zimbabwe

Motives and causes for trouble are:

Poverty, hunger, access to water and resources, food price increase, lack of money, financial collapse, high rate of unemployment, high rate of taxes, lack or abuse of human rights, corruption, megalomaniacs, exploitation of manpower (slavery) and resources, ignorance towards citizens, lack of democracy, dictatorship, mega land ownership, political interests, demands for independency (separation), martial laws suppressing people or minorities, apartheid, ethnic conflicts, military coup, extreme ideologies and dominance of religion (fundamentalism), and collective religious psychosis.

We obviously must differentiate between different dimensions:

- Some trouble spots are focused on a small location or areas.
- Some trouble spots are small, but exaggerated from media.
- Some trouble spots encompass entire nations and its neighbors.
- Some trouble spots have roots that go back centuries.
- Some trouble spots have roots that go back 50-60 years.
- Some trouble spots started years ago or are rather an 'event'.
- Some trouble spots are simply the result of a previous war.
- Some trouble spots show geopolitical fights between super nations.
- Some trouble spots are caused from foreign states by proxy activities.
- Some trouble spots have continuous demonstrations, riots, or unrest.
- Some trouble spots have active war like activities.
- Some trouble spots have grown due to foreign states meddling in.
- Some trouble spots have periodical or continuous terrorist attacks.
- Some trouble spots are expressing extreme tensions between states.
- Some trouble spots fall in the categories: genocide, war crimes, ethnic cleansing and crimes against humanity

There must be ways to solve trouble spots! Some factors are hindering already from the beginning:

- All trouble spots are fundamentally caused by, politicians who are unable to deal correctly with the resources, and the needs and wants of their folk.
- Some trouble spots are fundamentally caused by religious, especially fundamentalist differences; sometimes triggered or abused by politicians.
- Here and there is an opposite group or are some politicians lured, seduced, or abused by external governments with hidden interests.
- Some trouble spots are fundamentally and thoroughly caused, triggered, and heated up from foreign governments following their special interests. We can even search for the hidden 'secondary effects': Trouble is created to deviate (distract) people's attention from other fields or areas or activities. Trouble can also be ignited to indirectly making money (e.g. selling weapons, increase of food prices, giving loans to governments).
- The top global trouble spot since 1948 is Israel with its Arab neighbors. Some Israelis (Zionists) have stolen the land with the fake and insane argument that God gave them this land some 3000 years ago. This trouble spot has caused wars and endless misery to the Arab and Palestinian people. Half of the world was and still is in danger of being roped into a World War III because of this trouble spot. The Zionist regime has begun genocide, war crimes, ethnic cleansing and crimes against humanity. Thousands of politicians tried to solve this problem by

talking, negotiating, mediating. This approach will never lead to a solution.

- Most of the trouble spots could be solved. But the mind of the responsible people is not working well, blocked from stubbornness, narcissism, and religious bubbles. The fixation on fundamentalist understanding is simply a psychological matter that can be solved. There are also strategies of mediation that absolutely all politicians do not have in their mind and mediation programs. There are too many politicians involved in mediations that have no idea about the mind and soul of people, and their skills and strategies are ridiculous.

- There are the conceited and arrogant capitalist mediators and politicians that think they can solve the problem with weapons, money and Western models of 'democracy'. They also think that they can solve a trouble spot within months or a year. These people should first solve the problems they have at home. And they have immense dangerous problems at home.

- The UN as a possible mediator has terribly failed in the past. A major cause is that the United States with their Jewish-Zionist interests dominates the UN behind the scene. Therefore from there, there is no potential to solve any heavy trouble spot. Ban Ki Mon has shown at the NAM Conference in Teheran (28.8.2012) that he is a ridiculous puppet of Israel's and UN' interests; he disqualified himself as a mediator. [87] It also shows how rotten the UN is!

- We must accept that there are trouble spots that need a decade to be solved in a sustainable way. Western politicians always want fast success of their activities to use it for their own career interests. As politicians have their own trouble at home, they are never free of interest in a mediation setting. Not even this complexity can they see; so, how can they see the true and genuine path of solution for another folk, group or country?

---

[87] http://www.presstv.ir/detail/2012/09/02/259492/nam-leaders-support-iran/

3.10. Unemployment

- In many countries the rate of unemployment is disastrous: 8-25% and up to 30-50% of the youth do not have a job.
- Hundreds of millions worldwide do not have a job! Billions of people are underemployed or get a wage that does not allow for a humane life.
- 80% of working people in the industrial nations are scared of losing their job and see no future perspectives.
- Many well educated, professionals are finding it difficult if not impossible to find a decent and suitable job or they are simply underpaid.
- For more and more couples, the creation of a family becomes a financial nightmare; love is gone and the relationship is in a permanent stress.
- Additionally, real estates, food, and consumer goods are all becoming more expensive; but the wages have stagnated or decreased for a decade.

Unemployment causes:

- Low self-esteem
- Decrease of self-confidence
- Permanent state of fear
- Distress
- Tense inner state
- Extreme frustration
- Sleeping disorder
- Unhappy state
- Bad mood
- A lot of quarrels
- Alcoholism
- Depression
- Aggression
- Suicide
- Exaggerated smoking
- Passivity
- Isolation
- Feeling of shame
- Mentally low activity
- Emotional weakness
- Loss of creativity
- Feeling down
- Despair
- Helplessness
- Discontentedness
- Emotional regression
- Compliance
- Conformance
- Tendency to obey
- Tendency to take orders
- Servility / submissiveness
- Mental disorder
- Psycho-somatic reactions
- Unhealthy eating
- Higher risk of accident
- Labor unrest
- Separations and divorce
- Destruction of family life
- Lack of care for one's children
- Lack of care for health

Impact in the Psychical Organism:

- Decrease of constructive thinking
- Imbalanced interpretation
- Ignored genuine inner needs
- Disinterest in spiritual qualities
- Preponderantly negative feelings
- Very low power of and interest in love
- Reduced control of perception
- Disinterest in personal development
- Strong defense mechanisms
- No satisfaction or fulfillment

→ Work is a genuine inner need. Work is also a real need to make life.

- Politicians do always have work, but they never have an idea what it means not to have work or to have part-time work that does not allow for making a living.
- The high unemployment rates in European Countries and in the United States show that politicians are unable to correctly do their job.
- A rate of 10% is an extremely serious problem; a rate of 20-25% is a terrible disaster; a rate of 30% or more is an outrageous catastrophe. The responsible ministers should be fired immediately!
- If the head of a state with very high unemployment rate can't solve this problem, then he is in the wrong place.
- High unemployment rates show clearly that politicians responsible for this field are unable to think in complex networks, to find pioneering solutions, and to efficiently govern the apparatus towards solutions. These politicians are always agents of a systemic corruption in their country. Their mind is unable to manage such tragedies and disasters!
- High unemployment rates are essentially caused by a wrong construction of the production fields, the neglected field of the small firms of production, a high lack of vocational education (especially technical and educational fields), miserable working attitudes of the majority of citizens, an exaggerated service sector (i.e. tourism), a blown up public administration, and the globalization that is at the core and the roadmap for an 'imposed' global governance.
- The actual financial crisis shows us another field of causes: luring and seducing the citizens for consumer loans (100% - 120%) mortgages, and

luring and seducing the politicians to 'easy public debt' preponderantly to pay their corrupt system. These politicians behaved like naïve children.

- The worst of all is that the financial earthquakes in such countries are fully planned and triggered from the mega-banks. In general from banks (that had only the focus of multiplying money) in order to destroy societies and entire states. Politicians did not learn anything from history!

- Finally we can observe a re-armament and endless wars for the past 20 years, triggered and managed from the United States, NATO and the European Union. The costs of wars and re-armament for 20 years cover all the public debt of these countries! This means: without these wars, America and Europe would flourish and develop in balance. We have here again this roadmap of deicide that is in the hands of the Jewish-Zionist Masters! Seen from here, the private banks such as Goldman Sachs and Co are just the tools used to destroy countries and to trigger wars. And this will have no end in the coming decades. The evil roadmap is also working in Asia. [88]

Normative statement: Political abettors of the deicide roadmap must be brought to justice and must be fired; must be put in prison. Europe must become free from foreign military bases (and occupancy), free from the economic supreme masters, free from systemic corruption, and free from this insane neo-capitalism. That's the only way to find back the outstanding collective inner potentials and cultural values that have created in the past immensely valuable expressions of human values.

Normative statement: The evil military and economic octopus having most of the world under control must be eliminated. The roots of this terrifying cancer must be eliminated. Europe is in highest danger of totally collapsing. The only system that is relatively neutral is the military of each country. They must save the values of their constitution and eliminate all the Trojan horses everywhere.

Or is there another solution?

---

[88] http://www.globalresearch.ca/dangerous-crossroads-america-pressures-asean-bloc-to-contain-china/

3.11. Public Debt and Financial Disasters

(See also Schellhammer: Economics III. 2012, p. 299-300)

Some examples about debt and losses (increases are to be expected with every year):

- Bank losses: approximately $1,600 billion
- Loss of real estate values (US and UK): $4,650 billion
- Damage to the world economy: $4,200 billion
- Destruction of asset values: $50 trillion
- Financial Governments spent $10.8 trillion on bailouts
- $3.6 trillion was spent on the bailout in the US
- $2.4 trillion on the bailout in the UK
- $3.2 trillion on the bailout in other rich nations
- $1.6 trillion was spent by China and other emerging nations
- The US spent the equivalent of 25.8% of its GDP
- The UK spent the equivalent of 94.4% of its GDP
- In the UK the cost (debt) per person is $50,000 (£31,250)
- The collapse of the Spanish property market resulted in €360 billion of bad debts. Spain has over one trillion public debt.
- The United States reached public debt of $16 trillion (end of August 2012).
- Over the next five years, the UK government debt is expected to rise from £600 billion to £1.4 trillion, while the US national debt could double to $10 trillion.
- The global debt has reached $75 trillion. [89] [90]
- Germany 2010: Public debt rises to €2 trillion: The debts of the German Federation rose nearly 22% (€230.3 billion) to €1,284 billion. The debt of the German States stood at €595.3 billion at the end of 2010. The debt of the municipalities and local authorities stood at €119.4 billion. [91]

- ☞ The entire global financial system is a gigantic Ponzi scheme. It is designed to keep everyone enslaved to perpetual debt.
- ☞ A monstrous debt psychosis has infected most politicians. They all wanted to solve the economics problems of their society with money for which they have not worked before. They all lied to their citizens saying

---

[89] http://thewe.cc/contents/more/archive/us_debt.html
[90] http://usdebt.kleptocracy.us/
[91] http://alpari-forex.com/es/news/1220558.html

that everything is 'normal' with debt and it produces prosperity for everybody.

❦ A huge majority of politicians, lawmakers, ministers, and heads of state have not been and are not prepared for their job and responsibility. They have not learned anything from history, about economics, and the very fast changing world. They have a brainwashed mind from the media and believe like their naïve citizens that the media really report the truth. Even those who have studied political science and economics are brainwashed and manipulated with selected and distorted knowledge. They all have sold their country to the supreme masters of economics. No intelligence! No Spirit!

❦ It is an outrageous crime against humanity that politicians worked and work with increasing public debt to finance their rotten state administration, their systemic corruption, and their neo-colonialist war road map of neo-capitalistic imperialism.

❦ Nobody has a realistic plan to pay back these public debts. It will need 200 years if we also consider the (high) interest rate. At least the 8 following generations will have to pay for the inability of the politicians today. Or an unimaginable war will solve the problem, but create even worse problems.

❦ Many nations have lost their collective soul and their autonomy due to public and private debt. Who is the winner? The true winner is not on the visible political stage!

The World Economic Forum says that we need to grow the total amount of debt by another $100 trillion over the next ten years to 'support' the anticipated amount of 'economic growth' around the world that they expect to see …

❦ Giving loans on a level of hundreds of billions, to other countries always lead to a reduction of the independence of countries and creates an external control through foreign financial institutions.

❦ Certain banking sectors can never stop to offer loan traps, to put people and governments and entire countries into more and more trouble.

❦ Who will pay back in the future all the actual public debt and additionally these $100 trillion debts over the next 10 years?

❦ It is a lie that billions or trillions of additional debt will lead to economic growth. Those governments who need billions need this money to first pay their apparatus, their internal obligations (e.g. pension and unemployment payments), and pending interest of 'old' debts. With that no economic growth is created.

- If a country in economic trouble gets one trillion with an interest of 7-12% then it must create new (pioneering) production entities and later they must be able to sell these products with a profit that is higher than this trillion plus the interest during the given period. This is not possible and leads to a total collapse if many other countries try the same game. The sole winner is the lender bank that has doubled the amount of money within 10-13 years.

- Those lawmakers, ministers, and heads of state that try to solve financial trouble, to economically survive, and to create higher living standard with public debt have learnt nothing from history. They always repeat the same mistakes – and this for probably more than 2000 years. It leads always to a ruined state, a ruined folk, a ruined culture, and in the end to wars that make everything much worse. The winners are always the same kind of people.

- Who says that economic growth is always and everywhere the right thing to achieve? Who says that the Western living standard is the right model for the entire world, for all folks and cultures? These winners that are always the same kind of people for centuries, even millenniums, say and repeat this as a kind of mantra that is simply the trap for the sham! They are the monstrous scammers, the most dangerous octopus on earth!

4. Power and Powerlessness

4.1. Political Systems

"(The term) 'Government' refers to the institutional processes through which collective and usually binding decisions are made." [92]

Imagine: 30 (or 100) people use the term 'government' in a discussion. Now we ask them what they mean when using this term. We can be sure that we will get many different responses. We will also get different responses between a group of politicians and a group of people talking about 'government'.

'Institutional processes' we understand as processes that occur within the political system. The system it self does not take any decision. People in office take decisions. Are there decisions that are not binding? What kind of decisions, are not binding?

"Government is more commonly understood to refer to the formal and institutional processes that operate at the national level to maintain public order and facilitate collective action. The core functions of government are thus to make law (legislation), implement law (execution) and interpret law (adjudication)." [93]

What are these 'institutional processes'? Here it says 'decision making processes'. In that sense 'government' means 'the system of decision making processes'. This is not about algorithm, not about mathematical models of probability or a game theory. It's about humans that take decisions based on rules given by the system. Taking decisions a human must have the indispensable knowledge and mental skills in order to take the right (efficient) decisions. Some important questions arise:

- What are the abilities these humans must have to take the right (efficient) decisions?

---

[92] Heywood, p. 26
[93] Heywood, p. 26

- Are all their decisions really in the interest of the citizens?
- A human is not a rational apparatus; a human is a complex organism. And seeing all humans together, they form a very manifold 'collective organism'. Do politicians know how these organisms function?
- About what do these special people take decisions?
- Does the rules of the system allow taking the right (efficient) decisions?
- Does the system provide the right knowledge (information) in order to take the right decisions?

We can construct the term 'government' as a system with some specific sub-systems or (dynamic) characteristics:

- The decision making agents in the system
- The information providers (media, advisors, lobbyists)
- Information, knowledge (sources, disposition)
- Structure of proceeding (official channels or quality steps)
- Rules (communication, exchange of information, taking decision
- Abilities of the agents (communication, negotiation, argumentation)
- The subjects that are objects of decisions
- Practical frame conditions (e.g. local distance between the agents)
- The interests that flow in decision making processes

Considering other description from the author the term 'government' also includes:

- Formal processes
- Institutional processes
- To maintain public order
- To facilitate collective actions
- To make laws
- To implement laws
- To administrate

"To govern means to rule or to control others. Government can therefore be taken to include any mechanism through which ordered rule is maintained, its central features being the ability to make collective decisions and the capacity to enforce them." [94]

To govern is the core activity of the government. The components of the term 'to govern' are based on the author:

---

[94] Heywood, p. 26

- To rule
- Mechanisms to control
- Capacity to maintain the rules
- The ability to make collective decisions
- Embedded in institutions and in institutional processes

→ The more we identify the components (sub-systems and elements) that form part of the term 'government, the better and more constructive we can analyze, interpret, conclude and simply discuss this matter.

→ If we understand the 'core elements' as the center of a system, then we already know: there are other indispensable parts (sub-systems) that are crucial (or: immanent) to govern, rule, make decisions, etc.

"A political system or regime, on the other hand, is a broader term that encompasses not only the mechanisms of government and the institutions of the state, but also the structures and processes through which these interact with the larger society." [95]

The author differentiates between 'government' and 'political system' (or: regime). We would rather prefer drawing here a corresponding system (or model) as a base for discussing this matter.

The core elements about the term 'political system' from the author are here:

- Regime (which means: system, characteristics, order, but also governance, etc.)
- Mechanisms of government
- Institutions of the state
- Structure of interactions with the citizens
- Processes of interaction with the citizens
- Interrelations between the complex whole
- Interrelations between powers, wealth, resources in society
- Organization of economic life
- The way everything operates through the government

"Political system: A network of relationships through which government generates 'outputs' (policies) in response to 'inputs' (demands or support) from the general public." [96]

---

[95] Heywood, p. 26
[96] Heywood, p. 26

In a very general view given from the author:

- A political system is a network
- A political network consists in relationships
- A political system generates an output
- A political system has an input (from the public)

'Input from the public' is very simplified, a bit. A political system has many more different inputs: lobbyism, politics of the Central bank, advisors and experts, pressure groups, international relations, the media, the bureaucrats, and 'the invisible hand' also has its fingers in the network. We can even understand the taxes (and other financial income) as an input.

➔ A political system doesn't work without its agents and without money! In that sense a political system is an organism with measurable (countable) and non-measurable and non-rational vivid factors.

"A political system is, in effect, a subsystem of the larger social system. It is a 'system' in that there are interrelationships within a complex whole, and 'political' in that these interrelationships relate to the distribution of power, wealth and resources in society. Political regimes can thus be characterized as effectively by the organization of economic life as they are by the governmental processes through which they operate." [97]

This is indeed a very large social system and we must ask if it does make sense to create such a large system in opposite to the system of 'government'. The whole is so much extensive that we can easily miss seeing the single parts of the system. We have already shown that the term 'politics' and 'political science' can be easily manipulated at least it contains and excludes different parts.

➔ Based on our result in chapter one, we see here in the description of the term 'political system' a huge lack of elements.
➔ Economic categories can never encompass all factors that form the processes in a political system.
➔ A political system is much more than the managing apparatus of distribution of power, wealth and resources.

"Aristotle held that governments could be categorized on the basis of two questions: who rules and who benefits from rule?" [98]

---

[97] Heywood, p. 26
[98] Heywood, p. 27-28

Indeed, these two questions are the core questions for many things in life: There are actions or events or incidents and a way to understand and manage this complexity. The second question gives us in most cases the right answer. It's similar to the detective's questions, which he investigates about a given murder: What are the motives? Who benefits from this murder? We must extend the two questions from Aristotle. They are too much focusing on too small perspectives. We can create more relevant questions:

- Who rules?
- Why can a person or group rule?
- Who benefits how from rules?
- Who looses what from rules?
- Is a ruler free to act (in a democratic process) or hidden forced to act?
- What are the declared motives (interests) to rule?
- What are the hidden motives (intentions) of a specific ruling action?
- What are the consequences of a specific ruling action?
- What are the collateral effects from a specific ruling action?
- What are the short term and long term effects from a specific ruling action?
- How does a specific ruling action affect human's mind and behavior?
- Which human values are respected and promoted from a specific ruling action?
- Which human values are ignored or destroyed from a specific ruling action?

"Aristotle's purpose was to evaluate forms of government on normative grounds in the hope of identifying the 'ideal' constitution. In his view, tyranny, oligarchy and democracy were all debased or perverted forms of rule in which a single person, a small group and the masses, respectively, governed in their own interests and therefore at the expense of others. In contrast, monarchy, aristocracy and polity were to be preferred, because in these forms of government the individual, small group and the masses, respectively, governed in the interests of all." [99]

The ideal from Aristotle leads today to very serious questions:

➔ What is the 'normative ground' in governance?
➔ What is the difference between tyranny and democracy if today democracy is (in America and Europe) totally perverted and abused for imperialistic purposes?

---

[99] Heywood, p. 27-28

"Totalitarism is an all-encompassing system of political rule that is typically established by pervasive ideological manipulation and open terror and brutality. Totalitarism differs from both autocracy and authoritarianism in that it seeks 'total power' through the politicization of every aspect of social and personal existence. Autocratic and authoritarian regimes have the more modest goal of a monopoly of political power, usually achieved by excluding the masses from politics. Totalitarism thus implies the outright abolition of civil society: the abolition of 'the private'. Totalitarism regimes are sometimes identified through a 'sixpoint syndrome':

1. An official ideology
2. A one-party state, usually led by an all-powerful leader
3. A system of terroristic policing
4. A monopoly of the means of mass communication
5. A monopoly of the means of armed combat
6. State control of all aspects of economic life." [100]

We can observe in the United States:

- Reduction of human rights
- Limitation of freedom
- All-embracing control of citizens
- Brainwashing through the media
- A hidden dictatorship
- A self-fabricated terrorism
- A global imperialistic politics with military and money
- Death penalty
- 95% control of the media by 5-6 owners, operating also globally
- State control of businesses (through extensive regulations)
- One de facto ideology: Global governance and economic profit
- Neo-colonialist dominance and expansion with debt-means
- Total control of all money movements (economic life)
- A two-party-system where differences are irrelevant
- The control through corporations
- The Jewish-Zionist dominance in governmental processes

And we can observe the same development in most European Countries, Great Britain included.

How far away is this from dictatorship, fascism, and a totalitarian regime? What are the human values of the differences?

---

[100] Heywood, p. 29

"The first and second worlds were further divided by fierce ideological rivalry. The first world was wedded to 'capitalist' principles, such as the desirability of private enterprise, material incentives, and the free market; the second world was committed to 'communist' values such as social equality, collective endeavor, and the need for centralized planning. Such ideological differences had clear political manifestations. First world regimes practiced liberal-democratic politics based on a competitive struggle for power at election time. Second-world regimes were one-party states, dominated by 'ruling' communist parties. Third-world regimes were typically authoritarian, and governed by traditional monarchs, dictators or simply the army. The three-worlds classification was underpinned by a bipolar world order, in which a USA-dominated West confronted a USSR-dominated East." [101]

The author divides three political blocks:

- Capitalist first world
- Communist second world
- Developing third world

The division criteria between the first and second world is ideological rivalry. And the third world is characterized by a low level or lack of living standard. Does this help us to understand the world? Can politics operate with such a blinded division? Is such a division correct?

- This is old-fashioned ideological thinking and has not much to do with the global reality.
- The author enormously trivializes differences between governments respectively countries.
- The communism from Marx, Lenin, and Stalin has gone. It seems that the author doesn't know that. Communism today is much different.
- The term 'communism' can fill easily 1000 pages to describe. Has the author ever been in North-Korea and Belarus?
- Does the author know that there are huge differences between Saudi-Arabia and Iran, or Afghanistan and many other Islamic states?
- Switzerland is a capitalistic state and India is also a capitalistic state; even China includes capitalistic characteristics, and so does Russia. What are the differences?
- The author understands communism as centralized planning, collective endeavor, and social equality. We have extreme and rigid central planning through regulations in USA and EU! We have an immense disequilibrium

---

[101] Heywood, p. 29

in wealth, wages, and economical power in general. We have a dehumanized population in USa and EU through media and high living standard. What is the value of such capitalistic developments?

☞ The author constructs his world based on the Bush era: the axis of the evil. But we could argument that the axis of evil is Israel-Jewish Zionism-USA and Europe.

☞ Since more that 100 years Great Britain, Germany, France, Italy, the United States and Israel are the most evil warmongers with international dimension. We could divide these states on earth on the criteria: 'aggressive, bellicose operating globally or internationally'.

☞ We also could divide the nations by religious criteria: Christianity that has killed and massacred an estimated one billion humans. And what can be said of the Islamic states? How is the picture in Buddhist states? And what do we, and thousands of other authors, since 2000 years say about the Jewish folk?

☞ Selling students such primitive and ideological views as 'knowledge' is unfair and amoral. This is not science! It's a way of dictatorship, manipulating, brainwashing, and shaping the opinions and character of students.

➔ To find a correct systemic approach politics and political science need a new set of multi-variant characteristics that gives a useful and correct picture about the different nations! And this picture must include human values and the state of the mind and soul of people, and also the state of the nature, including contamination.

The liberal democracy claims to have the following characteristics:

"Liberal democracy (consists in):

- Constitutional government based on formal, usually legal, rules
- Guarantees of civil liberties and individual rights
- Institutionalized fragmentation and a system of checks and balances
- Regular elections that respect the principle of 'one person, one vote; one vote,
- One value' party competition and political pluralism
- The independence of organized groups and interests from government
- A private-enterprise economy organized along market lines." [102]

---

[102] Heywood, p. 30

The components of liberal democracy are:

- Formal, usually legal rules
- Civil liberties
- Civil rights
- Institutionalized fragmentation
- System of checks (control)
- Regular elections
- Respecting the citizens vote
- Party competition
- Political pluralism
- Independence of organized groups
- Independence of government's interests
- Private enterprise economy

Questions arise about this kind of democracy:

→ Is there a non-liberal democracy somewhere on earth?
→ Is a 'conservative' or 'green' democracy different to these characteristics?
→ Is a monarchy also a democracy?
→ Are there differences compared with a republican democracy?
→ What is the value of a democracy if the banking world and the corporations rule this so called democracy?
→ Where is the democracy if a few people rule 80% of the global media?
→ Where is democracy if everywhere the 'invisible hand' of the Jewish-Zionist body has taken hold?
→ How many regulations are sustainable until liberal democracy dies?

☞ Some constructions of terms can lead to a very distorted understanding.

"New patterns of economic development have brought material affluence to parts of the third world, notably the oil-rich states of the Middle East and the newly industrialized states of East Asia, South Asia, and, to some extent, Latin America. In contrast, poverty has, if anything, become more deeply entrenched in parts of sub-Saharan Africa, which now constitutes a kind of 'fourth world'." [103]

These new developments create a lot of confusion with the classical terms that determine 'systems':

---

[103] Heywood, p. 30

- Third world countries become capitalistic.
- Third world countries become industrialized.
- 'Third world' countries with extreme increase in poverty are now the 'fourth world' countries.
- Industrialized countries have incredible increase in poverty.
- There is in some countries an increase of democratization.

"The phrase 'third world' is widely resented as being demeaning, because it implies entrenched disadvantage. The term 'developing world' is usually seen as preferable." [104]

- Some constructions of terms can lead to a very distorted understanding.
- The classification in first, second, third, and forth world countries does not match with the reality of more than 180 countries on earth.
- A classification (criteria of a classification) can distort and demean the value of a country.
- A classification (criteria of a classification) can also distort and over-value a country.
- The usual criteria of such a classification are very artificial, even ideological, and do not respect the manifoldness of 'qualities' in a country and of its citizens (e.g. mind, soul, behavior, realized human values). Political science offers us a purely or preponderantly economic categorization.

The main question is with which criteria we can categorize the countries. No system of classification relies on one single criterion. The author sees the problem and proposes eight categories (or factors):

"No system of classification relies on a single all-important factor. Nevertheless, particular systems have tended to prioritize different sets of criteria. Among the parameters most commonly used are the following:

- Who rules? Is political participation confined to an elite body or privileged group, or does it encompass the entire population?
- How is compliance achieved? Is government obeyed as a result of the exercise or threat of force, or through bargaining and comprise?
- Is government power centralized or fragmented? What kinds of check and balance operate in the political system?
- How is government power acquired and transferred? Is a regime open and competitive, or is it monolithic?

---

[104] Heywood, p. 30

- What is the balance between the state and the individual? What is the distribution of rights and responsibilities between government and citizens?
- What is the level of material development? How materially affluent is the society, and how equally is wealth distributed?
- How is economic life organized? Is the economy geared to the market or to planning, and what economic role does government play?
- How stable is a regime? Has the regime survived over time, and does it have the capacity to respond to new demands and challenges?" [105]

A new system of classification (typology); we summarize the criteria:

1) The ruler and the political participation
2) Means to achieve compliance (threat, bargaining, and compromise)
3) Centralized or fragmented government (checks and balances)
4) Ways to achieve power; open, competitive, monolithic regime
5) Distribution of rights and responsibilities (government, citizens)
6) Level of material development (living standard parameter)
7) Organization of economic life, role of government
8) Stability of a government (capacity to respond to new challenges)

We have here qualitative and quantitative parameters. How can quantitative parameters transformed into quantitative parameters (a scale)?

There is always a 'more' and a 'less', but different qualities or types do not necessarily include 'better' or 'worse'.

A comparison of different patterns of regime presumes standard values that all countries would need to achieve. This is an ideological cheat.

There are many folks and people that have a different way of living, different cultures, different religions, differently dominant human values, different geographical conditions (e.g. climate), and different environments (nature). To bring all countries on the level of the same yardstick is extremely arrogant and conceited.

Every country has his history and roots that are century or millennium old. Some countries may need another century to go through an indispensable enlightenment; others should run today for enlightenment. The development of a country together with the evolution of its folk has an intrinsic dynamic or intrinsic interference.

---

[105] Heywood, p. 31

It is a requirement of democratic rules that each folk can decide themselves about their development and future. Telling other countries what is right in matters of governance becomes very fast Western (capitalistic) hubris and leads to imperialistic ambitions, called 'neo-colonialism'.

→ Before the Western governments and academic institutions of political science tell other (third world) nations what is right for their regime and folk, they all should better ask themselves: Is everything of high importance correct in our country?

→ No other country and folk has brought to the entire world so much misery and suffering as the Western world with its Christian religion!

"This approach highlighted, for instance, differences between codified and uncodified constitutions, parliamentary and presidential systems, and federal and unsanitary theory, which became increasingly prominent in the 1950s and 1960s. This approach concerned less with institutional arrangements than with how political systems work in practice and especially with how they translate 'inputs' into 'outputs'." [106]

The author shows us the key regime features from the 19th and earlier twentieth Century consisting in political factors, economic factors, and cultural factors. He misses to mention religion, which is much more than a culture. The regime types that can be identified in the modern world are, corresponding to the author:

- Western polyarchies
- New democracies
- East Asian regimes
- Islamic regimes
- Military regimes
- We add: Western oligarchies

"Polyarchy can be understood as a rough or crude approximation of democracy, in that it operates through institutions that force rulers to take account of the electorate. Its central features are as follows:

- Government is in the hands of elected officials.
- Elections are free and fair.
- Practically all adults have the right to vote.
- The right to run for office is unrestricted.
- There is free expression and a right to criticize and protest.

---

[106] Heywood, p. 32

- Citizens have access to alternative sources of information.
- Groups and associations enjoy at least relative independence from government." [107]

The Western polyarchies already have converted into hidden oligarchies:

- The government is not anymore in the hands of elected officials; it is in the hands of the economic supreme masters.
- Elections are free and fair, but some groups dispose of immense money and the media operate in shaping the citizens' opinion in the interest of the 'oligarchs'.
- The right to vote doesn't say anything if the votes are about significant matters in relation to real democratic participation. 20,000 lobbyists have much more say behind the curtains.
- The right to run for office is unrestricted, but hopeless without significant money and influence. This right should be restricted and determined with human factors, including integer personality, professional knowledge and skills.
- Free expression and demonstration do not change anything in the main political stream.
- Access to other sources of information is limited by the citizen's ability and education. The powerful propaganda through the main media is unbreakable.
- The independence of heads of state, prime ministers, presidents and Chancellors is a myth. As soon as they are in office they will get the message they don't have the say but must obey the order from the 'invisible body'.
- The wars triggered from the Western world since 1991, the economic crisis today, the increasing extreme rate of unemployment, the heavily increasing poverty in USA and EU, the outrageous public debt, the lost generation of today, the actual wars and bellicose activities from USA and EU show us who has the say and what matters with 'regime'. Have a look at the Middle East and from there at Asia and Russia.
- The author has forgotten to say that money rules the world, money together with military power, and nothing else. The concentration of money today shows us who has the say.
- The author also ignores the systemic corruption that forms essential part of governance, not only in Spain, Italy, and Greece, but in a majority of countries, including the United States where we can identify a total systemic corruption.

---

[107] Heywood, p. 33

🖝 The approach from the author is very narrow-minded and short-sighted. It seems that he has no idea about the reality of regimes nowadays.

An essential characteristic of polyarchies is: "Individualism is often seen as the most distinctive of western values, stresses uniqueness of each human individual, and suggests that society should be organized so as to best meet the needs and interests of the individuals." [108]

The value 'uniqueness of each human individual' is without doubt superior. But it is a myth that ignores the real characteristics of humans:

🖝 The big lie here is that humans are absolutely not equal.
🖝 The understanding of 'human individual' is not clarified here.
🖝 95% of humans are not usefully formed, are malformed in their mind, are imbalanced in their mental functions, don't develop and use their mental capacities, are brainwashed with ideologies and fake religions, and are shaped from the economic and political world as a greedy 'consumer'.
🖝 80-95% of all humans are stupid, unable to love and live human values, are liars, cheaters and neurotics, are a mass of 'rats' that contribute nothing to the psychical-spiritual human evolution or the quality (culture) of a society, don't respect the nature and the world of animals, but produce only waste and sewage, and toxic mental energy.
🖝 Such an understanding of humans favors ego-centrism, mass brainwashing, anti-social attitudes and lifestyles, and also abuse of human's manpower.
🖝 The uniqueness of a human must be formed, educated, and shaped to be 'unique'.
🖝 For the western folks and politics all humans of other countries are anyway under-humans, evil humans, unworthy humans.

"Western polyarchies are characterized by a diffusion of power throughout the governmental and party systems." [109]

'Diffusion of power' sounds interesting and to be a positive value. But 'power' is not simply power. Taking decision about a new train line is not the same as taking decision to invade Iraq, Libya, Afghanistan, or the Balkans. Taking decision in favor of genetic modification of food is not the same as taking decision for an increase of taxes.

---

[108] Heywood, p. 33
[109] Heywood, p. 34

We have in Europe and the United States different systems of power, for example:

- Coalition government
- Separation of power between executive and assembly
- Bicameral system
- Multiparty system
- Proportional representation
- Federalism
- Codified constitution and a bill of rights

Is it really important to find out which of them is the best system? Are all these systems really better than a single party system, a centralized government, and a unicameral system (etc.)?

We have in a majority of European countries and in the United States a series of mega-problems:

- Increase of poverty, decrease of the middle class, gigantic public debt and also private debt, highest rates of unemployment, lost young generation, high contamination, high rate of mental disease and behavior disorder, an extreme critical development towards dehumanization, destruction of the eco-systems, a collective brainwashing of unseen dimension in history, permanent wars triggered in other countries, a rigidity of regulations and control of all citizens that destroys this liberal individualism (or 'uniqueness of each human individual'), a loss of all superior human values, and etcetera.
- The de facto system of power is relative to the individuals in office. The use of power can never be better than the people that practice this power. A huge majority of these individuals do not have the necessary integrity, character, spirituality, knowledge, and skills to use the power, to promote humans' evolution, and to lead a folk or to solve collective problems.

We also identify the same problems and many more or other kind of mega-problems in many non-European countries around the globe, even much worse pictures of society and human life in some countries. So we must assume that the kind of 'democracy' and governance is irrelevant in respect to these problems that already have become of global importance and urgency.

"The USA is also the most overtly religious of western regimes, and it is the only one, for instance, in which Christian fundamentalism has developed into a major political force." [110]

Now we have to come to the probably most explosive issue in governance: Christian fundamentalism is a major political force. Fundamentalism refers to the Old Testament. There are the Evangelists, the Mormons, and other Christian Churches that are preponderantly rooted in this unholy book full of falsifications, fairy tales, fabrications, lies, myths, anecdotes, disfiguration of real history, full of protagonists and places that never existed and events that never happened, and etcetera. These Churches are fundamentally in coalition with the Jewish religion (and Zionism) that has the same roots (the Old Testament). The Jewish religion and Zionism claim to be the sole authentic folk and inheritors.

- As a logical consequence fundamentalism is and produces mental insanity.
- The American governance is heavily influenced by religious insanity.
- The Catholic Church is fundamentalist and shapes governments in Europe.
- Religious insanity (or sham) shapes the mind of politicians and citizens.
- The alliance between fundamentalist religion and governance is evil.
- As money rules the world, the supreme economic masters must be rooted in this fundamentalist religion; they understand themselves as the authentic inheritors of God's mission their forefathers received (Genesis I, verse 28).
- Herewith we have identified the worst hornet's nest in the political system.

But the western World declared 'communism' as the worst and most evil political system. The characteristics of communism are in the view of the author:

"Communism, in its simplest sense, is the communal organization of social existence on the basis of the collective ownership of property. As a theoretical ideal, it is most commonly associated with the writings of Marx, for whom communism meant a classless society in which wealth was owned in common, production was geared to human need, and the state had 'withered away', allowing for spontaneous harmony and self-realization:

- Marxism-Leninism is the 'official' ideology.

- A communist party that is organized on the principles of 'democratic centralism' enjoys a monopoly of political power.

---

[110] Heywood, p. 34

- The communist party 'rules' in the sense that it dominates the state machine, creating a fused state-party apparatus.
- The communist party plays a 'leading and guiding role' in society, controlling all institutions, including the economic, educational, cultural and recreational institutions.

Economic life is based on state collectivization, and it is organized through a central planning system." [111]

Let's assume that all ideologies have some good, some bad, and some completely wrong or stupid characteristics. However, an ideology is always an idea, a complex idea that includes human and social values, and is confronted with a very complex and mostly very difficult and critical reality.

The Western World has generally the Capitalism as their superior ideology. Politicians and Western science of politics see Communism as their arch enemy. Both have failed terribly which we have proven with the state of humanity and the planet. The worst factors in the global mega-parameters are the regicide and deicide. And deicide is a western made roadmap.

We identify some essential characteristics of communist political system:

- Democratic centralism
- Monopoly of political power
- Central power rules the state machine
- There is only the state-party-apparatus
- One party rules and guides society
- One party controls everything in society
- Economy is based on central planning

The communist system itself doesn't make the state and governance. There are people in charge using and abusing the system. These people have a mind and soul. They are always confronted with the specific circumstances in their country that are sometimes too big to solve within a short period. And they have their real or invented enemies.

---

[111] Heywood, p. 35

Therefore we have to distinguish between the systemic structure reflecting an ideology, and the people in office more or less believing the ideology. Foreign propaganda (psychological war) and economic measures (used as a tool for economic war) can damage and destroy any other country's political and economic system. Rearmament is also a tool to destroy the economy of another country.

Monopoly of power, centralized regulations of everything, control of all human's economic activities, and one-state-party is certainly not really tasteful. It ignores the human's different potentials and talents. It ignores the indispensable psychical-spiritual development of the individuals. It ignores the public education that should prepare people for mastering life. It ignores many human values. It also ignores the cultural differences (ways of living), especially those who are related to the nature (geological environment) and history.

Marxism-Leninism failed. But did this ideology with its political practices fail due to the ideology? Or have there been (since the beginning of the twentieth Century) also internal forces such as fundamentalist religions, systemic corruption, and people in charge with a tremendous lack of integrity, professional (political) knowledge, and political skills? Did the communist system fail due to Western economic wars and their propaganda machine full of lies? Did this communist ideology fail due to Hitler's breach of contract having started a war against Russia? As each political system in the past has a dynamic factor which leads periodically to a development of the political system, how could this communist system have developed without such destructive internal and external influences?

"The process of democratic transition has been both complex and difficult, highlighting the fact that democracy should not simply be viewed as the 'default position' for human societies. New democracies not only lack developed democratic political cultures but they also have to handle the strains produced by the external forces of globalization as well as rapid internal change." [112]

We identify here between the lines the usual triumph of the Western Capitalism. The same simplification and polarization, distorting history, we also have found in all classical books about study of economics.

---

[112] Heywood, p. 35

The values of a real democratic system and a real democratization are without doubt in general desirable. But the democratic political culture must be taken under a critical view.

→ A real democracy requires well educated people, also psychologically and spiritually, and especially for mastering life and understanding democratic politics.

→ A real democracy requires well educated people in charge which includes integrity, professional (political) knowledge, a well-balanced and developed mind, global and economic knowledge, and a series of special skills.

→ A real democracy requires transparency, a debt-free public administration or at least sustainable public debt for sustainable projects of society's interest, and independent agents in charge.

→ A real democracy requires a system that is free of systemic corruption, free of corporative dominance, free of religious dominance, free of power abuse, free of (external) public debt, and also a result of a cultural development that can't be forced or speed up with military intervention or trade punishments.

🌢 The Western model of democracy can serve as a frame with some specific valuable and constitutive criteria. But selling the Western model of democracy is nowadays simply a way of aggressive imperialistic politics.

🌢 It seems that the author is driven here by a 'democratic psychosis' that is nothing more than a bubble or an immense lie.

🌢 It is a very undemocratic attitude from America and Europe to impose the Western model of democracy on other nations using military force or proxy entities, or other 'punishments', or luring their leaders with gigantic amounts of money.

🌢 Since more than 20 years the US Army and NATO have triggered and executed terrible wars and have committed outrageous war crimes without having asked the citizens if they want it and see it as necessary for protecting their own country. Never the American folk and the European folks would have or would agree today such evil and satanic imperialism. This has absolutely nothing to do with a true democracy.

"Confucianism is a system of ethics formulated by Confucius (551-479 BCE) and his disciplines that was primarily outlined in *The Analects*. Confucian thought has concerned itself with the twin themes of human relations and the cultivation of the self. The emphasis on *ren* (humanity or love) has usually been interpreted as implying support for traditional ideas and values, notably filial piety, respect, loyalty and benevolence. The stress on *junzi* (the virtuous person) suggests a capacity for human development and potential for perfection realized in particular through education. (...) Confucianism has been seen, with Taoism and Buddhism, as one of the three major Chinese systems of thought, although many take Confucian ideas to be coextensive with Chinese civilization itself." [113]

"East Asian regimes tend to have similar characteristics. Firstly, they are orientated more around economic goals than around political ones. Their overriding priority is to boost growth and deliver prosperity, rather than to enlarge individual freedom in the western sense of civil liberty." [114]

Without doubt there are countries that need economic growth in order to provide the necessary resources for the satisfaction of the basic needs of their folk.

Talking about 'to enlarge individual freedom' requires first to know what is meant with the word 'freedom' and 'civil freedom'.

There is not much freedom if the products and services for basic needs of a folk are not allocated and not affordable for all citizens.

The word 'freedom' suggests something like 'unlimited freedom'. But there is never an unlimited freedom, and freedom requires responsibility and skills to use the freedom in a sustainable way.

Freedom of speech has two sides. On the one side it is of highest value and indispensable of the human evolution. Not being allowed to substantially criticize a system or people in public charge (political and religious) suffocate any development of collective interest or necessity. On the other side, what 95% of people talk in public and on the Internet (about politics, human values, God, religion, the truth, and etcetera) is mere toxic mental rubbish that can convert into very destructive effects in a society.

---

[113] Heywood, p. 36
[114] Heywood, p. 37

"China's acceptance of capitalism has blurred the distinction between it and other East Asian regimes, profound political contrasts survive. China, in political terms at least, and North Korea, in both political and economic terms, are unreconstituted communist regimes, in which a monopolistic communist party still dominates the state machine." [115]

- What the author tells us here is pure ideological scrap. It is very short-sighted and superficial, covering the real political and historic context.
- North Korea is exposed to an imperialistic, very bellicose 'arm' established in South Korea for imperialistic interests all over the Pacific.
- China has its own very bad experiences, especially with the British government and imperialistic expansion since more than 100 years.
- The 'monopolistic communist party' is a pejorative word. Does the author know what the everyday political reality there is?
- The word 'China's market Stalinism' does not reflect the real economic world of China. Here again the author operates with an ideological template suggesting that 'democracy' is the sole right alternative.

"In Japan and 'tiger' economies such as Taiwan and Singapore, growth is now based largely on technological innovation and an emphasis on education and training, whereas China continues, in certain respects, to rely on her massive rural population to provide cheap and plentiful labour." [116]

- The Japanese soul has been broken and humiliated to the core with the two nuclear strikes from the Americans, militarily absolutely unnecessary.
- The 'tiger economy' is nothing more than compensation for the lost human values and to forget the inner pain and the broken soul.

"Theocracy (literally 'rule by God') is the principle that religious authority should prevail over political authority. A theocracy is therefore a regime in which government posts are filled on the basis of the person's position in the religious hierarchy. This contrasts with a secular state, in which political and religious positions are kept strictly separate. Theocratic rule is illiberal in two senses. First, it violates the distinction between private and public realms, in that it takes religious rules and precepts to be the guiding principles of both personal life and political conduct. Secondly, it invests political authority with potentially unlimited power, because, as temporal power is derived from spiritual wisdom in this type of regime, it cannot be based on popular consent or be properly constrained within a constitutional framework." [117]

---

[115] Heywood, p. 37
[116] Heywood, p. 37
[117] Heywood, p. 37

Considering that all big religions are archaic religions and basically not better or worse than Christianity, theocracy is really a story for the archaic Age.

But how do we see the situation if the Archetypes of the Soul with all its inner processes, also the supreme Archetypes of the Soul, both rooted in the activity of the 'spiritual intelligence', and the entire complexity calls for all humans for a holistic psychical-spiritual development? What it this concept is the 'true religion' for al humans and all cultures and folks on earth? Should such an understanding form part or pre-condition for politics and political career?

"Islam is not, however, and never has been, simply a religion. Rather, it is a complete way of life, defining correct moral, political and economic behavior for individuals and nations alike." [118]

"Shari'a: Islamic law, believed to be based on divine revelation, and derived from the Koran, the Hadith (the teachings of Muhammad), and other sources." [119]

One aspect here is substantial and crucial: A true religion can never separate its teaching from the complex mind that is being formed already during the prenatal time (as described in chapter 2.5. and 2.6.) and the responsibility of individuals and institutions (state) for forming or re-forming (through schools and individually) the psychical functions and training the right way of operating with the spiritual functions (dreams, meditation), and the knowledge and skills that are indispensable for living and holistically growing.

- The Western democracies and probably all democracies on earth ignore this true inner life! What a disgrace! Herewith the values of a democratic system fall down by 95%, like shares of a public corporation.
- It is not the Western duty to teach the Masters of the Islam what is a true religion. They have to find it out themselves, even if it takes 100 years or more.
- The 'divine revelation' has been abused a million of times in the history of mankind. There is only one source that can provide such 'knowledge': the dreams and with that the vivid (not copied or ordered) fulfillment of the Archetypes of the Soul. And that requires immense inner performances.

---

[118] Heywood, p. 38
[119] Heywood, p. 38

"Whereas most regimes are shaped by a combination of political, economic, cultural and ideological factors, some survive through the exercise, above all, of military power and systematic repression. In this sense, military regimes belong to a broader category of authoritarianism. Military authoritarianism has been most common in Latin America, the Middle East, Africa and South East Asia, but it also emerged in the post-1945 period in Spain, Portugal and Greece.

The key feature of a military regime is that the leading posts in the government are filled on the basis of the person's position within the military chain of command. Normal political and constitutional arrangements are usually suspended, and institutions through which opposition can be expressed, such as elected assemblies and a free press, are either weakened or abolished." [120]

- The Western countries could only survive due to its economic and military power.
- There is no country on earth that has converted in such an insane military institution like Europe and the United States.
- There is no country on earth that has so much damaged, killed people, and destroyed other nations' infrastructure and political systems than Europe and the United States.
- The true 'regimes' are those with an insane military structure behind so called Western democracy.
- Indeed, all Western political systems are occupied by civil agents and not by military officers or generals. But does it say who really governs the country?
- The true rulers of the Western world are neither on the political stage nor on the military stage, but they trigger the wars. That's Western militarism! So, what's the difference between Western democracy and military regimes?

Up to now we don't really know what 'democracy' is. We could say it is a political system that allows citizens to vote, to elect specific individuals for an office in the government. Therefore the system has some specific rules that allow to vote. Lincoln's statement, a million times quoted, said: a government of, by and for the people. In other words or our interpretation: Individuals that form part of the people are elected by the people to govern for the people. So, five questions arise:

---

[120] Heywood, p. 39

1. Who are the people?
2. How far should the people's political participation go?
3. What does 'govern' mean and include?
4. What is to govern in the interest of people?
5. How far does this ruling go into the people's life?

Some critical thoughts:

1) A majority of people are naïve, credulous, conceited, submissive, cantankerous, stubborn, talk before they think (are blabbers), have no idea about society and the world, are neurotics and narcissists, have no significant knowledge or very narrow ideas about politics, are totally undeveloped mentally, ignore their soul (inner life) and human values, never stand for the truth, are unable to love, don't use their mind for living and resolving problems, are heavily overcharged in their unconscious mind, over-estimate themselves, are not really responsible for their life, etc.

☞ Stupid people should have a say in a democratic system?

2) In most democratic systems people can go voting, electing individuals of a political office, and sometimes decide about local projects. If we consider the environment around a process of voting, we identify some critical factors: the media shape opinions, mostly based on vague facts and much distorted around such facts. Those individuals (or political parties) that dispose of much money have logically much more chance to win. Eloquent individuals with enough knowledge about mass psychology have better chances than others. People are programmed with ideology, dogmas, and opinions, mostly a result of their biography. 95% of people do not have any political understanding. A huge majority does not understand what the classical words that are used for seduction and lure means. At least people can express their views and interests. What are their interests? How are their views? A majority has a very narrow view and very ego-centered interests.

☞ Ego-centered and narrow-minded people without substantial political knowledge should have a say in a democratic system?

3) There are many ways to govern. The term 'democracy' does not determine the system (e.g. centralized government or not, direct or representative democracy). We also can't simply deduce from this term the way to govern. In most so-called democratic countries people can't vote about neo-colonialist and imperialistic activities and wars. They can't vote about many matters politicians take decision, for example all kind of regulations, reduction of privacy, and control of their money.

- Once the individuals elected for a political office, these people do what they want; in most cases it does not cover the interests of people.

4) What is to govern in the interest of people?

The term democracy does not give a limit nor does it determine the 'untouchable' privacy. Why should everybody be allowed to have and drive a car? Why should everybody allowed to take an airplane for long distance holidays? Is genetic modification of food in the interest of people? Is the over-exploitation of oceans in the interest of people? Is all the tasteless junk-food in the interest of people? Are wars in the interest of people?

- To govern in the interest of the people, the masses, can lead to a catastrophe and ruin a country.
- The governments have very little commitment in providing people with healthy (and tasty) food or in protecting healthy air and the resources for the future generations.

5) How far does this ruling go into the people's private life?

A liberal individualism allows much more freedom than many other ideological positions. Other tendencies nowadays want to control and regulate everything in people's life and business. Politicians in America and Europe have already drastically reduced the private realm or meddle in the private life of people using the media (e.g. shaping opinions and ways of living, moral categories)

- Proclaiming 'democracy', 'freedom' or 'humanitarian' values is much abused and perverted in the national and international business of politics.

De facto, a long list of political parties claims to be 'democratic': the communists, the liberal, the conservative, the republicans, the socialists, the 'green' party, the 'grey panther' (representing the interests of elderly people), the Christ-social party, the social democrats, and others.

There is a modern development that is called 'neo-corporatism'. The interests of corporations, including banking, is organized, privileged and institutionalized in order to influence policy. The ruling class or elites have the say, but after elections rarely the citizens. Parliamentary democracy has become a theatre pretending democratic processes. It doesn't matter which political party is in power.

The economic oligarchy replaced democracy; and nobody wants to see it. So, why should we further discuss pluralism, multiculturalism, and democracy? It's all irrelevant today, in America and Europe.

- The genuine value of democracy is lost. Human values in political projects and decisions are to a large extent ignored. The truth has no place in the political business. It's all about increase of growth (GDP) at any price.
- The people's democracy doesn't exist anymore. Did it ever exist?
- All the wars provoked, triggered and executed from America and European countries since 120 years – today from the US Army and the NATO – never wanted from the people, show us: democracy never existed, it's a myth covered with the freedom of (opulent) consumption, of satisfying narcissism, of unlimited offers for pleasure and entertainment.
- All forms of democracy in Europe and the United States are an outrageous failure and lead to the destruction of the planet; even to a WWIII.
- Political declarations about democracy are a crude piss take.

In general we identify some faults in the system:

- → The people are disconnected as soon a candidate is elected and in office.
- → The power of the head of state is too extensive, not controlled enough.
- → The institutional influences are much stronger that the voice of the people.
- → Those who control the monetary system are not controlled enough by the government. And the government is not controlled enough by the people.
- → A high or all-embracing governmental centralization is already 75% dictatorship.
- → A representative democracy intrinsically leads to an oligarchy and goes further on a path towards dictatorship.
- → The fact that people can vote about projects and elect individuals for an office does not mean that the system operates democratically.
- → As most big media are in the direct or indirect power of selected individuals who on the other side are part of a hidden pressure group, the Western democracy has become a chimera.

4.2. Political Ideology

What is a political ideology?

A hypothesis describes an assumption about the existence of one variable or of the interaction of two or more variables (or facts). A hypothesis is always the start of a scientific work. A hypothesis must be proven. A 'conspiracy-theory' is a hypothesis about an assumed existent conspiracy.

A theory describes the way of interaction between two or more variables. It tries to explain a dynamic interaction. Cause and effect is here a matter of interpretation that sometimes is obvious and sometimes is also a matter of further research.

A thesis is either a diploma work or a statement that has to be proven.

An ideology is a way of seeing the world. In a broader sense an ideology is a concept or sum of thoughts about the world. In a general way we can say, an ideology is a way of philosophical thinking about matters of politics and society.

An ideology contains ideas, thoughts, facts, theses, hypotheses, theories, presuppositions, assumptions, attitudes, norms, rules, paradigms (model, model of thought, sample, example, leading line, and ideal), meanings and interpretations.

The critical nature of an ideology is the fact that it always implies meanings, human values, and a scale of good-bad, better-worse, constructive-destructive, efficient-inefficient, more-less, progressive-regressive, and a scale expressing priorities, importance and urgencies.

An ideology always starts from a position: the state of the mind and soul of a person and its environmental conditions. The position is the reality in the inner 'screen' of a person that contains the result of the perception about the inner and external world.

Most ideologies contain also elements of a doctrine, a kind of infallible, immovable, and not changeable political 'dogma' (like the dogmas in Christianity). Such elements that are not comprehensible or common sense always produce imbalance and fights; it leads to strife and in the end to wars.

→ The only critical component that characterizes ideology as non-scientific and reprehensible (must be rejected) is when a component becomes a 'natural', non-provable and non-comprehensible infallible principle and all the rest consists in facts and theories.

Nevertheless there are infallible, immovable, and not changeable valuable characteristics.

Humans have a mind and this is always since ever and forever like that. This statement does not say anything about the quality and efficiency of its capacities build up during life. But there is a lot of knowledge that explains which functions are rooted in the mind. We can also say: We never start building the second floor when the first floor is not prepared. We start building a house with the cellar or ground floor, never with the roof. Other examples: before we change something we should explore and know what it is about. A person can never drive a car if he has no idea how driving a car is working. A living room totally full of old furniture can't be fully re-furnished if (most of) the old stuff remains in the room. Or: Continuous important imbalance in human's mind and soul always has critical long-term effects. If one small wheel of a watch is damaged, then the watch doesn't work. A grain of sand in the gearbox can damage and block the functioning of the entire gear box.

Or: The psychical-spiritual development of a person is a dialectic holistic process. In general, there are psychological and spiritual principles that are 'infallible'. One can't steal a higher state of development. Without a complete catharsis of the unconscious mind, the complete fulfillment is never achievable. Or referring to the Archetypes of the Soul we can say: these inner processes are infallible, absolutely indispensable and not changeable or manipulated by a person. Infallible is also the statement: Humans can never manipulate the spiritual intelligence, but always the intelligent functions of the mind.

In that sense we conclude: Ideologies always indispensably include 'infallible principles' of the human's nature and life. The cheat is also always given: declaring a principle as infallible 'eternal law' produces criticalities, like the grain of sand in the gearbox. In other words: a manipulated 'infallible dogma' in a system of thought that creates criticalities. This is the very first critical aspect of ideologies.

Another critical aspect is the natural matter mentioned above: the state of the mind and soul of a person and its environmental conditions. The position is the reality in the inner 'screen' of a person that contains the result of the process of perception about the inner and external world. Therefore it is logical that different ideologies exist and it is nothing 'bad' at all. The critical problem is that people with different ideological concepts in the mind understand them as the 'best' and 'most unique' with eternal validity. Stubbornness and stupid cantankerousness can lead to very critical social matters. In that sense:

→ The neurosis of people plays an immense role in discussing ideologies and the characteristics of social sciences.

Ideology understood as a concept of thought, facts, theses and theories are indispensable, in science and politics. But we must respect: As human evolution (individual and collective) is always in a process of development. Political ideologies are also a reflection of a given reality from a specific epoch.

→ From a scientific and practical point of view ideologies are not principally to reject, except if they are as a whole made 'absolute' due to embedded parts that are nothing more than 'political dogmas'.

Based on these considerations we want to have a closer lock at the political 'isms' such as liberalism, socialism, conservatism, etc. Our comments and interpretations are based on the above given understanding of ideology.

Summarized statements from Heywood, p. 44:

- Ideology is not simply a worldview. No ideology can encompass the entire world.
- Ideology is more than a developed social philosophy. It reflects the human realities together with the institutional and natural environment.
- Abusing ideology as a political weapon is a neurotic or amoral human factor, not a factor that is part of ideology.
- Humans can discuss why creeds and doctrines are not useful and very often dangerous. But an ideology consists in much more than creeds and doctrines.

Summarized statements from Heywood, p. 44:

- An ideology is not per se an instrument of social control to ensure compliance and subordination. People convert an ideology into such an instrument.

Summarized statements from Heywood, p. 45:

- An ideology is much more than a set of ideas. It includes many facts, proven realities, proven theses, common sense, comprehensible statements, and elements from the real world of politics and society.
- Political action is rarely simply the result of an ideology. The human reality and objective circumstances have an immense impact in political action.
- Using the world 'overthrow' here converts all ideologies to something pejorative and evil. The intention to overthrow a political system shows a way to achieve changes. But there are legitimate and constructive ways to make changes. Changes form part of human evolution.
- Each human should periodically 'make account' of his way of living and state of his life. It is nothing bad for the political world to make periodically account about the state of society and the political activities.
- It is something very normal that humans have desired visions for their life, formulate aims they want to achieve. Therefore also the agents in the political world should or must make (and revise) periodically desired visions and aims.
- People have an idea of a 'good life'. Depending on their given circumstances these ideas can much differ between humans. It is also 'normal' and desirable that politicians make their idea of a 'good society'.
- The way to achieve a desirable good life or desirable good society depends on many practical factors and a huge complexity of given circumstances. They're efficient and less efficient, short and long ways to achieve objectives. A dispute about such ways is something normal between people and political agents or groups. This has nothing to do with ideology.
- Strategic considerations about achieving aims are only one side of the 'ways' to achieve an aim; the other side is that people always want to achieve something within a very short period. People and also political agents must accept: Mistakes in the past have a price to resolve the mess. Some critical situations need many years can even take 10, 15 or 25 years to be changed to the good (the vision, aims). In general, aims of high value encompassing the entire society require more than 15 years in achieving. This has nothing to do with ideology, but much with real circumstances.
- The huge majority of people want to possess without having worked for it. They want a house or a car, although it's not appropriate considering

their material and psychological capacity. The same problem we identify in the world of politics. And this also has nothing to do with ideology.

- All known ideologies have a very archaic understanding of humans and human life, which in the end includes society or living standard. Herewith starts the fundamental problem. Such a foundation can only create very crucial problems and logically the methods to master these problems are also 'archaic'. That's why politics since centuries go in a circle and miss bringing forward the true human evolution. This has to do with ideology.
- There is in most societies a neurotic fault in the political activities and in discussions about political aims and means. For pure reason of pleasure, envy, greed, ego-centrism, narcissism, and compulsion in destroying, the agents, drag every other ('hostile') idea, aim or measure in the mud. This has nothing to do with ideology.
- It is a very common dynamic strategy of people and political agents while arguing about an objective matter, they use it to fight on a personal (relationship) level to be the winner (the top dog), to reduce and destroy the power of the counterpart, and to implicate the other person (or group) in his neurotic conflict. And this has absolutely nothing to do with ideology.
- Another human factor in the political world (and in general) is that people would rather kill a counterpart than to question, to revise their own creeds, beliefs, attitudes, interests, aims, visions, and measures or strategies. Most politicians are in general cowards and hypocrites, also in their fixation of an ideology. And this is part of the psychopathology and certainly not of ideology.

Now, we want to collect and discuss some characteristics from different classical ideologies. We ignore here that today some characteristics have strongly lowered their importance or have a different understanding between nations.

(We collected information form Heywood, p. 45-69. We cannot guarantee the entire correctness.)

1) Liberalism

- Laissez-faire capitalism (guarantees prosperity)
- Individualism
- Unique identities of humans
- Supreme importance of the human
- Humans are of equal moral importance
- Reduced importance of the collective body
- High importance of the development of individuals

- Performance and abilities lead to the 'good'
- Individuals make their own moral decisions
- Freedom is the core value (to enjoy)
- Freedom stays above equality, authority, justice
- The world is of rational structure
- Individuals are able to make wise judgments
- Individuals are the best judges of their own interests
- Importance of progress
- Importance of capacities of humans to resolve matters
- Individuals are 'born equal', at least in moral terms
- Humans are different in talents and willingness to work
- Equal chances to realize their unequal potentials
- Meritocracy: talent + hard performance
- Toleration in thinking, speaking, valuing, acting
- Pluralism in moral, cultural and political diversity
- Importance of intellectual progress
- Free market (includes free competition)
- Natural strife for harmony between rival views and interests
- Authority operates with consent or willing agreement
- Authority arises from 'below', grounded in legitimacy
- Limited government (to avoid developments towards tyranny)
- Faith is placed in self-help, responsibility, entrepreneurship

Comments to 1):

To give highest importance to humans and to understand humans as 'unique' is certainly a key requirement for all ideologies. But the understanding is extremely archaic and cut and dried. But humans need education, are shaped already from prenatal time. All psychical-subsystems must be formed, trained, and shaped, each subsystem in balance with the other systems. The entire development of humans is embedded in different social contexts, starting with the family.

One the one side an individual must become an own identity (becoming a unique identity), but we can't separate human life from the social (collective) context. In that sense it doesn't make sense to give reduced importance to the collective. It is wrong to say that individuals are 'born equal', at least in moral terms. Moral attitudes have a strong emotional component that already shapes a fetus in the prenatal time. In the best case we can say: biologically 'born equal'.

As long as humans are not holistically formed and trained (mental functions), they can't make 'wise' judgments. To be the 'best judge of one's own interest' promotes ego-centrism that leads together with neuroticism and narcissism to individual and collective criticalities. It's a huge over-estimation to assume humans want to perform, are willing to work hard, and to develop and use their potentials (talents).

Unlimited freedom doesn't exist, and if somebody or a group tries to get it, the result will end in an extreme imbalance that creates individually and collectively damages. The right use of freedom requires a well-formed mind, much knowledge, and a series of skills to master life and to perform in the professional world. Laissez-faire attitude allows those who already have much, to get much more at the costs of the collective. Fact is, in the modern times of today performance alone doesn't guarantee success. To master life one must acquire a lot of knowledge and learn the appropriate skills. The natural strife for harmony between rival views and interests is a fairy tale.

The 'free market' is an illusion and leads humanity to the doom which we can easily see with the actual public debt, the concentration of money, the absolute amoral business doing of the banking world, and the mega-parameters that shows us how much the corporations and the modern life style already have destroyed the world. The dominance of the media in the hands of a few people is another proof that a free market is a lie as soon somebody wants to grow with little money at disposal. The thousands of regulations for the business world also paralyze any 'healthy' free market with a 'healthy' free competition.

Toleration in thinking, speaking, valuing, and acting is indispensable. But if tolerance becomes unlimited and destroys human values and the Archetypes of the soul, then the entire community loses the evolution. 'The ideal of 'equal chances to realize their unequal potentials' is also a myth. The importance of intellectual progress must be seen in the interrelation with all other mental 'sub-systems', including the 'spiritual intelligence' and the 'love capacity'. We cannot put 'intelligence' hierarchically on the top. If humans form part of the world, the world is never preponderantly 'rational', rather emotional, stupid, ignorant, arrogant, lazy, neurotic, etc.

We can say 'faith' is placed in self-help, responsibility, and entrepreneurship or 'hard working'. But if the parents and social environment are rather emotional, stupid, ignorant, arrogant, lazy, neurotic, and etcetera, then there is very little change for such 'faith'.

Governmental authority can't operate with consent or willing agreements. Authority doesn't arise from 'below', grounded in legitimacy. The supreme masters of the economy govern the governments and from there, together with their media power entire folks and continents. However, the superior governmental floor is disconnected from the folks and the real problems of society embedded in a global dimension.

🖢 Either the authors of such ideology and their followers are very naïve; blinded, and shortsighted, with low knowledge about the reality, or this ideological concept is a treacherous construction to deceive the folks and to operate freely and invisibly on the economic stage behind the curtains.

2) Conservatism

- Tradition: desire to conserve virtues, respect endured customs, institutions
- Wisdom of the past, 'tested' structures and practices
- Promoting stability and security (social and historical belonging)
- Limitations of human's rationality
- To consider the infinite complexity of the world
- Experience, history, pragmatism
- Practical goals
- Beliefs as an attitude or approach to life
- Humans are imperfect: limited, dependent, security-seeking
- Humans are morally corrupt: selfishness, greed, thirst for power
- A strong state, strict laws, stiff penalties
- Society is a vivid organism with indispensable structures
- Family values, values of community
- Importance of health and stability of society
- Gradation of social positions and status
- Differing roles and responsibilities
- Importance of mutual obligations and reciprocal duties
- Care for the less fortunate
- Authority is always exercised from 'above'
- Authority provides leadership, guidance, support
- Leadership as a result of experience and training
- Freedom requires responsibility (obligations, duties)
- Having property is vital, gives security, a certain independence
- Property is an exteriorization of people's personality (performance?)

Comments to 2):

Here is no picture about the human's mind and soul. Except: humans are imperfect and corrupt. And their rational capacity is limited. As politicians are humans, they also are imperfect and corrupt, and their rational capacity is also limited. This is a much reduced, very superficial, arrogant and archaic understanding of humans. A very disputable picture!

The political answer can only be the 'authority' that orders, control, and punish from 'above'. Logically it also leads to a strong state, to strict laws, stiff penalties, and strong leadership, guidance, and support. The political answer is authoritarian. But are these leaders really 'mature', 'wise', and do they have the necessary knowledge and skills, including integrity?

The wisdom of the past means everything and nothing at the same time. There is certainly valid wisdom, but also old-fashioned 'ideas' about life that doesn't match with the modern world. Some customs may be still valuable, but the modern world needs new customs that are adapted to the real life. Some virtues are always valuable; others are only for the past archaic human theatre.
There are values of high importance: security, stability, health, and family values. Care for the less fortune is a matter of defining the line of poverty. The practical (pragmatic) approach is strong and discussible.

A new understanding of society has practical consequences: society is a vivid organism, with indispensable institutions, role distribution and responsibilities. People and the agents in the political world must be trained for understanding and managing this organism. We can understand freedom here as a freedom that is limited through this organism and requires also responsibility for the organism.

- Experiences and history is always a source for new knowledge and new ways of dealing with matters of life. But do the people learn from their experiences? Do politicians learn from history? Not much!
- Although the understanding of society is here within a frame of evolution and within the vivid 'organism', the single elements are not related with each other, difficult to identify an intrinsic network, and a contrived authority on the top of all. That's rather against an immanent dialectic nature of evolution.
- We identify here a forced and imposed management of society and the folk, letting the folks at the bottom to simply obey.

3) Socialism

- Human beings are a social creature
- Humans are linked by the existence of a common humanity
- Individuals are shaped by social interactions and participation
- Individuals are a members of a collective body
- Individual behavior results from social factors (rather than innate qualities)
- Humans share and are bonded to a common humanity
- Cooperation comes before competition
- Collectivism comes before individualism
- Competition breeds resentment, conflict, and hostility
- Equality is of highest (and superior) value
- Social equality guarantees social stability and cohesion
- Material benefits should be distributed on the basis of need
- Basic material benefits should not be distributed on merit and work
- Satisfaction of basic needs is a prerequisite for human existence
- Participation in social life is a basic need
- Social classes are categorized in distribution of income and wealth
- Rejection of oppressed and exploited working class

Comments to 3):

Also here we identify a much-reduced understanding of human's mind and soul. The idea that all humans are social creatures implies that they are also individuals with a mind that must be shaped, formed, and trained within the intrinsic potentials. The idea of collective organisms is real, but not the entire story.

Yes, humans are shaped by social interactions and participations, but there are many more factors that shape a human, including self-reflection and all kind of education. To be linked with a community full of stupid and neurotic people is rather a pain and hinders a genuine psychical-spiritual development.

Cooperation and competition do not exclude each other. The view is extremely polarizing and that doesn't reflect a healthy understanding. Above that more than 50% of humans are lazy, lazy-minded, have their heavy inner burden, and a much reduced inner development. Seen as a 'body' it becomes a paralyzed body. Competition with rules is a creative force that can bring forward the evolution (or progress).

The collectivism is an important dimension, but it is exaggerated and ignores that each human has a privacy and uniqueness to be shaped, strengthened, and expressed. That all humans are 'equal' requires saying in which characteristics they are 'equal'. Humans are not equal! Here is an immense lack of balance. The reality is forced artificially.

Indeed, first of all humans have genuine and indispensable needs that must be respected and satisfied. One billion people living in extreme poverty and an additional two billions in significant poverty damages the entire state, the environment, the culture, the individuals, and the planet. Participation in social life is indeed a basic need that is nowadays with social communities on the Internet completely alienated from real human encounter and participation (of living, growing, and managing life).

Defining social classes or social groups is not wrong. The problem is which characteristics form 'classes' or 'groups' in a way that is helpful for its living and development. Exploitation of workers, but also of the natural resources, today of entire states, and of the planet as a whole is a matter of supreme criticality.

- ☞ Although we can identify important aspects of humans and society, the entire concept is extremely imbalanced. In the end it requires a very authoritarian leadership that would not be necessary with an appropriate understanding of humans and its education.
- ☞ Although some concerns even today are of highest importance, the entire packaging through 'collectivism' is rather a bit like a strait jacket.

4) Marxism

- Economic life and the working conditions are of highest importance
- Economic and class factors determine development
- Immutable 'laws' drive history forward, and not the agents
- The driving force of human development is dialectic (interactive)
- Labor is reduced to being a mere commodity
- Workers are alienated from products, process, and fellow workers
- Workers are hindered in being a creative and social being
- Unalienated labor is the source for human fulfillment & self-realization
- Worker subsist through selling labor and are 'wage slaves' (exploited)
- Workers are paid less than the 'surplus value' from their work
- Only the ruling class has economic ownership and economic power
- There is an irreconcilable conflict between ruling class and proletariat
- Highest importance: Production to satisfy genuine human needs

There is a lot here of highest importance today, although written in and for the epoch 100 years ago. The economic life with all its amoral doing and the exaggerated consumption today show us the actuality of Marxist concerns.

Also the critical description of the position of the working class still has highest actuality from China to Europe and the United States. The ruling classes today, called 'the elites' are on a path of unstoppable global destruction (humanity as a whole, societies, and the eco-systems). This process of destruction we call 'decide' as it leads to the elimination of the creation.

In general the societies with high living standard have created a collective self-alienation that already dehumanizes a majority of humans.

- The humans with their mind and soul (inner life) and all their inner potentials, the potential psychical-spiritual development, are fully ignored.
- The conflict between ruling class and the folk is not irreconcilable. There are solutions today that can lead to a new level of enlightenment and human evolution. But the ruling class and also the people need a very heavy lesson first and foremost.

5) Fundamentalism

There is also the environmentalism and more 'isms', but of interest to add here is a short general thought about fundamentalism.

The core characteristics that shape this 'ism' are:

- Principles declared as the irremovable truth
- The texts are infallible and sacred, given from God
- The elements are religious and infallible creeds
- Politics must be founded on these 'dogmas' (beliefs)
- Social life must be founded on religious principles
- The principles promotes selflessness
- The principles require devotion from humans

- Fundamentalism entirely ignores the process of forming and shaping the mind and soul of humans. The understanding of humans is extreme archaic and never sustainable for the future.
- The understanding of religion is rooted in the Ancient times; maybe it was right and useful at that time for leading the folks. But today it's a path towards elimination of all factors that characterizes a human.

- Fundamentalism ignores that each human is responsible for his psychical-spiritual development. We also entirely miss here a useful concept of humans.
- Not even the religious dimension reveals any tin bit of the 'spiritual intelligence'. Such construction can never promote human's evolution.
- Fundamentalism only strengthens and satisfies the power greed of the religious and political ruling class.
- Fundamentalism is extremely authoritarian and based on myths, fairy tales, fabrications, and illusions. It favors paternalism and mental-spiritual slavery.
- Fundamentalism has no understanding that also religion should have an evolutionary learning dynamic like science. It also ignores the fact that whatever a wise man or prophet wrote and said in the past, was conditioned and determined from the personal mental state (inner development), and the collective mental, economic, political and religious conditions.
- All kind of religious fundamentalisms ignore the inner archetypal processes, the Archetypes of the Soul to make vivid, and the supreme Archetypal processes that are a special mission.
- Fundamentalism is based on collective brainwashing and manipulations, never on inner archetypal experiences that result from extensive and profound elaboration of self-knowledge and all these archetypal processes.
- Fundamentalism is an unlimited, psychotic hubris and a frightening abuse of the word 'God'.

Short summary: The all-covering intrinsic faults

→ All ideologies are based on an image (concept) about the species 'human' that is very superficial, much reduced, archaic in its core, naïve in it's destructive potential, ignorant concerning the holistic processes of forming and shaping, unaware of the complexity of human values and genuine inner needs.

→ All ideologies do not consider the interdependences between rational intelligence and spiritual intelligence, love capacity and genuine inner needs, feelings (emotions) and the unconscious mind, the gender characteristics and the inner opposite pole.

→ All ideologies do not consider the extremely distorted and suppressed state of the inner psychical function, and the extreme imbalance between all the sub-systems in the mind of people.

→ All ideologies do not consider that human's behavior and moral character are the result of the forming and shaping of all the inner psychical-spiritual sub-systems.

→ All ideologies do not consider the manifoldness of human values and genuine inner needs, and the high value of being (incarnated) on this earth.

→ All ideologies do not consider that the core meaning of human's life is to explore and develop all the inner psychical-spiritual functions in order to become a balanced and centered 'unity' and 'totality'.

→ All ideologies do not consider that all kind of stupid, naïve, blinded, amoral, evil, destructive, perverse, and insane behavior of humans is the result of unformed, wrongly formed, malformed, ignored, suppressed, and distorted psychical-spiritual functions.

→ All ideologies do not consider that also a huge majority of politicians (agents in the field of politics) have preponderantly unformed, wrongly formed, malformed, ignored, suppressed, and distorted psychical-spiritual functions.

→ All ideologies do not consider that most problems of and in the political world and on or of the planet are made due to the critical way people are formed and shaped.

→ All ideologies do not consider that the biography of people (including 4-6 generations) and the history of the folks (centuries, millenniums) are not simply the past to forget or copy, but also a real energetic presence forcing to repeat all the conflicts and evil doing in the past until it's reconciled and brought forward with new learning.

→ All ideologies do not consider and mainly have absolutely no idea about the Archetypes of the Soul and the supreme Archetypes of a variety of missions (professional and spiritual) that give to the entire humanity the principles, rules, aims, meaning of life, and the path for the solutions of the entire global 'humane organism', called 'humanity' or 'mankind'.

→ No matter which ideology a human is representing and does stand and fight for, they are all in the same essential ways deficient. They are all on the path of deicide, which means: they dehumanize all humans, destroy the planet, ban the truth, take the piss out of the capacities of love and the inner Spirit, cover their inner (insane) deficiency and falseness with (more) lies and distortion, and they menace and punish all those that reveal and stand for the supreme values of humans and humanity.

Political Parties

Political ideologies are represented and practiced by political parties. An overview over the bundle of political parties in different countries, we can find those who represent the discussed ideologies, and others that represent their own combination of the above discussed characteristics. Political parties consist in the characteristics of their ideology.

Therefore it is needless to enter into the practical world of the political parties. They all have the same deficiencies corresponding to their ideology. But there are two practical aspects of high importance that we can shortly question:

1) How do they transform their ideology into practical politics?
2) How does the system of parties influence their practical program?

We try an explorative approach to shape the perspectives of answers:

Political parties need members, want to grow locally and even nationally. A huge majority of possible member candidates are not much interested in reading and analyzing political (ideological) programs. They all have direct and real concerns.

A political party can't tell to possible members that they have to change their opinions and their lifestyle in order to become a member of their party.

A political party can't tell to member candidates that they have first to acquire knowledge and skills in order to become a 'competent' member.

Logically a political party must much reduce the ideological 'mission' and to find out the relevant opinions and concerns people have. From there they must draw their program and 'marketing' that matches with the people's mind. This is the pragmatic way to build up an attractive program and to increase the amount of members.

Since 20 years there are new political parties that try to find a new approach: they inform people, teach them about realities, shape them in moral attitudes and opinions, educate the people, and mobilize as much people as they can for their practical programs. To mention are here especially the environmental parties and the 'green' parties. Here and there new parties arise on a local level that fights for specific concerns and projects.

There are political parties that operate preponderantly with black-and-white labels such as left, right, progress, liberty, equality, tradition, nationalism, and etcetera. They all try to find new members or voters with emotionally striking labels. A hidden strategy is to create a certain rational but more unconscious fear of the 'enemies' (a competing party).

Political parties are the starting point for a political career. To be elected for an office in a (local, provincial) government, a candidate is at the beginning an active member of a political party. Rarely an independent individual can make political career; in the best case on a local level.

Members of a political party with specific duties are strongly active in a network of relationships within the hierarchy of the national party-systems. The entire network of political parties founds and moves the policies, the interests and goals. The bigger a party, the more power it has.

Today in Europe we observe a significant decline in the interest of people to become a party member. Who wants to become a party member? What are the qualifications (knowledge and skills) and personal motives of the candidates and party members? Who can start, once a party member, a career within the party and for an office in a (local, provincial) government?

There is a slogan with a wise core: Reality is the truth; or: reality shows the truth. What is the reality in a society? The list of gorgeous criticalities is long. The visible problems of a society are only the tip of the iceberg. And all problems have an invisible creeping development until they come out on the superficiality. We also have to consider that all big problems have a momentum during its creeping development and future oriented within a perspective of forecast (5, 10-20 years).

- Therefore heavy criticalities in a society reveal the deficiencies of politicians in the past 5, 10, 20 or even 30 years.
- Therefore heavy global criticalities reveal the deficiencies of a majority of politicians around the globe in the past 5, 10, 20 or even 30 years.

- There is no convincing argument that today candidates for a political office or actual agents in a political office do have much less deficiency than those in the past 30 years.
- The immense criticalities of societies, of humanity and the planet today require minimum 25 years to be fully and all-sided balanced on a sustainable path of solutions. Are there members of a political party or incumbents of an office today that can think in networks and a perspective of 25 years? The political system based on a 4-year period of election doesn't allow operating on bigger time perspectives, except short-termism.
- We conclude: the motives to become a member of a political party and to make political career is not founded in professional knowledge and skills that the criticalities of today and tomorrow can be solved with. The motives are ego-centered and preponderantly irrational.
- In a rather vulgar way: Each sleazy toad with enough money, highly eloquent, nepotistic, corrupt and theatrical, ignorant in all critical matters of society, and with a network of people sharing something, can find the way in a political office.
- Hence the skills for winning an election, that are different to governing are consistently applied and have resulted in the systemic failures that are detailed in this book.

4.3. State and Political Structure

What is the difference between a political structure and the state? To find an answer we need first to clarify the term 'state'. A definition consists first in general description.

"The shadow of the state falls upon almost every human activity. From education to economic management, from social welfare to sanitation, and from domestic order to external defense, the state shapes and controls, and where it does not shape or control it regulates, supervises, authorities or proscribes. Even those aspects of life usually thought of as personal or private (marriage, divorce, abortion, religious worship and so on) are ultimately subject to the authority of the state." [121]

The components of a state as described in the quote are:

- Education
- Economic activities
- Social welfare
- Sanitation
- Domestic defense
- External defense
- Etcetera

The state is also an active agent in collective and private fields:

- Shapes
- Controls
- Regulates
- Supervises
- Authorizes
- Proscribes
- Etcetera

Important to be aware of, is that also marriage, divorce, abortion, religious worship (etc.) fall under the regulations from the state.

---

[121] Heywood, p. 89

➜ The state is an entity consisting in specific institutions that are active in the interest of managing all matters of collective and selected matters of the individual life (citizens) within a specific territory.

"The term 'state' has been referring to a bewildering range of things: a collection of institutions, a territorial unit, a philosophical idea, an instrument of coercion or oppression, and so on. This confusion stems, in part, from the fact that the state has been understood in three very different ways, from an idealist perspective, a functionalist perspective and an organizational perspective." [122]

➜ A state can be defined (or discussed) under the ideal, functional, and organizational perspective.

"What is the state?

- The state is sovereign. It exercises absolute and unrestricted power in that it stands above all other associations and groups in society.
- State institutions are recognizably 'public', in contrast to the 'private' institutions of civil society. Public bodies are responsible for making and enforcing collective decisions.
- The state is an exercise in legitimation. The decisions of the state are usually (although not necessarily) accepted as binding on the members of society because, it is claimed, they are made in the public interest or for common good; the state supposedly reflects the permanent interests of society.
- The state is an instrument of domination. State authority is backed up by coercion; the state must have the capacity to ensure that its laws are obeyed and that transgressors are punished.

The state is a territorial association. The jurisdiction of the state is geographically defined), and it encompasses all those who live within the state's borders, whether they are citizens or noncitizens. On the international stage, the state is therefore regarded (at least in theory) as an autonomous entity." [123]

Characteristics of the state are:

- Sovereignty
- Unrestricted power

---

[122] Heywood, p. 90
[123] Heywood, p. 91

- Superiority
- Public bodies
- Making decisions for the collective
- Enforcing its decisions
- Exercises in legitimation
- Decisions are binding for citizens
- Operates in the interest of the folk
- Instrument of domination
- Has supreme authority
- Has a right of coercion
- Can punish (legitimated violence)
- Forces to obey
- Operates within a determined territory

→ De facto all these activities are operated by, agents in office. In that sense the state becomes a humane face.

→ What a state is allowed to do or must do through its agents is a matter that humans (the citizens of the state's territory) decide.

→ A state is an abstract (constructed) system consisting in many abstract (constructed) sub-systems.

→ A state is a verbal (written) construction from humans in order to manage all things, natural beings, all humans' existence and activities.

→ The state is the owner of the territory. The state can sell (or rent) a limited amount of land to citizens or entities and the citizen or entity (as new owner) can use it and sell (or rent) it to other citizens (or entities).

→ We can also say: The owner of a state is the entire folk and the agents in the state-system operate in the interest of all citizens (or: representing the interests of the folk/citizens).

→ There are territories, known also as 'state', where the owner of a territory (and of the state) is a royal or aristocrat person or entity.

There are certain differences between 'state' and 'government':

"The state is more extensive than government. The state is an inclusive association that encompasses all the institutions of the public realm and embraces all the members of the community (in their capacity as citizens).

Government is part of the state.

- The state is a continuing, even permanent, entity. Government is temporary: governments come and go, and systems of government can be reformed and remodeled.

- Government is the means through which the authority of the state is brought into operation. In making and implementing state policy, government is 'the brains' of the state, and it perpetuates the state's existence.
- The state exercises impersonal authority. The personnel of state bodies is recruited and trained in a bureaucratic manner and is (usually) expected to be politically neutral.
- The state, in theory at least, represents the permanent interest of society. That is, the common good or general will." [124]

→ The state encompasses everything that is on its territory.
→ The state is a permanent entity, although during history very variable.
→ A government is temporary as its system can be changed.
→ A government is temporary as its agents change periodically.
→ The government is the operating entity of the state.
→ The bureaucratic apparatus administrates the state.
→ The state represents the common will of its citizens.
→ The government represents the partisans' (the people's) will.

The development of globalization has created an immense imbalance in the understanding and functioning of a state. Big corporations have become a disproportional influence in governance. The banking system, especially big banks, has acquired a national and international (global) power through money concentration and control of money flow that undermines the entire system of governance and of the functions of the 'state'. All kind of democracies around the globe have become misbalanced and distorted and are under the dominance of the economic entities.

☞ The concept of 'democracy' has always been a chimera. Since 2000 years the banking system always has controlled and 'governed' from the ambuscade (subversively) the folks, the governments, and with that the states and its activities.
☞ The Christian Churches have always shaped, formed, brainwashed and manipulated the people's mind and soul. Through that and above that the Christian Churches also had an immense influence in all kind of governments and policies. Still today the Christian Churches have an immense influence in the definition of a state and in its governance.

A state and its governmental and administrative entities play an immense role that affects the life of individuals, the collective, and international relations.

---

[124] Heywood, p. 91-92

On the one side of a scale we have the 'minimal state':

"The institutional apparatus of a minimal state is thus limited to a police force, a court system and a military of some kind. Economic, social, cultural, moral and other responsibilities belong to the individual, and are therefore firmly part of civil society." [125]

On the other side we have the 'totalitarian state': [126]

The discussion about the right form of democracy and governance become obsolete if we consider the developments of the last 20 years:

"The central feature of economic globalization is the rise of 'supraterritoriality', the process through which economic activity increasingly takes place within a 'borderless world'." [127]

"If borders have become permeable and old geographical certainties have been shaken, state sovereignty, at least in its traditional sense, cannot survive. This is the sense in which governance in the twenty-first century has assumed a genuinely post- sovereign character. It is difficult, in particular, to see how economic sovereignty can be reconciled with a globalized economy. Sovereign control over economic life was only possible in a world of discrete national economies, and to the extent that these have been, or are being, incorporated into a single globalized economy, economic sovereignty becomes meaningless." [128]

🖙 Since 30 years globalization increasingly has corroded many states and governments around the globe, the entire European Union, the United States, Canada and other capitalistic states.

"The power and significance of the state has also been affected by the process of political globalization. However, its impact has been complex and, in some ways, contradictory. On the one hand, international bodies such as the United Nations, the EU, NATO and the WTO have undermined the capacity of states to operate as self-governing political units. [129]
Fact is:

🖙 Western democracy is eroding, even disfigured and perverted.

---

[125] Heywood, p. 99
[126] Summarized statements from Heywood, p. 102, 8
[127] Heywood, p. 103-104
[128] Heywood, p. 103-104
[129] Heywood, p. 103-104

- Western democracies have lost much of their sovereignty.
- More centralized regulations have reduced the citizen's free realm.
- The UN is dominated by the US and Jewish-Zionist interests.
- The UN has converted into an impotent apparatus.
- The NATO is the new extended arm of the United States.
- The bases of the US military occupy many European States.
- European countries can't act ignoring or go against the interests of Israel.
- The entire Balkans and all nations in North Africa are the battlefields of imperialist interests.

"A growing range of decisions (for example, on monetary policy, agricultural and fisheries policy, defence and foreign affairs) are made by European institutions rather than by member states. This has created the phenomenon of multilevel governance." [130]

- Democracy and trade have become a Trojan horse for building up the 'Fourth Reich'.

"The WTO, for example, acts as the judge and jury of global trade disputes and serves as a forum for negotiating trade deals between and amongst its members." [131]

- Trade has a lot to do with (over-) exploiting resources of other countries, raw material, fish, arable land, and (cheap manpower), etcetera.
- Trade also puts many nations into the debt trap that makes them dependent from foreign governance and foreign monetary power.
- Trade is insofar a political matter as it determines the economic territories a country gets for its interests. It's simply about distributing the slices of the cake.

Above that we have to consider the very evil political activities and attempts:

- All the wars since 1991 (Gulf war I, Gulf war II, Balkan war, Afghanistan war, Iraq war, the wars in Libya, the subversive destruction of Tunisia, Egypt, today Syria, and tomorrow probably Iran) have destroyed entire nations, killed millions of people, decomposed entire governments and destroyed entire infrastructures of these states.
- Above that military activities from the US Army are breaking down in Yemen and Pakistan the entire political system of this country.

---

[130] Heywood, p. 103-104
[131] Heywood, p. 103-104

- All these war activities for more than 20 years have cost the citizens over $50 trillion and the produced damages in other countries also have a cost on the level of $30-50 trillion. The citizens in Europe and the United States have to pay for it!

- "Several years after 9/11 architect Richard Gage formed Architects and Engineers for 9/11 truth, an organization that has grown to include 1,700 experts. The plans of the towers have been studied. They were formidable structures. They were constructed to withstand airliner hits and fires. There is no credible explanation of their failure except intentional demolition." [132] "The 9/11 myth is the pillar of another fabrication, the so-called "Global War on Terrorism" and constitutes the one and only pretext for the U.S. imperialist war on the world, responsible for the death of millions of innocent civilians." [133]

- This is all made by the European Union and the United States, both declaring to be 'democratic'.

- Most values of political importance such as democracy, peace, freedom, and humanitarian aid are abused, disfigured, distorted, and totally perverted from its genuine meaning. This is the Western way of doing politics.

To show how democratic politicians and governments operate with words we can take the slogan 'smoking kills' with all its images on the cigarette package. There must be a complex statistic behind such a slogan and the following political measures that have been taken for example in Europe. But citizens only get a figure saying how many people died due to smoking. Some critical approaches show the problem:

First of all, the statistic does not say if all these people died due to lung cancer or respiratory illnesses. It does not say if these smokers really died from nicotine. Nicotine contains a variety of chemicals and also simply pesticide. A difference is not made between the effects of these chemicals and of nicotine. Smoking also produces particles of grim. Is it the grim particles (fine dust) that kill or is it the nicotine or the cigarette paper that is also chemically elaborated?

---

[132] http://www.globalresearch.ca/on-911-doubts-were-immediate/
[133] http://www.globalresearch.ca/911-facts-fiction-and-censorship/

Towns, especially big towns and cities, but also areas close to roads (and train rails) with high traffic are highly contaminated from different kinds of fine dust, chemicals, fumes, and oil heating (winter, grim particles). New cars have during 6-12 months inside a variety of chemical emissions that can affect the respiratory apparatus and the lungs. A cruise ship has the same amount of toxic emission as 50,000 cars. Cruise ships continuously leaving a port, entering a port, and operating at a port immensely contaminate the area and can produce lung cancer and other respiratory illnesses.

Working in any kind of a mine results in breathing immense amount of fine dust and also of used chemicals. Does a smoker working in a mine or living near a mine (20 km radius) die from smoking? People working with pesticide (e.g. agriculture) may be smokers and die from smoking. Or do they die from the combination of smoking and inhalation of pesticide particles, or only from the pesticide nano-particles? There are many jobs where smoking people are exposed to chemicals that emanate by using them. There is no scientific research about how the manifold chemicals and smoking interrelate.

Seen as a whole, the statistics do not say anything about the cocktail-effects together with smoking; nor do they say that the main factor is not smoking, but the inhalation of fine dust or of toxic chemicals.

- The same game goes on with the manifold values of the democracy as mentioned above. It's the same way politicians and individuals in power operate with the people. We conclude: 'Smoking kills' is a big lie and it shows the way politicians and the government operates in general with the citizens about most political matters.

- In Chapter 3 we developed an extensive picture about global contamination, the contamination of the chain food, the air, and the environment in general. There are many more sources tickling like a bomb, for example all the chemical bombs and warship wrecks with millions of tons of oil sunk, and rusting on the bottom of the North Sea and the oceans. There are also tens of thousands of barrels with (very toxic) nuclear material on the bottom of the oceans. Billions of people consume through food and inhale many toxic particles. Billions of people will probably get ill in the future, will die, or 50-65% of newborn babies will have organ deficiency. All governments hide this outrageous criticality that will affect all lives on earth and can even lead humanity to its extinction.

- These are some examples showing the perverse falseness of the authorities in the Western governments. This is called 'democracy' or 'democratic governance in the interest of the people'.

Europe – together with Great Britain and the United States as the leading power, triggered from the stage behind the curtains by the Jewish-Zionist supreme economic masters – has become the 'Fourth Reich', a totalitarian dictatorship that allows its citizens to consume as much as they can, to drive a car as often as they can, to eat and drink as much as they can, to have sex as much and however they can or want, and to have fun as much as they want.

With collective contamination, with their all-embracing media brainwashing, and with the 50,000 consumer goods on offer at amazing shopping malls, they have damaged the brain, the mind and soul, of a huge majority – as much as they could.

As for example the German people can see every week on one of their TV-channels a report or movie about the Second World War, about how evil this totalitarian state was, how evil Hitler and his SS were, and how sad this war sceneries were, they all think today: "Thank God, today we live in a democratic paradise of high living standard with much freedom! The Satan is anyway far away in Iran and North Korea. Our great government brings democracy to the world and much humanitarian aid."

It remains to add: 100-150 years ago the same regimes destroyed the whole of Africa, have stolen every thing there, and destroyed most infrastructures and killed most folks. And the same political spirit (with the same religion) the Western countries conquered the world 300-500 years ago, also have stolen every thing there, and destroyed most infrastructures and killed most folks.

→ History repeats itself until it's understood, reconciled, and renewed, no matter how or what the political system is called.

4.4. Media and Politics

Political institutions and single politicians in office are not used to directly communicate with the citizens. They do not inform the folk about what's going on within the country and around the globe. They do not explain their projects, nor do they 'educate' people in politics.

The media provides most information about political matters: public and private television, radio, newspaper, magazines, movies, and their websites. These mass media are the communication channel between the citizens and the political institutions.

DISNEY, owner of ABC, Touchdown Pictures, Buena Vista, Hollywood Pictures, Caravan Pictures, Miramax Films, the production of documentaries A & F, TV History Channel, Discovery, Disney and others; AOL / Time Warner, which owns CNN, HBO, Warner Brothers, Castle Rock, Time, Sports Illustrated, People, Fortune, Entertainment, Money, Netscape and others;

VIACOM, which includes CBS, Paramount Pictures, Simon & Schuster, Pocket Books, Blockbusters, Showtime, MTV, The Movie Channel & Nickelodeon, BET, Nickelodeon, etc..;

GENERAL ELECTRIC, owner of NBC, CNBC, MSNBC, Bravo, Universal Pictures, and thirteen television stations, and closely linked to the arms and aerospace industries;

RUPERT MURDOCH'S NEWS CORPORATION, owner of Fox TV, DirecTV, TV Guide, New York Post, The Weekly Standard, 20th Century Fox, MySpace and large holdings in Sky TV and others;

Bertelsmann AG, one of the world's largest media corporations, has the European RTL-TV, Random House, Bantam Dell, Doubleday, Alfred A. Knopf, Vintage Books, and others.

The first five are registered as American and the last one is German. It would make sense to find out who the owners are of the most important media groups around the globe. They represent a religion, an ideology, financial interests of the elite, and an orchestrated media power strategy in order to influence (condition, brainwash, manipulate) humanity.

It is also of highest importance to find out what the media do not say about the state of humanity and the earth, and the hidden actors of politics, religion, economy, industry and media.

Six Jewish Companies Control 96% of the World's Media [134] [135]

The media use and abuse a great variety of mechanisms for propaganda:

- When people are afraid, they don't think rationally. And when they can't think rationally, they'll believe anything.
- Go after the person's credibility, motives, intelligence, character, or, if necessary, sanity.
- Where anti-racists are accused of racism, or in the climate change debate, where those who argue for human causes of the phenomenon are accused of not having science or facts on their side.
- Why lie about the historical facts, even when they can be demonstrated to be false? Well, because dogmatic minds actually find it easier to reject reality than to update their viewpoints.
- If you can find a group to blame for social or economic problems, you can then go on to a) justify violence/dehumanization of them, and b) subvert responsibility for any harm that may befall them as a result.
- Violence becomes synonymous with power, patriotism and piety.
- Bullying and yelling works best on people who come to the conversation with a lack of confidence, either in themselves or their grasp of the subject being discussed.
- The idea is to deliberately confuse the argument, but insist that the logic is airtight and imply that anyone who disagrees is either too dumb or too fanatical to follow along.
- With morality politics, the idea is to declare yourself and your allies as patriots, Christians and 'real Americans'.
- Because the speaker has been blessed by God to speak on behalf of all Americans, any challenge is perceived as immoral.
- Being repetitive, being ubiquitous and being consistent. The message must be repeated over and over, it must be everywhere and it must be shared across commentators.
- The disdain for education and other evidence of being trained in critical thinking are direct threats to a hive-mind mentality.

---

[134] http://www.freepress.net/ownership/chart
[135]

http://theunjustmedia.com/Media/Six%20Jewish%20Companies%20Control%2096%25%20of%20the%20World%E2%80%99s%20Media.htm

- Any attempt to bring the discussion back to the issue at hand will likely be called deflection, an ironic use of the technique of projection/flipping.
- The more someone is losing their temper in a debate and the more intolerant they are of listening to others, the more you can be certain they do not know what they're talking about.
- The fact that a lot of people believe something is not necessarily a sign that it's true.

In Italy it is the Berlusconi media group, in Europe we have the Bertelsmann group, in Great Britain we also identified a concentration of media ownership[136] , in France we have the same concentration operated by Sarkozy's friends[137]; 'Agence France-Presse' is the world's third-largest news agency[138]; and in Spain we have identified some important entities and individuals that have most of the important Spanish Media in their hands.[139]

→ There is a significant ownership network behind the media corporations that connects with super rich individuals, (private) banks, and the Church.

Worldwide most important media information sources are CNN, BBC, Reuters, and Associated Press. A majority of newspapers around the globe use these sources (paying a fee).

Statistics say that Americans watch 6 hours television per day, Germans estimated 3.5 hours which we consider as a European average. Additionally people read newspapers, magazines, and visit also Internet news sources.

A few media corporations (owners) dominate the policy about information and cinema around the globe. They cover a huge part of the world and deliver the people with a main stream of selected and prepared information. Humans' life is daily penetrated from information preponderantly from these sources.

- The global media power is immense, all-area covering, and absolutely dominant.
- Most information is elaborated, selected, re-shaped, filtered, commented, and fully controlled within a given information policy.
- There is a lot of information of highest importance that these mega empires never give out to the people.

[136] http://en.wikipedia.org/wiki/Concentration_of_media_ownership
[137] http://en.wikipedia.org/wiki/Concentration_of_media_ownership
[138] http://www.guardian.co.uk/media/2010/jul/05/nicolas-sarkozy-french-media
[139] http://www.elblogsalmon.com/sectores/quien-esta-detras-de-los-medios-de-comunicacion-en-espana-infografia-actualizada

- The given manifoldness (pluralism) of media, which could balance the selection of media information, is suffocated by economic and imperialist interests.
- All news on standard TV edition with a usual emission time of 15 minutes covers not even one hundredth of the important information. There is no time space for any deeper or more complex thought about any information.
- People are bored, unsatisfied, angry, moody, tired, preoccupied, and hungry for sensations. People want entertaining information. They are not interested in serious ideological or mental stuff or in complex criticalities. Bad news is good if it produces a feeling of sensation or adrenaline. The 'bad' always must be on the 'other side'.
- These media have the power to stigmatize, defame, and demonize any person and to destroy any career of any politician or 'authority' in a society or nation. They can do so with any folk of another culture and religion. They always can enlarge any 'hair in the soup' of any person and 'sell' this as the 'evil' or 'inacceptable' matter. And these media do so whenever it is of their ideological, religious, political, or economic interest.
- Not a thousand experts and not 40.000 individuals in relevant positions have any chance to be listened, not even if they have information or a project that is of supreme importance for a folk or for humanity. Not the most pioneering projects of a small group or of an individual have ever a chance to be considered from the media for reporting; except if it is to their economic interest and does not endanger their position.
- Due to economic reason the media must entertain, must simplify, must trivialize, must avoid challenging the consumer, must sell illusions, and must give to the people what they like.
- These media have immense power without responsibility. They globally facilitate and promote what they want. In that sense they are global players in the world of globalization without being called to account. They destroyed entire cultures, have broken worldwide local lifestyles, have created around the globe a 'westernization' or 'Americanization' without being responsible for the critical collateral effects.
- With unscrupulousness on a level of Goebbels, they shape the mind of their customers: they distort Russian and Chinese politics, all the imperialistic doing in North Africa, the events in Syria, the situations with Iran, the military activities from the US Army and the NATO around the globe. They would never question Jewish matters from the Second World War or the foundation of Israel, or Zionism (as a political-religious ideology and politics), the exploitation and contamination that is destroying all eco-systems and so on. They would never question the

9/11 operation or the 'Bin Laden' myth, or the bellicose proxy activities of America's secret services in many countries; etc.

- Media provides patterns of knowledge, behavior, attitudes, opinions, values, ideas, interpretation, and lifestyle. They sell their self-fabricated realities. 10.000 times, 100.000 times and a million times the same pattern from all the different media, together with the appropriate images (photos or movies), and the consumer has fully integrated these patters in his mind as the 'true reality' and the 'right way'. This is called 'brainwashing'.

- How do we have to interpret the fact that the supreme economic masters have the control over these media groups via financial channels?

Western media allocate and 'sell' through their channels the tools and 'food' that destroy all genuine human values, humanity as a whole. All kind of mad and lovely movies bombard the youth, the teenagers and the never growing old teenagers with occultism, black magic, supra-natural science fiction, zombies, vampires, Satanism, devil, skeletons, skulls, sorcerers and magical powers, dark forces, violence, games to train killing or to find killing is 'cool', baby fuckers, child abusers, murders of girls and women, the mad and possessed, the monster tyrants, cannibals, heavy metal music, secret codes and rites, Lady Gaga, neo-punk fashion, wild sex, "sex, drugs and rock 'n' roll", alcoholism, pork fest, party drugs for fun, drugs as lifestyle, Cabbalistic, nihilism, screaming, shouting, execration of sinister fear. Everything is practiced and used that makes people crazy, permanently dissatisfied, aggressive, uncontrolled, explosive, addicted, and etcetera; everything is produced and used that dehumanizes and vulgarizes humanity. In one word starting already in the early childhood towards the parents and teachers: "The truth is shit! Fuck you, I do what I want!"

- This mass culture provided from the media is meticulously calculated, fabricated with hypnotic and narcotic entertainment in order to destroy already the babies' mind and soul, to dumb the youth, to infantilize the adults; in general to destroy the ability to think, to be responsible, to love, to take care, to trust, to feel secure, to learn, to live genuine spirituality, to become a balanced and powerful individual, to have genuine faith, and to find fulfillment in the soul.

- All the masses must be brought into one channel, one tube, and one line of dehumanization. This is part of a gorgeous master plan of regicide and deicide.

- We, the Western (Christian and Jewish) super race, have the right given from God, to exploit every vivid and non vivid thing on earth, to take away the land from any country that is 'non-western', to kill every member of other races and religion, to destroy every infrastructure and culture from every country, to dominate the rest of humanity ordering them how they have to be and to live. It's cool and it makes us the 'unique supreme race' chosen from God to fulfill the 'divine' mission.

- The power of the big mass media is immeasurable and its abuse unlimited. Who are these people that rule the media and the economies from the hidden stage? What happened to them that they can be so illimitably satanic?

The consequences for politicians:

→ Political agents are permanently confronted with the media power.
→ Politics must adapt their self-presentation that conforms to the media principles.
→ Politics must 'sell' their policies consumer-friendly.
→ Politicians can never say the truth about the state of humanity and the planet.
→ Politicians can't call the media for account.
→ Politicians must be very cautious with the information they give out.
→ Politicians must fabricate their messages in a way the consumers like and wish to get.
→ How is the relation between governments and economics, if the governments have astronomic public debt owing to entities that are controlled by the supreme economic masters?

4.5. Politics and Religion

In general we are focusing in our explorations the Western world that includes the Christian religion. Christian religion has always been the 'left hand' of Western politics. Therefore it is appropriate to give a short critical picture about Christian religion.

A true life

We give some key words showing what we mean with 'true life': Human being, life, love, joy, zest for life, lust, full of life, satisfaction, happiness, hope, justice, peace, power of the inner Spirit, centered in the inner Spirit, all-embracing life, totality, completeness, balance, openness, light, confidence, aim, psychical-spiritual evolution, fulfillment, conjunction of the real and spiritual world, fulfillment of the Archetypes of the Soul, source of life, catharsis, renewal, reconciliation, forgiveness, salvation, redemption, and presence of God!

Defeat of the truth

All wisdom, all human values (love, hope, truth, peace, justice, spirit, the Archetypes of the Soul, etc.) and all the wise men together never stand a chance against politics, the financial power, the media, the industry, the official religion and the huge masses (billions) of brainwashed, blind, neurotic, malformed and driven people.

Add to that the fact that the state of humanity and the earth is so catastrophic and heading towards the complete annihilation, and that people will be squashed and hardly have room for their psychical and spiritual freedom.

The search for the truth in the Christian religion leads people to incomprehensible facts. Nothing in the entire universe can be so brutally devilish as the lies and the falseness of the Christian religion, its deeds and its consequences.

On the other hand the search for the truth leads to the truth about religion. With that the total breakthrough is given. But the people don't want the truth behind all the lies, distortions and falsifications. Even those that uncover the lies of the religion, politics, economy, industry and business world don't want the real truth.

It seems that there is only one last remedy to get the people to open their eyes. The collective unconscious first needs to explode globally. This will bring an end to the 3000-year-old Jewish-Christian history, marked by lies, distortion, falsification, perversion, brutality, lunacy, psychopathy, psychosis, megalomania, suffering and pain, murder and wars and provide the foundation for a new beginning.

Today there is not one word related to the spiritual and religious concern that has not been misused, disfigured, falsified, emptied, or perverted. With only a few million exceptions, seven billion people are brainwashed and totally disfigured in their truthful being and becoming.

➔   Most politicians need a new enlightenment.

Corrupt religion

- Politicians of the Christian-oriented party need their naive, blind followers.
- Politicians in general want this type of human being, so that they can do what they want.
- The military needs this type of human being, as a soldier, as submissive cannon fodder.
- The military can declare their military action as act of God, and "in the name of God".
- The industry needs this type of human being, to make maximum profit.
- If the Pope and the Bible lie, Christians believe the lies, so also politicians can lie.
- The big media have it easy with their games of deceit and distortion.
- Brainwashing, manipulation and propaganda only functions with this type of human being.
- Most of the billionaires base their wealth and their power on this type of human being.
- If the people are focused on the suffering of Jesus Christ, then they bear a lot of suffering.
- If the people are fixed on the after life and the relieving Paradise, then they accept poverty.
- If the people believe in the authorities of the Church, then they protest very little against state powers.
- If the people are psychically and spiritually weak and submissive, then the politicians are strong.
- If religion can deceive people without being detected, then those in power can as well.

- If people have their soul at the mercy of the Church, then they give their life at the mercy of those in power.
- If people let themselves be exploited by the Church, they let themselves be exploited by the state.

Those in power around the world, the leaders in politics and the economy as well as the elite think they are the winners in this power game. But history teaches us: The last winner standing is always the papacy und with that the institution that leads the entire Christianity (the churches of the world church council included). Those that rule heaven (the souls of all people including those in power in the economy and government) rule (with the illusionary world of Dogma) the people (humanity) and with that the world: this was and is the politics of the Roman-Catholic Church and of the Christian religion since the creation of the first Vulgate.

Herewith the papacy determines war and peace on earth; even if the religious power loses, it will ultimately always be the winner, during war and after war. Politics uses and misuse religion. And religion uses and misuses politics. This is how it has been 1000, 2000, 3000 and 5000 years ago; and this is how it will go in, until the new, genuine, truthful and evolutionary religion reaches its breakthrough – or until both eliminate each other together with humanity as a whole.

Christian dogmas

All the Christian dogmas, teachings and practices have got absolutely nothing to do with any part of the psychical-spiritual life (the inner life) of a person, of psychical-spiritual development, and of a constructive self-forming for living and growing with love and the inner Spirit.

➔ Christian dogmas, teachings and practices completely ignore what makes a person to a genuine human being.

What kind of love and relationship do the people live with their partner if they mutually ignore all these aspects of inner life we all have? And what is the result? It is the same kind of result as the one expressed and produced by the Christian dogmas, teachings, and practices! Lies and games and sadistic suppression everywhere, over and over again, with the result of a complete neurotic being and living, not rarely psychopathic! This produces an immense hidden suffering and failure worldwide!

Christian dogmas, teachings and practices do not express any ability to understand people's real inner psychical-spiritual life.

That's why we have contamination and climate change with is consequences, the destruction of the world of nature and animals, an incredible amount of victims of traffic accidents, wars and terrorism, misery, poverty, and countless amoral and criminal people around the globe.

Christian Churches also teach: not being Christian is a lost being and life, and therefore all non-Christians are evil and bad people, never people of God. Logically they can't get to heaven. That's why most of the Christian Churches want the total collapse, the last big war, the destruction of the earth, and the elimination of humanity: to show to the rest of the world's souls that they are the only religion that has the truth and therefore that they are the sole folk going to heaven.

→ Very neurotic! Very perverse! Totally psychopathic! A frightening danger for humanity and the earth!

Sources of Christianity

- The Book: Chaotically plugged together anthology of unrelated texts that hundreds of anonymous authors, publishers and copywriters created, reworked, translated, falsified and 'improved'.
- It is proven, that the texts from the Bible (Old and New Testament) were always continuously changed.
- Political power interests always played a role in the creation of the Bible texts.
- It is proven, that much did not and could not have happened as stated in the Old Testament.
- There are many oral and written sources of unknown origins and stories.
- Some texts date back to the time 250-100 BC, others from the time around 539 BC.
- The 5 books of Moses were not written by Moses; they are also not 3200 years old.
- Historical facts were inflated, distorted, mixed up and placed into a different time.
- There are many unknown authors and thousand fold editing of the texts over many centuries.
- Many essential untruths have been determined in the Old Testament.
- The texts of the Bible that relate to previous times were only written down much later.
- The essential texts of the Bible (Old Testament) originate from the late 7th century BC.
- There are countless contradictions in the Bible.

- In the Bible there are Commandments that without doubt originate from the Old Babylonia, from the Hammurabi Codex.
- In many old civilizations there were myths about floods, also in India, China and America.
- Much already originated from the Epic of Gilgamesh from the Mesopotamian region.
- There are many parallels between the Bible (Old Testament) and the Epic of Gilgamesh.
- Most of the religious customs and values have their roots in the Asia Minor and Egyptian region.
- The archaeological analysts come to the conclusion, that the Old Testament is fully the work of subsequent editors.
- All the analysts see the Pentateuch as a 'mosaic from different sources'.
- The Bible itself turns out to be an artifact with many erratic statements from different societies.

➔ Do the politicians know about these critical sources?

Creation of the Bible

- The authors of the four Gospels are unknown; the names are made up.
- The four Gospels were written around 70-100; the authors are unknown.
- The Pauline epistles came about around the year 50. But Paul did not know Jesus, knew nothing about him.
- J.C. died around the year 30; and there is not a single witness from the time.
- Numerous religious texts are not integrated; the Apocrypha.
- There is no biographical knowledge about most of the protagonists in the Old Testament and the New Testament.
- Nobody knows, what Jesus Christ taught (said). There is practically nothing concrete that one knows about this person. And yet, in the Bible it constantly says: "And Jesus said…"
- Selected texts indicate little about truth and falsifications within a text.
- Many texts do not have any declared authors and no authenticity as "source text".
- There are many Early Christian texts and fragments that were not integrated into the Bible.
- There are ways of reading and interpreting that can never lead to a single truth.
- There are almost as many text forms as there are copies.
- Translators are not always precise; sometimes also not concentrate, careless or incompetent.

- Changes and compositions always had to conform to the views and interest of the papacy.
- The Bible is a conglomerate of copies of copies and translations of translations.
- Texts can be forged, texts can be wrongly translated, new texts can be added, the meaning changed through sentence construction, something of one's own can be integrated, something can be "put right" (in order to falsify), texts can be excluded, etc., and the originals can be burnt.
- Critical books always ended up on the list of forbidden books since the beginning of the Christian state religion.
- The Bible was written by completely different, mostly unknown people with differing ideas and views and at different times.
- The Bible is the book of the Christian churches that has been thousand fold changed always according to private, ecclesiastic and political interests.
- The Bible today is created to a complete work, of all the previous reigning interests of the past 3000 years.
- The Bible can never be the pure "word of God" and the "dictation of the Spirit". There are no comprehensible reports, apart from a few archetypal dreams, that also need to be put into question.
- Nothing, absolute nothing is "authentically" documented about the prophets, Abraham or Moses, Christ, the Apostles, the Gospels or from God and Spirit.
- Nothing in the Bible or in the Church is "error-free", "unflawed", "untouchable", or "infallible", especially not the Pope or the Magisterium.
- If everything is declared as the "word of God", then one obtains a grotesque, chaotic, neurotic and schizophrenic image of God; it appears that everything has gone astray on a fatal religious Psychosis.
- The environment of the origination of the "Holy Scriptures" is not "divine", rather: Power, wars, hate, power struggle, political interests, intrigues, murder, papal crimes, perversions, powerful and influential people, forgers, religious evildoers, etc.
- The many gruesome events of mass murder that according to the Bible were arranged, advocated, supported or even accomplished by a vengeful God himself are absolutely insane.
- The Roman-catholic Churches since a long time a rigid, even fossilized, psychopathic power apparatus, rooted in thinking from the Middle Ages, still as devilish as the inquisition of the times.
- The worldview of the Bible, including the ideas about the creation of the world and the human being correspond to the spiritual horizon and knowledge of human beings from around 2000-3500 years ago.

- 2000 years of Christian and Christian Church history have prevented timings and contexts to be seen scientifically and historically in true form.
- In its history Christianity has probably killed, murdered, and let starve and die over one billion people.

➔ Do the politicians know about this critical creation of the Bible?
➔ If the politicians know about this critical creation of the Bible, why do they not inform the people about?

Content of the Bible

- The Old Testament is based on testimonies and talks of the creation of the earth, the prehistory of mankind, the election, the history of salvation. The contents are put together out of a variety of texts: Tales, stories, law collections, testimonies, pieces of wisdom, chronicles, liturgical and poetical texts, lamentations, love songs, family sagas, legends...
- The aim of the one-God-movement was and is, to create a world epic as collection of historical scrolls, memories, sagas, popular tales, anecdotes, Kingly propaganda, prophecies and ancient composition, partly original, partly copied from previous editions.
- The creation of the world according to old Sumerian beliefs is similar to the stated one in the Bible.
- The birth of Moses, his childhood and youth are consistent with legends from the time in the Mesopotamian region.
- The exodus from Egypt with Moses never happened.
- The Ten Commandments can already be found – in somewhat different form – already in the Egyptian Books of the Dead.
- Nearly everything is legend and never historiography.
- Most of the texts are adapted to the political interests of the given times.
- The savage story, that Abraham sacrificed his son at the will of God, is legend.
- The mass exodus of the Jews from Lower Egypt, from the Delta region, never happened.
- Monotheism was not an invention of the Israelites.
- Jericho never had a wall and did not even exist at the time that Joshua was said to have conquered it.
- A federal state of Israel and Judaea never existed.
- Countless conceptions and tales in the Bible originate from other civilizations and religions.
- Essential parts of the story of Israel played out very differently from the way the Bible portrays.
- A settlement of Israel through Abraham never happened.

- Different archaeologists place the time of Abraham in different epochs, which differ by up to 1000 years.
- The contradictions in the story of Abraham are indications that Abraham hardly could have even existed.
- Biblical and archaeological information indicates a concoction of cults.
- There are historical facts that make it impossible that Isaac ever existed.
- The whole story about Jacob is false.
- All the portrayed facts and findings are clues, that the legends about Joseph were a complete invention.
- The incidents of the 12 sons of Jacob in Egypt are to be seriously put in question.
- The ascertained data from excavations in Egypt are not compatible with Moses data from the invented Pentateuch.
- A mass exodus from Egypt under Ramses appears to be completely implausible.
- There are no indications of any mass exodus under a Moses.
- The exodus of 600.000 people from Egypt is invented.
- The invented Moses could not have been hindered by Edom.
- Myths are subsequently condensed into historical fact.
- Moses' laws: It is incomprehensible, why God would promise a land that first needs to be conquered with war and religious-racist mass murder.
- The exodus from Egypt is a conglomeration of legends from different epochs.
- The book of Joshua is a collection of sagas, heroic tales and local myths.
- An over 100 year, invasion under Joshua could hardly have occurred.
- The factual life of Israelites is hardly described in the Old Testament.
- A "golden age" of Israel under David and Salomon is simulated.
- There are no archaeological findings of the structures of a kingdom of David.
- Large kingdom or a central administration, as portrayed in the Old Testament with a temple city Jerusalem, did not exist in the times of Judah.
- The people in Israel-Palestine were up until the end of the 8th century B.C. illiterate.
- The Genesis (1st book of Moses) is a concoction of various nomadic tales.
- The archaeological findings, or rather the non-findings clearly indicate that the invasion under the King Josia did not take place.
- With false stories about the King Omri, Ahab and Isebel the true story of Israelis camouflaged according to plan and Jerusalem placed at the center.

→ Do the politicians know about all the fabrications of the Bible?

→ If the politicians know about this critical fabrication of the Bible, why do they not inform the people about?

The unholy Bible

60 Gospels existed in the first centuries. At the end, the ecclesiastic authorities chose 4 editions, written between the years 70 and 120. Not a single one has been written by an eyewitness! And not one original Gospel exists, not even first transcripts. The authors of the original texts are unknown. No apostle has ever written such texts! Nobody has written down what Jesus said. The first 100 years after his death no historian even took notice of him.

Countless copyists redacted and copied over and over again the texts of the Holy Bible, added, changed or deleted pieces. Over 2,000 diverse text variations and 250,000 variations of reading exist today. And these texts are translated today with many errors into 1,100 languages and dialects!

These texts in a rarely accountable manifoldness are simply mission letters, mythological tales, religious edifications, legends, with a lot of anecdotes and fictional stories, with each copywriting new additions and eliminations, smaller and bigger changes. All texts are made by unexampled lies, falsifications, and displacements. The contradictions are countless. The constitution of the Holy Bible does not allow for an understanding of these texts as 'holy' or 'inspired from God'.

In the Gospels you will find innumerable statements that are quoted billions of times by churchgoers: And Jesus said: "…"; or: "I am …". Fact is: Nobody knows what Jesus said! Such words are even presented as authentic words of God! This is called 'brainwashing' and 'manipulating with lies'.

Critical Bible research says: All stories in the Old Testament and New Testament are legends, myths, sagas, fictions, anecdotes, full of manipulation and deceit. The Bible is a chaotic and corrupted collection of texts. There is practically no real historical substance. The four Gospels are never a biography of J.C.!

Today it is proven that the Christian dogmas already existed in the Middle East and Far East, at Jesus' time as well as thousands of years before his epoch: the spiritual procreation, the physical resurrection, the mother of God, the son of God, the savior, the messiah, the prophet, the angels, the devil, God, the eternal life, the paradise, hell, the miracles, the dogma of the trinity, the crucifixion as a sin offering, the story about Adam and Eve, the natural death as a punishment, the creation as the beginning of the salvific history, and all the sacraments such as baptism, the remission, the last supper, etc. Nothing is new and authentically Christian in that sense!

Considering the development of these texts it is an absurdity to allege that God has written or dictated these texts, or that these texts have been written by inspiration through God. There, where lies don't lead further, there is the need for an untouchable 'belief'. It's absolutely perverse to teach and claim: our belief lives from the relationship to the Holy Bible, inspired by the Holy Spirit. But indeed: the belief can't be better than these texts.

All the Christian dogmas, teachings and practices have got absolutely nothing to do with any part of the psychical-spiritual life (the inner life, the psychical-spiritual organism) of a person, of psychical-spiritual development, and of a constructive self-forming for living and growing with love and the inner Spirit. Christian dogmas, teachings and practices completely ignore what makes a person to a genuine human being.

→ If the politicians know about this sham in the Bible, why do they not inform the people about?
→ If the politicians don't know about this sham in the Bible, how can they be 'competent' politicians and managing their duties in a professionally objective way?

Insane Apostles' Creed

This is how the blinded and mentally lost Christian talks:

- All men know God, but reject Him
- God has written these words
- Sinners cannot understand the good news of the Gospel
- The Sinners cannot accomplish salvation
- Salvation is a gift of God
- Salvation is given freely, by grace through faith
- As Christians we have to imitate Christ's humility
- Faith is a gift of God
- First drawn to faith by the Holy Spirit and then man can believe

- Jesus said faith the size of a mustard seed is sufficient to bring salvation
- Jesus said: I say to you, unless one is born again he cannot see the kingdom of God
- All men are born spiritually blind and dead in their trespasses (sin)
- The preaching of the gospel are the means by which God grants the gift of faith
- Spirit can work faith in human's heart
- Faith in God is not blind
- Faith in God is based on His character and His promises

→ The Apostles' Creed in reality means: "I believe in an enormous amount of improvable and non comprehensible statements and a confusing nonsense of empty words that has got nothing to do with the Archetypal processes of the Soul, and above that practically can't be put in relation with the psychical-spiritual and real life of human beings."

→ This is pure taking the piss! If politicians don't see and understand this deceiving and insane reality, how can they be 'sane' politicians?

Our Father submission

The Church teaches: The Father in heaven is the prayer that Jesus Christ has told us to pray. – But nobody knows what Jesus Christ has taught!

This prayer has no essential aspects of human life. The psychical-spiritual Archetypes of the Soul are not addressed. People are drilled to obedience and subordination in the belief, not to an active work, not to the psychical-spiritual growing. People do not have to learn anything here.

People are not allowed to acquire knowledge and skills to appropriately live their human being.
The prayer Our Father has no practically realizable content. The prayer Our Father is an emotional brainwashing and a magic manipulation with the purpose to abuse the longing of the people for a life with God and Spirit!

→ An atrocious lie and scam that politicians obviously support!

Hail Mary psychosis

Hail Mary: We don't know anything about this woman. Authentic historic reports do not exist. We have no document proving that she has elaborated a high psychical-spiritual level or that she has lived it.

This prayer is addressed to a myth. There isn't the slightest element about an Archetype of the Soul, about being a woman and being a mother as reality and value. There is nothing, absolutely nothing in this myth that we can value as a realizable real ideal of being a woman and being a mother.

Therefore: this prayer is the most absurd, perfidious and sadistic humiliation of all women and especially of all mothers. The person praying is directed by force and manipulated towards an ideal of a woman which in that kind never existed and can never exist. And the men, speaking this prayer, become brainwashed mummy boys that can never build up a real, genuine and human relationship with a woman.

➜ This is dire madness that politicians obviously support!

Mechanisms of belief

The shocking hidden psychological mechanisms of religions and spirituality are:

1. Happiness and fulfillment are displaced to the transcendental life (after death) instead of realizing them as psychical and spiritual values in this world.
2. Deviance of beliefs is punished as against God in order to sustain one's system of beliefs and the religious institution.
3. The identification with the almightiness of God or the founder of the religion – and with the religious teaching – serves as a compensation of a weak self-identity.
4. Constrained sticking to beliefs is based on a magical defense of sexual drive and of the innermost devotion to the partner in a love relationship between man and woman.
5. The immature tie in the adult age to the parents is transferred to the church and the religious teachings.
6. Autonomous intelligence, reason and the Spirit are powerless in front of fundamentalist and dogmatic beliefs. This extinction is produced with the purpose that emotions can bind unhindered identifications.
7. Believing in salvation through God and the founder of a religion together with real and suggested guilt produce an act of slavish obedience up until complete self-abandonment.
8. Defense of belief serves the need for power, the greed to "know it all", the narcissistic obsession to be recognized, and the protection of benefit.
9. Expectation of salvation is projected (displaced) to the founder of a religion and the church and its representatives as a result of rejecting the psychical-spiritual evolution – the inner process of salvation.

10. The per se valuable readiness to devote one's being and life to God is forced with menace through blind believing and with restrained indoctrination.
11. Religion and spirituality without elaborating the Archetypes of the Soul with the inner Spirit, experienced with dreams and meditation, is a morbid confusion!

Motives to believe

- Humans are lazy, lazy to think, sluggish, superficial and don't want to learn anything.
- Humans want easy, fast, simple and direct solutions for their salvation.
- Humans are submissive to authority, easily deceivable and easily enslaved.
- Humans are like blind sheep, driven herd animals and followers.
- Human are cowardly and fearfully paralyzed by social pressure.
- Humans believe in "holy lies" because they themselves lie, live in lies.
- Humans believe in archaic nonsense, because they themselves are archaic.
- Humans want to belong, otherwise they are alone and excluded.
- Humans do not want to take responsibility for the truth.
- Humans need the belief, in order to live their quarrelsomeness.
- Humans cannot give up their belief, because they are stubborn.
- Humans live their sick cantankerousness with their belief.
- Humans are scared of the shock that the truth can release.
- Humans have such a small ego, that they refurbish it with belief.
- Humans think they are better with their belief, than non believers.
- Humans are scared of life and therefore cling to their belief.
- Humans themselves play a false, deceitful, deceiving game in life.
- Humans are psychically on the stage of development of a small child.
- Humans can live their own, open or concealed arrogance with their belief.
- Humans choose illusions over the strong facts of life and humane being.
- Humans hope for the redemption of their unconscious complexes with belief.
- Humans compensate their human weaknesses with their belief.
- Humans have enormous concealed guilt, partly real and partly self suggested.
- Humans increase their extremely low and bad self-value with their belief.
- Humans expect help from God and J.C. instead of helping themselves.
- Humans compensate their weak, instable self-confidence with their belief.
- Humans flee from themselves and their own inferiority with their belief.
- Humans think that with belief they can tame their, "unworthy" compulsiveness and lust.

- Humans see their life as unworthy and low; create balance with belief.
- Humans cannot live themselves and need the "mother church".
- Humans have not been loved and hope to receive the love of God with their belief.
- Humans have experienced suffering and in their belief experience comfort and relief.
- Humans strengthen their own imperiousness and their tyrannical personality.
- Humans don't have a genuine self-identity and find it in their community of believers.
- Humans conceal with their extremely low psychical-spiritual development with their belief.
- Humans do not have any substantial self enlightenment and do not want any.
- Humans do not want to see, how their own parents are completely archaic.
- Humans suppress their hate of their father, mother and life with their belief.
- Humans are sickened by themselves, their own body and flee into belief.
- Humans have an increased feeling of triumph, being in the "true" belief.
- Humans are submissive and masochistically bonded in their drive to religion.
- Humans are orally unsaved and nurture themselves through fixation on belief.
- Humans do not have any substantial knowledge, to question themselves or others.
- Humans are scared, to look at themselves in the inner mirror.
- Humans are scared, to recognize the devilish lies of the church.
- Humans fear to recognize themselves, how they are deceived by the religion.
- Humans loose their ground, when they recognize "infallible" truth as a lie.

The lost Christian

- The Christian, who believes in lies and forgeries, is himself the victim and a liar and forger.
- The Christian, who believes in the distortions and falsifications, will himself be distorted and even falsified.
- The Christian, who believes in absurdities, becomes absurd himself and lives in an absurd manner.

- The Christian, who believes in a corrupt work and corrupt leadership, becomes corrupt himself.
- The Christian, who believes in dogma, is stubborn, inflexible, rigid and compulsive.
- The Christian, who believes in the self-righteous teachings of the church, becomes self-righteous himself.
- The Christian, who believes in the oppressive rules and commandments, becomes the oppressor himself.
- The Christian, who believes in the miracles of Jesus, then hopes for a miracle and loses his life.
- The Christian, who believes in the dehumanization of Jesus and Mary, dehumanizes himself.
- The Christian, who believes in the intervention of God on earth, is kidding himself.
- The Christian, who believes in help by means of worshipping the cross or a wall, ends up in madness.
- The Christian, who believes in the vile spiritual fraud, he will even cheat and dupe.
- The Christian, who believes in absurd magic rituals, he himself lives with stupid magical attitudes.
- The Christian, who believes in the cross of death and suffering, lives in constant fear of death and suffering.
- The Christian, who believes in the content of religious songs and sings along, ends up in psychosis.
- The Christian, who believes in the salvation of the church, is lazy, naive, gullible, stupid and ignorant.
- The Christian, who believes in the doctrine of Adam and Eve, is a mentally poor, lost creature.
- The Christian, who believes in the perverse sexual teachings of church leaders, becomes somewhat perverse.
- The Christian, who believes in celibacy and the religious ideal of the woman, is never able to love.
- The Christian, who believes in the high dignitaries of the Vatican, can never distinguish God from the devil.
- The Christian, who believes in the magic of redemption and salvation, is lazy and becomes more and more rotten.
- The Christian, who believes in the power of the "Urbi et Orbi" blessing, is a hypocrite and a coward.
- The Christian, who believes in neurotic, psychopathic and psychotic teachings, becomes so himself.
- The Christian, who believes in the teachings of the diseased labyrinth, will find no escape and only war.

- The Christian, who believes in God's help on the battlefield, is himself guilty of being at war.
- The Christian, who believes in the transformation of the St. Mass, becomes a danger to humanity.
- The Christian, who believes in dogmas without the psychical-spiritual organism, will never find himself.
- The only solution and salvation: The inner consummation of the Archetypal Processes of the Soul!

Enough drama

Enough already with this idiotic dogmatic blabber, with this sick belief, with this mentally ill and insane stupid and infantile ideas about Christ and God and the after world and about that what Christ taught 2000 years ago. Enough already with all these lies!

Enough already, how Christians have suppressed, raped, tortured, exploited and enslaved over one billion people, if not up to several billion people. Enough already, how Christians have again and again robbed, murdered and killed entire folks with abhorrent wars – and today continue the same way with indescribable arrogance, greed, falseness and bestial lunacy!

Enough already, how office holders lie, betray and fool all the Christians, even the entire humanity, with their religious psychosis, and how they brainwash, manipulate and exploit their souls for their concealed backstabbing greed for power! Christians, the folks and the politicians, once and for all need to ask themselves, why they prefer this unholy Bible – full of archaic, diabolic, and toxic rubbish – and all the Christian illusions, lies and falseness over the truth.

Characteristics of belief

The words "I believe..." are used in many ways:

- I believe in God, in God, the creator of..., the Holy Spirit, the Paradise / I believe in J.C., the Holy Bible, the Holy Mary, the Prophet Mohammed / I believe that J.C. made miracles, left the world physically /
- I believe that humans have a soul, living eternally / I believe in angels that help me to manage my life / I believe in the all-embracing power of love / I believe that the inner Spirit always speaks the truth / I believe that animals and plants have a soul /
- I believe in the word of my father, of the authority X / I believe that everything will go well / I believe that humans must live morality / I

believe in democracy as the correct political ideology / I believe that there is a cosmic energy /

- I believe that human being's minds form psychical energy that radiates / I believe in the ability of person X to do … / I believe in the message X…, etc.

The words "I believe…" have different meanings:

- I believe: in something concerning the other world = convinced without proof
- I believe: in the absolute truth of what person X wrote 2,500, 2,000, 1,500 years ago
- I believe: in something that will happen = I conclude, I interpret, I suppose, I hope
- I believe: in an ability concerning a person = I suppose, I hope, I am sure, I trust
- I believe: in specific moral, rules, norms = that they are correct and necessary
- I believe: in scientifically proven knowledge and facts = scientific knowledge and facts are correct and true; etc.

The statements "I believe …" have different sources of knowledge:

- Texts written in the nearer past, or the far and very far past
- Words said by a person declared to be trustworthy due to X
- Knowledge declared to be true by very old religious authorities
- Knowledge declared to be true by old institutions of high reputation
- A statement of a recognized person (authority) in a system of society
- Conclusion based on facts, calculations, analysis, interpretation
- A result of natural or social science, declared to be proven regularity
- A result of journalistically explored and documented facts, incidents
- Personal experiences from a trustworthy person, e.g. friend, scientist
- Summary of collective experiences proven to be correct / true
- Real personal experiences, single incident or repeated experiences
- Elaborated life knowledge considered to be useful and worthy wisdom
- Personal conclusions of experiences, single incident or repeated experiences
- Experiences of dreams that they speak right judgments and the truth
- Experiences of meditation that they speak right judgments and the truth
- Experiences with manifold senses that they give correct information
- Comprehensible and provable, traceable and reproducible experiences

The history of humanity is a labyrinth of colossal lies, deceit, cheat, distortion, displacement, fabrications, manipulations, exaggerations, extenuations, overstatements, and abuse of the truth and of power or for any personal or institutional profit, so that for any religious or spiritual statement we require an efficient way with clear rules to attain a comprehensible and provable, traceable and reproducible experience about the so called "truth".

We also must take into consideration that the truth about terrestrial, human or transcendental matters is very complex and can be described with words, images and symbols in many ways and a variety of meaning-elements, with very different accents and views. The truth is by the majority of realities not static and simple, but manifold, complex, and evolutionary. The idea that the transcendental world of the souls and the entity called 'God' (whatever it is) is static, never learning and never in any kind of process is a stupid, very naïve understanding.

Belief and Religion

Do we need a religious belief that is a labyrinth of colossal lies, deceit, cheat, distortion, displacement, fabrications, manipulations, exaggerations, extenuations, overstatements, fairy tales, legends, fantasies, absurd teachings, crimes and genocides, robbery and wars, slavery and human exploitation, psychopaths and megalomaniacs, injustice and inhumane, and abuse of the truth and of power or for any personal or institutional profit?

No! Humanity doesn't need such a religious belief anymore! It would never lead out of the dark labyrinth! It will never bring humanity's evolution forward. It will destroy the planet and the entire humanity. In any case, there is not much truth in all-religious teachings around the globe!

The essential question is: Do we need a religion or spirituality with "knowledge" that is thoroughly or mostly not comprehensible and not provable, not traceable and not reproducible by new experiences based on clear and practicable methods?

No! Humanity doesn't need such kind of religious and spiritual pseudo-"knowledge"! Religious and spiritual knowledge must be comprehensible and provable, traceable and reproducible.

Religious and spiritual knowledge always depends on the mental state of humans. Inefficiently or wrongly shaped (formed) psychical functions (subsystems of the mental organism) and a disrupted and conflictive interaction between all the psychical-spiritual functions or subsystems can never reach a clear, useful, and complete picture of the transcendental realities, nor a correct and complete picture about humanity and the world.

A religious and spiritual belief that is not based on and not linked with the mental (psychical-spiritual) organism and with the indispensable conditions of mastering human life is useless and meaningless. True religious and spiritual knowledge – about the soul of humans, the other world, and the divine world – requires the fulfillment of the Archetypal Processes of the Soul! This process is the only way that opens the door to comprehensible and provable, traceable and reproducible transcendental knowledge.

Religious Knowledge

Fact is: All humans have a psychical-spiritual organism. Science speaks here about the 'mind' or the 'psyche'. This organism consists of psychical functions: perception, intelligent functions, emotions (feelings), I-functions, consciousness, defense mechanisms, inner needs, love capacities, an inner pole of the opposite gender, the spiritual intelligence (the inner Spirit creating dreams), and the unconscious mind with norms, attitudes, values, suppressed and unsolved matters ('complexes') and the biography that has been formed since the prenatal time.

On the one hand the Archetypal Processes of the Soul aim to form all psychical functions to optimal efficiency (to function) for personal development and an optimal balance and interaction between the subsystems.

On the other hand these processes require and form behavior skills for mastering life and managing oneself within the process of growth during the entire life course. We can identify these learning processes as psychological and educational topics. There is no need to categorize such processes as 'religious' or 'spiritual' or as a 'belief'-concept.

With that all this so-called 'religious knowledge' is based on quality and efficiency of the formed (shaped) psychical and spiritual functions. All the evil behavior of humans is basically a result of wrongly formed, deformed, distorted, malformed, unformed, ignored, neglected, and imbalanced functions as a complex unity in permanent interrelation.

The question remains: Are there (in these archetypal processes) also functions, inner realities, inner experiences, and processes we can identify and categorize as 'religious' or 'spiritual'? Yes, there are!

Religion and Moral

Religion teaches a lot about morality, moral values, the way to live (life style), and laws that determine many aspects of daily life. Religions guide their members in determining between right and wrong, good or bad. Rules and laws define concepts of right and wrong. Religion and laws form a unity. Such moral rules and laws discipline behavior. The concepts of morality are as manifold as the religious teaching. Such rules and laws order life matters such as marriage, divorce, contraception, sexuality, children behavioral education, behavior, clothing, rituals, celebration, and also violence, physical punishment, abuse, slavery, cruelty, torture, death penalty, and wars, etc. The understanding of sins is manifold, contradictory, conflicting, and perverse.

The history shows us: Religious morality can include all kind of evil doing. Christianity has killed during its history an estimated one billion people, entire folks, raped every vivid being and robbed every non-vivid thing. There is no need to understand religion as an ethical mission, ordering people the right or good way of living and doing. Today we have the Human Right codex, a wide understanding of human values, a variety of utilitarian and humanistic ethics, and in general an extensive field of laws that regulates things, life and business.

The question remains: If there is a God, if people have a soul and will eternally live in the other world, how could this affect or additionally contribute to a universal constructive morality and ethical concept on terrestrial life?

New Understanding of Religion

A new understanding of religion does not need any belief as a foundation. Nevertheless, faith is a general human matter, indispensable in human life and between people. Faith also means hope. Religions use the word 'faith' for the relations to God, J.C., the incumbents, etc. We understand faith basically as "trust" in a person or institution.

Trust is first a natural disposition, but should be based during life on reliable and reproducible experiences. We understand the term 'belief' as related to something incomprehensible, not provable, not traceable, not reproducible and referred to the transcendental world, especially to divine entities. Belief is always directed to a dogma, to a part of a fundamentalist concept. A new understanding of religion does not need such belief attitudes.

A new understanding of religion (religious and spiritual knowledge / teaching) arises from several sources to be experienced from any intelligent and educated human.

This is the foundation of a new universal religion:

- The spiritual intelligence (the inner Spirit) giving to humans messages through creating dreams.
- There are archetypal dreams of immense spiritual meaning that no human mind can construct.
- Experiences with dreams reveal: there is a spiritual source knowing everything about the real world.
- Experiences with dreams reveal: there is a spiritual source knowing everything about the other world.
- Experiences with dreams reveal: there is a spiritual source knowing everything about the divine entities.
- The result of the right way of meditation reveals the same spiritual intelligence as creator of messages.
- The mental energy (e.g. telepathy) lets us experience that there is a psychical and cosmic energy.
- There are specific rituals that operate with cosmic energy letting people experience the cosmic energy.
- All Archetypes of the Soul can be reproduced with energetic rituals letting people experience its meaning.
- There are the Archetypes of the Soul, the principles that mark the process of a holistic development.
- There are higher Archetypes forming spiritual experiences about God, the other world, and much more.
- There is the power of love that shows us a transcendental capacity to transform and enrich human life.

These sources of spiritual or religious experiences reframe human understanding, life, and the higher meaning of life. Also the evil behavior and mind of people get a new frame and understanding with these spiritual realities.

It is naïve and stupid to think a human could ever see, experience and understand the truth of the source of human life and the truth about the other world and the divine entities without any effort and performance, without going the path of the psychical-spiritual development towards completeness and totality, towards the supreme fulfillment of the soul.

The price to get the comprehensible, provable, traceable and reproducible knowledge of the source, the origin and aim of humans is: humans and the entire mankind must go through the Archetypal Process of Individuation! This is the new core essence of religion. It has always been like that and always been distorted in order to abuse humans, species, nature, and things. The divine project probably will take another millennium.

And those who want to become experts in these transcendental and spiritual matters must go through the higher archetypal processes for spiritual (religious) professionals of the new universal religion. These professionals can explore and research the eternal divine source of life, the other world, the new frame of morality, and the ultimate meaning of human life. The explorations and learning processes will never end in the third millennium.

All religions and spiritual concepts must first clear out their sick dogmatic rubbish and all the scam elements, superstitions, and fairy tales. And then they must live, explore and reintegrate the above mentioned foundation of the new universal religion. It is self-evident that such a catharsis and renewal of religion and spirituality can have many ways of verbal and cultural expression, of imagination (visualization) and meditation, of priorities and preferences, of practical rituals and celebrations, of institutional management, of teaching, and of ways of living.

Living rooted in these spiritual and transcendental realities is the key for all global solutions and personal fulfillment of humans. The evolution of mankind can only continue within the frame of this new universal religion! All other options will end in the destruction of the planet and the doom of mankind in less than a century.

→ The failure of politics is deeply rooted in the Christian religion.

Wise Men

Without a doubt we can assume, that today around the globe there are people that are very wise, that seek and live a genuine inner spirituality. They have learnt a lot about life and about people, learnt a lot about the deepest meaning of love, about hope, the truth, justice, peace, and the innermost meaning of life. They experience the spiritual power inside through meditation, contemplation and many also through their dreams. They all belong to the most valuable people that exist on earth.

These wise people have experienced and know, how much most people ignore their inner being and how these people are and live totally self-alienated. They have experience and know about the inner suffering of billions of people.

They also know about how the lies, the life lies, the cheating and deceiving, the falseness and evilness, the distortion and twisting create endless suffering, despair and hopelessness.
All these wise people have deep in their heart, the desire, that people around the globe find their fortune and their fulfillment, that freedom and justice reigns over the earth, and that all people find within themselves the inner transcendental source. Many of the wise people, women as well as men, have a certain smaller or bigger access (inner experience) of the existence of the transcendental world that means they found the spiritual world.

Many of these wise people, partly also members of an official religion, are actively anxious, to help other people find their way to psychical-spiritual fulfillment. Many may have their own, somewhat bizarre ideas about spirituality. Certain organizations however are extremely astray and even teach, absurd ideas and practices; we won't touch on this critical aspects here.

We can certainly assume that such wise people existed over and over again over the past centuries amongst many civilizations around the globe and that they always existed. They also existed 1000, 2000, 3000 and more years ago in all civilizations around the globe. They told people about their experiences, shared their knowledge and organized themselves in communities. Already in the second subsequent generation this word of mouth knowledge become alienated from its substance, manipulated, distorted and misused for different interests. Subsequently people created legends out of this substance and these – later biographically unknown people – were given names and a story.

There are wise men as protagonists in the Bible. There are also prophets, men of God, saviors, messiahs, priests, teachers of wisdom, enlightened personalities and those sent by God – however one wants to define those terms. Most probably most of these very wise men failed out of known reasons: power of the established religious institutions, political and local cultural circumstances. The masses could neither read nor write; most of these people were overwhelmingly poor, stupid, submissive to authority, and had a magical experience of their existence.

One had to sell the people supernatural illusions, already based on the reason of (word of mouth) marketing. The failure of such a mission is practically preconditioned. Only fragments of their being, actions and teaching stood the test of time; partially mixed creatively or with strategy, with other ideas and knowledge from other cultures and with distorted (untruthful) historical facts. With that given individual or institutional interests, most of the genuine, authentic knowledge was extremely or even totally distorted.

→ Do politicians get advice from wise men? Do they ever consider getting advice from wise men?
→ Why do politicians fear and avoid wise men? They have fear that they lies would be uncovered and they would have to stand for the truth.

Christianity has the Crucifix that expresses the core message of its religion. This is the meaning of this symbol:

🦗 Death penalty like the electric chair or the lethal injection today!
🦗 Corpse: dead, the end, sadness, suffering, hopelessness, darkness, forlornness, and absence of God!
🦗 No hope, no love, no care, no zest, no justice, and no power of the inner Spirit!
🦗 No life, no joy of life, no happiness, no satisfaction, no lust, and no fulfillment!
🦗 Accusation, reproach; stirring up hate, depression, fear, guilt, rage and revenge!

The Life Symbol (Circle-Cross-Mandala) offers an alternative:

🦗 Human being, life, love, joy, zest for life, lust, full of life, satisfaction, happiness, hope, justice, peace, power of the inner Spirit
🦗 Centered in the inner Spirit, all-embracing life, totality, completeness, balance, openness, light, confidence

- Aim, psychical-spiritual evolution, fulfillment, conjunction of the real and spiritual world, fulfillment of the Archetypes of the Soul, source of life
- Catharsis, renewal, reconciliation, forgiveness, salvation, redemption, and presence of God!

The importance:

- What does a human need for its psychical-spiritual evolution?
- What does humanity need for its psychical-spiritual evolution?
- On which of both symbols should governance being founded?
- Is there an ideological (political) alternative for humanity's psychical-spiritual evolution?

5. Government Failures

(Extracts from Schellhammer: ECONOMICS III)

5.1. Political Failure

"There are also government failures – situations in which the government intervenes and makes things worse. Government failures are pervasive in the government – the government is always failing in one way or another." [140]

➜ Indeed, governments sometimes make things worse with their interventions.
➜ The government is always failing in some way or another because the economy is a failure.
➜ Failure is part of life as nobody is perfect; life is a learning process, also for economists.

"The business of governments is to keep the government out of business – that is unless business needs government. (Will Rogers)" [141]

➜ This is an opinion. It is more: it leads to the destruction of society and democracy.
➜ Nothing can be worse on earth than to give all the market power to economists.

"Government failures – when the government intervention in the market to improve the market failure actually makes the situation worse." [142]

➜ The author doesn't give here a list of concrete failures. The picture is a terrible simplification.
➜ Political failure must be seen and interpreted in the complex network of the real economics.

"Why are there government failures? Let's briefly list some important reasons:

---

[140] Colander, p. 71, 72
[141] Colander, p. 485
[142] Colander, p. 485

1. Government doesn't have an incentive to correct the problem. Government reflects politics, which reflects individual's interests in trying to gain more power for themselves. Political pressures to benefit some group or another will often dominate over doing the general good.

2. Governments don't have enough information to deal with the problem. Regulating is a difficult business. To intervene effectively, even if it wants to, government must have good information, but just as the market often lacks adequate information, so does the government.

3. Intervention in markets is almost always more complicated that it initially seems. Almost all actions have unintended consequences. Government attempts to offset market failures can prevent the market from dealing with the problem more effectively. The difficulty is that generally the market's ways of dealing with problems work only in the long run. As government deals with the short-run problems, it eliminates the incentives that would have brought about a long-run market solution.

4. The bureaucratic nature of government intervention does not allow fine-tuning. When the problems change, the government solution often responds far more slowly...

5. Government intervention leads to more government intervention. Given the nature of the political process, opening the door in one area allows government to enter into other areas where intervention is harmful. Even in those cases where government action may seem to be likely to do some good, it might be best not to intervene, if that intervention will lead to additional government action in cases where it will not likely do well.

The important point to remember is that government failures exist and must be taken into account before making any policy recommendation. That's why real-world economic policy falls within the art of economics, and policy conclusions cannot be drawn from the models of positive economics." [143]

→ The economic arrogance is speaking here. These people only want to dethrone the kings.
→ An incentive to correct the problem is in the mission to lead the folks and the entire society.
→ Politicians and economists have individual interests in trying to gain more power/rewards for themselves.

---

[143] Colander, p. 499

→ Governments don't have enough information to deal with problems; same for economists.
→ Challenge for economists: Almost all actions in human's life have unintended consequences.
→ The difficulty is that dealing with negative externalities only works in the long run (inertia).
→ The real disaster: Bureaucratic nature of government intervention does not allow for any fine-tuning.
→ The source of the coming doom: the nature of economics and the corporation's motives.
→ It's obvious that economists hate political interventions; it could damage their profit drive.
→ Real-world economic policy is an art: and where is the science that follows scientific rules?

"For the government to correct the problem, it must

1) Recognize the problem.
2) Have the will to do something positive about the problem.
3) Have the ability to do something positive about the problem.

Government seldom can do all three of these well. Often the result is that government action is directed at the wrong problem at the wrong time." [144]

→ Do the economists realize the outrageous problems they have and create worldwide?
→ Having a will is great; having stupid masses and economic psychopaths is a nightmare.

"Economic policy is, and must be, applied within a political context. This means that political elements must be taken into account. Politics enters into the determination of economic policy in two ways, one positive and one negative. Its positive contribution is that politicians take market failures and failures of market outcomes into account when formulating policy. Ultimately the political system decides what externalities should be adjusted for, what is a desirable distribution, what rights are above the market, and when people's revealed demand does not reflect their true demand. To the extent that the government's political decisions reflect the will of society, government is making a positive contribution." [145]

---

[144] Colander, p. 537
[145] Colander, p. 537-538

→ Why can the economic system not decide what negative externalities should be adjusted?

→ Political elements must be taken into account; but it's more: governments must find back their freedom of operation (from the economic institutions) and teach the economists how they have to take human factors, the nature, and the planet into account.

"The political reality is that, in the short run, people are often governed by emotion, swayed by mass psychology, irrational, and interested in their own rather than the general good. Politicians and other policy makers know that; the laws and regulations they propose reflect such calculations. Politicians don't get elected and reelected by constantly saying that all choices have costs and benefits." [146]

→ In opposite to that, we can say: economists and the money masters are governed by ego-lunacy, unlimited greed, megalomania, psychopathy, and psychosis. They use mass psychology, abuse the irrational mind of humans, and they are only interested in their own profit, ignoring the evolution of humanity.

→ In general we could not find substantial criticism and suggestions for politics and governments. But the entire tone reflects a deep hostility towards politics in general as if these economists would want to dethrone governments and to fully control the entire political systems.

→ Seen from the other side, with a certain understanding, the economists and business people (all levels) are frustrated in such a way by the stupid, ignorant, arrogant, incompetent, and good-for-nothing in the world of politics, so that the economic intelligence must put them in traps.

Example of a Political Failure

3.2.2011: Obama's speech; he claims: "the leadership that made the U.S. (is) the light of the world." In other words: Obama claims the U.S. to be "the predestined nation, the only one that can save mankind". This implies that he is the new Messiah saving the world; and the U.S. is the chosen folk from God. "God bless the United States of America", he was saying.

Confucius: "Signs and symbols rule the world, neither words nor laws." Today we must say: Corporations rule the world and the politics, not politics. The meaning of signs and symbols of corporate groups dominate people. States have de facto converted into corporate groups.

---

[146] Colander, p. 538-539

Their only creed is ultimately greed for money for power, which is fueled by lust. In their agenda, they all have the complete destruction of all Archetypes of the Soul.

There are hundreds of thousands of CEOs, owners of corporate groups, politicians and religious leaders who have acted during decades with their megalomania, paternalism, extreme greed, stubbornness, sick narcissism, arrogance, falseness and scrupulousness, perversion, amorality and a religious psychosis or political lunacy.

The psychological and material question is always the same: Who is the profiteer of such mad politics and legal mendacity? Who is the profiteer of such governmental criminality "in the Name of the Creator and the Almighty God"?

5.2. Lobbyism and Pressure Groups

Over 13,500 (2009) and estimated 17,000 lobbyists (2012) work in Washington to influence the entire American government. Money spent for lobbyism 2011: more than $3.5 billion [147]

16,500 lobbyists are working to influence the European Union in Brussels. [148] Other sources mention up to 30-35,000 lobbyists.

In the US, corporations spent an average of $200,000 a year on lobbying every politician elected to state legislatures. [149]

The United States, the European Union and many other countries are significantly manipulated, dominated, controlled, abused and exploited by hundreds of thousands of lobbyists, CEO's, institutions, personalities, secret service agents, (co-) owners of banks and corporate groups or educational institutions. Many of them are originally rooted in interests of other nations.

Nepotism, favoritism and informal understandings between businesses, officials and politicians in many places lead to inefficiency and gross waste of resources.

Macroeconomic conclusions:

→ Lobbyism radically undermines democracy and legal governmental power.
→ Lobbyism works in the interest of the rich, the superrich, and the corporations.
→ There is no powerful lobbyism for the citizen's everyday interests and concerns.
→ There is no powerful lobbyism for the small and medium sized firms' interests and concerns.
→ There is no powerful lobbyism that protects the human values and a basic ethics.

---

[147]
http://wiki.answers.com/Q/How_many_people_work_as_lobbyists_in_the_nation's_capital_today
[148] http://www.pacteurope.eu/pact/wp-content/uploads/2012/04/European-Lobbying-EN.pdf
[149] http://en.wikipedia.org/wiki/Lobbying_in_the_United_States

→ Lobbyism disfigures and manipulates the importance of the macroeconomic parameters.
→ Lobbyism is not a democratic institution in the interest of their concerns and never in the interest of general balanced governance.

There are other pressure groups and economics groups, trade unions, unions or associations of commerce, agriculture and labor. But these groups also do not represent the interests of the people. Greenpeace and Transparency International have a public voice, but they also do not cover the concerns of the citizens.

Citizens are a sum of individuals that have no private voice, apart from the yearly elections and votes. Governmental agents are not in a direct contact with the citizens, apart from occasional events (celebrations) and some communal information on their Website. Citizens can go for strike or demonstrations. The police reaction is well known around the globe. New social movements have practically no significant influence in governmental decision-making processes. The favored Western individualism has drastically reduced the readiness and ability for solitarian action and participation in matters of common interests. A political renewal from the 'bottom' has no chance. There is no organization, no money, no big group, and no leader that could unify a mass of people in order to become a strong political voice.

People live in a cultural, economic and political rootlessness. A huge majority also lives in a spiritual and religious rootlessness. Considering the high unemployment rates in Europe and the United States, the risk to lose the job is high. Small firms and self-employed people can easily lose customers if they try to get a voice with 'new ideas' or pioneering projects'. Economic fear makes people obedient and submissive or at least close-mouthed.

5.3. Politics, Power and Money

General explorations:

With politicians it is first and foremost always about money: money for their own pocket, their privileges and guarantees for a future to follow their political career.

Instead of serving the people, politicians first serve themselves, their morbid narcissism and their 'clubs', and the interests of corporations. This makes them fall easy prey to blackmail. They are secretly blackmailed or lured for whatever and whenever. Rarely are they politicians out of vocation or for genuine ideological reasons; but always out of self-interest.

Many governments sell or lease agricultural land and provide licenses for others to exploit the resources in their countries. This serves the corporations, the elite, but never the population; especially not as a measure against poverty or unemployment.

Governments misuse and misspend far too much money from taxpayers for their own protection. For the same purposes they continuously create new laws to limit the rights of the citizens and increase the size of the elite's wealth (economy).

Most government officials have no comprehensive knowledge of the real situations faced by their own people, and of global humanity or the planet's best interests. They are unable to think in complex networks that focus on the past, the present and the future.

When politicians don't know how to deal with conflicts due to a lack of knowledge, skills and personal character, they react with brutal force. They are not capable of identifying the conflict as a result of their own failures. They are not capable to engage in dialogue with the citizens and together to work out solutions. Austerity measures are an example of stupid reactions.

Most politicians are adept at exaggerating, understating, sweet talking, glossing over, lying, cheating, forging, seducing, manipulating, maneuvering and coming to terms. For these leaders, almost every means is justifiable to achieve their objectives and to use every possible loophole including covert extortion.

Most politicians have an idea of mankind from the middle Ages. Practical politics has not changed since 500 years in its fundamental principles. They 'lead' their people and yet know nothing about human beings or the inner being of humans.

Many politicians misuse God and religion for their own perverse political games.   They violate the   values that earlier pioneers in their own people fought so hard to acquire. Slavery, the conquest and imperialism of the past have merely changed in form and appearance.

Most politicians do not want truth. The logical conclusion is simple: they are never in the position to solve the big problems in their own country let alone the critical state of humanity and the planet. They always talk about the (essential) growth of the economy, never about quality and balance and never about the 'true human life'.

Most women in politics simply copy the patterns of men. In this sense they are nothing but masculine women. The genuine qualities of real (natural) women are not welcome in politics and also not in religion. Also as a result of this politics (and religion) their doing will and must fail.

The state administration, the servant of power is a massive Moloch. Most people that work within the state administration are absolutely incapable of reacting to imbalance and of dealing constructively with the individual situations of citizens. Most of them suffer from feelings of inadequacy in their 'elevated' positions and compensate by working to the letter. Their completely inefficient apparatus sucks up millions if not billions and in spite of supposedly serving the people treats them like human biomass, dealing with them like industrial mass production. Politicians prefer it like this! It's always their mother behind!

Politicians experience maximum lust at the destruction of the Archetypes of the Soul, for example love, truth, marriage and family, the development of the inner life and the power of the inner Spirit. With that they destroy themselves and they destroy the future of their own children, of their population, and of humanity as a whole. This is the way it goes in Marbella, Madrid, Zurich, Berlin, Paris, London, in the United States, in Israel, in the whole capitalist coalition as well as in other countries, completely infected with European capitalism (imperialism), not to talk about contaminated Christianity over 800 years. Such development is the result of a roadmap from the masters behind the curtains.

In January 2011 a Swiss politician of highest executive position said (we translate): "I recommend to every woman, that she should get herself a man who is active in the military. Everything else is like at the discount store; you never really know what you are buying." This attitude we already know from the Nazis and from Hitler's loyal followers.

An insider speaks about the financial power: 7.7.2011 - Hillary Clinton reviews Spanish government and applauds their servility. She said at the visit of President Zapatero and the King Don Carlos: "There is virtually no important global or military challenge that we are not working on together." Even before that visit, Trinidad Jiménez, Minister of Foreign Affairs cleared all possible doubt by stating that "close cooperation between the U.S. and Spain will be visible in the political, economic and military spheres." Zapatero and the King have sold Spain to foreigners – read: to America; it means: to the owner of the corporation called 'United States'. [150] No Spaniards can see it because no media and no responsible people are talking about it!

Who are these masters destroying societies everywhere with their financial power? What are their true primordial motives? Sexual frustration? Psychopathy? Megalomania? Narcissism? Madness? Religious Psychosis? The roots of all their inner conflicts lie in the failure of their forefathers 2,000 years ago! Through that they have lost their status as 'chosen folk from God'. They have roped in the entire world into their collective unconscious conflict, burdened themselves increasingly with immense guilt and inner pain.

The summer-winter time regulation in Europe is an excellent example to show what politicians do. At the time, when they introduced this change, they had a respectable aim (reducing consumption of electricity). This was a very expensive implementation. Soon they found out that the aim can't be achieved. And today, decades later, we still have this stupid time change which costs a lot of money twice per year. The world of animals get confused twice per year and hundreds of millions people as well need to adapt their biorhythm and are confused during 1-3 weeks. Now today, no politicians want to put this on the political table aiming for a compromise by continuing with 'back to normal' in the middle of one hour forward and one hour back. It's about public money wasted for nothing and probably for the coming decades or centuries!

---

[150] http://english.pravda.ru/world/europe/07-07-2011/118420-Clinton_reviews_Spanish_government_applauds_servility-0/

The history of the past 10 years teaches us: The neo-capitalistic coalition, US-Army and NATO, chases foreign heads of states and ministers claiming that they have stolen a lot of money from their folks, built up enormous private wealth. Do you remember Ghaddafi ? Mubarak? There are more in Africa for example. At the same time many banks, corporations, and individuals get richer and richer on a level of billions of dollars and they get increasing power over trillions of dollars and Euros. We must interpret: the governments, the 'kings' in the past, have become the 'servants' of the new 'kings' that have been previously the servants of the 'kings'. In all cases the folks pay the price. That's the supra-dynamic of macroeconomics. It's not surprising that the classical books about economics do not describe and analyze the real business world, but feed the students of economics and business with 80% junk and 20% facts that are of superficial or low importance.

The common people are blind, brainwashed, misled and deceived, too lazy to think, deformed by the education system, rotten by religion and focused only on their own daily physical and material needs.

Macroeconomic conclusions:

→ Governments generally have far too much money at their disposal. It makes them insane.
→ Governments and politicians are secretly blackmailed or lured for corporate interests.
→ Governments have become the servants of the major corporations and banks.
→ Most government officials have no comprehensive knowledge of the citizens' situations.
→ Governments have no holistic knowledge about the state of humanity and the planet.
→ Ministers are not capable to engage in dialogue with the citizens and the small firms.
→ Government's practices: understating, lying, distorting, manipulating, and maneuvering.
→ Practical politics has not changed since 500 years in its fundamental principles.
→ Governments misuse God and religion for their own perverse political games.
→ Politicians talk about the growth, but never about quality and balance of life standard.
→ The state administration, servant of power, is a massive Moloch, absorbs too much money.

→ Politicians experience maximum lust at the destruction of the Archetypes of the Soul.

→ The neo-capitalistic coalition, US-Army and NATO, chases foreign head of states and ministers claiming that they have stolen a lot of money from their folks for their own sake.

Mediterranean Governance

Governmental spending is of prime importance in macroeconomics: The Spanish government has earned more than a trillion Euros over the past 25 years from tourism as well as from the sale of properties to foreigners (especially in the Mediterranean areas, Balearic Islands, Canary Islands). During the same time the European Union provided further billions to Spain. The Costa del Sol, Costa Blanca, Mallorca raked in billions if not hundreds of billions in taxes, duties and fees.

What did the Spanish government do with these huge amounts of money? They let 2 million homes be built that can't be sold now at prices with 60% profit because if they would have insulation protecting from the summer heat and the winter cold like is usual for example in Germany; and they destroyed with the urbanizing madness up to 80% of all natural areas along the ocean.

The attitudes in the world of business and politics are outrageous: corruption and rip off are as high as in an underdeveloped African country. Now, we can imagine where the money is gone. It must compensate another problem: We estimate that around 65% of all members of local governments, including the heads of village or town councils, do not have the necessary knowledge and skills, nor the character and personality qualities to lead their folk and to manage the duties of their job in a permanently changing world with increasing global problems. They live and work with a mind from the previous époque, always adoring their mothers.

A highly relevant macroeconomic question is: Where exactly did this money go? One thing is certain, the money did not go to a nationwide efficient infrastructure (public transport, sewage system, renewable energy, technological research, renewable energy, public education and especially advances in vocational education), nor into a solidly founded and all-sided economy in their underdeveloped Southern regions.

Working hard with excellent professional attitudes is a foreign concept for the majority of Spaniards. They all prefer waiting for the masses of tourists that bring fresh cash every summer. Spain's technological pioneering development is a Fata Morgana. Not many Spaniards want to get their hands dirty and to sweat or to learn some complicated technical stuff. Above that they are too lazy to learn for life and work. The mothers of this young generation feed their mal-educated and pampered kids and tell them: 'Just get a job in the state administration or work in a bank like your father.'

Bull fighting (killing) is a pleasure for Spaniards. The bull is a symbol since millenniums for fertility, male potency, strength, power, and male pride. These Spaniards, probably especially women and mothers, have fun to kill these male attributes. A sick world with economic consequences: impotent men at home, in the governments, in the pioneering production, and in the free market.

That is why today Spain has its self-inflicted financial crisis and its extremely high unemployment. The same questions have to be asked for Greece, Italy and other Mediterranean regions. Economic science should investigate and explain with its theories! What is certain is that not even with a trillion-Euro-bailout from the IMF and the European Central bank the economic problems of Spain, Italy, and Greece could be solved. A macroeconomic consequence will be: Spain, Greece, and half of Italy will fall into the state of a 'developing country'.

Macroeconomic conclusions:

➔ The way governments spend public money is of prime importance in macroeconomics.
➔ Many governments have no long term perspective in spending public money.
➔ The attitudes for human values in the world of business and politics are outrageous.
➔ Working hard with excellent professional attitudes is a prime condition for the economy.

The 9/11 Attacks and the Costs of War

The 9/11 attacks on the World Trade Center in New York is probably still vivid in most people's memory. It was an act of terror, ordered by Osama Bin Laden, so they say.

Yet 3,000 scientists (!) in the USA put this into question: they say the events never occurred as they have been portrayed in the media and presented by politicians. They say the buildings could never have collapsed alone because of the airliners' impact. The buildings were 'prepared' with special explosives on all floors in order to create the downfall. The whole scenery of those events was orchestrated by the secret service of the US (CIA) and Israel (Mossad). It is not a matter of economic science to find out here the truth.

The aim they say was to create a reason for war, to invade and occupy Iraq. This however is said to also be but a small element of the global plan for a 'One World Order' of the capitalist coalition, including the occupation and possession of oil fields around the globe and the weakening of Russia, China and the whole Islamic world.

Of high economic interest is the financial aspect of terrorism:

How many people died through terrorist attacks, orchestrated by Bin Laden, Al-Qaeda and other similar groups around the world? There were some 3,000 from the World Trade Center. To these can be added perhaps 1,000 deaths from individual terrorist attacks around the world. This does not include terrorist outrages in Iraq, given that these are understood as part of the war. We are perhaps talking about 4,000 deaths to date since 9/11 caused by 'terrorists'. This adds up to approximately 400 victims per year or 33 per month. This is indeed a terrible tragedy, a miserable suffering for those left behind and obviously not justifiable.

But let us compare these figures with some other figures:

➔ Over 42,000 deaths from Road Traffic Accidents in Europe alone (every year).
➔ 380,000 deaths from fine dust (cars), in Europe alone (every year).
➔ Over 46,000 deaths from Road Traffic Accidents in America alone (every year).
➔ 400,000 deaths from fine dust (cars), in America alone (every year).
➔ Millions of deaths around the world due to contamination, also every year.
➔ 3-4 billion people living in poverty, so that 1,000 people can earn billions.

Do you understand? Something is wrong here with the economic theories: The proportions are not comprehensible: Wars to fight terrorism with around 4,000 victims spread over 10 years, or 33 victims per month. At the same time trillions of dollars are spent on weapons and all the wars since 9/11. And we can relate the figures with the victims from road traffic accidents per year. Such disproportions indicate extreme lies!

Macroeconomic conclusions:

→ Governments do not want the truth and measure realities with different scales.
→ Governments distort values of high human importance in order to rectify evil doing.
→ Governments ignore the economic and human factors of road traffic accidents.
→ Governments have double faced moral and perverse attitudes in matters of wars.

The Holocaust Law as a Principle of Economics

We do not want to explore here the historical events of war and the Holocaust, nor the figures and circumstances of the real genocide. It's sad anyway. Our interest is: In many states there are laws that prohibit anyone from critically investigating or even critically expressing oneself about the Holocaust.

In actual fact most of the critical investigations do not deny the Holocaust; the murder of Jews during the Second World War. The critical statements and observations are usually related to the alleged number of '6 million Jews' and about the subject matter of what can be defined as murder and what can be defined as war victim. Here it's about a fact of figures and the interpretation of a word.

Critics claim that it was never 6 million Jews who were murdered, that such a figure is impossible. One thing can be said as a matter of fact: It is not important if it was 6 or 3 or 'only' half a million victims. It is and will remain a terrible genocide.

The economical and psychological consequences however are extremely different: Compensation payments and collective (German) guilt as a means for endless political manipulation (blackmail and extortion) come to a new light. Israel and generally affected Jews have received billions of DM, USD and EUR to date. Here it's about benefit or profit; either way it's about money.

As a follow up, one must also integrate the judgment of other collective murders in the 19th, 20th and 21st century. From what figure can one talk about 'genocide'? To this topic there are far worse hypotheses (evil allegations?): Jews (Zionists) proposed their plan to Hitler of murdering millions of Jews, in order to subsequently claim the right to Palestine and as blackmail for massive financial payments in the future. We can compare the figures and interpretations with the figures of victims of private car traffic accidents since 50 years: higher than the victims of WWII and this for the sake of industrial profit and governmental taxes! Here and elsewhere with human topics (e.g. absolute poverty, hunger, dirty water, etc.) it's about externalities, collateral damages. There are always enormous collateral damages with wars (e.g. Vietnam, Afghanistan, and Iraq).

There are at least 100 historical and scientific questions that would need to be clarified to this Holocaust matter. The Holocaust laws prohibit this. These circumstances (figures, interpretations, comparisons) make the whole Holocaust affair extremely suspicious: indeed something very explosive is being covered up, something that nobody is allowed to uncover or discuss.

Digging in the marsh is strenuous and in the end nobody wants to know the truth. Revealing the truth is collectively punished: in a relationship, in a family life, in the social life, in the industry (production), in the world of religion, politics and the science of economics or the real economy.

On the other side digging and fully showing the truth is a fundamental principle of science, also of social science, but thoroughly missed in the neo-capitalistic science of economics!

Macroeconomic conclusions:

➔ Politicians hide or manipulate macroeconomic parameters or they simply lie about them.
➔ Macroeconomic facts are 'elaborated' to make people and corporations feel comfortable.
➔ The collective pays for the failure of authorities, institutions, corporations, and government.
➔ The way governments operate with facts, figures, interpretations, comparisons is distorted.

5.4. Maturity of Politicians

The Defense Minister in Germany (May 2011) was a 39 year old attorney. The Foreign Minister is a homosexual, married to a man. From a psychoanalytical view we must say: Never can a 39 year old have the maturity, moral integrity, life experience and wisdom necessary for such a position. Age alone surely does not provide the wisdom and moral integrity. The life experiences alone neither. Homosexuality is a very complicated neurosis, marked by a disturbance in the balance of the male and female pole; also in a deep libido disorder to the mother and father. On top of that the use of the 'Marriage'-Archetype for a same-sex relationship is a desecration of the eternal 'Marriage'-Archetype. That's a political cabaret!

In Spain there was (2011) a government minister who was born in 1971 and another in 1976; both are women. Never can a 35 or 40 year old person have the maturity, moral integrity, life experience, human knowledge, personal psychical-spiritual foundation, knowledge and skills to manage a government department with global perspectives, and the corresponding wisdom necessary for such a position. That's also a political cabaret!

Give to such a government a 100 billion, 300 billion or 500 billion Euros bailout, and then, after a few years go look for the money – you will need 50 years to find out where the money is gone. That's a macroeconomic issue, nothing new for many developing countries, e.g. in Africa!

The people should start to think about what relevant skills and psychical-spiritual preconditions (free from neurosis, psychosis and psychopathy) a person should have in order to be in a position of the highest political responsibility in order to carry out and manage in the interests of the people.

This question should be asked around the world, regardless of culture or form of government. It is especially valid for church office holders (e.g. minister, priest, monk, bishop, cardinal, Pope) and for religious teachers of all kinds. In the future, those who violate the Archetypes of the Soul should never be allowed to fill top leadership positions in a society if humanity wants to have a good future!

It has been clear for a long time now that the people in Europe and America feel that governments have long lost touch with the healthy and genuine needs of the people. The citizens say: 'governments and political leaders cheat, lie, twist and distort'. They only act in their own interest. They are doing nothing against poverty in their own country. They are doing nothing for the long-term benefit of their citizens. So, herewith we are back to macroeconomics!

Macroeconomic conclusions:

→ A majority of politicians lack maturity, moral integrity, life experience and wisdom.
→ Neurotic, psychotic and psychopathic politicians can't properly manage the concerns of a society.
→ Governments have long lost touch with the concerns and genuine needs of the people.
→ The arrogance and ignorance of politicians towards their own folk is beyond imagination.

5.5. The Perversion of Power

We present here a longer part of an article admitting that we can't prove the truth; but it shows a picture widely known around the globe:

"I was involved in the payment, in the direct payment in cash to a person who killed the president of a foreign country. I was in the meeting where it was decided to give this cash money to the killer… I know that certain people who are Bilderbergers were involved in such orders…. We had to pay on the instructions of foreign powers for the killing of persons who did not follow the orders of Bilderberg or the IMF or the World Bank for example…. the biggest banks in Switzerland are involved in unethical activities…. its trillions, completely unaudited, illegal and besides the tax… most of the directors of Swiss banks are not locals anymore, they are foreigners, mostly Anglo-Saxon, either American or British… they destroy our society and destroy the people world wide just for greed. They seek power and destroy whole countries, like Greece, Spain, Portugal or Ireland and Switzerland will be one of the last in line. And they use China as working slaves. And a person like Josef Ackermann, who is a Swiss citizen, is the top man at a German bank and he uses his power for greed and does not respect the common people. He has quite a few legal cases in Germany and also now in the States. He is a Bilderberger and does not care about Switzerland or any other country… They have huge amounts of money available and use it to destroy whole countries…. The real aim is to destroy Europe…. the big Swiss banks, because they are not Swiss anymore, most of them are led by Americans…. a kind of exclusive elite club that has all the power and everybody else is impoverished and down…. The EU is under the iron grip of Bilderberg….

…The big banks are training their staff with Anglo-Saxon values. They are training them to be greedy and ruthless. And greed is destroying Switzerland and everybody else… We are confronted with really ruthless criminals, also big war criminals. It's worse than genocide. They are ready and able to kill millions of people just to stay in power and in control…. Question: In the structure of Bilderberg, is there an inner circle that knows the plans and then there is the majority who just follow orders? Answer: Yes…. Bilderberg was founded by Prince Bernard, a former member of the SS and Nazi party and he also worked for IG Farben, who's subsidiary produced Cyclone B." [151]

---

[151] http://www.henrymakow.com/revelations_from_a_swiss_banki.html

The main issue here is not the people in this event or the content itself. It is about 'democracy' that has been a hollow word for a long time. The oligarchy of the capitalistic financial markets has the power. The population merely serves for the exploitation for their 'One World Government' aims. Rarely somebody gets into the government without a lot of money or without being promoted by 'important' personalities and institutions.

Politics serves those that have and want to have more. More recently politics serves the political and religious psychosis: For the new World Governance. This also means: against Islam. With this the people will once again have the never ending religious war at their doorstep like every few centuries.

Remember the 'Crusades' from the 12th to the 14th century. This is exciting for the Pope! It has been like this since 2,000 years. Religion abuses politics and politics abuses religion. Both in turn misuse the people. Who is the actual culprit here? What has this got to do with macroeconomics? A hypothesis could be: it was and still is only about stealing money or making profit.

'Justice' today is in many democratic (and other) countries nothing but a lie. Laws protect political crimes, political corruption, political mendacity and hypocrisy. The judicial system is a macroeconomic pillar that allows to operate businesses and to manage life and wealth.

When you look at the outcome, then you know what is wanted or approved. This is what the governments, and the politicians want and approve:

- The people are helpless.
- The people are ensnared.
- The people are lied to.
- The people are brainwashed.
- The people need to be blind.
- The people should shut up.
- The people should not think.
- The people are chained to credit.
- The people are allowed to buy a car.
- The people should suffer from emissions.
- The people must suffer in general.
- The people are allowed to have a cell phone.
- The people should lose themselves in the Internet.
- The people are allowed to have fun.
- The people can speculate.
- The people should consume.
- The people should use credit cards.

- The people should be (relatively) poor.
- The people can have a swimming pool.
- The people can have a walkway.
- The people should feel lust when shopping.
- The people should go to the doctor.
- The people should go to the pharmacy.
- The people can go on holiday.
- The people cannot have a soul.
- The people should not ask questions.
- The people should see lies as the truth.
- The people should see neurosis as something healthy.
- The people should see lunacy as a mission.
- The people should experience narcissism as wellbeing.
- The people should get meaningless things for cheap.
- The people must adapt.
- The people who are critical need to go into psychotherapy.
- The people who do not follow the lunacy must be punished.

There are too many politicians that are imprisoned in pathogenic narcissism, neurosis and psychopathy, perverse lunacy, obsession and greed, lies and falseness, intrigues and maneuvers. They only serve themselves, the elite and their power.

Many ministers and head of states in Europe and elsewhere do not govern; they do execute the orders from the supreme masters. They barely serve the people. They all disregard and abuse the Archetypes of the Soul. They are far too uneducated for the issues they manage, especially in their understanding of the psychical-spiritual being.

There are many laws that merely serve politicians themselves, their power, the wars, the elite, the exploitation and misuse and in many cases infringe the basic rights of every human being. The Holocaust laws hinder the truth and the exact (objective, neutral) establishment of the truth; it serves the lies and hidden benefits.

On the other hand new laws must be established to prohibit the brainwashing of people. New laws are also necessary for the protection of the environment, the planet and every human being. Too many laws and forms of punishment are only there to oppress the people, create mistrust and hatred and to ultimately sow fear and suffering. All those who created these laws must be held accountable, absolutely all of them.

Macroeconomic conclusions:

→ Too many laws and forms of punishment are only there to oppress the people.

→ 'Justice' today is in many democratic (and other) countries nothing but a lie.

→ Politics serves the political and religious psychosis: For the new World Governance.

→ Religion abuses politics and politics abuses religion. Both in turn misuse the people.

5.6. Economic Destruction of Democracy

"The power elite consist of those with tremendous amounts of both wealth and power in our world. Like any group, the power elite has both individuals and factions which are inclined to promote their own self-serving interests, and those who are more interested in serving the greater good. Many scholars who have spent considerable time studying this group have found that there are factions within this elite group which at times fight against each other, while at other times they work together for common goals." [152]

The elites do what all elites do. They launch more wars, build grander monuments to themselves, plunge their nations deeper into debt, and as it all unravels they take it out on the backs of workers and the poor. [153]

The collapse of the global economy, which wiped out a staggering $40 trillion in wealth, was caused when our elites, after destroying our manufacturing base, sold massive quantities of fraudulent mortgage-backed securities to pension funds, small investors, banks, universities, state and foreign governments and shareholders. [154]

The elites, to cover the losses, then looted the public treasury to begin the speculation over again. They also, in the name of austerity, began dismantling basic social services, set out to break the last vestiges of unions, slashed jobs, froze wages, threw millions of people out of their homes, and stood by idly as we created a permanent underclass of unemployed and underemployed. [155]

As Sigmund Freud grasped in 'Beyond the Pleasure Principle' and 'Civilization and its Discontents' human societies are as intoxicated and blinded by their own headlong rush toward death and destruction as they are by the search for erotic fulfillment. [156]

And the elite are all at the mercy of finance. Who owns the significant financial institutions and who has the say in the world of finance?

---

[152] http://www.hidden-knowledge.net/lessons/05a_power_elite
[153]
http://www.truthdig.com/report/item/this_time_were_taking_the_whole_planet_with_us_20110307/
[154] http://www.rense.com/general93/next.htm
[155] http://www.bibliotecapleyades.net/sociopolitica/sociopol_globalelite62.htm
[156] http://www.studioeight.tv/phpbb/viewtopic.php?f=12&t=22492

The elites destroy the core of societies in Europe and America; also in this way for example:

British society is witnessing a swift end to traditional family life with 46% of children now born to unmarried mothers... nearly half of all children will go through the trauma of seeing their parents divorce before they are 16....A child in a single-parent family is 75% more likely to struggle at school, 70% more likely to become addicted to drugs, 50% more likely to develop a drinking problem and 35% more likely to be unemployed in adulthood. [157]

In Germany a third of singles are against marriage. Many unmarried Germans want to remain unmarried. Only 43 per cent of them can imagine getting married sometime in the future.

On the Internet and in the media one can find many critical observations with respect to politics. The facts of yesterday are forgotten or covered up with new facts. A lot is interpreted and assessed subjectively. Depending on the side of the political questioning or the analysis one will find completely different pictures of a concern.

By using a few examples we intend to motivate questions and hypotheses, which could lead to further questions and meticulous investigations. One or the other critical observations may be seen as a conspiracy or allegation.

We understand the political topics and facts here as a starting point for economic hypotheses, which the science of history and economics, free from ideology and specific interests should explore.

Macroeconomic conclusions:

➜ All mentioned critical aspects of political acting lead to immense misuse of public money.
➜ Lack of political integrity, knowledge and skills produces immense loss of public money.
➜ Political mismanagement causes poverty, amorality, immense collateral damages, and costs.
➜ The weak success of democracy has been destroyed and sold to the financial elite.
➜ Politicians are humans and as a human they have destroyed hundreds of millions of lives.

---

[157] http://www.presstv.ir/detail/175459.html

→ Governments in America and Europe are responsible for 4 billion lives in extreme misery.
→ Coward ministers and head of states are fully responsible for wars and its consequences.
→ The best possible pioneering and advanced concept, theory and practice of micro- and macroeconomics can't have success with ignorant, amoral, coward, hypocritical, neurotic, psychotic, and psychopathic politicians.
→ New pioneering and vanguard academic programs, free of the insane neo-capitalism, must be offered in order to build up a new generation of leaders that will save humanity and the planet.

5.7. Systemic Faults in Politics

- Those who want to make political career have to go up a very challenging ladder.
- First of all they have to decide about an ideology and with that the right political party.
- As a member of a political party it's a must to be active and all-over friendly to get attention.
- The candidate must expand his connections and stay in contact with promoters.
- A candidate has many competitors but all claim to have the right leadership power.
- A candidate is always confronted with other members that proclaim their solutions.
- At the basic level of a political career a candidate must regularly contact many citizens.
- Once the candidate sits in a local or provincial parliament, he has stronger competitors.
- On this higher level the candidate must knock at many doors to present himself.
- Even if at this political low level, the candidate will be lured from all kind of lobbyists.
- Now, the candidate wants a seat in the provincial government. He must travel a lot.
- To become known by the party members and the citizens is indispensable: time consuming.
- The day arrives; the candidate sits in the provincial parliament. Strong fights start.
- The candidate is lost since many cooks want to prepare the same menu; to have a say.
- Practical constraints dissolve ideological ideals and force to distorted compromises.
- After a first year, the provincial minister finally understands how it works between the doors.
- There is a lot that he didn't know and he feels that he does not have the appropriate knowledge.
- Politicians do not have much time for further education or for collecting information.
- The information the provincial minister gets on the table are selected information.

- From now on his plans and decisions are based on selected information and compromises.
- After 2 years the candidate realizes that he is simply a manager of the ongoing machine.
- Starting the third year the minister must already carefully think about the next elections.
- He can bring forward some projects, bring in new stimuli; but everything is micro-level.
- With the fourth year he must begin to spend up to 40% of his time for the next election.
- The provincial minister finally has become a member of the national committee party.
- Now he is fully engaged in the next elections and in meetings all over the country.
- He learnt to speak in a way that he gets majority supporters to get a national minister seat.
- Such activities are very time consuming (at public cost) and require promising a lot of 'benefits'.
- The candidate for the upper echelon has little time for his family; has already lost his soul.
- He learnt to twist, distort, trivialize, lie, deviate, deceive, and operate in a clandestine way.
- Finally he gets the national ministerial seat and the games continue on a perfidious level.
- Most of the resort is completely new for the beginner; he talks a lot and plays down the tasks.
- Every day some lobbyists knock at his door, or send him information with demands.
- He spends 40% of his time with telephone calls, talking, reading documents, meetings or travelling.
- He is the defense minister now, but he has no idea about the devilish geopolitical games.
- Although he is used now to practice Machiavelli's principles, he is naïve towards others.
- After two years he finally realizes that he is imprisoned in a dark labyrinth without exit.
- He needs much of his time to protect his seat for the future with the soft soap principle.
- With the end of the third year he learnt not to touch the hot potatoes and to hide the truth.
- His ideology, ideals, and political values are gone; remain as verbal relics in his speeches.

- At the next election he loses the seat and gets an interesting job from a corporation.
- The following ministers, a majority new, restart at zero, and change the previous decisions.

Most probably a majority of politicians and members of governments do not even have 5-10% of the knowledge and skills of critical network thinking in our Economics I, II, and III.

In contrast to that, the masters of economics know very well how they operate with their study books and in the world of corporations and banking.

The supreme masters manage their project during their entire life. And then one of their children becomes the successor. These people have their institutional power legacy through generations. They do not need the voice of the stupid citizens. They are the genius master minders and laugh about the naïve (democratic) politicians they have in their iron fist through public debt, media control, and other tools.

→ The key fault is: such a democratic system never allows for a long-term management of national projects and there are too many competitors that always claim to have a better solution.
→ From some governments one can get the impression that the innermost drive the politicians have lies in their biography since early childhood: always the father, the mother, the teacher, the professor, the priest and finally their partner (husband, wife) had the last word and these politicians had no say at all in their private life. But now, as politicians they blindly compensate with far too much incompetence and immaturity, but with the same stubbornness they experienced and the defiance they had when they were in the age of the terrible twos.
→ From this view it's not surprising that the masters of economics go for their throat and dance on their nose.

5.8. History of Wars

The history of wars is horrifying. No one could believe it. The presented list below is probably not complete and does not give deeper knowledge about the agents, the countries, the places and the motives. For further interest: we have summarized the list from the data given by Wikipedia. [158]

Probably this list should be better in the appendix. But I recommend to go through here, page by page, each time closing the eyes shortly (seconds) and to contemplate a second about realities of wars since ever and today, and even with a glimpse towards the future of wars in the coming decades.

Another suggestion is to create some ideas about what could have been done with these quadrillions of money (costs for the wars and the damages, and the loss of economic potentials). If the reader feels strong enough, then he can visualize all the suffering and misery created by all these wars. The weight of this suffering and misery also reaches quadrillions of pain and tears.

List of wars in the last 2000 years

Start	Finish	Name of Conflict
43	96	Roman conquest of Britain
58	63	Roman–Parthian War
60	61	Boudica's Uprising
66	73	First Jewish–Roman War
69	69	Year of the Four Emperors
101	102	First Dacian War
105	106	Second Dacian War
115	117	Kitos War
132	136	Bar Kokhba revolt
161	166	Roman–Parthian War
166	180	Marcomannic Wars
184	205	Yellow Turban Rebellion
190	191	Campaign against Dong Zhuo
194	199	Sun Ce's conquests in Jiangdong
216	216	Parthian war of Caracalla
225	225	Zhuge Liang's Southern Campaign

---

[158] http://en.wikipedia.org/wiki/Lists_of_wars

228	234	Zhuge Liang's Northern Expeditions
247	262	Jiang Wei's Northern Expeditions
263	263	Conquest of Shu by Wei
279	280	Conquest of Wu by Jin
291	306	War of the Eight Princes
376	382	Gothic War
421	422	Roman–Sassanid War
502	506	Anastasian War
526	532	Iberian War
527	527	Iwai Rebellion
533	534	Vandalic War
534	537	Wars against the Moors
535	554	Gothic War
541	562	Lazic War
572	591	Roman–Persian War
588	588	First Perso-Turkic War
598	614	Goguryeo–Sui Wars
600	793	Frisian–Frankish wars
602	628	Byzantine–Sassanid War
613	628	Transition from Sui to Tang
619	619	Second Perso-Turkic War
627	629	Third Perso-Turkic War
629	630	Emperor Taizong's campaign against Eastern Tujue
632	633	Ridda wars
633	644	Muslim conquest of Persia Part of the Muslim conquests
634	1180	Byzantine–Arab Wars
634	635	Emperor Taizong's campaign against Tuyuhun
638	638	Emperor Taizong's campaign against Tufan
639	642	Muslim conquest of Egypt
640	648	Emperor Taizong's campaign against Xiyu states
644	668	Goguryeo–Tang War
645	646	Emperor Taizong's campaign against Xueyantuo
650	758	Khazar–Arab Wars
656	661	First Fitna
670	676	Silla–Tang Wars
672	672	Jinshin War
680	1355	Byzantine–Bulgarian Wars
680	692	Second Fitna
711	718	Umayyad conquest of Hispania
715	718	Frankish Civil War
717	718	Siege of Constantinople, part of the Byzantine–Arab Wars
732	732	Battle of Tours
735	737	Marwan ibn Muhammad's invasion of Georgia

751	751	Battle of Talas
755	763	An Lushan Rebellion
772	804	Saxon Wars
854	1000	Croatian–Bulgarian wars
869	883	Zanj Rebellion
955	955	Battle of Lechfeld
941	941	Rus'–Byzantine War
977	978	War of the Three Henries
993	993	First Goryeo–Khitan War
999	999	Battle of Svolder
1010	1011	Second Goryeo–Khitan War
1014	1014	Battle of Clontarf
1015	1016	Cnut the Great's conquest of England
1018	1018	Boleslaw I's intervention in the Kievan succession crisis
1018	1019	Third Goryeo–Khitan War
1019	1019	Toi Invasion
1030	1030	Battle of Stiklestad
1043	1043	Rus'–Byzantine War
1048	1308	Byzantine–Seljuq Wars
1051	1063	Zenkunen War
1065	1067	War of the Three Sanchos
1066	1088	Norman conquest of England
1083	1089	(disputed) Gosannen War
1096	1099	First Crusade Part of the Crusades
1101	1101	Crusade; Part of the Crusades
1145	1149	Second Crusade; Part of the Crusades
1147	1242	Northern Crusades; Part of the Crusades
1156	1156	Hōgen Rebellion
1160	1160	Heiji Rebellion
1169	1175	Norman invasion of Ireland
1179	1179	Battle of Jacob's Ford; Part of the Crusades
1180	1185	Genpei War
1185	1204	Uprising of Asen and Peter
1189	1192	Third Crusade Part of the Crusades
1202	1204	Fourth Crusade Part of the Crusades
1206	1324	Mongol conquests
1208	1227	Livonian Crusade; Part of the Crusades
1209	1229	Albigensian Crusade; Part of the Crusades
1213	1221	Fifth Crusade; Part of the Crusades
1214	1214	Battle of Bouvines
1215	1217	First Barons' War
1228	1229	Sixth Crusade; Part of the Crusades
1242	1249	First Prussian Uprising

1248	1254	Seventh Crusade; Part of the Crusades
1260	1274	Great Prussian Uprising
1262	1262	Berke–Hulagu war
1264	1267	Second Barons' War
1266	1266	Battle of Benevento Part of Guelphs and Ghibellines
1270	1270	Eighth Crusade; Part of the Crusades
1271	1272	Ninth Crusade; Part of the Crusades
1282	1302	War of the Sicilian Vespers
1296	1328	First War of Scottish Independence
1302	1302	Battle of the Golden Spurs
1308	1308	Teutonic takeover of Danzig (Gdańsk)
1315	1315	Battle of Morgarten
1315	1318	Irish-Bruce Wars
1321	1322	Swedish–Novgorodian Wars
1323	1328	Peasant revolt in Flanders
1326	1332	Polish–Teutonic War
1331	1333	Genkō War
1332	1357	Second War of Scottish Independence
1337	1453	Hundred Years' War
1341	1364	Breton War of Succession; Hundred Years' War
1375	1378	War of the Eight Saints
1380	1380	Battle of Kulikovo
1383	1385	1383–1385 Crisis
1380s	1390	Tokhtamysh–Timur war
1385	1424	Forty Years' War
1386	1404	Timur's invasions of Georgia
1402	1402	Battle of Ankara
1407	1427	Fourth Chinese domination
1409	1411	Polish–Lithuanian–Teutonic War
1410	1411	Ming–Kotte War
1414	1414	Hunger War
1419	1419	Ōei Invasion
1419	1434	Hussite Wars
1422	1422	Siege of Constantinople
1422	1422	Gollub War
1425	1454	Wars in Lombardy
1431	1435	Polish–Teutonic War
1431	1435	Lithuanian Civil War
1444	1444	Battle of Torvioll
1453	1453	Fall of Constantinople
1454	1466	Thirteen Years' War
1455	1485	Wars of the Roses
1456	1456	Siege of Belgrade

1462	1462	The Night Attack
1467	1477	Ōnin War
1467	1479	War of the Priests
1470	1471	Dano-Swedish War
1471	1471	1471 Vietnamese invasion of Champa
1474	1477	Burgundian Wars
1475	1479	War of the Castilian Succession
1480	1480	Siege of Rhodes
1482	1484	War of Ferrara
1482	1492	Granada War
1492	1494	First Muscovite–Lithuanian War
1494	1498	Italian War
1495	1497	Russo-Swedish War
1499	1504	Italian War
1499	1499	Swabian War
1499	1503	Ottoman–Venetian War
1500	1503	Second Muscovite–Lithuanian War
1503	1505	Landshut War of Succession
1505	1517	Portuguese–Mamluk naval war
1507	1508	Third Muscovite–Lithuanian War
1508	1516	War of the League of Cambrai
1509	1509	Battle of Diu
1509	1512	Ottoman Civil War
1510	1514	Hvar Rebellion
1510	1510	Portuguese Conquest of Goa
1512	1522	Fourth Muscovite–Lithuanian War
1514	1514	Battle of Chaldiran
1515	1515	Slovenian peasant revolt
1516	1517	Ottoman–Mamluk War
1519	1521	Polish–Teutonic War
1519	1521	Spanish conquest of the Aztec Empire
1520	1521	Revolt of the Comuneros
1521	1526	Italian War
1521	1523	Swedish War of Liberation
1522	1522	Siege of Rhodes
1524	1526	German Peasants' War
1526	1530	War of the League of Cognac
1526	1526	Battle of Mohács
1527	1697	Spanish conquest of Yucatán
1527	1528	Hungarian campaign
1529	1543	Ethiopian–Adal War
1529	1529	First war of Kappel
1529	1529	Siege of Vienna

1529	1532	Inca Civil War
1530	1552	Little War in Hungary
1531	1531	Second war of Kappel
1531	1572	Spanish conquest of the Inca Empire
1532	1555	Ottoman–Safavid War)
1534	1536	Count's Feud
1534	1537	Fifth Muscovite–Lithuanian War
1535	1541	Toungoo-Hanthawaddy War
1536	1538	Italian War
1537	1548	Conquistador Civil War in Peru
1542	1546	Italian War
1542	1543	Dacke War
1546	1547	Schmalkaldic War
1548	1548	Burmese–Siamese War
1551	1559	Italian War of
1552	1556	Kazan War
1552	1552	Siege of Kazan
1554	1557	Russo-Swedish War
1558	1583	Livonian War
1562	1598	French Wars of Religion
1563	1564	Burmese–Siamese War
1563	1570	Northern Seven Years' War
1567	1872	Philippine revolts against Spain
1568	1569	Burmese–Siamese War
1568	1571	Morisco Revolt
1568	1648	Eighty Years' War
1569	1573	First Desmond Rebellion
1569	1570	Rising of the North
1570	1573	Ottoman–Venetian War
1571	1571	Russo-Crimean War
1573	1573	Croatian-Slovenian peasant revolt
1578	1590	Ottoman–Safavid War
1579	1583	Second Desmond Rebellion
1580	1583	War of the Portuguese Succession
1580	1589	Ottoman–Portuguese Conflicts
1583	1588	Cologne War
1584	1593	Burmese–Siamese War
1585	1604	Anglo-Spanish War
1590	1595	Russo-Swedish War
1592	1598	Japanese invasions of Korea
1593	1606	Long War (Ottoman wars)
1593	1617	Moldavian Magnate Wars
1594	1603	Nine Years' War (Ireland)

1596	1596	Cudgel War
1599	1605	Burmese–Siamese War
1600	1611	Polish–Swedish War
1602	1663	Dutch–Portuguese War
1603	1618	Ottoman–Safavid War
1605	1618	Polish–Muscovite War
1609	1614	War of the Jülich succession
1610	1614	First Anglo-Powhatan War
1610	1617	Ingrian War
1611	1613	Kalmar War
1614	1615	Burmese–Siamese War
1617	1618	Polish–Swedish War
1618	1648	Thirty Years' War
1618	1648	Dutch Revolt Part of the Thirty Years' War
1619	1682	Ahom–Mughal conflicts
1620	1621	Polish–Ottoman War
1621	1625	Polish–Swedish War
1623	1639	Ottoman–Safavid War
1625	1625	First Genoese-Savoyard War
1626	1629	Polish–Swedish War
1627	1627	First Manchu invasion of Korea
1628	1631	War of the Mantuan Succession; Thirty Years' War
1632	1634	Smolensk War
1633	1634	Polish–Ottoman War
1634	1638	Pequot War
1635	1659	Franco-Spanish War
1636	1637	Second Manchu invasion of Korea
1639	1639	First Bishops' War (Three Kingdoms)
1640	1640	Second Bishops' War; Wars of the Three Kingdoms
1640	1652	Catalan Revolt
1640	1668	Portuguese Restoration War
1640	1701	Beaver Wars
1641	1653	Irish Confederate Wars, Wars of the Three Kingdoms
1641	1644	First War of Castro
1642	1646	First English Civil War, Wars of the Three Kingdoms
1643	1645	Torstenson War Part of the Thirty Years' War
1643	1645	Kieft's War
1644	1646	Second Anglo-Powhatan War
1644	1674	Char Bouba war
1644	1651	Scotland in the Wars of the Three Kingdoms
1645	1669	Cretan War
1648	1657	Khmelnytsky Uprising
1648	1649	First Fronde

1648	1649	Second English Civil War, Wars of the Three Kingdoms
1649	1651	Third English Civil War, Wars of the Three Kingdoms
1649	1653	Mughal–Safavid War
1649	1653	Cromwellian conquest of Ireland
1649	1649	Second War of Castro
1650	1653	Second Fronde
1651	1986	Three Hundred and Thirty Five Years' War
1652	1654	First Anglo-Dutch War
1652	1689	Russian–Manchu border conflicts
1654	1667	Russo-Polish War
1654	1660	Anglo-Spanish War
1655	1655	Peach Tree War
1655	1660	Second Northern War
1656	1658	Russo-Swedish War
1657	1658	Dano-Swedish War
1658	1660	Dano-Swedish War
1662	1665	Burmese–Siamese War
1663	1664	Austro-Turkish War
1665	1667	Second Anglo-Dutch War
1665	1709	Kongo Civil War
1666	1671	Polish–Cossack–Tatar War
1667	1668	War of Devolution
1670	1671	Stenka Razin Rebellion
1672	1676	Polish–Ottoman War
1672	1678	Franco-Dutch War
1672	1674	Third Anglo-Dutch War Part of the Franco-Dutch War
1673	1681	Revolt of the Three Feudatories
1675	1679	Scanian War Part of the Franco-Dutch War
1675	1676	King Philip's War
1676	1681	Russo-Turkish War
1681	1707	Maratha War of Independence
1683	1699	Great Turkish War
1683	1699	Polish–Ottoman War; Part of the Great Turkish War
1683	1684	War of the Reunions
1684	1699	Morean War Part of the Great Turkish War
1685	1685	Monmouth Rebellion
1686	1700	Russo-Turkish War
1687	1689	Crimean campaigns
1688	1697	Nine Years' War
1689	1697	King William's War Part of the Nine Years' War
1689	1691	Williamite War in Ireland
1689	1692	Jacobite Rising in Scotland
1695	1696	Azov campaigns

1699	1700	Darien scheme
1700	1721	Great Northern War
1701	1714	War of the Spanish Succession
1702	1713	Queen Anne's War. War of the Spanish Succession
1702	1715	Camisard Rebellion
1703	1711	Rákóczi's War for Independence
1707	1708	Bulavin Rebellion
1710	1711	Russo-Turkish War
1711	1715	Tuscarora War
1712	1716	First Fox War
1714	1718	Ottoman–Venetian War
1715	1717	Yamasee War
1715	1715	First Jacobite Rising Also called "The Fifteen"
1718	1720	War of the Quadruple Alliance
1721	1763	Chickasaw Wars
1722	1725	Dummer's War
1722	1723	Russo-Persian War
1728	1733	Second Fox War
1733	1738	War of the Polish Succession
1735	1736	Miao Rebellion
1735	1739	Russo-Austrian-Turkish War
1739	1748	War of Jenkins' Ear
1740	1748	War of the Austrian Succession
1740	1742	First Silesian War
1741	1743	Russo-Swedish War
1744	1748	King George's War
1744	1745	Second Silesian War
1745	1746	Jacobite Rising
1746	1748	First Carnatic War
1749	1754	Second Carnatic War
1752	1757	Konbaung-Hanthawaddy War
1754	1763	French and Indian War
1756	1763	Seven Years' War
1756	1763	Third Silesian War
1757	1763	Third Carnatic War
1758	1761	Anglo-Cherokee War
1759	1760	Burmese–Siamese War
1761	1763	Spanish–Portuguese War
1763	1766	Pontiac's War
1765	1767	Burmese–Siamese War
1765	1769	Sino-Burmese War
1766	1769	First Anglo-Mysore War
1768	1768	Louisiana Rebellion

1768	1774	Russo-Turkish War
1768	1772	Bar Confederation
1774	1775	Pugachev's Rebellion
1775	1776	Burmese–Siamese War
1775	1782	First Anglo-Maratha War
1775	1783	American Revolutionary War
1776	1794	Chickamauga Wars
1778	1779	War of the Bavarian Succession
1779	1783	Anglo-Spanish War
1779	1781	First Xhosa War
1780	1784	Fourth Anglo-Dutch War
1780	1784	Second Anglo-Mysore War
1781	1781	Revolt of the Comuneros (New Granada)
1785	1786	Burmese–Siamese War
1785	1795	Northwest Indian War
1786	1787	Shays' Rebellion
1787	1787	Burmese–Siamese War
1787	1791	Austro-Turkish War
1787	1792	Russo-Turkish War
1788	1790	Russo-Swedish War
1788	1789	Theater War
1788	1930s	Australian frontier wars
1789	1792	Third Anglo-Mysore War
1789	1793	Second Xhosa War
1791	1804	Haitian Revolution
1791	1794	Whiskey Rebellion
1792	1792	Polish–Russian War
1792	1792	Burmese–Siamese War
1792	1797	War of the First Coalition
1793	1796	War in the Vendée
1794	1794	Nickajack Expedition
1794	1794	Kościuszko Uprising
1795	1806	Miao Rebellion
1796	1796	Persian Expedition
1797	1797	Burmese–Siamese War
1798	1802	War of the Second Coalition; French Revolutionary Wars
1798	1800	Quasi-War
1798	1798	Irish Rebellion
1798	1799	Fourth Anglo-Mysore War
1799	1803	Third Xhosa War
1799	1800	War of Knives Part of Haitian Revolution
1801	1805	Temne War
1801	1805	First Barbary War

1801	1801	War of the Oranges
1802	1805	Second War of Haitian Independence
1802	1805	Second Anglo-Maratha War
1803	1804	Burmese–Siamese War
1803	1805	First Kandyan War
1803	1803	Emmet's Insurrection
1803	1806	War of the Third Coalition Part of the Napoleonic Wars
1804	1804	Battle of Sitka Russian colonization of the Americas
1804	1813	First Serbian Uprising Serbian revolution
1804	1804	Castle Hill convict rebellion
1804	1810	Fulani War
1804	1813	Russo-Persian War
1805	1811	Egyptian Revolution Part of the Napoleonic Wars
1805	1805	Janissaries' Revolt
1805	1810	Franco-Swedish War Part of the Napoleonic Wars
1805	1805	Haitian Invasion of Santo Domingo
1806	1807	War of the Fourth Coalition Part of the Napoleonic Wars
1806	1812	Russo-Turkish War; Part of the Napoleonic Wars
1806	1807	British invasions of the Río de la Plata
1806	1807	Ashanti-Fante War
1806	1811	War of Christophe's Secession
1806	1811	Vellore Mutiny
1807	1808	Janissaries' Revolt
1807	1818	Mtetwa Empire Expansion
1807	1814	Peninsular War Part of the Napoleonic Wars
1807	1814	Gunboat War Part of the Napoleonic Wars
1807	1812	Anglo-Russian War; Part of the Napoleonic Wars
1807	1809	Anglo-Turkish War; Part of the Napoleonic Wars
1808	1810	Rum Rebellion
1808	1809	Finnish War
1808	1809	Spanish Restoration in Santo Domingo, Napoleonic Wars
1808	1808	Bantam Conquest
1808	1809	Dano-Swedish War; Part of the Napoleonic Wars
1809	1809	War of the Fifth Coalition Part of the Napoleonic Wars
1809	1810	Quino Revolution Part of the Spanish American wars
1809	1810	Tyrol Rebellion Part of the Napoleonic Wars
1809	1812	Burmese–Siamese War
1809	1825	Bolivian War of Independence, Spanish American wars
1809	1824	Peruvian War of Independence, Spanish American wars
1810	1818	Argentine War of Independence, Spanish American wars
1810	1811	Tecumseh's War
1810	1810	US Occupation of West Florida
1810	1817	Merina Conquest of Madagascar

1810	1820	Punjab War
1810	1826	Chilean War of Independence, Spanish American wars
1810	1810	Conquest of Hawaii
1810	1818	Amadu's Jihad
1810	1813	Lamu Expansion
1810	1821	Mexican War of Independence, Spanish American wars
1811	1811	Invasion of Java
1811	1811	Tonquin incident
1811	1812	Fourth Xhosa War
1811	1811	Ga-Fante War
1811	1815	Arakanese Uprising
1811	1811	Battle of Las Piedras Part of the Spanish American wars
1811	1812	Cambodian Rebellion
1811	1812	Korean Revolt
1811	1811	Paraguayan Revolt
1811	1812	Owu-Ife War
1811	1818	Ottoman–Saudi War
1811	1823	Venezuelan War of Independence; Spanish American wars
1812	1812	French invasion of Russia Part of the Napoleonic Wars
1812	1814	War of the Sixth Coalition Part of the Napoleonic Wars
1812	1815	War of 1812
1813	1814	Creek War
1813	1813	Peoria War
1814	1814	Swedish-Norwegian War; Part of the Napoleonic Wars
1814	1816	Gurkha War
1814	1816	Ashanti–Akim–Akwapim War
1814	1814	Hadži Prodan's Revolt Part of the Serbian revolution
1814	1876	Argentine Civil Wars
1815	1815	Second Barbary War
1815	1817	Second Serbian Uprising Part of the Serbian revolution
1815	1816	Spanish reconquest of New Granada
1815	1815	Second Kandyan War
1815	1815	Hundred Days War of the Seventh Coalition
1815	1815	Neapolitan War Part of the Hundred Days
1815	1815	Temne-Susu War
1817	1864	Caucasian War
1817	1818	Third Anglo-Maratha War
1817	1819	Ndwandwe–Zulu War
1817	1818	First Seminole War Part of the Seminole Wars
1817	1817	Pernambucan Revolt
1818	1819	Fifth Xhosa War
1818	1828	Zulu Wars of Conquest
1819	1820	Bolívar's campaign;New Granada Spanish American wars

1820	1822	Ecuadorian War of Independence
1820	1823	Trienio Liberal
1820	1823	Ottoman–Persian War
1820	1875	Texas–Indian wars
1821	1823	Brazilian War of Independence
1821	1832	Greek War of Independence
1821	1837	Padri War
1821	1829	Spanish reconquest of Mexico
1821	1848	Comanche–Mexico War
1822	1844	Haitian occupation of Santo Domingo
1823	1831	First Anglo-Ashanti War
1823	1826	First Anglo-Burmese War
1825	1825	Decembrist revolt
1825	1828	Cisplatine War
1825	1830	Java War
1825	1825	Franco-Trarzan War
1826	1828	Russo-Persian War
1827	1827	Winnebago War
1828	1829	Gran Colombia – Peru War
1828	1834	Liberal Wars
1828	1829	Russo-Turkish War
1829	1829	Chilean Civil War
1830	1830	July Revolution French Revolution
1830	1831	November Uprising
1830	1831	Belgian Revolution
1830	1847	French conquest of Algeria
1831	1834	First Siamese–Vietnamese War
1831	1832	Baptist War
1831	1833	Egyptian–Ottoman War
1832	1832	Black Hawk War
1833	1840	First Carlist War
1834	1836	Sixth Xhosa War
1835	1835	Malê Revolt
1835	1836	Toledo War
1835	1836	Texas Revolution
1835	1842	Second Seminole War
1835	1845	War of the Farrapos War of Tatters
1836	1839	War of the Confederation
1837	1838	Lower Canada Rebellion
1837	1838	Upper Canada Rebellion
1838	1838	Battle of Blood River
1838	1838	Mormon War
1838	1839	Pastry War

1838	1839	Aroostook War
1839	1839	Honey War
1839	1842	First Anglo-Afghan War
1839	1842	First Opium War
1839	1851	Uruguayan Civil War
1841	1845	Second Siamese–Vietnamese War
1841	1842	Sino-Sikh War
1841	1842	Dorr Rebellion
1843	1843	Wairau Affray Part of the New Zealand land wars
1843	1849	Dominican War of Independence
1844	1844	Franco-Moroccan War
1845	1846	First Anglo-Sikh War
1845	1846	Flagstaff War Northern War New Zealand land wars
1846	1864	Navajo Wars
1846	1846	Hutt Valley Campaign Part of the New Zealand land wars
1846	1846	Dutch intervention in Northern Bali
1846	1847	Seventh Xhosa War
1846	1848	Second Carlist War War of the Madrugadores
1846	1848	Mexican-American War
1846	1848	Wanganui Campaign Part of the New Zealand land wars
1847	1901	(Chan Santa Cruz occupied)
1901	1933	(Last of skirmishes) Caste War of Yucatán
1847	1855	Cayuse War
1848	1849	Praieira revolt
1848	1848	Revolutions of 1848 in the Italian states
1848	1848	Greater Poland Uprising
1848	1848	French Revolution
1848	1848	Revolutions in the German states
1848	1849	Revolutions in the Habsburg areas
1848	1848	Wallachian Revolution
1848	1848	Sicilian revolution of independence
1848	1848	Dutch intervention in Northern Bali
1848	1849	First Italian War of Independence
1848	1849	Second Anglo-Sikh War
1848	1849	Hungarian Revolution
1848	1851	First Schleswig War The Three Years' War
1849	1850	Dutch intervention in Bali
1849	1855	Burmese–Siamese War
1849	1924	Apache Wars
1850	1865	California Indian Wars
1850	1864	Taiping Rebellion
1850	1853	Eighth Xhosa War
1851	1852	Platine War War against Oribe and Rosas

1852	1853	Second Anglo-Burmese War
1853	1874	Miao Rebellion
1853	1856	Crimean War
1854	1860	French conquest of Senegal
1854	1861	Bleeding Kansas
1855	1856	Nepalese-Tibetan War
1855	1858	Yakima War
1855	1856	Rogue River Wars
1855	1855	Battle of Ash Hollow
1855	1856	Puget Sound War
1855	1867	Punti–Hakka Clan Wars
1855	1858	Third Seminole War part of the Seminole Wars
1856	1857	Campaign
1856	1860	Second Opium War Arrow War
1856	1857	Anglo-Persian War
1856	1873	Panthay Rebellion Du Wenxiu Rebellion
1856	1857	1857 Cheyenne Expedition
1857	1858	Indian Rebellion, India's First War of Independence
1857	1858	Utah War
1857	1860	Ecuadorian–Peruvian territorial dispute
1858	1858	Coeur d'Alene War
1858	1858	Fraser Canyon War
1858	1862	Cochinchina Campaign
1859	1859	Second Italian War of Independence
1859	1863	Federal War
1859	1860	Hispano-Moroccan War
1860	1860	Paiute War
1860	1873	Russian Conquests of Central Asia
1860	1861	First Taranaki War Second Maori War
1861	1883	Occupation of Araucanía
1861	1865	American Civil War
1861	1867	French intervention in Mexico Franco-Mexican War
1862	1862	Dakota War of 1862
1862	1877	Dungan revolt Muslim Rebellion
1863	1863	Ecuadorian–Colombian War
1863	1865	Dominican Restoration War
1863	1863	Naval battle of Shimonoseki Part of the Japanese Civil War
1863	1864	Bombardments of Shimonoseki Japanese Civil War
1863	1863	Bombardment of Kagoshima Anglo-Satsuma War
1863	1865	January Uprising
1863	1864	Invasion of Waikato Third Maori War
1863	1865	Colorado War
1863	1864	Second Anglo-Ashanti War

1863	1866	Second Taranaki War Part of New Zealand land wars
1864	1865	Uruguayan War
1864	1865	Mito rebellion Kanto insurrection
1864	1864	Hamaguri Rebellion and First Choshu expedition
1864	1864	Second Schleswig War Second Danish-German War
1864	1864	Tauranga Campaign
1864	1865	Bhutan War
1864	1868	Snake War Cheyenne and Arapaho War
1864	1865	Russo-Kokandian War
1864	1870	Paraguayan War
1864	1866	Chincha Islands War
1865	1865	Powder River Expedition
1865	1865	Morant Bay rebellion
1865	1870	Hualapai War
1865	1868	Basuto-Boer War
1865	1866	Bukharan-Kokandian War
1865	1868	East Cape War Part of the New Zealand land wars
1865	1868	Russo-Bukharan Wars
1865	1865	Hyogo naval expedition Part of the Japanese Civil War
1866	1866	Second Choshu expedition
1866	1866	Austro-Prussian War
1866	1868	Third Italian War of Independence Austro-Prussian War
1866	1868	Red Cloud's War
1866	1869	Cretan Revolt
1866	1866	French Campaign against Korea
1867	1875	Comanche Campaign
1867	1874	Klang War Selangor Civil War
1868	1868	Glorious Revolution (Spain)
1868	1869	Titokowaru's War Part of the New Zealand land wars
1868	1869	Boshin War War of the Year of the Dragon
1868	1868	Expedition to Abyssinia
1868	1872	War of the Abyssinian Succession
1868	1872	Te Kooti's War Part of the New Zealand land wars
1868	1878	Ten Years' War Great War
1869	1869	Haitian Revolution
1869	1869	Red River Rebellion
1870	1871	Franco-Prussian War
1871	1871	United States expedition to Korea
1872	1876	Third Carlist War
1872	1873	Modoc War Lava Beds War
1873	1913	Aceh War
1873	1874	Third Anglo-Ashanti War
1873	1874	Cantonal Revolution

1874	1874	Brooks–Baxter War
1874	1874	Saga Rebellion
1874	1875	Red River War
1876	1876	Shinpuren Rebellion
1876	1876	Akizuki Rebellion
1876	1876	Hagi Rebellion
1876	1877	Great Sioux War, Black Hills War
1877	1877	Nez Perce War
1877	1877	Satsuma Rebellion
1877	1879	Ninth Xhosa War
1877	1878	Russo-Turkish War
1878	1878	Bannock War
1878	1878	Lincoln County War
1878	1879	Cheyenne War
1878	1880	Second Anglo-Afghan War
1879	1880	Little War (Cuba)
1879	1879	Anglo-Zulu War
1879	1883	(Chile-Peru Peace)
1879	1879	Sheepeater Indian War
1879	1880	Victorio's War
1880	1881	Basuto Gun War
1880	1881	First Boer War
1881	1881	French occupation of Tunisia
1881	1899	Mahdist War
1882	1898	Mandingo Wars
1883	1914	Ekumeku War
1883	1885	First Madagascar expedition
1883	1886	Tonkin Campaign
1884	1885	Sino-French War
1885	1885	North-West Rebellion
1885	1885	Serbo-Bulgarian War
1885	1885	Third Anglo-Burmese War
1888	1888	Sikkim Expedition
1890	1890	First Franco-Dahomean War
1890	1891	Pine Ridge Campaign
1891	1891	Chilean Civil War
1892	1894	Second Franco-Dahomean War
1892	1894	War in the Eastern Congo
1893	1897	War of Canudos
1893	1894	Revolta da Armada
1893	1893	Franco-Siamese War
1893	1893	Conquest of the Bornu Empire
1893	1894	First Melillan campaign

1893	1894	First Matabele War
1894	1896	Fourth Anglo-Ashanti War
1894	1894	Donghak Peasant Revolution
1894	1895	First Sino-Japanese War
1894	1895	Second Madagascar expedition
1895	1896	First Italo-Ethiopian War
1895	1898	Cuban War of Independence
1895	1895	Japanese invasion of Taiwan
1896	1896	Anglo-Zanzibar War
1896	1898	Philippine Revolution
1896	1897	Second Matabele War
1897	1897	Greco-Turkish War
1897	1897	Benin Expedition
1897	1898	Tirah Campaign
1898	1898	Spanish–American War
1898	1900	Voulet-Chanoine Mission
1899	1901	Boxer Rebellion
1899	1902	Second Boer War
1899	1902	Thousand Days' War
1899	1902	(Malvar surrender) Philippine–American War
1900	1900	War of the Golden Stool
1901	1902	Anglo-Aro War
1902	1932	Unification of Saudi Arabia War
1903	1904	British expedition to Tibet
1904	1907	Herero War
1904	1905	Russo-Japanese War
1905	1905	Russian Revolution
1906	1906	Dutch intervention in Bali
1906	1906	Bambatha Rebellion
1907	1907	Romanian Peasants' Revolt
1908	1908	Dutch intervention in Bali
1908	1909	Persian Civil War
1908	1908	Dutch-Venezuela War
1909	1910	Second Melillan campaign
1909	1911	Wadai War
1910	1920	Mexican Revolution
1910	1919	Border War; Part of the Mexican Revolution
1911	1912	French conquest of Morocco
1911	1912	Italo-Turkish War
1911	1912	Xinhai Revolution
1912	1913	First Balkan War
1912	1916	Contestado War
1912	1933	United States occupation of Nicaragua; Banana Wars

1912	1912	Negro Rebellion Part of the Banana Wars
1913	1913	Second Balkan War
1914	1921	Zaian War
1914	1918	(Armistice)
1914	1914	United States occupation of Veracruz; Banana Wars
1914	1915	Maritz Rebellion
1915	1934	United States occupation of Haiti Part of the Banana Wars
1915	1917	Senussi Campaign Part of World War I
1915	1916	National Protection War Anti-Monarchy War'
1916	1917	Kaocen Revolt
1916	1916	Easter Rising
1916	1924	United States occupation, Dominican Republic
1916	1918	Arab Revolt
1917	1917	February Revolution
1917	1917	October Revolution
1917	1922	Russian Civil War
1917	1918	Soviet-Turkish War; Part of Russian Civil War
1917	1921	Ukrainian War of Independence
1918	1918	Finnish Civil War
1918	1918	Georgian–Armenian War
1918	1919	German Revolution
1918	1919	Greater Poland Uprising
1918	1919	Polish–Ukrainian War
1918	1920	Georgian–Ossetian conflict
1918	1920	Armenian–Azerbaijani War Part of the Russian Civil War
1918	1920	Estonian War of Independence, Russian Civil War
1918	1920	Latvian War of Independence Part of the Russian Civil War
1918	1919	Lithuanian–Soviet War
1918	1919	First Saudi-Hashemite War
1919	1919	Lithuanian War of Independence (War Bermontians)
1919	1919	Polish–Czechoslovak War
1919	1919	Hungarian–Romanian War
1919	1922	(Armistice)
1919	1919	Third Anglo-Afghan War
1919	1919	Portuguese Monarchist Civil War
1919	1920	Italo-Yugoslav War
1919	1921	Polish–Soviet War
1919	1919	First Silesian Uprising
1919	1921	Irish War of Independence
1919	1922	Greco-Turkish War
1920	1920	Franco–Syrian War
1920	1921	Franco-Turkish War
1920	1920	Vlora War

1920	1926	Rif War
1920	1920	Polish–Lithuanian War
1920	1920	Second Silesian Uprising
1920	1920	Turkish–Armenian War
1920	1920	Zhili–Anhui War
1920	1921	Guangdong–Guangxi War
1921	1921	Red Army invasion of Georgia
1921	1921	Third Silesian Uprising
1921	1921	Iranian events
1921	1922	East Karelian Uprising
1922	1922	First Zhili–Fengtian War
1922	1923	Irish Civil War
1924	1924	August Uprising
1924	1924	Second Saud–Sharif War
1924	1924	Second Zhili–Fengtian War
1925	1925	Incident at Petrich
1926	1928	Northern Expedition
1926	1929	Cristero War
1927	1950	Chinese Civil War
1928	1929	Afghan Civil War
1929	1929	Sino-Soviet conflict
1929	1930	Igbo Women's War
1930	1930	Yen Bai mutiny
1930	1930	Central Plains War Part of Chinese Civil War
1930	1932	Sino-Tibetan War
1931	1932	Japanese invasion of Manchuria
1931	1934	Kumul Rebellion
1932	1932	Constitutionalist Revolution
1932	1932	Ecuadorian Civil War
1932	1932	Shanghai War
1932	1935	Chaco War
1932	1933	Colombia-Peru War
1934	1934	Soviet invasion of Xinjiang
1934	1934	Austrian Civil War
1934	1934	Saudi-Yemeni War
1935	1936	Second Italo-Abyssinian War
1936	1939	Great Arab Revolt in Palestine
1936	1939	Spanish Civil War
1937	1937	Islamic rebellion in Xinjiang
1937	1945	Second Sino-Japanese War
1938	1938	Battle of Lake Khasan
1939	1939	Hungarian Invasion of the Carpatho-Ukraine
1939	1939	Slovak–Hungarian War

1939	1939	Italian invasion of Albania
1939	1939	Battle of Khalkhin Gol
1939	1945	World War II
1939	1940	Winter War Part of World War II
1940	1941	Franco-Thai War Part of World War II
1941	1941	Ecuadorian–Peruvian War
1941	1941	Anglo-Iraqi War Part of World War II
1941	1944	Continuation War Part of World War II
1943	1949	Ukrainian Insurgent Army insurgency
1944	1945	Lapland War Part of World War II
1944	1953	Guerilla war in the Baltic States
1944	1949	Ili Rebellion
1944	1947	Jewish insurgency in Palestine
1945	1946	War in Vietnam
1945	1949	Indonesian National Revolution
1945	1946	Iran crisis
1946	1954	First Indochina War
1946	1949	Greek Civil War
1947	1947	Paraguayan Civil War
1947	1948	Indo-Pakistani War
1947	1948	Civil War in Mandatory Palestine
1948	1950	Pre-Korean War insurgency
1948	1949	Arab–Israeli War
1948	1948	Costa Rican Civil War
1948	Ongoing	Internal conflict in Burma
1948	1960	Malayan Emergency
1948	1948	Operation Polo
1950	1951	Invasion of Tibet
1950	Ongoing	Korean War
1950	1958	Kuomintang Islamic Insurgency in China
1950	1967	Retribution operations
1952	1956	Tunisian War of Independence
1952	1960	Mau Mau Uprising
1953	1953	Iranian coup d'état
1953	1959	Cuban Revolution
1953	1975	Laotian Civil War
1954	1959	Jebel Akhdar War
1954	1962	Algerian War
1955	1972	First Sudanese Civil War
1955	1975	Vietnam War
1956	1956	Hungarian Revolution
1956	1956	Suez Crisis
1957	1958	Ifni War

1958	1959	North Vietnamese invasion of Laos
1959	1959	Tibetan uprising
1959	2011	Basque conflict
1960	1961	Campaign at the China–Burma Border
1960	1966	Congo Crisis
1960	1996	Guatemalan Civil War
1961	1970	First Kurdish–Iraqi War
1961	1961	Bay of Pigs Invasion
1961	1961	Bizerte crisis
1961	1991	Eritrean War of Independence
1961	1961	Invasion of Goa
1961	1975	Angolan War of Independence; Portuguese Colonial War
1962	1964	Tuareg Rebellion
1962	1970	North Yemen Civil War
1962	1962	Sino-Indian War
1962	1966	Indonesia–Malaysia confrontation
1962	1976	Dhofar Rebellion
1963	1967	Shifta War
1963	1963	Sand War
1963	1974	Guinea-Bissau War of Independence Portuguese War
1964	1979	Rhodesian Bush War
1964	Ongoing	Colombian armed conflict
1964	1974	Mozambican War Independence; Portuguese Colonial War
1964	Ongoing	Insurgency in Northeast India
1964	1964	Zanzibar Revolution
1965	1965	Dominican Civil War
1965	1966	United States occupation of the Dominican Republic
1965		Indo-Pakistani War
1965	1979	Civil war in Chad
1966	1969	Korean DMZ Conflict
1966	1966	Samu Incident
1966	1989	South African Border War
1966	1988	Namibian War of Independence
1967	1967	Six-Day War
1967	1975	Cambodian Civil War
1967	1970	Nigerian Civil War
1967	1967	Chola incident
1968	1970	War of Attrition
1967	Ongoing	Naxalite–Maoist insurgency
1968	1989	Communist Insurgency War
1968	1998	The Troubles
1968	1968	Warsaw Pact invasion of Czechoslovakia
1969	Ongoing	Islamic insurgency in the Philippines

1969	1969	Football War
1969	1969	Sino-Soviet border conflict
1969		Ongoing Papua conflict
1970	1971	Black September in Jordan
1971	1971	Bangladesh Liberation War
1971	1971	Indo-Pakistani War
1972	1974	First Eritrean Civil War
1973	1973	Yom Kippur War
1974	1974	Turkish invasion of Cyprus
1974	1991	Ethiopian Civil War
1974	1975	Second Kurdish–Iraqi War
1975	2002	Angolan Civil War
1975	1991	Western Sahara War
1975	1990	Lebanese Civil War
1975	1989	Cambodian–Vietnamese War
1975		Ongoing Insurgency in Laos
1975	1975	Indonesian invasion of East Timor
1976	1983	Dirty War
1976	2005	Insurgency in Aceh
1977	1992	Mozambican Civil War
1977	1977	Libyan–Egyptian War
1977	1978	Ogaden War
1977	1977	Shaba I
1978	1978	Shaba II
1978	1978	South Lebanon conflict
1978	1979	Uganda–Tanzania War
1978	1987	Chadian–Libyan conflict
1978		Ongoing Kurdish–Turkish conflict
1979	1979	Sino-Vietnamese War
1979	1990	Sino-Vietnamese conflicts
1979	1983	Kurdish rebellion in Iran
1979	1982	Civil war in Chad
1979	1989	Soviet war in Afghanistan
1980	1992	Salvadoran Civil War
1980	2000	Internal conflict in Peru
1980	1988	Iran–Iraq War
1980	1981	Second Eritrean Civil War
1981	1981	Paquisha War
1981	1986	Ugandan Bush War
1982	1982	Falklands War
1982	1982	Ndogboyosoi War
1982	1982	1982 Lebanon War
1982	2000	South Lebanon conflict

1982	1982	Ethiopian–Somali Border War
1983	1983	Invasion of Grenada
1983	2009	Sri Lankan Civil War
1983	2005	Second Sudanese Civil War
1983	1988	Kurdish Rebellion; Part of the Iran–Iraq War
1984	1987	Siachen conflict
1985	1985	Agacher Strip War
1987	1987	Sino-Indian skirmish
1987	1993	First Intifada
1987	1988	Thai–Laotian Border War
1987	Ongoing	Lord's Resistance Army insurgency
1988	1994	Nagorno-Karabakh War
1989	1991	Mauritania–Senegal Border War
1989	1990	United States invasion of Panama
1989	1992	Civil war in Afghanistan
1989	1989	Romanian Revolution of
1989	1996	First Liberian Civil War
1989	Ongoing	Insurgency in Jammu and Kashmir
1990	1990	Invasion of Kuwait
1990	1991	Gulf War Kuwait
1990	1993	Rwandan Civil War Elements of the French Army
1990	1995	Tuareg rebellion Mali
1991	1991	Ten-Day War Slovenia SFR Yugoslavia
1991	1992	South Ossetia War South Ossetia
1991	1994	Djiboutian Civil War Djibouti
1991	1995	Croatian War of Independence Croatia
1995	1991	Bosnia and Herzegovina
1991	1991	SAO Krajina
1991	1991	SAO Western Slavonia
1991	1991	SAO Eastern Slavonia
1991	1992	SFR Yugoslavia
1992	1995	Republic of Serbian Krajina; Republika Srpska
1991	2002	Sierra Leone Civil War Sierra Leone
1991	2002	Algerian Civil War Algerian government
1991	Ongoing	Somali Civil War
1991	1993	Georgian Civil War
1991	1991	Uprisings in Iraq
1992	1992	East Prigorodny conflict North Ossetian
1992	1996	Civil war in Afghanistan. Taliban
1992	1992	War of Transnistria
1992	1993	War in Abkhazia
1992	1995	Bosnian War Bosnia and Herzegovina Croatia
1992	1994	Croat–Bosniak War

1992	1997	Civil war in Tajikistan
1993	2005	Burundi Civil War
1993	Ongoing	Ethnic conflict in Nagaland
1994	1997	Iraqi Kurdish Civil War
1994	1994	Chiapas Zapatista Army of National Liberation Mexico
1994	1994	Civil war in Yemen Democratic Republic of Yemen
1994	1996	First Chechen War, Chechen Republic of Ichkeria Russia
1994	1999	Caprivi conflict Namibia Caprivi Liberation Army
1995	1995	Cenepa War Peru Ecuador
1995	2009	Insurgency in Ogaden
1996	2006	Nepalese Civil War CPN Nepalese government
1996	2001	Civil war in Afghanistan
1996	1997	First Congo War AFDL
1997	1997	Rebellion in Albania Albania
1997	1999	Republic of the Congo Civil War Republic of the Congo
1997	1997	Clashes in Cambodia Hun Sen (CPP)
1997	2008	Pool Department insurgency
1998	1998	War in Abkhazia (White LegionForest Brotherhood
1998	2002	Civil war in Chad, Movement for Justice
1998	1999	Kosovo War NATO
1998	2000	Eritrean–Ethiopian War Ethiopia Eritrea
1998	2003	Second Congo War Dem Rep of Congo
1998	1999	Guinea-Bissau Civil War Rebels led by Mané Guinea-Bissau
1999	1999	Kargil War India Pakistan
1999	2000	East Timorese crisis East Timor
1999	2001	Insurgency in the Preševo Valley FR
1999	2003	Second Liberian Civil War Liberians
1999	2007	Ituri conflict
1999	1999	Invasion of Russia IIPB
1999	2009	Second Chechen War Russian Federation
2000	2005	Second Intifada Israel Hamas
2001	2001	Indian–Bangladeshi border conflict
2001	2001	Insurgency in the Republic of Macedonia
2001	Ongoing	War in Afghanistan
2002	Ongoing	Operation Enduring Freedom – Philippines
2002	Ongoing	Operation Enduring Freedom – Horn of Africa
2002	2002	Operation Defensive Shield
2002	2007	First Ivorian Civil War
2002	Ongoing	Insurgency in the Maghreb
2003	2010	War in Darfur
2003	2011	Iraq War
2003	Ongoing	Balochistan conflict
2004	Ongoing	War in North-West Pakistan

2004	2007	Central African Republic Bush War
2004		Ongoing Conflict in the Niger Delta
2004		Ongoing Shia insurgency in Yemen
2004		Ongoing South Thailand insurgency
2004	2009	Kivu conflict
2005	2010	Civil war in Chad
2005	2008	Mount Elgon insurgency
2006	2011	Fatah–Hamas conflict (Brothers War)
2006	2006	Lebanon War
2006		Ongoing Mexican Drug War
2006	2009	War in Somalia
2007		Ongoing Operation Enduring Freedom – Trans Sahara
2007	2009	Tuareg rebellion
2007		Ongoing Civil war in the Republic of Ingushetia
2008	2008	Invasion of Anjouan
2008		Ongoing Cambodian–Thai border dispute
2008	2008	Djiboutian–Eritrean border conflict
2008	2008	South Ossetia war
2008	2009	Gaza War
2009		Ongoing Sudanese nomadic conflicts
2009		Ongoing Insurgency in the North Caucasus
2009	2009	Boko Haram Uprising
2009		Ongoing South Yemen insurgency
2009		Ongoing War in Somalia
2010		Ongoing Yemeni al-Qaeda crackdown
2010	2010	South Kyrgyzstan riots
2010	2010	Kingston unrest
2010	2011	Ivorian crisis Second Ivorian Civil War
2011	2011	Libyan civil war
2011		Ongoing Egyptian War on Terror in Sinai
2011	2012	Yemeni revolution
2011		Ongoing Syrian civil war
2011		Ongoing Sudan internal conflict
2011		Ongoing South Sudan internal conflict
2011	2012	Operation Linda NchiPart of the War in Somalia
2011		Ongoing Libyan factional fighting
2012		Ongoing Tuareg rebellion
2012	2012	South Sudan–Sudan border conflict
2012		Ongoing East DR Congo conflict
2012		Ongoing Conflict in Lebanon Part of the Syrian civil war

➔ **1100 Wars in 2000 years!**

→ Estimated 300-500 war-like conflicts with significant victims can be added!
→ 1945-2012: Estimated 270 wars plus estimated 130 war-like conflicts!
→ 1900-2012: Estimated 300 wars plus estimated 150 war-like conflicts!

Without doubt we can say: All the precious genuine human values related to the Archetypes of the Soul, which many folks have explored and developed during centuries or millenniums, must be protected with military power. All the precious common goods of a society, including culture that has been performed without having stolen its resources and without having exploited other folks must be protected with military power. This is because there are countless evil people in power that only want to steal the land and the results of performances of other folks.

But also without doubt we must say: A huge majority of all wars and war-like conflicts are due to insane satanic rulers, very evil people with (economic) power, deficient and arrogant governments, archaic religions, and very stupid blinded people.

Wars will continue. The military power alone from the United States and the NATO has the power to destroy the planet 3-5 times with nuclear bombs and weapons of mass destruction. We can add Russia, China, and other nations that have a similar power to respond to the capitalistic imperialistic warmongers.

There is not a thin sign on this earth that allows forecasting a better future than the big Armageddon within 35-40 years. Additionally to this very frightening perspective the planet will also hit the entire humanity with the iron whip of its natural energy; and this will not take 100 years.

The rats for the wars

- The Franco-Prussian War (Franco-German War) 1870-1871
- The First World War 1914-1918
- The Second World War 1939-1945

An estimated 120-150,000,000 people died due to these wars, became handicapped (named at that time 'gimps'), or seriously injured through these wars, directly or indirectly. Millions of women became widows and millions of children became orphans. Millions more have lost their home and everything.

And the Germans did not learn anything up to today from these dire experiences, today again going to war as part of the NATO to Afghanistan in order to eliminate terrorists, a fabricated myth. Did the British people learn anything from their own imperialistic history of wars? Did the Americans learn anything from the Vietnam War? Did they learn anything from Goebbels' propaganda methods? Not at all!

This picture alone shows us exemplarily for many more wars:

1) The folks were and still are very submissive, naïve, obeisant, ignorant, stupid, and blinded to authority, because they need a 'father' that looks well after them, accepts them, praises them, gives them the 'right rules' for a good way of living, and promises them a good life in the future. Christianity has prepared them and continues preparing them for this subordination promising them a place in the paradise. Their rigid and brutal fathers and the frigid mothers, both unable to love have done their job and continue doing this job today for the service in the Army or Church.

2) The heads of states, the ministers, and the entire governments show herewith their true face by throwing their folks into battles, immense suffering and misery: false, aggressive, arrogant, hypocrites and cowards, perverse, psychopathic, archaic, despotic, evil, and satanic; and some very naive. The relationship between government and the folk was always and still is today perverted: the folk serves the interest of the agents in the governments and economics – also and especially in modern democracies.

Hallelujah: "He died for the fatherland. He died for God and Jesus Christ. Hundred million people and much more died, or became handicapped, widows or orphans for the fatherland, for God and Jesus Christ." With their taxes and obeisance the victims have paid themselves their horrifying, fearful and tearful destiny.

🖐 How long does it take and which experiences do the European, the British and American people need until they understand that they are only rats for the governments to be used for their megalomania and insane politics, rats also for the capitalistic economics whose supreme masters are the main profiteer from wars who ever wins a war?

The history of wars clearly shows us:

🖐 All political concepts in the past and in the present have failed in achieving peace on earth and eliminating the roots of all wars.

- All religious concepts in the past and in the present have failed in achieving peace on earth and eliminating the roots of all wars.

- All technical, intellectual, cultural, and spiritual developments and achievements since 2000 years up to today have failed in achieving peace on earth and eliminating the roots of all wars.

- All leaders and managers in all institutions (systems) of society in the past and in the present have failed in achieving peace on earth and eliminating the roots of all wars.

- All achievements for a high living standard and all concentration of money and wealth have failed in achieving peace on earth and eliminating the roots of all wars.

- All achievements for justice and the appropriate human rights, human values, and ethics have failed in achieving peace on earth and eliminating the roots of all wars.

- All kind of international institutions, from the UN to a hundred other continental and global institutions, have failed in achieving peace on earth and eliminating the roots of all wars.

- All achievements for public education from the kindergarten up to universities have failed in achieving peace on earth and eliminating the roots of all wars.

- All the constitutions, laws, and regulations for the society's business and life of all states have failed in achieving peace on earth and eliminating the roots of all wars.

- All mass media, all the valuable books that have ever been written, all knowledge about humans, society and politics have failed in achieving peace on earth and eliminating the roots of all wars.

- All modern offers for entertainment and pleasure have failed in achieving peace on earth and eliminating the roots of all wars.

- All the 'freedom of speech', the 'freedom of movement', and the 'freedom of consumption' have failed in achieving peace on earth and eliminating the roots of all wars.

- The efficiency and success of international relations is very low and in most cases a basket case. The entire concept of international relations has failed in achieving peace on earth and eliminating the roots of all wars.

- All the accredited public and private education, especially social sciences (psychology, education, philosophy, economics, and politics) have failed in achieving peace on earth and eliminating the roots of all wars.

- All wise men and women, all humans with an excellent genuine faith and with high skills and top-knowledge in the interest of society and humanity, philosophical and practical, have not had and did not succeeded in achieving peace on earth and eliminating the roots of all wars.

We can add here shortly another insane capitalistic issue: Since the 'car' was invented we estimate 100-150,000,000 (direct and indirect) victims, calculated by all possible accidents and contaminations from the mining to the production and the use of cars. The contamination from all traffic systems has produced another 150-200,000,000 victims; maybe more than 500,000,000 victims if we add contamination in general).

- Most of the technology since around 150 years is an incredible failure at gigantic costs of humans' mind and lives, the planet, humanity, and peace on earth. Technology with its education is accredited. Everything that human's mind and soul needs is not accredited but ignored or banned.
- We conclude: behind all the wars and the traffic-systems are the same insanity, amorality, lack of human values, and deficiency of the mind and soul of people and especially of the leaders in politics and economics.

In a short-sighted view we could say: The reason is because humans are predators, beasts, animals, rapacious monsters, a failure of biological evolution, and de natura nothing more than 'vivid evil beings'. Adding the state of humanity and the planet today, we could cynically say: A huge majority of humans are monstrous mental and spiritual gimps. But this view misses the ignored mental and spiritual potentials with its requirements for humans' evolution.

99% of the potentials in human's mind and soul are ignored, malformed, distorted, suppressed, perverted, and some potential simply abused for eco-centered interests and rapid satisfaction.

95% of humanity has not learnt that for everything in life and also for psychical-spiritual development hard and strenuous performance on a daily or weekly basis is required.

95% of humanity has not learnt the indispensable skills and knowledge in order to understand the potentials of the mind and soul and how to manage the psychical-spiritual development that is the immanent (archetypal) superior meaning of life.

Religions and public education have never discovered, explored, and taught the 'spiritual intelligence', the critical and constructive power of the unconscious mind, and the Archetypes of the Soul as the supreme potential for humanity's evolution.

There have been prophets, Messiahs, and very wise men and women that have explored, found and taught the 'spiritual intelligence', the critical and constructive power of the unconscious mind, and the Archetypes of the Soul as the supreme potentials for humanity's evolution. But they did never get a voice to reach a folk, especially the established religion and governments.

The quadrillions of tears, the immeasurable weight of suffering and misery due to all these wars are today still hanging around the globe like an energetic black and heavy cloud, full of pain and guilt, forcing humanity to continue and continue with wars either to understand and reconcile and learn for a new evolutionary path, or to be eliminated through further wars and human made disasters (e.g. contamination).

There is since ever a collective oath: "Do never explore, find and teach the 'spiritual intelligence', the critical and constructive power of the unconscious mind, and the Archetypes of the Soul!" Today the entire humanity has to pay the price for this satanic 'rule'; and the people that will live on earth in the coming 500-1000 years will still have to pay for the damages that this oath has produced and still does unstoppably produce.

Normative statement: The rulers in all systems of society, including religion, in the past and today are responsible for this oath inherited from their forefathers and transferring this legacy to the next generation. They all must be brought to justice, impeached and convicted!

If the young generation today doesn't want to see the failure of their parents and forefathers, the failure of education and the archaic religions, and if they do not want to learn from these failures with all its consequences, and acquire the new Enlightenment of the 21st Century, then they will experience again a future of endless wars and finally the end of the GDP-Race.

- In this book here, also in the 'Trilogy on Economics', in 'Deicide', and in many more books I have written, I give the proof that humanity has a chance to reach a new Age of human evolution.
- In the 'Trilogy on Economics' and in 'Deicide' I also present the structure and principles of the 'Roadmap 25Y' (Y = years) for humanity's leap in the psychical-spiritual evolution, the indispensable program for the 'biological evolution' of humanity.

5.9. Enlightenment for the 21st Century

The book from Orrell David (about the economic myths) gives us essential suggestions and ways of thinking for a new approach of politics: [159]

- Is politics based on measurable parameters?
- Is political action predictable?
- Is the result of political actions predictable?
- Can we describe politics by scientific political 'laws'?
- Is politics made up of independent individuals?
- Does politics make people happy?
- Can an unstable politics create stability?
- How is the gender balance in politics?
- Is politics rational?
- Is politics efficient?
- Is politics fair?
- Where does the actual politics lead us?

The same questions we put on the table for economics. Our analysis of these questions resulted in: NO! Not at all! Economics is an ideology, an illusionary fabrication from imbalanced minds and politics is an ideology as well.

The core answer for politics is: Forecasting politics (effects of politics) is in the best case possible on a mainstream level of the mega parameters. These mega parameters (Chapter 3) form some kind of a mega organism. And this organism is already heavily damaged.

Humanity as a whole is a mega organism. The planet is a mega organism. All governments on earth together form a mega organism. These organisms consist in natural, political, economical, religious, educative, psychological, and spiritual factors. If these organisms are affected from mega criticalities in all these factors, then we can forecast its development: It will lead to the doom within 35-40 years.

---

[159] Orrell David. EconoMyths. London 2010

494

We have an extreme individualism in the collective. Individualism doesn't make anyone happy. We have a herd behavior in all relevant systems of society. Herd behavior is stupid. Trends and rumors as well as catastrophes produce emotions that influence humans' behavior. Human's behavior is also strongly influenced by all systems of society. Politics can be seen herewith as a part-system of an immense mega network with countless links, nodes, and interactions. Every part-system has inputs from all directions and outputs also in all directions.

How can people (and politicians) constructively deal with such immense inputs and outputs in an environment full of disequilibrium? How can people (and politicians) take rational decisions? How can people (and politicians) satisfy their self-interests if they are already dehumanized? How can people (and politicians) be independent if they are mentally enslaved and driven from the collective unconscious (the energetic 'cloud')?

Seen in a general way, each human has a certain social network. There are the couples, parents, siblings, friends, and colleagues. There are the social networks that are 95% artificial. There are the neighbors, the friends of one's children und their parents. There are the people working in retail and services to which humans are in a short contact daily, weekly, or occasionally. Some individuals have up to 10 or 20 in their personal network; others have not even one or in the best case 2-3 humans in their social network. Individuals participating in special groups (hobby, sport, etc.) have more people in their network. A folk consist in such patterns of social networks. In countries like Great Britain, Germany, France, United States, etc., are millions of such independent patterns of network that are not linked with each other. These social patterns are isolated units. The social permeability between social patterns is limited. Their inner guidance is low, miserable, distorted, or inexistent.

Sociology categorizes people in social classes. The criteria for determining social classes are varied: economic status, education, professional status, religion, and reputation (authority status). Social patterns have a tendency to be more or less homogenous in relation to such categories. There is rather a low permeability between social classes however they are determined. In that sense social patterns have limited hierarchical class permeability. There is no inner guidance within a class or between hierarchical classes.

A social pattern consists of a close circle that includes strong emotional ties and tends to be relatively stable. The more extensive circle is formed by sharing certain attitudes and interests, and is mostly time limited and very flexible. Social patterns tend to mutually confirm and reinforce a high part of the given attitudes, ways of thinking and interpreting, ways of judging, etcetera, and the behavior patterns that forms a lifestyle or a way of mastering life. Social patterns are more stable in rural areas, villages, and small towns; more flexible and variable in big towns and cities (social anonymity).

We can understand a social pattern as a vivid organism consisting in individuals with a mind and soul, and with certain characteristic behavior patterns they share. The way the mind and soul ('inner life') are formed and shaped, determines behavior of the people; ignored here external influences that direct and conditions people's behavior. If one or more members of a social pattern have malformed psychical functions, much disintegrated psychical and spiritual sub-systems, which leads in neuroticism and narcissism (and other mental and behavioral disorder), then the entire social pattern is affected and has a tendency to mutually reinforce such 'ill' components. 'Ill' components of social patterns can have an effect in the entire social organism similar to a disease, a cancer or any destructive mental or behavioral 'energy'. We can conclude that individualism always has a social taker and counterpart, and therefore also individualists are affected (however) from 'ill' parts of social patterns in their social environment.

Our approach here has some important consequences for politicians and the governmental operations in general:

→ The manifoldness of social patterns on the different 'social class' levels cannot form one voice against a government.
→ Agents of political structures are highly or totally disconnected from such social patterns and its varied pattern-'diseases'.
→ Political agents can operate against the collective or ignore the collective up to a certain level without being in danger.
→ However the state of the mind and the behavior of such social patterns are, low, deficient or 'ill', up to a certain amount of patterns it does not put in danger the political decisions and activities.
→ Individual protesters, self-immolations, hunger strikes, demonstrations (with hundred thousand or a million participants), intellectual groups (or initiatives), and even pressure groups such as Greenpeace or Transparency International, do not hinder a government to do what they have on their agenda.
→ If a very hot critical point is reached in a society (for example highest unemployment rate, poverty, and scarcity of primary products and

services for the needs of people), then the entire social system (the sum of social patterns) forms automatically a mainstream against the government. Sometimes a religion promotes it (unifying people), sometimes a religion hinders it (hold them down, stupid and submissive).

→ The more the majority of social patterns are mentally and behaviorally low in quality (efficiency) and low in 'health', the more difficult it becomes to implement renewal, pioneering changes, or even directing the folk towards a new way of living.

→ Significant changes, implemented from a government, require a period of one generation. Only wars, proxy bellicose activities, dictatorship with military control, and immense natural catastrophes affecting entire nations, a continent or even the planet, can make significant changes in a society within a short time.

→ A democracy can never be better than the mental and spiritual qualities of the people and of the manifold social patterns, which are expressed in people's behavior, lifestyle, and beliefs. The manifold social patterns today on earth have everywhere become ill and mad, broken and rotten from a mechanical and rational control and exploitation of the nature, of humans, and of society. The sham of religion, the arrogance of governments, and the stupidity of people have made it possible.

→ The right to vote, the freedom of speech and religious belief and movement, a high living standard, the free market, the right to acquire properties, and the protection of privacy alone does not make for a democracy. With all these democratic values a government can still operate as a (hidden) dictatorship or (partly visible) oligarchy in the sole interest of the visible elites and the invisible supreme economic masters.

→ Disrespecting the educational psychical-spiritual need of the mental and social organism of humans and ignoring its capacities and potentials for fulfillment, for making a living and contributing to the society leads to the destruction of society, humanity and the planet.

In the vivid part-systems of a society and the planet people live and act according to their social pattern. Additionally societies are established with all their manifold infrastructures. Mistakes, failure, deficiency, disturbances, perturbations, breakdowns, disasters, (long term) instability, extreme events, risks and opposite forces in mutual fight are everywhere. We also must add the self-interest of individuals, groups, and institutions of all kind.

This mega organism doesn't work rationally or efficiently. It is per se unstable and its development as a whole is 'mathematically' unpredictable. Is there a hidden dynamic 'law' of interaction and natural systemic 'feedback', which could be used for determining collective aims, for management and control, and finally for prediction?

If there is not such thing like a 'law' or principle, then the entire global 'organism' is unstable, in the best case short-term controllable and stable within a very limited frame and time period. In general, we can never force these systems in a rational frame without paying the price of complete dehumanization and destruction of the planet.

→ We should also consider that everything has a meaning for humans and therefore everything also has an emotional and irrational component.

Sure is, optimal equilibrium, balance, fairness, satisfaction, and efficiency is not static and essentially today not given in the mega organism (humanity and the planet together) as described above. In some sub-systems or sub-sub-systems there may be a kind of short-term and relative equilibrium, satisfaction and efficiency, but at what costs (of other sub-systems)?

Humans and institutions get all the time feedbacks from other systems or sub-systems or sub-sub-systems. The state of the planet, for example, gives us a very clear feedback. Global poverty can also be seen as a feedback, for example; extreme imbalance of wealth and wages, or deficiencies of governance and self-interest of politicians. Mental disorder and many human made illnesses, obesity included, are a feedback.

In other words: political decisions and political behavior always get feedbacks in many ways. The sham of Christianity (or archaic religions in general) produces all kind of feedback, which we can identify on a mental level or a behavior level (individually or collectively), or on the effects of individual and collective acting (living) ruled by dogmatic belief.

Is there a utility category or a drive theory, an instinct theory, or a general motivation theory based on the pleasure-factor (emotion) that could serve as a rational parameter for the creation of a 'law' or principle that is useful for governance? Economics understand 'money' as a rational factor (thing): "Money governs". But money is never simply a rational factor. Politicians see the GDP as a rational factor; but this parameter does not create stability and equilibrium in the complex 'organisms'. In case of a given growth, this parameter ignores the negative externalities. This kind of orientation for doing politics is very dumb (see: Schellhammer, Economics III).

The whole world is thoroughly governed by the dominance of men. Mental male characteristics, excluding the female characteristics, create imbalance and becomes thoroughly destructive in politics, economics, religion, and in the world of business. Female characteristics are everywhere inferior to male characteristics (see: chapter 2.5.).

→ Wars and the destruction of the planet and the global poverty are man-made. Wars are always 100% man made, even if there are some bellicose women on the political stage. Psychologically, we can say men are left-brain-driven added with a high testosterone level.

It's a lie that governance (politics) is rational, calculable, measurable, objective, impartial, just or controlled. And the politicians as an individual themselves are far away from such characteristics. Politics is ferocious, untamable, devious, irrational, ego-obsessed, asymmetric, biased, imbalanced, hegemonic but submissive to economics (partly to archaic religion), false and evil, permanently in struggle for power, with everything we know from Machiavelli.

Politics is permanently colliding with all systems, nationally and globally, human oriented and planet (ego-systems) oriented. Politics permanently ignores its negative externalities (at home and overseas). Political systems are rigid, inflexible, an authoritarian structure that breaks the human nature, the nature of the eco-systems, and all human values and tools for holistic efficiency. The permanent fight on the political stage is about money, about getting more taxes, or about austerity measures – and never about mankind's evolution under national and global perspective.

→ Politics and politicians thoroughly ignore and dehumanize the mind and soul of the people (and of their own).
→ With exclusive rational characteristics politics is contra-evolutionary; they simply have no idea about mind and soul.

The entire political system is 'unsatisfiable' in terms of power, reputation, fame, money, and economic growth. The stress that arises from all these fights, also arises from greed (for power), needs, and wants, enormously imbalances the mind and soul of the agents. So, how can they create a relative and progressive equilibrium in a society? Such people can never be rooted in their soul. They are not rooted in wisdom, in ethics (human values), in attitudes of love, in the truth, in humility, in graciousness, courage, and spirituality. If they are rooted in an ideology, they live and operate like from a mini boat in the middle of the ocean with high waves around. Logically politicians generate in the society and the world what they are themselves and what the political system allows them to operate.

THE EARTH HAS TAKEN BILLIONS OF YEARS TO NURTURE. HUMANITY HAS EXPERIENCED MORE THAN A BILLION VICTIMS DUE TO INSANE WARS, SUFFERING AND MISERY. TODAY WE EXPERIENCE A PERMANENT HUMAN MADE IRREVERSIBLE DESTRUCTION OF ALL CREATURES, ALL RESOURCES, AND ALL THE ECO-SYSTEMS. WE HAVE EXPERIENCED AND EXPERIENCE SINCE 1900 UP TO THE 21ST CENTURY WARS AND WARS OVER AND OVER AGAIN, JUST TO BECOME TEMPORARY MASTERS OF A PART OF THE EARTH.

Since 1945, the US has attempted to overthrow more than 50 governments, most of them democratically elected. It has attempted to suppress a populist or national movement in 20 countries. It has grossly interfered in democratic elections in at least 30 countries. It has dropped bombs on the people of more than 30 countries. And it has attempted to assassinate more than 50 foreign leaders. [160] And they continue doing so.

WE ARE A BLINK OF AN EYE AWAY FROM ARMAGEDDON. STUPIDITY IN ALL SOCIAL CLASSES UP TO THE TOP ELITES IS MORE DESTRUCTIVE THAN NUCLEAR BOMBS. This is the glorified Western democracy! This is what the political science teaches us to do or to accept as a 'natural phenomenon': pure insanity and unstoppable decide!

In case you are still not convinced with the given knowledge and facts in this book, I want to come back to the mega parameter 'contamination' and add some facts that show you the insanity and deicide dogs body politicians:

Contamination of humans' body: [161]

"Hundreds of industrial chemicals, pollutants and pesticides are pumped back and forth from mother to fetus through umbilical cord blood (2005).

…413 industrial and consumer product chemicals found that the babies averaged 200 contaminants in their blood (2004) … In total, the babies' blood had 287 chemicals, including 209 never before detected in cord blood.

[160] http://www.globalresearch.ca/americas-war-next-stop-iran-who-will-save-us/
[161] http://www.organicconsumers.org/school/newborns071505.cfm
http://watoxics.org/chemicals-of-concern

…Many of these chemicals can disturb development of the endocrine system and of the organs that respond to endocrine signals in organisms indirectly exposed during prenatal and/or early postnatal life; effects of exposure during development are permanent and irreversible.

…The scientists found that trans-generational exposure can result from the exposure of the mother to a chemical at any time throughout her life before producing offspring due to persistence of endocrine-disrupting chemicals in body fat, which is mobilized during … pregnancy and lactation.

…U.S. industries manufacture and import some 75,000 chemicals."

➔ Billions of humans and the entire world of species are affected!

Chemicals in human's body produce: [162]

- Cognitive disability, intellectual disability, developmental delays
- Chronic hostile, aggressive or disruptive behaviors
- A generalized slowing of physical and /or mental reaction

➔ Billions of humans and the entire world of species are affected!

Mental effects of the 42 most important chemicals, some examples: [163]

- Behavioral changes
- Emotional instability
- Emotional reactivity
- Insomnia
- Memory loss
- Headaches
- Delayed hypersensitivity reactions
- Developmental brain damage
- Reduced learning
- Dizziness
- Loss of motor control
- Decrease in spatial learning
- Growth retardation
- Behavioral changes
- Panic attacks
- Depression

---

[162] http://www.minddisrupted.org/documents/Mind%20Disrupted%20report.pdf
[163] http://www.mcsbeaconofhope.com/42_common_toxic_chemicals_and_th.htm

- Fatigue
- Concentration
- Short-term memory
- Decreases in reaction time
- Disruptions in memory and understanding
- Sexual and sleep disorders
- Brain cell degeneration

→ Billions of humans and the entire world of species are affected!

Body effects of the 42 most important chemicals, some examples: [164]

- Respiratory irritation
- Lung damages
- Brain, liver and stomach tumors
- Cardiac abnormalities
- Eye irritation
- Uncoordination
- Heart attack
- Leukemia
- DNA damages
- Kidney damage
- Allergic reactions
- Breast cancer
- Liver- lung- & enzyme damage
- Antibiotic allergy
- Muscle cramps
- Fetal damage
- Immune damage
- Red blood cell damage
- Asthma
- Central and peripheral nerve damage
- Neurologic damage
- Gastro-intestinal problems
- Heart muscle damage
- Heartbeat changes
- Bronchitis
- Childhood bronchitis
- Fetal death
- Birth defects

---

[164] http://www.mcsbeaconofhope.com/42_common_toxic_chemicals_and_th.htm

- Menstruation system damages
- Hearing loss
- Skin damage

→ Billions of humans and the entire world of species are affected!
→ Billions of humans will die the coming decades due to contamination!

Impeachment

- Contamination of humanity is a global program, affects also the planet and all eco-systems, including the food chains. Contamination is the result of the modern technology and 100% man made. Psychologically, we can say male politicians are left-brain-driven added with a high testosterone level; or they have simply become mad due to the 'legal' power they have.
- This kind of contamination has reached the level of global genocide. The governments are responsible for all these developments. Together with the picture about wars we have given above, the systems of politics and governance is a complete failure – or a satanic tyranny behind the backdrop of 'democracy'.
- The failure of politicians, of the members of political parties, of the parliaments, of the ministerial offices, and of the heads of states is outrageous. They do not deserve a thin bit of respect or trust from their folks. They do not deserve that the citizens respect the laws, regulations, and state administration (bureaucracy).

On the other side as long as the folks are too lazy to work (perform) hard, thoroughly lazy-minded, unwilling to learn a lot, stupid, infantile, naïve, greedy, blabber-mouths, disinterested in the human values and the Archetypes of the Soul, rejecting profound self-knowledge and being responsible for their psychical-spiritual development, rejecting to work life long (as much as health allows), and obsessed from 'possessing without having worked for it', obsessed also from having a good living standard with mobile phones, cars, and other comfortable gadgets, meat every day, fun and entertainment, unlimited consumption with loans, but thoroughly rejecting the truth and glorifying the lies and falseness and decadence, they do not deserve anything better than a tyrannical government that puts them in re-educational working camps.

Conviction

- Politicians that are abettors of the deicide and unwilling to respect the Archetypes of the Soul do not deserve a place in the paradise.
- The people that reject the Archetypes of the Soul and hard learning and working as the foundation of their living do not deserve a place in the paradise.

■ Humanity needs a new secure path with a new system of governance and politics, of economics and public education, of religion and spirituality!

Hope for Humanity

After 30 years of extensive research, I have cracked the mystery of humanity.

Human beings have achieved immense breakthroughs over the past 2,000 years, from technology to science. While cavemen could barely light a fire, today we can sit in a spacecraft and visit the moon. While Kings and rulers took months to get a message to their counterparts abroad back a few hundred years, today they can pick up the phone and press a button and alter humanity's path forever in a matter of a few seconds.

Unfortunately, despite technological advances and breakthroughs in sciences, the mystery of humanity has barely been tackled. Pioneers such as Sigmund Freud and Carl Gustav Jung dared to challenge contemporary thoughts during their times and explore the depths of the inner life. Such vanguard visions unfortunately stagnated in the rat race towards fame and fortune, with their legacies merely being exploited as opposed to researched and developed. What any corporate CEO will confirm in today's fast-pace world is that we need research and development to sustain advances. The same goes for the mystery of humanity, for religion, for economics, for politics, and for education.

The situation is simple: While humans have strived to explain all kinds of questions, the most important questions have remained unanswered. A quick Google search reveals some of the most asked questions humanity poses: "What is the meaning of life? Is there a God? Why is there suffering and death? What happens when I die? Who am I?" 7 billion people ask the most important questions day in and out, without getting a satisfactory answer, which forms the foundation of human life and of society.

Humanity needs a new educational perspective that provides fulfillment for billions through democratic and dogma-free education, which includes answering the most important questions in life.

The young generation today is facing a bleak future of contamination, of total financial collapse, economic turmoil, social unrest, endless regional and perhaps even global wars and a complete lack of realistic and long-term job perspectives.

■ **The need and urgency for a new Enlightenment for the 21st Century is of highest importance in order to give hope to humanity.**

Billions of people around the globe have questions about life, love, relationships, spirituality, sexuality, dreams, emotions, feelings and inner conflicts on a daily basis. Billions of people do not understand the critical development of societies and the world as a whole. Billions of people do not understand the rotten world of politics. The entire humanity is trapped in a dark labyrinth of self-destruction and in the best-case scenario invented bubbles of hope.

The concept of the Archetypes of the Soul offers all the answers, tools and skills as well as the capacity and conditions for developing the 'cracked mystery of humanity' and for giving to billions of people a peaceful future with the start of a new evolutionary Age.

The agents in the world of politics, economics, religion, and education must found their governance and management of society in the cracked mystery of humanity.

■ **The new Enlightenment for the 21st Century is herewith proclaimed.**

■ **Catharsis and renewal is the challenge to make it work for the future.**

Is politics for human evolution possible?
YES!

It requires an all-embracing catharsis
It requires a complete new concept of mankind
It requires a new understanding of human life
It requires a complete new concept of public education
It requires a new understanding of politics and economics
It requires a fundamentally new understanding of religion
It requires the integration of all Archetypes of the Soul
It requires a leadership that guarantees personality integrity
It requires leaders that are top trained with a pioneering spirit
It requires minimum 25 years to achieve significant renewal

If this catharsis and renewal is globally not wanted, the price is the elimination of humanity and the destruction of the planet!

Deicide or Renewal – You decide!

The 'Roadmap 25' is developed in Economics I, II, and III.
And in the book 'Deicide'.

Literature

Colander, D.C.: Microeconomics. 8th Edition. McGraw-Hill 2010. New York

Boucher David & Kelly Paul: Political Thinkers. From Socrates to the Present. University Press 2nd Edition 2009. Oxford, N.Y.

Ellis William: Politics, Aristotle. A Treatise on Government. IAP, 2010. Las Vegas, Nevada

Haddock Bruce: History of Political Thought. 1789 to the present. Polity Press 2005. Cambridge UK

Heywood Andrew: Politics. 3rd Edition 2007. Palgrave Macmillan. London UK

Knight Julian: British Politics for Dummies. John Wiley & Sons Ldt. Chichester. West-Sussex, 2010, UK.

Krugman Paul, Wells Robin, Graddy Kathryn: Essentials of Economics. Worth Publishers 2011. New York

Lynch Philip, Fairclough Paul: UK Government & Politics. 5th edition 2012, Deddingtou, Oxfordshire UK.

Mankiw N. Gregory, Taylor Mark P.: Economics. 2nd edition. South-Western Cengage Learning. 2011. Hampshire. United Kingdom

McConnell Campbell R., Brue Stanley L., Flynn Sean M.: Macroeconomics, Principles, Problems, and Policies. 19th edition 2012. McGraw-Hill. New York

McDowell Moore, Thom Rodney, Frank Robert, Bernanke Ben: Principles of Economics. 2nd European Edition. McGraw-Hill Higher Education 2009. Berkshire

Orell David: Economyths. Icon Books Ltd, 2012. London UK.

Voegelin Eric: History of Political Ideas. Volume II, 5th edition 1997. University of Missouri Press. Columbia.

Wootton David: Modern Political Thought. Readings from Machiavelli to Nietzsche. Hackett Publishing Company, Inc. 2nd Edition 2008. Indianapolis

Books from Schellhammer Edward:

Trilogy on Economics. Spain. 2012
Deicide. Spain. 2012
Practical Psychology. Spain. 2012
Evolutionary Human Education. Spain. 2011 (German Edition)

For further information:
English: http://www.rcigi.com/about/books/
German: http://de.rcigi.com/buecher/

Made in the USA
Charleston, SC
07 November 2012